PHILIP II … N
IM…

ASPECTS OF GREEK AND ROMAN LIFE

General Editor: H. H. Scullard

PHILIP II AND MACEDONIAN IMPERIALISM

J. R. Ellis

THAMES AND HUDSON

First paperback edition 1986

Printed and bound in the U.S.A.

CONTENTS

PREFACE 6

CHRONOLOGY OF PHILIP'S REIGN 14

I MACEDONIA: PEOPLE, LANDSCAPE AND TRADITION 21

II THE ATHENIAN ALIGNMENT 45

III THE CHALKIDIAN ALIGNMENT 66

IV TOWARDS A GREEK SETTLEMENT 90

V THE UNEASY PEACE 125

VI BREAKDOWN 160

VII THE SECOND GREEK SETTLEMENT 181

VIII PHILIP, ALEXANDER AND PERSIA 211

APPENDIX 235

SELECT BIBLIOGRAPHY 240

NOTES 245

INDEX 309

PREFACE

To a large extent the rise and fall of Philippic studies as well as the flux in attitudes towards Philip and his Macedonia have been governed by an inadequacy of sources – or at least of balanced sources. In broad terms the available evidence contemporary with the reign of Philip is not Macedonian but Greek; and at that mainly Athenian; and at that mainly anti-Macedonian. It is of course no absolute bar to the comprehension of any two opposing viewpoints that the one is expressed (even superlatively expressed) and the other distorted or altogether absent. Our almost total dependence on Tudor sources for the reign of Richard III has not prevented in recent times a more equitable study of the last Plantagenet. Julio-Claudian and late fifth-century Athenian studies have now begun to rise above the limits imposed by Tacitus and Thucydides respectively. The trouble with bias is not that it exists – not even that at times it may utterly dominate the evidence. What really matters is that it may go unrecognized; or, more often, improperly recognized.

There has recently been admirable illustration* of what is (or ought to be) a truism of historiography in general, that the development of Philippic studies over the past three centuries has been critically influenced – not to say determined – by the contemporary circumstances of the successive generations contributing to it. In the mid-nineteenth century, at a time of unparalleled social and political reform in his own country, for example, George Grote saw in the Greek city-state the sublimest expression of human individualism. To him, by consequence, Philip was the aggressor of the age, the 'destroyer of freedom and independence in the Hellenic world'. To the school of especially German historians who wrote in the aftermath of the successful unification movements of the later nineteenth century Philip appeared, on the contrary, to be the far-sighted unifier of a Hellenic motley (as the Englishman Hogarth saw him soon afterwards). The

* A. D. Momigliano, *Studies in Historiography* (London 1966) 56ff.

attitude of the historian has been the product to a significant degree of his own circumstances.

But that is inevitable. It is indeed the stuff of history, the exploration by a society of its own personal relationship with the past. (So each generation, as an act of selfconsciousness or as a means of fixing its identity, needs to rewrite it.) But in this particular case what is more serious is that, since all the sources are Greece- or Athens-oriented, the historian's viewpoint has been in practice the expression not so much of a relativity between himself and Philip as of his prior attitude towards the contemporary Greek world and, in particular, towards the Athenian *polis*. Thus, to those to whom the oratory of Demosthenes was the voice of freedom raised courageously against the dark forces of barbarian totalitarianism, Philip was – as one has said – no better than a Hitler, and Aischines his Quisling. To those whose political sensitivities were offended by the recalcitrant particularism of the Greek *polis*, by Demosthenes' fruitless attempts to resurrect those heroic days of a century earlier when Athens established her freedom to plunder and enslave the rest, Philip was a sort of prior-day Bismarck of the Hellenes.

While investigation of the impact of Philip on Athenian history is far from an unworthy occupation, it is as incomplete by itself as the study of the Persian Wars as an exclusive phenomenon of Greek history. The fourth century BC needs its Macedonian viewpoint. What the present work attempts to do, in a small way, is to evaluate Macedonia's own needs and interests, so far as they may be recovered, and the consequent internal constraints acting upon her domestic and especially foreign policies, with respect, at any rate, to the reign of Philip II.

It may be that the reader, like the author, will conjure to mind a picture of Philip the man. There will be those who are familiar with the small body of sayings attributed to him and with the little stories collected by much later authors purporting to reveal his character. It is my own view that these are by and large useless. Then there are such indications as contemporaries very occasionally give (Aischines, for example, on the king's charm towards the Athenian ambassadors in 346), which may, according to prejudice, be taken to disclose the real Philip – or no more than the political Philip. For Philip was, whatever else, a politician; and there are those who think of politicians as the little boy of popular myth thought of policemen, those he had always heard about and then those more benevolent gendarmes who bought him icecream to soften his judgement: there are the bastards and there are the cunning bastards. This book is not a biography. Such an exercise on the basis of such evidence is not possible. Thus it is not given the obvious title: Philip II of Macedon. For if it is naïve to speak of the causes of fourth-century Macedonian imperialism in terms of Philip's personal outlook (whether his supposed restless belligerence or, alternatively, some farsighted zeal for Hellenic unity), it must be the height of folly to do so on the basis of the sort of pseudo-evidence for it that survives.

And yet this has often been done. The remarkable explosion of social and military energy that propelled Macedon in hardly more than three decades from the periphery to the centre of eastern Mediterranean affairs has been put down to the private compulsions of one man. Certainly, the contributory and instrumental effects of Philip's early morale-boosting victories in 359 and 358 and his acquisition two years later of the rich Pangaian area beyond the Strymon have been given due weight. The necessary existing resources have not been overlooked, the large available manpower, the bounteous and secure food-supply and already better than modest reserves of copper and tin, gold and silver. But what is missing is the reagent, the factor or factors directly responsible for the massive forces now released for the first time. In the age of mass media the galvanic role of one man alone may be superficially credible, but hardly in a large and diverse ancient state.

If there had been in the past any single major reason for the impotence of Macedonia against its traditional predators – the Illyrians, Athens, Olynthos, even at times Thebes and Sparta – it had been the crippling absence of unity that was exploited time and time again by those with their own interests to serve. The primary manifestation of this disunity, admittedly shadowy even on the few occasions our sources allow some light to penetrate the curtain of obscurity, was the antagonism between Upper and Lower Macedonia, west and east.

But in Philip's reign, as the curtain lifts a little, a change takes place. Mostly dimly, but perceptibly, through such agencies as the transplantation of population-groups, the large-scale dilution of the noble *hetairos* class and the institution of the Royal Pages, a single nation takes shape. Even clearer in this process is the role of the army, probably in any case the only Macedonian institution capable of a pervasive and comprehensive national role. Through the subordination of the regionally recruited *taxis* to the nationally organized militia, by the provision of attractive monetary and status inducements to loyal service in the national body, by the making feasible continuity of service in it by grants of land at least to the officers and probably to their men, and particularly by the laying of a heavy emphasis on an institution whose natural orientation was towards its apex rather than its extremities, there grew during this reign an allegiance to the single nation, through its army, and to the king-commander as the single head.

There can be little doubt as to the centrality of Philip's part in the process. While the vital elements were already there the realization of their potential was his achievement. But if the army was at once the instrument and the expression of the new unity it was all the more essential that military objectives were constantly in mind and, more important, that military successes were won, lest it turn the newly found energies in upon itself and the state. While, that is, the revolution was at least shaped by Philip's own determination and perception, he was as bound as anyone else by its implications; he was the rider of the tiger he had released.

This is not to say, however, that Philip can have occupied the Macedonian throne in 359 already convinced that military expansion would provide all or indeed any of the answers to his difficulties. In the context of the first years of his reign, when to survive must have been ambition enough, expansionary imperialistic aims were the indulgent fantasies of a dreamer. But here again we have suffered at the hands of our sources. Our most impressive contemporary author, Demosthenes, does not touch on Philip until the end of the 350s (although Demosthenes' Athens had already been formally at war with him for several years), by which time Macedonia was becoming a power to be reckoned with, and he judges this king's early reign in the light of the achievements of later years. The same is true of other sources. These northern fringe-dwellers of the Hellenic world were simply not noticed by literate contemporaries until Philip's successes compelled their attention; and, when they did notice, they naturally saw in the previous years an inevitable and, worse, calculated rise to that level of prominence and influence. But when Demosthenes, in a speech on another subject in 351 (*On the Rhodians* 24), implicitly chides his fellow Athenians with dismissing Philip as a person of no account, we should not miss the obvious: that that, even yet, was how he could be seen.

In 359, with a multitude of dangers pressing upon him and his factious kingdom, Philip had, among other things, to face a question that had constantly exercised his predecessors: where would he find a protective alliance reliable enough to allow him reasonable security in the Aegean context while he endeavoured to ease the pressures from his immediate neighbours and within Macedonia? At that time, in fact, the choice was not difficult. Athens appeared currently within reach of the power she had exercised over her fifth-century alliance. In the late 360s, as the ineffectual sanctions of the Persian king's Common Peaces were increasingly recognized as the mere bluff of the preoccupied, and as the last remnants of Spartan power fast dissipated, Athenian ambitions in the Aegean (like those of Thebes by land) had become more and more transparent. Philip sought refuge under the expansive umbrella of Athenian power.

But little more than two years later the Athenian alliance was torn apart by the revolt and secession of some of its wealthiest and most powerful members. Here the king faced a second critical decision. He was in no position to assist his embattled ally, not least because he himself had no navy, so he might either chance his fortunes utterly on the strength and determination of Athens or cast himself loose in search of another support. His choice was the correct one; in 355 the Athenians were to accept the ultimatum of the Persian Artaxerxes Memnon and, humiliated and exhausted, surrender their claims on the growing naval alliance. Absolved of the need, by the end of 357, to subordinate his own interests to those of his ex-ally, Philip took Amphipolis. With Athens' own problems absorbing all of her energy and resources, he need fear no immediate consequences. By ceding the rich Anthemous valley and assisting in the suppression of Poteidaia – the magnitude of the concessions neatly underscoring the weakness from which Macedonia bargained – he won the alliance of the Olynthians and, with the reassuring presence of a friendly Chalkidian League at his Aegean side, was able to continue the tasks of building his army, reorganizing his state and strengthening its frontiers.

From 356 Macedonian influence began to spread beyond the frontiers, in Thrace and Thessaly. From his involvements during these years it becomes clear from what directions the king expected danger would come, for, whereas on the western, northern and northeastern sides little more was done than to launch the occasional punitive or preemptive strike, to the east and south, on the other hand, he devoted considerable time and care to the establishment of firm relations and reliable governments. Along the Aegean coastline of Thrace, moreover, he systematically picked off the maritime towns that might serve as bases for any resurgent Athenian naval power. But in 353 defeat came close to expunging all his achievements. In the shock wave that passed through his allied and buffer states following a serious loss in Thessaly, influence in eastern Thrace passed to Athens, to whom the Olynthians too began making overtures of peace, and in several other areas the Macedonian links were dislocated. Some of the damage was repaired quite quickly, thanks mainly to the remarkable success of Philip's Thessalian campaign of 352. But the strains in the Macedonian relationship with Olynthos remained to be repaired and its interests in eastern Thrace to be recovered.

However, although the kingdom could even yet offer no overwhelming challenge to the major Greek states, the Thessalian triumph of summer 352 might be seen as a portent – welcome to some, chilling to others. Most importantly, Philip's successes had brought him to the point where he stood on the threshold of central and southern Greek affairs, affairs which must concern him vitally as they had some of his predecessors, and affairs over which he need not even take any initiative to become involved, for he already had allies (including the Thessalian League and, by this time, perhaps Thebes) who would relish his participation in the debilitating Sacred War in Central Greece. It is at this point that his third critical decision had to be made; and, to understand it, we need to keep in mind the internal socio-military pressures in Macedonia, which by now must have been a factor impressing itself on the king's attention, and to apply some hindsight.

In 338/7, after the conclusion of Common Peace among the Greek mainland states (the so-called League of Korinth), Philip proclaimed his intention to lead eastwards a crusade that would enlist the Hellenes as his allies. He withdrew then from Greece and never saw it again; and neither, probably, would his son Alexander have returned there had dissensions not broken out on his father's assassination. The League of Korinth, that is, marked the end of the deliberate extension of Macedonian influence in the Greek peninsula. But a careful examination of the king's purpose in negotiating with Athens the Peace of Philokrates eight years before that time indicates that what he achieved in 338/7 had also been his intention in 346. It was this purpose – to make Greece safe for his own withdrawal for the greener pastures of Anatolia – that he must have determined upon at the end of the 350s or very early in the 340s. In its execution Hellas was to be a source of co-operation, assistance, even inspiration (and, above all, he must be certain that it would not erupt in his rear), but it was not in that direction that he sought to give rein to the military energies of his own society. When it came to the search for longer-term and profitable military objectives it was to the barbarians of Asia Minor that he turned.

Thus, around 350 as the Chalkidian alliance slipped away from him, he laid his plans for the master-stroke that would follow the now expedient obliteration of Olynthian power. The most potent coalition he must fear among the Greek states was that of Athens and Thebes. In the immediate future it was not a likely event, but the one way to ensure that the hoplite army of Thebes, its strength so convincingly demonstrated (to the cost, among others, of Macedonia) during the 370s and 360s, would never be used against him was to strip from the Thebans the foundation of their power, the Boiotian and other neighbouring areas under their domination. To balance and control a weakened Thebes he would make use of Athens, upon whose co-operation he would depend. To this end he designed the Peace of Philokrates. Under its regulation would be established, in effect, a co-hegemony over the Greek world, with the Athenians again free to control the seas and able, at least with Macedonian support, to maintain peace among the Hellenes. Access to her Black Sea grain sources would be guaranteed Athens by her ally's control of Thrace. As Philip's military needs drew him towards Asia Minor, Athens' navy would render assistance and stand ready to open its economic resources to Aegean trade. Fundamentally, of course, the partnership would be unequal; but against this the Athenians would be able to balance the rewards accruing to them.

In many ways such an arrangement had been foreshadowed not long before in the relationship between Persia and Sparta in the Common Peaces of 387/6 and the 370s. In these, in effect, the one power stood as guarantor, the other as executor of a hegemonial structure imposed upon the Hellenic states. But where the Common Peaces had broken down – in the failure of Persia to prevent the growth of Athenian naval and Theban land power and in the inability of the depleted Spartan population and its reactionary army to match the Theban hoplite on the battlefield – the Peace of Philokrates might have stood firm, based on what would be the strongest army and what was already the strongest navy of the Hellenic peninsula.

Such a settlement of Greek affairs was not to be. Nearly a decade was lost as Philip struggled at first to save and then to replace a peace aborted just before birth. Its substitute, the League of Korinth, was in at least one sense the inferior of the ill-starred predecessor, in that its realization had to follow a war whose fears and hatreds must blunt the possibilities of willing association among recent adversaries. But its effect was much the same – or would have been had its architect and engineer not been struck down soon afterwards by the assassin's dagger.

It is thus the general conclusion of this study that Philip (as much as Alexander after him) was no solitary phenomenon of Macedonian or Greek history, materializing from nowhere without impetus, explanation or context. Philip did contribute much of his own to the shaping of what can only be thought of as a major social and military revolution, initially by his skilful organization of the necessary means of survival and later by his recognition and exploitation of the forces he had released in doing so; and to this positive and dominant theme the debility of a Greek world racked for many decades by war and dissension played a matching counterpoint. But the expansive force itself, perhaps largely the product of a newfound security and confidence, came to exist in a sense separately from the king and to govern his actions and policies. To say only this, however, is to suggest that Macedonian imperialism was undiscriminating and undirected, which, as this work attempts to show, is not the case. The course set by Philip may have gone unrecognized by some of his contemporaries, but not by all, and it is still indentifiable; and that, by means of a progressive investigation of the whole reign, is the major purpose here.

The spelling of Greek names has presented no less than its usual difficulty and has been tackled with no fewer than the usual inconsistencies. There is no particularly good reason in the twentieth century for Latinizing a Greek name and I have not done so where it was comfortably avoidable. As to Anglicized or the especially common Latin forms, the worst to be said of them is that they lend a spurious familiarity to what ought to be exotic and alien. A rough Upper Macedonian tribesman should sound more credible as Alexandros (better still with the Modern Greek stress accent on the second syllable) than as friendly, suburban Alexander. But since gentlemen of that name abounded I found it convenient to refer to the Alexanders of the Argead family while leaving their foreign and country namesakes unblemished. Otherwise, with Macedonian people and places (with the single exceptions of the kingdom itself and its king), the Greek form is retained. With other names the same convention is observed (*e.g.* Delphoi and Aischines), other than in cases of the very familiar (Aristotle and Athens) or the otherwise disagreeable to eye or ear (Cyprus, Thucydides and Thrace).

The extent of my heavy indebtedness to the scholarship of others I hope I have been able to make clear in my notes, appendix and bibliography. What I owe to the encouragement and advice of friends and colleagues is more difficult to record – not for lack of gratitude but for fear of omission; but I can not pass this opportunity of expressing my appreciation of help received at one time or another from Professors C. F. Edson, N. G. L. Hammond, M. M. Markle, R. D. Milns, G. le Rider and P. R. C. Weaver. My work has been materially assisted by the generosity of the Institute for Balkan Studies in Thessaloniki, the Myer Foundation together with the Australian Humanities Research Council and, especially, Monash University. To the British School of Archaeology at Athens, a convenient base for travel and an ideal milieu for reading and conversation, I owe several pleasant and fruitful months.

Monash University J.R.E.
Victoria, Australia
1975

THE CHRONOLOGY OF PHILIP'S REIGN

Abbreviations

c. = *circa*;	e. = early;	m. = middle;	l. = late
W = Winter	Sp = Spring	S = Summer	A = Autumn
i = January,	ii = February,	iii = March, etc.	

ATTIC MONTHS:

I = Hekatombaion	VII = Gamelion
II = Metageitnion	VIII = Anthesterion
III = Boedromion	IX = Elaphebolion
IV = Pyanepsion	X = Mounychion
V = Maimakterion	XI = Thargelion
VI = Poseideon	XII = Skirophorion

Note: in theory, i (January) coincides with the Attic month VII (Gamelion), ii (February) with VIII (Anthesterion), *etc.*, but in practice, since the Attic year lasted 354 days (in twelve months of 29 and 30 days alternately), the needs of periodic intercalation (when it was done properly: three 'full' months – i.e., of 30 days each – during each eight-year cycle) mean that coincidence between the two calendars can never be taken for granted. Thus, when Attic dates are known, I have given them; otherwise Julian months, seasons, years represent declining orders of chronological precision.

359 (W) Philip's accession.
Treaty with Bardylis; Philip marries Audata.
Macedonian troops withdrawn from Amphipolis.
Philip contacts Kotys of Thrace; Pausanias is killed.
Argaios at Methone; marches to Aigai; is defeated by Philip.
Peace with Athens.
(A ?) The Paionians are suppressed.

358 (Sp?) Bardylis & his Dardanians are defeated.
Upper Macedonia annexed.
Philip aids Aleuadai of Larisa; he marries Philinna.

357 (S) Athens recaptures Euboia from Thebes.
Macedonian alliance with Epeiros; Philip marries Olympias.
Athens forms alliance with the three Thracian kings.
(e.W) Outbreak of Athens' Social War.
(W) Philip takes Amphipolis; Athens declares war.

356 Philip takes Pydna.
(Sp) Macedonian/Chalkidian alliance.
Appeal from Krenides.
Theban attack on Phokis & Sparta in Amphiktyonic Council.
(S) Foundation of Philippoi.
Coalition: Ketriporis, Lyppeios & Grabos against Macedonia.
The Phokians seize Delphoi.
(I) Athens joins the northern anti-Macedonian coalition.
The birth of Alexander.
The northern coalition (minus Athens) is defeated.
Capture of Poteidaia, which Philip hands to Chalkidians.
Capture of Apollonia, Galepsos & Oisyme (or e. 355?).
Phokian alliances with Athens, Sparta & other Peloponnesians.

355 (Sp?) Philip again lends troops to Larisa to resist Pherai (?).
(X/XI) Neapolis appeals to Athens.
(m.S) Athens' Social War ends; her alliance crumbles.
(A) The Amphiktyony declares sacred war on Phokis.
(W) Philip invests Methone.

354 (Sp) The Phokian Philomelos takes the offensive in Central Greece.
Methone falls to Philip; he takes Pagai.
(S/A) He moves along Thracian coast, takes Abdera & Maroneia.
Philip/Kersebleptes agreement.
Chares attempts to ambush Philip's small fleet at Neapolis.
Thessalian request for further aid.
Philomelos falls at Neon; Onomarchos takes the Phokian command.

353 (Sp) Onomarchos convenes the rebel Amphiktyony; he campaigns successfully (in Sp & S) in Western Lokris, Doris, Boiotia & near Thermopylai, but is defeated near Chaironeia.
Chares captures Sestos & campaigns against Kersebleptes.
(S) Philip enters Thessaly & drives back Pheraian/Phokian allies.
(A) Onomarchos advances into Thessaly; the Allies defeat Philip & the Thessalians; Philip withdraws to Macedonia.
Kersebleptes accepts Chares' terms; alliance with Athens.
Athens sends cleruchs to the Chersonesos.
Olynthos declares friendship for Athens & requests alliance.

Artabazos & Memnon granted refuge at Pella.

352 (l.W) Onomarchos campaigns in Boiotia, takes Koroneia (& Korsiai & Tilphosaion?).
(Sp) Philip returns to Thessaly, is elected Archon of the Koinon (or S 353?).
Onomarchos marches towards Pherai; Chares sails for Pagasai.
(Sp/S) Philip takes Pagasai & defeats Phokians on Krokion Plain.
Pherai surrenders; Philip expels tyrants & marries Nikesipolis.
Cession to Philip of Pagasai & parts of Perrhaibia & Magnesia; Macedonian colony founded at Gonnoi.
(m.S) Philip advances to Thermopylai, finds it defended, withdraws.
(V) Philip reaches Heraion; alliance with Byzantion, Perinthos & Amadokos against Kersebleptes.

351 (Sp) Last meeting of rebel Amphiktyony.
Boiotian & Phokian troops in Peloponnesian War.
(I/II) Philip falls ill in Thrace.
(III) The Thracian campaign ends.
Philip's warning to the Chalkidians.

350 Campaigns in Paionia & Illyria?
Campaign in Epeiros; Arybbas becomes regent; Alexandros to Pella.

349 (S ?) Return of tyrants to Pherai.
(*c.* ix) Invasion of Chalkidike begins; Philip takes Stageira. (A) Demosthenes delivers Olynthiacs; Olynthian/Athenian alliance.
Philip expels Pheraian tyrants again.

348 (VIII–IX) Athenian intervention in Euboia.
(Sp) Philip resumes Chalkidian campaign.
(S ?) Aristotle leaves Athens.
(vi) Euboians bring news of Philip's friendship to Athens.
Philip invests Olynthos itself.
Capture of Phrynon of Rhamnous.
Ktesiphon sent to Philip.
(viii/ix) Fall of Olynthos.
Ktesiphon brings Philip's good will; Philokrates proposes peace-talks, & is prosecuted, defended by Demosthenes & acquitted.
(W) Euboulos' decree (Aischines goes to Arkadia).

347 (Sp/e.S) Phalaikos removed from Phokian command.
(I) Demosthenes & Philokrates enter Boulē.
Athens co-operates with Kersebleptes in setting up Thracian coastal fortresses.

(l.S) Philip intervenes half-heartedly in C. Greece.
(W) Siege of Halos begins.
Phokian triumvirate offers Thermopylai to Athens & Sparta.

346 (i) Athenian decree inviting Hellenes to join in war or peace.
(VII) Phalaikos recovers Phokian command.
(e. VIII) Iatrokles returns; Aristodemos reports; Proxenos' letter arrives; Embassy I leaves for Pella.
(m. VIII) Embassy I arrives in Pella.
(*c*.20. VIII) Embassy I leaves for home; Philip leaves for Thrace.
(*c*.27. VIII) Embassy I arrives home; reports to Boulē & Assembly.
(9–13. IX) City Dionysia (during which Macedonian envoys arrive?).
(18/19. IX) Athenian Assemblies vote for peace & alliance, but excise exclusion-clause from Philokrates' decree.
(23. IX) Surrender of Kersebleptes to Philip.
(24. IX) Athenians & their synod-members give oaths to Macedonian envoys; exclusion-clause reinstated *de facto*.
(3. X) Embassy II leaves Athens.
(*c*.26. X) Embassy II arrives in Pella.
(*c*.22. XI) Philip returns home to meet Athenian & other embassies.
(13. XII) Macedonians in Thermopylai; Embassy II arrives home.
(16. XII) Assembly confirms & extends alliance; promises aid.
(*c*.17. XII) Embassy III leaves for Thermopylai *via* Euboia.
Demosthenes & Timarchos impeach Aischines.
(*c*.18. XII) Philip despatches letter(s) requesting Athenian aid.
(*c*.20. XII) Assembly considers & rejects the request.
(23.XII) The convention between Philip & the Phokians.
(25. XII) Embassy III at Chalkis hears the news & turns for home.
(27. XII) Embassy III reports to Assembly at Peiraieus.
(I) Special Amphiktyonic Assembly at Thermopylai.
Athenian prisoners released by Philip.
(II) The Pythia held with Philip presiding; Athens abstains.
(III) Amphiktyons demand Athenian assent to recent decisions; Demosthenes: *On the Peace*; Athens backs down.
(IV) Autumn Pylaia.
(W – 346/5) Aischines successfully counter-impeaches Timarchos.
Antiphon tortured & executed.

345 (Sp) Amphiktyons support Athens over control of Delos.
Philip reorganizes population-groups.
He campaigns against Illyrian Pleuratos.
Isokrates: *epistle* 2.
(A) Megalopolis & Messene (*et al.*?) denied admission to Amphiktyony.

344 (S) Philip enters Thessaly, puts down revolts, garrisons Pherai under dekadarchy, reintroduces tetrarchic national government. Demosthenes goes to Peloponnesos as envoy.
(m/l. S) Philip sends Python to Athens; Demosthenes' *Philippic* II. Athens rebuffs Persian embassy.
(A/W) Hegesippos in Pella.

343 (Sp) Thebans press for Phokian reparations to begin.
(S) Philokrates impeached, flees.
Stasis in Elis & Megara.
Philip refuses aid for Kallias of Chalkis.
Pro-Macedonian factions dominant in Eretria & Oreos.
(A) Trial of Aischines.
Phokian reparations begin.
(A/W) Philip sends final offer of Common Peace to Athens & himself goes to Epeiros.

342 (W) Philip removes Arybbas, installs Alexandros on Epeirote throne; he adds Kassopeia to Molossian Koinon.
Athens sends troops to Akarnania & envoys seeking alliances in western Greece & the Peloponnesos.
(e.s.) Aristotle goes to Pella & then Mieza as Alexander's tutor.
(vi) The final campaign in Thrace begins.
(S/A) Hipponikos, Eurylochos & Parmenion in Euboia periodically.
Philip consolidates Macedonian hold on south coast of Thrace, forms alliance with Getai in the north; he marries Meda.
(A) Antipatros presides at the Pythia.
(W 342/1) Violence between Kardia & Athenian cleruchs in the Chersonesos.
Establishment of military colonies in Hebros Valley.
Macedonian herald (Nikias) kidnapped by Athens.

341 (Sp) Philip sends troops to Kardia; calls for reinforcements.
Diopeithes attacks Thracian towns.
Philip sends envoy, whom Diopeithes tortures & ransoms.
(Sp) Athens/Chalkis alliance.
(l. Sp) Demosthenes: *On the Chersonesos.*
(e.S) Hermias kidnapped, tortured & killed.
Demosthenes: *Philippics* III & IV.
(S) Philip defeats Teres & Kersebleptes, removes them from thrones.
(S/A) Oreos & Eretria taken by Athens.
(A) Demosthenes, Hypereides, etc., as envoys to Byzantion, Perinthos, Selymbria, Chios, Rhodos & Persia.

Philip campaigns on west coast of Black Sea.

(W 341/0) Demosthenes & Kallias canvass support in W. Greece & the Peloponnesos.

340 (l.W) Demosthenes & Kallias report great successes & hoodwink the Athenian *demos* into approving Euboian League under Chalkis.

(Sp) Philip attacks Perinthos.

Phokian reparations halved.

(m.S) Philip's letter ([Dem.] XII); the Macedonian fleet is escorted into the Propontis; Persian opposition.

(e.A) Philip invests Selymbria, advances to Byzantion.

He captures the corn-fleet.

(ix/x) Athens declares war.

Alexander defeats the Maidoi & founds Alexandropolis.

Chares bottles up Philip's fleet in the Black Sea.

(l.A/e.W) Phokion replaces Chares at the Propontis.

(?) Philip sends aid to the Skythian Ateas, but is rebuffed.

339 (l.W) Philip makes peace-overtures towards Byzantion, etc.

Tricking Phokion, he extricates his fleet.

(Sp/S) The Skythian campaign.

(Sp) Amphiktyonic charge of Amphissian sacrilege.

(v/vi) Amphiktyonic meeting at Thermopylai; campaign against Amphissa.

Thebes seizes Nikaia.

(S) The Macedonian army, after Triballian defeat, returns home.

(A) Sacred War declared against Amphissa; Philip elected Hegemon.

(x/xi) Philip occupies Kytinion & Elateia.

(xi) Macedonian & Athenian envoys at Thebes.

Theban/Athenian alliance; defence-forces in Gravia Pass & at Parapotamioi.

(W 339/8) Philip beaten back in two skirmishes near Kephisos.

338 (Sp) Philip tricks defence-forces in Gravia Pass; Parmenion captures Amphissa, moves to Delphoi, takes Naupaktos & hands it to Aitolians.

Athens, Thebes *et al.* fall back to Chaironeia.

(7.II) Battle of Chaironeia.

Athenian settlement.

Theban settlement.

Further settlements in Central Greece.

Isokrates' *epistle* 3.

(x/xi/xii) Settlements in the Peloponnesos.

Delegates called to Korinth; proposal of Common Peace.

337 (W/Sp) Second meeting at Korinth; Common Peace established; sacred war declared against Persia.
(Sp/S) Philip returns to Macedonia; he marries Kleopatra.
Exile (?) of Alexander & Olympias; both soon recalled.
Campaign against Illyrian Pleurias.
Marriages of Attalos to Parmenion's daughter & Amyntas to Kynnane.
Pixodaros affair (or Sp. 336)

336 (Sp) Advance-party under Parmenion crosses to Asia Minor; the Greek cities & islands begin to join the Common Peace.
(S) Marriage of Alexandros of Epeiros to Philip's daughter Kleopatra; the assassination of Philip.

CHAPTER I

MACEDONIA: PEOPLE, LANDSCAPE AND TRADITION

ONE IS HARD PRESSED TO COMPREHEND the lasting forces that shaped the character of the ancient Greek and his polis without a firm appreciation of the geographical and topographical features of his peninsula, features that more perhaps than anything else have borne the responsibility for the comparative continuity of Hellenic society through the ages in the face of immigrations, occupations, political dismemberment and arbitrary reconstruction. But not much less fundamental to the historical processes played out upon this peninsula are the very different characteristics of the southern Balkan region, whence it protrudes into the Mediterranean basin. If the predominating feature in the formation of the peninsular societies was the mountain-ranges that separated and circumscribed them in small inland and coastal spaces, that limited their agrarian capacities and forced many to turn their eyes to the sea for trade and communication, in Macedonia – though the mountains are there too – it was more the extensive, fertile plains carrying large populations of more loosely knit tribal organizations that shaped these frontier-people of the Greek world. The society nurtured on these plains was quite different from those of the bulk of the contemporary Hellenic world, in the fourth century BC still more akin in many ways to the heroic kingdoms of Homeric times.

KINGS AND KINGSHIP

For formal purposes the king himself was the state; in documents of state his name alone, ungarnished by title and uncomplemented by other executives, stood for Macedonia.[1] (Where the title – King of the Macedonians – was included, which is extremely rare at this period, it seems to have been only when the king was to be represented or addressed as an individual and not as the state.)[2] For example, in the Delphic hieromnemon-lists, by contrast with the delegates of all other Amphiktyonic tribes, whose representation was expressed in the form of ethnics, the Macedonians were styled simply 'those from Philip' or

Map 1 The Aegean Area

BLACK SEA
R. Hebros
THRACE
Selymbria
Perinthos
Byzantion
Heraion
aroneia
PROPONTIS
Ganos
Ainos
Kardia
Sestos
Lampsakos
MBROS
Abydos
PHRYGIA
Ilion
AIOLIA
MYSIA
Mytilene
ASIA MINOR
LESBOS
LYDIA
HIOS
IONIA
SAMOS
NAXOS
KARIA
KOS
LYKIA
RHODOS

'those from Alexander'. This however is not to be taken to mean that the king was regarded constitutionally as absolute ruler of the state – for there were certain qualifications to his power – but rather that circumstances had not yet arisen (or were in our period only now beginning to arise) to render inadequate the primitive concept of the king as the personification of the state. With the conquests of Philip, Alexander and the successors, with the dismemberment of the expanded state and with the appearance of several 'Macedonian' armies and several different king-commanders there first grew the pressing need of a more precise definition not only of the state itself but of the status of the king in relation to it. The confusion of the sources during this period of expansion and fragmentation (especially between 334 and the 220s),[3] during which theoretically national rulers acquired extra-national territory to which their claim as conquerors was automatic but which it will not always have been politic to treat as their private property, has given rise to some eccentric, legalistic theories, but these need not detain us here.

The origin of the monarchy is lost in antiquity but there is good reason for likening it to the Germanic chieftainship described by Caesar and Tacitus,[4] involving an elected military commander whose authority in peacetime was initially a function more of his personal standing and strength than of his office. Such systems may have gone back to a common Indo-European root.[5] By the time of the historical period, however, the Macedonian monarchy had evolved and solidified into something more formal but with residual traces of its beginnings. With such a theory in mind, as well as such features as the common informality between king and subject, scholars have often and rightly called the Macedonian ruler *primus inter pares*, presupposing origins in a system in which power pre-existing in the people is in a sense delegated to the king by acclamation, or *election* – as opposed to one in which power pre-existing in the person of the king is acclaimed or *recognized* by the people.[6]

In practical terms the king was leader in all military action unless he cared to commission subordinates to specific commands. He was chief priest, responsible for the religious obligations of the state and its people to their gods. Certain specified cases apart, he was supreme judge. But his power was limited – to an extent that no doubt varied according to the personal *auctoritas* of the individual monarch – by ancient law or tradition,[7] not necessarily the less real for being oral. In general this must have governed the proprieties of the king's actions with respect to his people and theirs with respect to him. It tended to restrain him from absolutism. In a difficult situation one of Alexander the Great's courtiers – not even a Macedonian – was to remind his leader that Macedonian kings ruled 'not by force but by *law*' –[8] this in a context where the king, by attempting to enforce on his own subjects the Persian practice of prostration, was in effect seeking to alter the legal (or at least the traditionally *proper*) relationship between ruler and subject. On the accession of a new king the Macedonians swore to him an oath of allegiance[9] and, if (in the absence of further evidence) we may judge by the similarly constituted, neighbouring Molossian state, this was an undertaking 'to serve (or guard) the kingdom according to the laws', to which the king responded with an oath 'to rule according to the laws'.[10]

There seem to have been two specific limitations on the powers of the ruler: he could not designate his own successor, nor did he have legal jurisdiction in trials for treason, to which he, the state, was a party.[11] As regards the former, the crucial question is whether the act of acclamation (*anadeixis*) by the army represented a form of selection or merely one of recognition. The aftermath of Alexander's death strongly suggests the former.[12] Although circumstances at that time were complicated by the lack of a clear successor the issue was resolved by an assembly of the whole army – or, rather, the expeditionary army then at Babylon. The leaders had their own various schemes and interests but the army as a whole was prepared and able to go its own way.[13] From the solution itself and from the expressed wishes of the army it is clear that there was a strong and natural preference for the nearest-born;[14] and no doubt under normal circumstances the eldest son always succeeded. But is is also evident that, as in this case where no clear-cut and obvious choice was open, the decision was in the hands of the army, however much it might be influenced by the machinations of the living or the preparations of the dead. Normally, that is, in practice this military power may have amounted to no more than a confirmation of what had been made inevitable by birth and training. But when no suitable prince was available it provided a mechanism for designating a successor from outside the immediate family. In the case of a king's death before his eldest son was old enough to rule it may have been normal nevertheless to acclaim the boy king and to appoint a regent-guardian – provided at least that there was not too long an interregnum to fill and that there was a suitable regent offering. But it must have been possible – and in this lies the only real difference between the Macedonian and a truly dynastic system – when extremely difficult circumstances made it imperative to find a successor mature enough and of sufficiently regal stature to command the kingdom's loyalty from the outset, to by-pass the natural recipient. As in the case of Philip II's accession this will have been an easier decision when the alternative to a very young son was a mature brother of the deceased.[15]

With respect to the jurisdiction of treason-cases, the king, through his personal authority and through the role he chose to play in the proceedings, might influence the decision, even practically put it beyond doubt;[16] but the judgement was not his. Obviously enough, he might investigate and prosecute a case of treason; as the state in person he was automatically, one would imagine, the plaintiff. But, as with the Roman Republican tradition described by Polybios, he (like the Senate) was responsible for the 'public investigation' while the people or the army (in Rome's case, the military assembly of centuries) was the sole judge.[17] In peacetime, according to Curtius, this function of the army was discharged by 'the people'.[18] While we can scarcely believe that in a country so dispersed as Macedonia any meaningful assembly of the people could be convened, we may perhaps take it that the reference is to the army organization when not actually under arms. As we shall see, it seems likely that no other national institution existed in any case.

HETAIROI

Around the king stood his people. In the military context, virtually the only one surviving, they appear to have been his Companions (*hetairoi*), the common soldiers and certain others referred to as the Macedonians of the camp[19] – possibly analogous to the Roman *capite censi* (*i.e.* citizens without property) and probably indigenous and enslaved subjects, serving as menials and camp-followers.

Unfortunately, the term *hetairoi* seems to have been used somewhat vaguely. It applied, for example, to a certain element of the army: the Companion Cavalry (or simply 'the Companions').[20] Near the beginning of Alexander's reign these must have numbered 3,300 or more, in as many as fourteen territorial divisions plus a so-called Royal Squadron.[21] But only a few years earlier it could be said by Theopompos that the *hetairoi* were no more in number than 800, that they owned large estates ('no less land than 10,000 of the richest Greeks with the largest estates') and that they included not only Macedonians but Thessalians and others from elsewhere in Greece.[22] They were distinguished – or they should have been, according to this most jaundiced of authors, who thought they were not – by their excellence. These were 'the Companions of the King', or 'the Companions of Philip.' The word thus seems to have a narrower and a broader sense – or perhaps a social and a military sense; from the noble, large-landowning class, whose heads of families were the king's barons, came also (from its younger men,[23] the sons and close retainers) the heavy cavalry force of the army. From the former came also the experienced commanders and administrators, a pool of talent on which the king drew for appointment to responsible positions.[24] It – or part of it – formed as well an inner circle, a council of elders who might advise the king and served as his personal retainers, very like the Homeric *hetairoi* or the *comitatus* in Tacitus' *Germania.*[25] It was a class which lived, fought and drank hard, which hunted and feasted for relaxation and whose interests – since, like those of the Spartans, its estates were tended by serfs – were primarily fostered by war.[26] During Philip's reign the *hetairoi* seem to have been swollen by numbers of new men, even non-Macedonians, whose status, conferred by the king, was confirmed by grants of land from conquered territories.[27]

SOLDIERS

The soldier-class, presumably the smaller landowners (in practice, perhaps, the remainder of the Macedonian citizenry), might serve the king as infantry – either in the regionally levied Foot-Companions (*pezetairoi*),[28] in the elite corps of Shieldbearers (*hypaspistai*)[29] or as light cavalry (*prodromoi*=scouts, or *sarissophoroi*=lancers).[30] In 334 the infantry component of the Macedonians under arms, both in Alexander's expeditionary force and in the home guard under Antipatros, was 30,000 or more, which included the 3000-strong Hypaspists (the Royal Bodyguard) and perhaps a total of twelve to fourteen territorial divisions of Foot-Companions.[31] The light cavalry were small in number; only 1000 or fewer seem to have served in the expeditionary army.[32]

SUB-CITIZENS

Of the lowest class we know even less.[33] There must certainly have been a substantial body of sub-citizens, increased hugely by the con-conquests of Philip, serfs like the Spartan *helotai* and the Thessalian *penestai*, whose labours on the land made economically and socially possible the operation of large citizen armies over long periods. It will have been from this element and perhaps from lower citizen groups with particular non-fighting skills that the groomsmen, servants, wagon-drivers, labourers and camp-followers in general were levied.

ARMY AND STATE

These four divisions within Macedonian society are presented to us almost exclusively in a military context by sources whose interest in the kingdom, outside that in the king and his more immediate retainers, was exclusively in its military achievements. But, even allowing for this bias, it is surprising that we learn almost nothing of other aspects of this society. Perhaps in institutional terms there was no other aspect. Military service was a part of the citizen's obligation to his state – which is to say, to his king. The oath of allegiance, whatever its form, in all likelihood embraced this. But other liturgies were owed by people to state. After the battle at the Granikos in 334, Alexander buried the dead and to the surviving parents and children of the Macedonians he granted remission from three forms of liturgy: personal service (presumably the military obligation) and two taxes, apparently local and national.[34] Taxes had to be collected, and this was probably effected in local administrative districts coinciding with the regional divisions in which troops were levied. In Lower Macedonia, since the time of Archelaos, such towns as Pella, Mieza, Aigai, Beroia, Alkomenai, Pydna and Aloros and, in the territories annexed by Philip, such towns as Amphipolis functioned as regional centres. In Upper Macedonia, where the population was less concentrated, the administrative system was grafted on to the indigenous structures in the tribal principalities, Orestis, Eordaia, Tymphaia, etc.[35]

But there is no sign of any administrative class or of state officials other than the military-officer element, which raises the presumption that even in the regionalized post-Archelaos system the whole country and all its districts were administered through the military hierarchy – a 'civil' organization which drew its executives from the parallel military structure and took its orders, like the army, ultimately from the top, the king-commander-state. Thus when Alexander remitted what appear to be military and civil obligations they both fell in reality under the same military heading.

THE KINGDOM

Such was the basis of the tough, rugged and bellicose society forming an effective shield across the top of the Greek peninsula. It was a frontier society preoccupied with the survivalist concerns of a people obliged to defend a land of relative plenty against pressures from the massive tablelands and the precipitous valleys to the north. Its own frontiers were extremely long, like 'a great circle, the southeastern segment of which is filled by the Aegean Sea,'[36] and they had to be carved out and maintained by the sword and the spear.[37]

The western border at Philip's death – to establish the mise-en-scène of his reign – was formed by the high, rugged Pindos range and its outriders Mt Petrino running between the Lychnitis and Prespa lakes, and Mt Touria, farther north. The Pindos divides the major part of the Hellenic peninsula in half, into a northeast and a southwest, and level with the top of the Aegean it separated the Macedonians from their kin, the Epeirotes, on the Ionian Sea. From its northwestern extremity the border ran eastwards by Mt Babouna and the northern limits of the Erigon river plain, turning farther northwards as far as Stoboi, at the confluence of the Erigon and the upper Axios, farther eastwards via Mt Messapion and after crossing the Strymon it followed the southeasterly line of Mt Orbelos and thence across to the Nestos, which formed the eastern frontier. The southern limits were defined by the Aegean coastline, including the peninsula of the Chalkidike, as far south as Mt Olympos and the mouth of the Peneios.[38]

For the kingdom itself the starting-point must be the three great river-systems that water, to some extent define and in fact created Macedonia.[39] The greater inhabited part of this land comprises tertiary and quaternary alluvial plains scoured out by the passage of these rivers from the massive ranges that dominate the Balkan hinterland and deposited below them. The Haliakmon and the Axios together with the Loudias and the Echeidoros built up the Emathian Plain and continue to precipitate heavy deposits of silt in the Thermaic Gulf. Farther to the east are the Strymon, with its long, oblique plain dominated by the modern city of Serrai, and the Nestos, flowing southeastwards at the foot of the Rhodope massif and southwards to its marshy Aegean mouth. Farther east again, the Hebros similarly dominates Thrace. The primary characteristic of all these rivers is their 'European' or 'Continental' type, as distinct from their 'Mediterranean' neighbours south of the Peneios; they flow throughout the year without drying up or even drastically reducing their volume during the hot summer months.

The Emathian Plain, north and northwest of the Thermaic Gulf, has always dominated Macedonia on account of its central position, its size and the comparatively ready access from it into most of the surrounding areas – rather than because of its superficially impressive naval situation. In fact this gulf, like most of the northern coastline (with the exception of parts of the Chalkidike), is poorly protected from the southwesterly gales or from the northeasterly Etesian Winds (the Meltemi) that sweep down across the plains in summer and early autumn. The gulf, moreover, even nowadays presents sailors with difficulties caused by silting from the efflux of four rivers into its waters. The modern vessel of any appreciable draught is obliged to hug the eastern coastline above the Chalkidike to avoid sandbanks opposite the mouths of the Haliakmon and Axios, in spite of the advantages brought by modern dredging

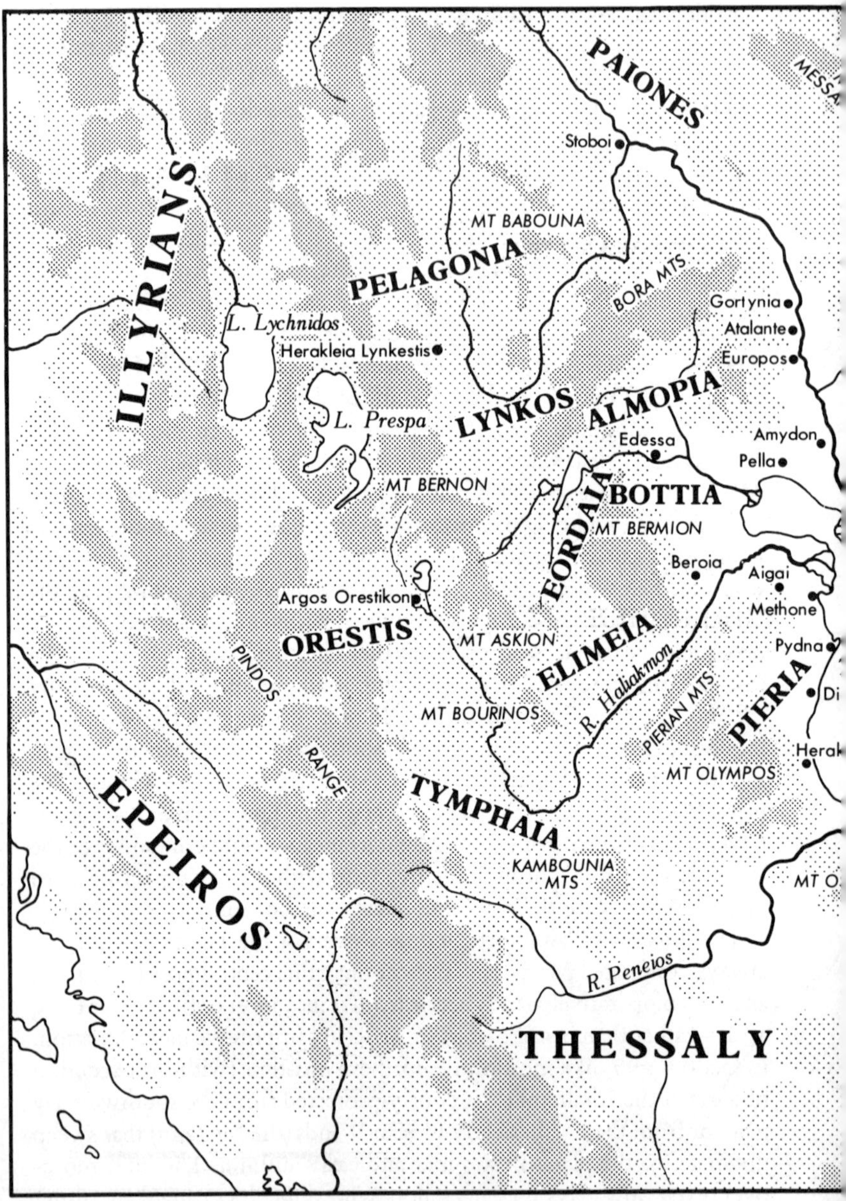

Map 2 Macedonia

RHODOPE MASSIF
SINTIKE
THRACE
MT MENOIKION
ODOMANTIKE
EDONIS
R. Strymon
BISALTIA
R. Angites
Philippoi
Abdera
Neapolis
MT PANGAIOS
Amphipolis
L. Koroneia
THASOS
L. Bolbe
Stageira
MYGDONIA
Anthemous
CHALKIDIKE
Akanthos
SAMOTHRACE
Olynthos
Poteidaia
Mende
Skione
LEMNOS
AEGEAN
SEA
N
1000 metres
200 metres
Sea level
PELION
0
20
40
60
80
100
Kilometres

techniques. Although the smaller ancient ship will have been less affected by this, the shallowness will certainly have contributed to the ease with which the waters were stirred up by the wind.

The Strymonic Plain, almost totally enclosed but for its narrow path between the hills at its mouth and the valley of the River Angites, which connects it with the inland Plain of Philippoi, is now the most fertile of the plains of Macedonia and Thrace; its significance in antiquity, however, lay more in its timbered and metalliferous environs. Except by the narrow coastal route the Strymonic Plain is approached only with difficulty from the west. The massive Krousia range and Mt Bertiskon extend from the low coastal hills for some 90 kilometres of almost impenetrable forest northwesterly to Mt Kerkine near Lake Prasias. On the east, except for the entry of the Angites valley, it is similarly shielded by Mt Menoikion, a continuation of the long Orbelos system and, near the coast, Mt Pangaion and Mt Symbolon.

The Plain of Philippoi (now dominated by Drama, 20 kilometres northeast of ancient Philippoi), is enclosed but for its connection with the Strymon. The only real passage to the east is that followed by the modern road from Kavala to its airport through the coastal hills. The plain was cleared and drained during the reign of Philip.

The plain of the lower Nestos may be passed over briefly. Only its smaller part – that west of the river-mouth – lay within Philip's Macedonia and in classical times it probably contained little more than marshlands. There is a conspicuous lack of ancient settlements on the coast between Neapolis (Kavala) and Abdera (near Cape Baloustro). Its main significance for Philip's reign is that the Nestos valley formed, with the Axios and the Hebros, one of the avenues of entry into the Aegean Basin from the areas north of Macedonia and Thrace.

West of the Emathian Plain three parallel mountain ranges run southeast and northwest, dividing western, or Upper Macedonia into two long, narrow series of valleys and small plains, the nearer drained by Lake Begorritis and its tributaries and the farther by the upper reaches of the Haliakmon. Both are terminated in the south by the Pierian and Kambounian ranges, which form the border with Thessaly, and in the north by Mt Babouna and its foothills at the top of the upper Erigon Plain and by Mt Touria, northwards of Lake Prespa.

THE ECONOMY

Thus the whole of Macedonia (as Philip left it) comprises a succession of five roughly parallel plains and valleys from the Pindos range to the Nestos, the broadest and most central embracing the head of the

Thermaic Gulf, and separated from one another by extensive ranges of mountains, penetrable only at intervals and not, especially in the west, without difficulty. The great bulk of the area is remote from the sea and little affected by it climatically – in marked contrast to more southern peninsular Greece. Winters, especially in the western uplands, are harsher and, especially nearer the coast, summers more oppressive and more unrelievedly hot than in the Mediterranean climate of Central Greece. At Monastir (ancient Herakleia Lynkestis) in southern Jugoslavia the January mean temperature is below freezing point and rises to 22°C in July, compared with coastal locations like Thessaloniki and Kavala, whose mean temperatures range from about 5°C to about 27°C with respect to the same months. In Athens the relevant figures are 9° and 27°.[40]

It is the fertility of the plains and the relatively high population-densities they sustain that account in large measure for the historical importance of the Macedonians, the frontier people of the Greek world. Cereals flourished (as they still do) in the large expanses available for their cultivation and horses, cattle, sheep and goats were grazed in abundance. Even now one-fifth of Macedonia is covered with forest and the mountains in antiquity were productive sources of timber and pitch;[41] the Dysoron-Bertiskon range and the high land of the northern Chalkidike in particular provided the best shipbuilding timber in Greece.[42] Game abounded. Herodotos mentions deer, boar, wild oxen and bears, as well as leopards, lynxes, lions and panthers.[43] Not unnaturally the hunt was a significant feature of the Macedonian economy and, for its youth, an important skill in the attainment of manhood. The man, however high-born, who had not yet succeeded in spearing his first boar without the aid of the net, was obliged, it is said, to sit at table instead of reclining with those who had established their manly prowess.[44] (In earlier days of lesser refinement, he who had not yet killed his first enemy was made to wear a halter instead of a belt.)

Copper and iron were available in considerable quantities and were mined and worked from the Late Bronze Age.[45] The same was true of gold and silver, the presence of which is attested from the silver mines of Damastion, north and east of Lychnitis,[46] to Philippoi in the Angites valley. Philip certainly mined the precious metal in the region of Mt Pangaion and in that of Damastion and very probably the silver mines of Mt Dysoron near Lake Prasias, which were first exploited by Alexander I, who derived from them one talent of silver per day.[47] The central town of the Pangaian area was Krenides, founded in 360 by Thasian islanders and refounded by Philip four years later as Philippoi.[48] The famous Asyla mines, which formed the basis of operations here and supplied undoubtedly his largest single source of revenue, were probably just east of Krenides, and returned an annual income of 1000 talents.[49] The principal other mining district near Pangaion was at Skaptesyle, south of the mountain and near the coast. It was said to have been owned at one time by Thucydides.[50]

With such resources Macedonia was self-sufficient. Such trade as passed over the frontiers was carried by land and the kingdom was in no way reliant on the sea. The population was large by Greek standards. When estimates must be based on the most indirect of information – arrived at mainly by extrapolation from military figures – clearly the imponderables are so great as to deter all but the foolhardy and the desperate. One has to guess first at the ratio of men under arms to the total military manpower available – done at best by analogy with other societies often hardly better known; then multiplication by a factor of 3½ or 4 may give a very general approximation to the total citizen population. This may in itself be a useful exercise, though its results can be expressed only in heavily qualified terms. But as regards the total population the larger problem for Macedonia – like that of the slaves for Athens and Rome – is the size of the subject element, those largely Thracian tribes that were not driven out at the conquest and occupation of their territory but apparently remained, some of them, to work the soil for their new masters. This 'rural proletariat' has been estimated as high as three fifths of the total population in 334, the only date for which we have moderately secure figures for men under arms.[51] Some control over the figures may be exercised by estimating the bearing capacity of the land,[52] but it is to be stressed that the following suggestions should be regarded only as the most general of indications.

POPULATION (IN 000S)

Adult male citizens			
– under arms in 334	35		
– not under arms in 334	50 – 60		
	Total	85 – 95	
Sub-citizens			50 – 80+
Total adult males			150+
	TOTAL POPULATION		500+

THE MAKEDONES

During the eighth and seventh centuries, as the result of a quite remarkable surge of expansive energy early in that period that has left archaeological remains far afield,[53] Illyrian tribes dominated the bulk of this area later to become Macedonia. One important site illustrating their presence – probably as a ruling military caste – is that near the neighbouring villages of Vergina and Palatitsia, on the foothills of the Pierian range overlooking the southwestern corner of the Emathian Plain, inland some 20 kilometres from Methone and seven or eight south of the banks of the lower Haliakmon.[54] Here the archaeological picture is of constant Illyrian occupation from *c.*800 BC until around the middle of the seventh century. Although this is only one of many such known to the excavator its importance – first of all, no doubt for its strategic situation – is noteworthy in the development of Macedonia. Farther southwards, on the slopes of Mt Titarion and the Pierian Mountains, together the northern extensions of Mt Olympos, were located the Makedones, giving their name to the area, Makedonis.[55]

In the early seventh century the Illyrian tribes occupying the northwestern corner of the Aegean area retreated quickly – for their roots were not deep – before a series of Thracian and Paionian thrusts, themselves under pressure from Kimmerian migrations southwards from southern Russia into the regions east and west of the Propontis.[56] The Illyrian strength contracted westwards and northwards towards their original (and later) homelands but they continued to occupy at least the uplands of western Macedonia-to-be, where they intermingled with the Molossian tribes that had survived their earlier expansion.[57]

EXPANSION

The Makedones somewhere near 650 BC became subject to a new and foreign ruling group claiming descent from the Temenid family of Peloponnesian Argos (a claim accepted in antiquity by both Herodotos and Thucydides as well as by the officials of the great festival of Olympia).[58] Their arrival is described by Herodotos[59] in a picturesque version which may have been circulated by the conquerors themselves to camouflage their dependence – in the assertion and perhaps the maintenance of their authority – on Illyrian assistance, for it was by way of Illyria that they had come and the Illyrioi still retained overlordship of this area, as the archaeological record at Vergina shows.

It was under this leadership, headed by Perdikkas I, the first of the dynasty of these Argeads, that the expansion of the Makedones began, probably in a movement northwards for the short distance to the southern bank of the Haliakmon. The Illyrian site at Vergina was taken and a capital established at this impressive point, ideally situated for a commanding view across the river and over the plain beyond. It was named Aigai, 'the place of goats' – a Delphic oracle later blessing its foundation in canting terms as 'the gift of aigis-bearing Zeus', a fertile place of flocks and 'gleaming-horned goats'.[60] During the century down to *c.* 550 BC the Argeadai Makedones extended their sway farther northwards over the areas of Bottia, Eordaia and Almopia. Driven before them the existing populations – or parts of them – migrated elsewhere, the Pierians apparently to the region of Mt Pangaion and the Bottiaioi into the hinterland of the Chalkidian peninsula. The Eordoi barely survived, their remnants settling at Physka in Mygdonia. The Almopes were similarly expelled, so we are told.[61] What we should understand, probably, is that while there were refugees there also remained a proportion of the original population as subject inhabitants of the conquered lands. The growing kingdom now stretched from west of Mt Bermion northwards to the Bora Mountains and eastwards to a narrow corridor held by Paionian tribes down the basin of the Axios. Beyond the river until the second half of the sixth century lay Thracian-dominated regions.

During this century of the rise of the Kingdom of Emathia the rule, according to tradition, passed successively through the hands of Argaios, Philippos I, Aeropos I and Alketas. But in the second half of the sixth, under Amyntas I (*c.* 540–498), the kingdom was extended and superseded. During his reign Macedonian domination extended as far as the mountain range bordering on the north of the Chalkidike, with the consequent annexation of part of Mygdonia, the valley of the Anthemous (the town or area of the same name was offered as a refuge by Amyntas to the exiled Athenian tyrant Hippias in 510)[62] and probably the narrow Paionian strip along the Axios (Amphaxitis).

Alexander I (*c.* 498–454), son and successor of Amyntas, increased the kingdom in the wake of the retreating Persian invasion-force to include the areas of the Krestones and Bisaltai, replacing their Thracian overlord. The territory of the Argeadai Makedones now extended northeastwards to Mt Kerkine, which bounds Lake Prasias on the north, and eastwards to the River Strymon – the whole of the area later described by Thucydides as Macedonia proper – as opposed to the related and allied but autonomous western uplands of Upper Macedonia.[63]

THE UPPER MACEDONIANS

It is unlikely that the Makedones had been sufficiently numerous or powerful to exert much influence on the upland tribes, among which an Illyrian element remained, but of which at least the southernmost were probably closely related to the Epeirotic tribes on and across the Pindos range.[64] But by the time of Thucydides 'the Lynkestai, the

Elimiotai and the other tribes of the uplands' were *Macedonian* (and elsewhere he refers to the first-named as Lynkestai Makedones).[65] It is thus clear that in the first three-quarters of the fifth century some degree of Macedonian power had made itself felt in the west – either, that is, during the reign of Alexander or in that of his successor Perdikkas II.

The evidence is slight, but these beginnings appear to be attributable to the former; and in this region too he may have profited from the Persian invasion of the Greek mainland. Apart from the likelihood of some penetration from Pieria into the more southerly uplands by Xerxes, which will ultimately have been to the advantage of his Macedonian 'satrap',[66] there are some signs of the establishment of a relationship from about this time between Elimeia and the Argead ruling house. We are told that a certain Derdas (apparently Derdas I, king of Elimeia) was the son of the Elimiote king Aridaios and was also cousin of the two sons of King Alexander I (Perdikkas and Philippos).[67] This presumably means either that Aridaios, himself an Elimiote, married a daughter of Amyntas I of Macedonia, or, if he was an Argead (which is more likely, since his name is common in the family), that he ruled the princedom with an Elimiote wife, who bore him Derdas, his successor.[68] Whatever the truth of it, the contact is clearly there, and it may even be a case of the temporary annexation of this upland region by the Argead kingdom; and it must date roughly to the time of Xerxes' campaign. If the influence of the central kingdom was not yet expanded farther north and northwest into Tymphaia, Orestis, Lynkos and Pelagonia, then at any rate it was by Thucydides' time. And if the inference is justified that such new relationships were born in enmity and distrust then that is consistent with their continuing pattern.

Significant are the terms in which Thucydides speaks of these associations: the uplands are, in his time, Macedonian in a sense – some allied and some subject – but they nevertheless retain their own rulers, unlike Lower Macedonia, which is under the rule of Perdikkas II.[69] These loose bonds amounted at best probably to mutual recognition of territorial limits, occasional treaties of friendship and, no doubt, at times the temporary acknowledgement of overlordship or of independence. Their troublesome and ephemeral nature may be seen in the attempts of the same Perdikkas (*c.* 454–413)[70] to subdue a recalcitrant and powerful Lynkestian monarchy, attempts made certainly with and probably also without the aid of the Spartan Brasidas.[71] A little earlier, after the revolt of Poteidaia from the Athenian Empire, the Athenians had exploited this divisiveness by enlisting the aid of Perdikkas' brother Philippos, along with Derdas I of Elimeia, in a campaign directed against the Macedonian king.[72]

In 382 Derdas II of Elimeia served in alliance with Amyntas III on the Spartan side against Olynthos.[73] Phila, probably the daughter of this prince, married Philip II either shortly before or shortly after his accession.[74] But such relationships were interspersed with the sort of enmity exemplified in the Elimiote alliance with Athens in 432. During the reign of Archelaos the king was forced to separate the Elimiote monarchy from his Upper Macedonian and Illyrian enemies by contracting a new marriage alliance.[75] Seventy years later, at the fall of Olynthos to Philip, among the prisoners taken was another Derdas, the king's own kinsman by marriage, brother of Phila.[76] He had probably gone into exile at the time of the king's marriage to his sister, whether in Philip's reign or in that of his predecessor, when Elimeia may have been finally annexed to the Argead kingdom. Of the Orestian monarchy we know almost nothing.[77] But we are better informed as to the sharp antagonisms traditionally dividing Lynkos and Pelagonia from the plainsmen of Lower Macedonia.

During the Peloponnesian War the Lynkestian king Arrhabaios seems to have been periodically at war with Perdikkas II, and this was indeed the normal state of affairs. Symptomatic of the fierce independence of this mountain monarchy was its proud claim to Korinthian Bakchiad descent.[78] While temporary agreements were occasionally expedient – for example, Arrhabaios appears as a friend and ally of the king in the Athenian/Macedonian treaty of 423/2[79] – he was certainly at war with Perdikkas around 418 and with Archelaos a few years later.[80] (On the latter occasion the Arrhabaios in question may have been the son of the former prince.) A Pelagonian, Menelaos, son of Arrhabaios, became and remained an Athenian citizen during the late 360s and the 350s, when Athens and Macedon were at war; he contributed aid and money to Athenian attempts on Amphipolis, which were being resisted by Perdikkas III.[81]

From the little information available to us it is of course impossible to trace relationships between the two Macedonias with any precision at all. But what we can say with some confidence is that almost whenever the activities of the upper kingdoms impinge on the attention of our sources – whether for this very reason or quite incidentally to it – the picture is markedly one of tension, mistrust and outright enmity. In Lower Macedonia the larger populations planted crops on the fertile plains; they lived a comparatively settled life on and around the estates of the Macedonian nobility and the king. In the western mountains, by contrast, the Upper Macedonians must have depended more on pasturage, with the rugged, shifting life-style that implies, in a harsh environment in which the transhumance of livestock is still practised.

Table 1: Genealogy of The Argead Dynasty: c. 540–298 BC

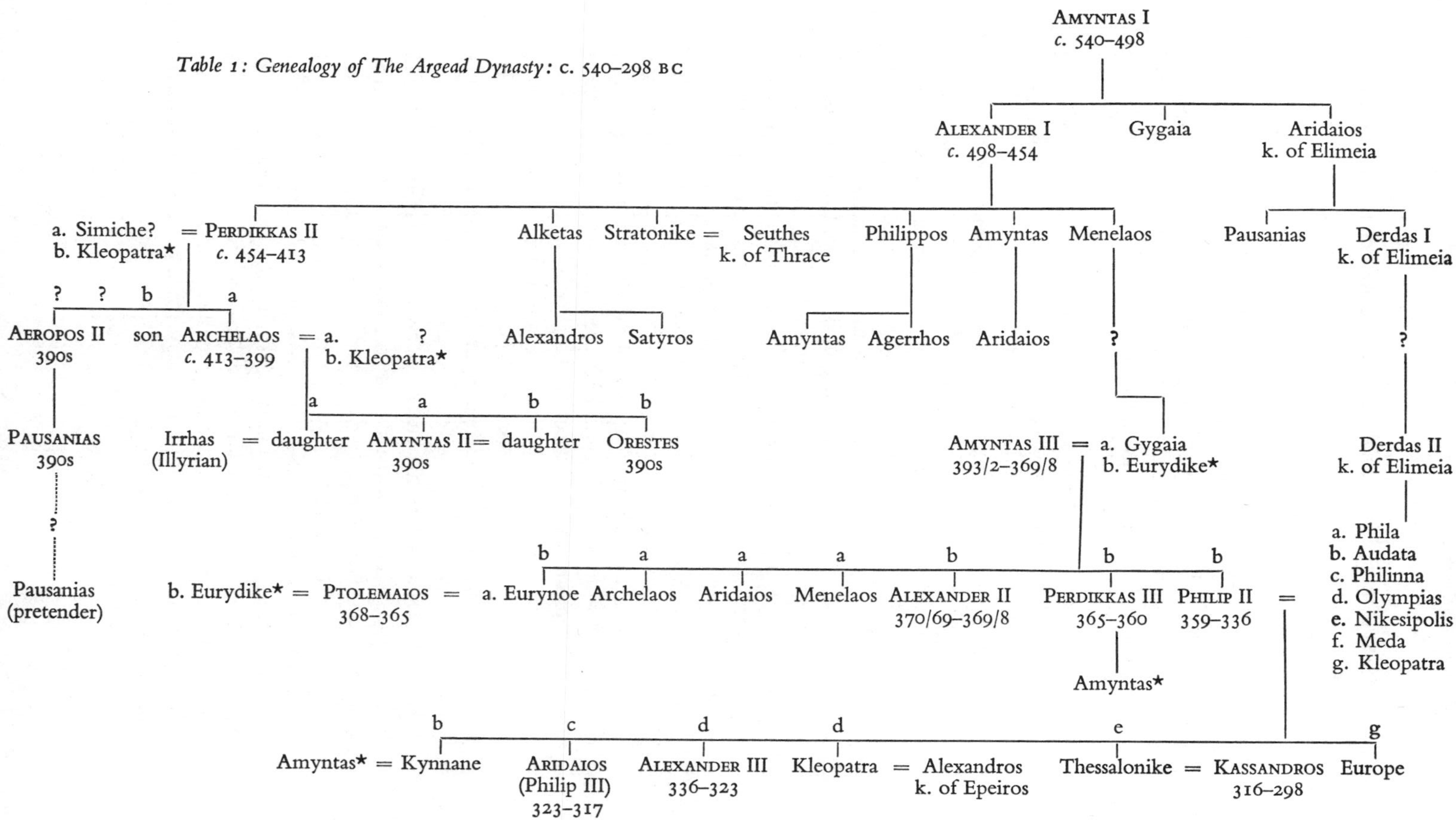

They lived a ruder life in smaller, more isolated communities, much more akin in many ways to the Illyrian tribes with whose fringes they were intermixed.

KING ARCHELAOS

Towards the end of the fifth century, then, Argead influence had extended intermittently into these western areas, but the important achievement of the previous decades had been the growth of the kingdom towards the east, as far as the Strymon. It was to some extent in acknowledgement of this that Archelaos (*c*.413–399), the son and successor of Perdikkas, removed his seat of government to Pella – although Aigai long remained the spiritual capital, burial-ground of the Argead kings and venue of some of the great occasions of state.[82] Pella lay northwest of the Thermaic Gulf on what was at that time either an inland extension of it or an inland water formed at an intermediate stage in the development of the gulf as silting impeded the access of the River Loudias to it.[83] Ideally situated with regard to the sea, yet (because the naval approaches from the gulf must have lain either up the river or through narrow and shifting channels in flat, marshy land) not especially vulnerable to seaborne attack, Pella, at its establishment as the capital, nevertheless provoked no Macedonian movement on to the sea, even though this was the period, at or just after the end of the Peloponnesian War, when the breakdown of Athenian power left a temporary vacuum between the shores of the Aegean. (Among the northern states it was the trading cities of the Chalkidian peninsula that profited from the Athenian decline.) Macedonia was a country whose resources were adequate to its needs and the economic basis and motivation upon which navies are built simply did not exist. Not until the reign of Philip II was any attempt (known to us) made to build a fleet, and that very limited in scope. Archelaos' motives must be sought elsewhere.

His new capital was more centrally placed in the extended kingdom, better insulated against incursions from the southwestern frontiers. The king may have been especially concerned at the proximity of the two Greek colonies, Methone and Pydna, with the latter of which he was at war early in his reign.[84] But there is some reason to believe that Archelaos' accession was dubiously achieved[85] and it is possible that he was also concerned to raise a new power-structure dependent on his own patronage away from the long-established nobility clustered about the old Argead court. Within a generation Pella was the largest Macedonian city.[86]

The kingdom was anything but homogeneous. During the acquisition of the original areas of Pieria, Bottia, Eordaia and Almopia, its kernel, although large bodies of pre-Macedonian occupants may have been expelled or slaughtered, one tribe or a small group of tribes from one part of Pieria could not fill and defend so large a space; indigenes in large numbers must have remained there in alliance or subjection to the newcomers. Expansion eastward of the Axios by the time of Perdikkas II had added diverse groups of Paionian, Edonic and Thracian stock. The kingdom was a conglomerate of tribal territories interspersed with small settlements acquired piecemeal over many generations. There can have been little sense of cohesion.

The response of Archelaos, so we may infer from indirect evidence, was to reorganize Lower Macedonia into a series of cantons dominated by and perhaps administered from central towns[87] – and it is perhaps also in this context that the transfer of the capital belongs. His attempts to strengthen the military capacity of the state probably accompanied the broader reform, with the new centres serving as agencies for recruitment. According to Thucydides there were, before the time of Archelaos, few strongholds and fortresses in the country; it was in his reign that the bulk of those known to him were constructed (presumably, therefore, late in his period of exile.)[88] Good military roads were built and the kingdom was generally organized more efficiently for war by provision for 'cavalry, arms and other equipment beyond what was achieved by all eight of his predecessors'. It was apparent to the Athenian author that the military capabilities were uneven; the cavalry was excellent (though perhaps not numerous) but the infantry was totally inadequate. Thus Perdikkas II, when meeting a Thracian invasion led by Sitalkes in 429, had not even considered levying the infantry forces but based the defence entirely (and on this occasion successfully) on his horsemen. It is likely, if we picture a Macedonian society comprising a pre-existing peasantry subject to the Makedones themselves, that a feudalistic structure combined with an agrarian economy could hardly produce anything, in territory eminently suitable to horse-breeding, but a horseborne landowning class together with an under-equipped motley of peasants and serfs.[89] The implication of Thucydides may be – though this is arguable – that Archelaos gave his attention not only to the cavalry, which was already effective, but to the creation of a proper infantry from the smaller landowners of Macedonian stock;[90] but the traumas of the decades to follow, which must have largely erased any advance he may have made in that regard, preclude any certainty.

Archelaos also – apparently to a more remarkable extent than any of his predecessors – deliberately fostered the spread of Hellenic culture, perhaps in the hope that it might override particularist local ideas and ideologies. Painters, musicians, poets – men of the stature of Agathon, Timotheos, Zeuxis, Euripides – travelled to his court.[91] It seems that in some ways the beginnings of a national identity, or at least the intention to establish one, may be attributed to this king. The more tragic then for the kingdom that its energetic leader was struck down in his prime with no heir strong enough to guarantee a stable succession.

ANARCHY AND INVASION

The state lapsed into near anarchy over the next few years. Orestes, the young and legitimate successor, was despatched by his regent Aeropos, who was followed briefly on the throne by his own son Pausanias[92] and, apparently at the same time, Amyntas II (another, younger son of Archelaos).[93]

The reign of Amyntas III began with the murder of Pausanias in 393/2. (Amyntas II was killed by the Elimiote Derdas.)[94] But although he reigned for 24 years this period was not as secure as its length might suggest.[95] His accession was the signal for an Illyrian invasion, against which the king contrived to strengthen himself through alliance with Olynthos, the powerful hegemon of the Chalkidian League.[96] But when the invasion came, probably in 392, it was so quickly successful that no help arrived. However, forced initially to abandon his capital, Amyntas was able, by making a grant of territory (probably including the Anthemous valley and the near-by area of Lakes Bolbe and Koroneia), to attract enough Olynthian assistance to regain control. Thessalian aid seems to have been involved. But the price of salvation was high. The Illyrians withdrew but on condition of an annual tribute, which continued for over three decades.[97] At about the same time Amyntas took as wife the Illyrian princess Eurydike, presumably as a further condition of peace.[98] Then, during the 380s, the alliance with Olynthos turned sour and this decade saw the installation of a rival king, Argaios, almost certainly the creature of the Olynthians, who ruled in opposition to Amyntas for two years (*c*.385–383) before he was expelled; at the same time Olynthos expanded so far into Macedonia that even Pella itself fell under its power. Only Spartan intervention between 382 and 379 restored the king to his capital and the lost territories to the kingdom.[99]

THE SONS OF AMYNTAS

Over the past century, since Argead authority had extended to the Strymon and into proximity to the cities of the Chalkidian peninsula and to Amphipolis, for which Athens still intermittently contended, Macedonia had become the prey of the major powers, Athens, Olynthos and Sparta. Vulnerable on its western and northern flanks to Paionian and Illyrian penetration and unable, for lack primarily of internal cohesion (for the efforts of Archelaos had had no time to take hold), to utilize its manpower and resources in its own defence, Macedonia was incapable of pursuing a policy of independence. Amyntas realized this and, observing the renascence of Athenian sea-power in the early and middle 370s, aligned himself accordingly in 375 or later. In 371 at the peace conference in Sparta the Macedonian delegate relayed the king's acquiescence in the Athenian claim on Amphipolis, a clear sign that Amyntas was prepared to submerge his local interests in the hope that a stable relationship with the revived naval power would pay higher dividends.[100] But the battle of Leuktra soon destroyed that hope and during the 360s the Macedonian kingdom swung back and forth between Athens and Thebes in their contest for northern influence. Indeed it soon emerged that the Athenians had insufficient interest in fulfilling treaty-obligations in the northern Aegean; the following two decades or so were to see a constant policy of unparalleled irresponsibility on the Athenian part, in which alliances were contracted without any real hope (or even intention) of carrying out the warranties assumed under their terms.

Alexander II (the first son of Amyntas and Eurydike), after a brief foray into northern Thessaly, relieving his ally Larisa from occupation by the troops of the tyrant house of Pherai but remaining to outstay his welcome, was pushed back by the advance of the Theban commander Pelopidas and retained his throne at the price of Theban alliance and the surrender (among other hostages) of his younger brother Philip.[101] Within the next year he was dead at the hand of his brother-in-law, Ptolemaios of Aloros, who married the queen mother, Eurydike, and reigned technically as regent for her second son, Perdikkas. During this reign there seems to have been a temporary renewal of alliance with Athens, for we hear of the intervention of Iphikrates to prevent an attempt on the throne by a certain Pausanias.[102] But a second northern campaign by Pelopidas in the summer of 367 brought Ptolemaios back into line with Thebes, which is reflected in his combination with the people of Amphipolis to resist Athenian ambitions there. At the renewal of the Theban alignment Ptolemaios was obliged to hand over fresh hostages and at this time the young Philip was restored. He had been in Thebes between 369 and 367. He was aged 13 or 14 at his surrender and 15 or 16 at his return and we can scarcely credit the stories circulated by some ancient and modern authors that learnt and developed at this time many of the military ideas with which he was to inculcate the Macedonian army a decade and more later.[103]

In 365/4 Perdikkas (the second son of Amyntas III and Eurydike) killed Ptolemaios and followed him on the throne. Later in his reign the anti-Athenian stance hardened to the extent that in the face of strongly renewed efforts by successive Athenian commanders to take Amphipolis Perdikkas allied himself with the threatened city, supplying troops for its defence.[104] The combination was successful and, since Athens' antagonism towards Olynthos was too strong to allow her to seek assistance from this quarter, she proved herself ultimately incapable of recovering her strength in the northern Aegean.

Confidently – overconfidently – Perdikkas now turned to handle the perennial enemy, the Illyrians. The tribute imposed by the Dardanians on his father had been continued by his elder brother and probably by Ptolemaios.[105] Following what was apparently a minor triumph in the northwest the young king mobilized his forces for a major strike against the Dardanian king, Bardylis, and the two armies met in battle.[106] The new optimism of the Macedonians was dashed. After the battle four thousand troops and the king lay dead. The victorious Illyrians began to mass for invasion. The Paionains of the upper Axios valley took the opportunity to plunder and pillage in their vicinity. Since the dead king's son was as yet very young, at least two claimants to the throne materialized to oppose Philip, now 23 years old, the youngest son of Amyntas III. His major rivals, Argaios and Pausanias, received backing from foreign powers which hoped to capitalize on the confusion.

Such, in early 359, was the inheritance of Philip II. None of his difficulties was unusual in Macedonian history, though rarely if ever had a new king faced such a barrage of them. In the ensuing years Philip was to find means of dealing with the external enemies of the kingdom. But no less serious and much more basic to the security and wellbeing of the state was the fact of its own disunity, the geographical, historical and possibly ethnic discontinuity between east and west, between Upper and Lower Macedonia. To remedy this would be not only to build a firmer defence against outside interests but to unleash a driving national energy that would in the end lead the Macedonians with remarkable success very much further afield than their present narrow but threatening horizons.

CHAPTER II

359–357
THE ATHENIAN ALIGNMENT

PHILIP'S INHERITANCE

THE DEFEAT OF PERDIKKAS by the forces of the Dardanian Bardylis could hardly have dashed more abruptly the Macedonian optimism that had provoked the clash.[1] Four thousand Macedonians lay dead with their young king. Depression lay heavy over the country, for not only was the external threat to Macedonia more immediately serious than for at least three decades, but the dead ruler's natural heir, his son Amyntas, was no more than a child. Enemies of throne and state on all sides gathered themselves to pounce. Paionian tribes in the north, never so well organized as to present a real threat in times of relative stability but now for the first time showing sufficient unity to boast an overlord, Agis (whose successor, at least, was to mint coinage in his own name),[2] began pressing downwards along the Axios valley in search more of plunder than of conquest; this was seen by the contemporary Ephoros, whose account of these first years is circumstantial and credible, as a sign of their 'contempt' for the Macedonians. The victorious Illyrians,[3] already occupying probably a substantial area of western Macedonia, began to mass for a concerted thrust to the heart of the kingdom. Old claims to the throne were revived and encouraged. Athenian hopes rose at the prospect that in the confusion a puppet might be installed who would aid rather than hinder their attempts to recover Amphipolis; their candidate was Argaios, almost certainly he who had ruled briefly in the late 380s as the creature of Olynthian expansion.[4] To the east a Thracian king, probably Kotys,[5] advanced his interests by supporting the claim of another exiled pretender, Pausanias, certainly the one who had tried, under the somewhat similar circumstances of 368, to seize it for himself – again, probably, with Chalkidian backing.[6] Seldom can any state have so nearly approached total dismemberment without utterly disintegrating.

But there was a respite and it proved enough. Perdikkas, at some time after the return, probably in 367, of his remaining brother Philip from hostageship in Thebes, had decided to establish the younger man in a command of his own.[7] Whether this amounted only to a grant of estates which would support him and a household of retainers and guards, or was the creation of some form of 'dukedom' is unknown (as is its location), but it is tempting to see here a connection with the marriage of Philip to the Elimiote princess Phila, daughter of Derdas II.[8] In 348 we find Phila's brother, another Derdas, among the Macedonians' prisoners at Olynthos.[9] His action in leaving the country (at a date unknown) and joining its enemies was possibly prompted by his displacement by Philip from the Elimiote throne. Since Phila, by her Macedonian and regal birth, ought to have enjoyed a high status at the Macedonian court and since, on the other hand, no more is ever heard of her, we should expect that she was married either very early in the reign, dying shortly afterwards, or before it began, in a marriage that did not survive the link with Illyria through the marriage with Audata (359) – or perhaps that she simply produced no child. Elimeia thus rates fairly highly as a candidate in the very tentative efforts to identify this land allocation. It was far from the blandishments of power at the court in Pella and at the same time strategically situated athwart the important inland passes between Macedonia and Thessaly.

Such a cession, wherever the land, was no doubt a gamble, there always being the chance that Philip might have used these resources to precipitate his own accession. At any rate, fortunately in the event for his country, he was able to assert successfully his own claim to the throne and was acclaimed King of the Macedonians.[10] When the decision of the army was called for, Philip was not the only possible candidate. Argaios and Pausanias can hardly have presented themselves, since, after their respective activities in the past, they must have lived in exile, as is confirmed by their appearance at this time in league with foreign interests. Three elder stepbrothers of Philip – Archelaos, Menelaos and Aridaios, sons of Amyntas III and his earlier wife Gygaia – were alive and may have been in the country in 359, though it is unlikely that they were serious claimants on the army's attention. It is probably later that the eldest, Archelaos, gave cause or pretext for his liquidation and the pursuit of his brothers.[11] But the most obvious contender for the crown, and under normal conditions its natural recipient, will have been the young Amyntas, son of Perdikkas III.[12]

As we have seen, while in practice the military assembly may normally have simply confirmed the succession of the eldest male son, it nevertheless could act otherwise. It might appoint a regent and guardian, or, if the natural heir were particularly young, it might presumably set him aside altogether – as the nine-year-old Philip V was later to be set aside in slightly different circumstances but by the same authority. In 359 the son of Perdikkas was at the most eight years old; he may, and this seems more likely, have been no more than a few months.[13] And if the assembly was as a rule guided by the custom of dynastic continuity, it did have the power to break this normal chain, such critical circumstances as those of 359 presenting the strongest justification for doing so. The young Amyntas was passed over, though he remained alive throughout Philip's reign, enjoying a position of some stature[14] – which we should lay to the credit of the confidence induced in the new king by his own industry and success and the undisputed high regard in which he was held by the majority of his vast subjects.

THRONE AND FRONTIERS

Philip's new role was unenviable, literally beset as he was on all sides; not at all the situation to inspire in him at this early stage the monumentally ambitious schemes sometimes attributed to him. However, in his handling of the immediate difficulties and his concurrent concern for the long-term problems he demonstrated from the outset the skill that continued throughout his reign to win him success.

The first requirement was time. It is unlikely that Perdikkas in 360/59 had been able to levy substantially more troops than Philip collected in 359/8, so that those now dead represented probably one third and possibly one half of the available manpower under arms. Of the survivors a great many, like defeated soldiers past and present, must have drifted away to their homes, frightened, dispirited and content only to cling to family and property as inconspicuously as possible. Curiously, delay was granted by the Illyrians, and this was crucial; but some explanation must be sought as to why Bardylis, recently victor in such decisive terms over the Macedonian army, did not press his advantage; not until more than a year later – and then on Philip's initiative and not his – was battle again joined. Ephoros (through Diodoros) recounts explicitly the Macedonian fears of what was to follow from this quarter and comments that Philip took over a Macedonia 'enslaved' to the Illyrians, and yet he offers no reason for so vital a delay. It seems necessary to surmise the negotiation by Philip of an armistice with his neighbour. At about this time, presumably in either 359 or 358 – that is, either before or soon after his Illyrian victory broke this Illyrian 'enslavement' – Philip took an Illyrian wife, Audata, probably the niece or daughter of Bardylis.[15] On her marriage the girl is said to have adopted the name Eurydike,[16] one which after the trail of blood and Illyrian associations left by her namesake (probably her cousin or aunt) was not likely, we may suspect, to be of Philip's choice. But if the marriage and the name were forced upon him then the likely date is early 359, when Macedonia would have been obliged to beg for terms, and not 358, after the defeat of the Dardanians, when any conditions laid down would have been at Philip's pleasure. The daughter born by Audata, Kynnane, remained at Pella to be married eventually to Amyntas Perdikka,[17] but the mother does not appear again in any source. If the marriage-alliance was contracted in 358 to seal the new peace then it was remarkably ineffective, because in only two years the contracting states were again at war. On the other hand, if dated to 359, such a treaty, including the marriage-bond, would explain the delay over this crucial year during which Philip was able to establish his own position, meet the most pressing internal problems, conciliate Athens and defeat the Paionians. No doubt such a treaty was humiliating, though in that regard hardly new to the Macedonians, but it was also necessary.

Dardanian honour was assuaged, for Bardylis in his extreme old age had re-established with a vengeance the now customary superiority of his tribe over the Macedonians; tribute payments were no doubt resumed and guarantees of submission received. We may only guess at other terms of the treaty. In all likelihood substantial areas of Upper Macedonia remained in enemy hands, especially Lynkos and Pelagonia, perhaps not without some co-operation from the local nobilities, and it is possible that guarantees were extracted regarding the Illyrian status there. Such conditions were little more than Bardylis had sought in the past, and they were now again sufficient. For Macedonia they provided a respite.

AMPHIPOLIS AND ATHENS

At the same time, it being plain that the most urgent Athenian contention involved the ownership of Amphipolis and that the Athenians were prepared to back their ambition with money and men, Philip withdrew from Amphipolis the military aid supplied by his brother and with gifts and promises beguiled the Paionians into a temporary peace.[18] At his accession Amphipolis was at least technically and probably in fact autonomous,[19] so that Ephoros' assertion that he withdrew from that city 'after first declaring it autonomous'[20] needs to be interpreted as an affirmation of its existing status. Sixteen years later in the Athenian Aischines' catalogue of Macedonian ingratitude and Athenian forbearance, in which we should expect over- rather than understatement, the orator can say only that Perdikkas 'fought on behalf of Amphipolis against our city'. Clearly, his action had entailed not the garrisoning of a subject city but military aid supplied to an ally, which Philip now simply recalled – hardly, as Demosthenes was to claim and as others have since thought, tantamount to an actual cession of the territory to Athens, since it was neither his to give, nor theirs, without first taking it by conquest, to receive.[21] This is, however, not to say that Philip's intention was not to create an impression of philathenian benevolence – that indeed was the whole point, for he urgently needed Athens' alliance – and he followed up with a request for a formal declaration of peace between the two states.

With the Athenians cogitating and the Paionians for the time quiescent, Philip was able to turn to his eastern frontier, whence the challenge of Pausanias came. With his Thracian and possibly eastern Macedonian support, known for his earlier attempt on the throne and for his royal blood, Pausanias must have appeared to pose a serious threat. But once again, promises and bribes were sufficient to undermine the endeavour. Philip appears to have entered into communication with Kotys before the latter's death and may even have travelled to meet him personally at Onokarsis.[22] Since the accession of the one and the death of the other fell in close sequence and, therefore, there can have been very little communication between them, it is very likely that the object of this intercourse was Pausanias, who was, in the event, abandoned and killed by his erstwhile supporter. The tripartite division of Thrace on Kotys' death[23] and the consequent struggles among his successors put paid for the time to any further Thracian ambitions in Macedonia.

In Athens the newly improved prospects of success over Amphipolis had the effect Philip wished on opinion there, and, far from the substantial support that might have been expected to follow any signs of success in Argaios' quest for the throne, the Athenians now hesitated over whether to abandon the Macedonian exile. Before receiving Philip's overtures, they had dispatched a force of 3000 hoplites with naval support under the command of Mantias,[24] but his orders were now evidently countermanded. Argaios was landed at Methone, a pro-Athenian Greek enclave on Macedonian soil and there virtually left to his own devices; Mantias and the bulk of his force remained at Methone while Argaios with his own mercenaries, his fellow exiles and it seems a few Athenians, perhaps volunteers from among the hoplites, set out for Aigai where they hoped to win favour. It is interesting to see, in view of Demosthenes' later accusations of duplicity on Philip's part over the whole question of Amphipolis, that the Athenians at that very time, finding promise in both of these horses, were cannily hedging their bets. Since Philip, as the man in control, was presenting a friendly aspect, official aid was withdrawn from his rival; but, in case of Argaios' success, the Athenian troops were close at hand to assist in his consolidation and to remind him of his obligations.

Making his way inland to the west, the pretender marched his supporters the 20 km or so across the northern foothills of the Pierian Mountains to the old Macedonian capital.[25] In strategic terms this was a well-situated base, commanding the northward-facing slopes with a useful view across the Haliakmon and the southern extent of the Emathian Plain, and dominating, with Methone, the southern coastal approaches to the kingdom. Further, as the old capital, Aigai may well have contained groups of potentially dissident noble families whose power had been eroded by the transfer of power to Pella some forty years before. Some such explanation seems called for by Argaios' hopes that without even resorting to force he might win over this city to his cause. But such hopes proved vain, and he began his retreat to Methone. With, at most, only 25 km. (each way) to travel there had been every chance of his escaping, if necessary, before Philip's forces could be mobilized and brought down from Pella, a good 60 km. away on the northern shore of Lake Loudias. But he had underestimated Philip's speed of movement or his ability to anticipate, for he was intercepted before reaching the coast. It is in fact very difficult to approach Argaios' likely route in secret from the northern side, most of his path lying across slopes commanding the whole panorama of the plain across which pursuit must come, and it may be that Philip was already in his area. At any rate, the surprise on top of the failure at Aigai was decisive and the royal forces had no difficulty in defeating the pretender, carefully distinguishing in the fighting and in the negotiations that followed between Argaios' mercenaries, many of whom were killed, the Macedonian exiles, who were taken prisoner, and the Athenian volunteers, who were released without ransom and with compensation for their losses.[26] Argaios at this point disappears from history.

By the middle of 359, then, Philip's standing as leader of the Macedonians is already high among his countrymen, his initial achievements, in keeping with most of those to follow, being characterized by an economy of military effort balanced – indeed, made possible – by skilful diplomacy and delicate timing. The loyalty of the people of Aigai had been considered suspect, at least by Argaios, but their choice – that between the younger brother of the dynamic Perdikkas, whose abilities were already becoming evident and who had in particular caused formidable Athenian support to melt away, and the pretender, whose only real chance of success had been at spear point – had been, in the event, a simple one. Philip's first known military engagement, although his opposition may not have been very impressive, had been an unqualified success and must have helped raise the army's morale.[27] In Athens, opinion, once hostile and then undecided, solidified in favour of the proffered peace. The withdrawal from Amphipolis and the deliberately generous treatment of the prisoners taken near Methone had advertised the attractions of Philip as ally rather than enemy, so that the alternative attraction of alliance with Olynthos and its league won little support among the Athenians.

The Olynthians in fact were surprisingly late starters. Quick in the past to press their northward interests, their first known appearance in 359 was as rival suitors in Athens when that city was already debating Philip's peace-offer (although it is just possible that they had been backing Pausanias' claim on the throne). We are to take the two bids as alternatives, of which Athens, in choosing one, must reject the other. As Demosthenes said, when support for the Macedonian agreement was gaining momentum, some Athenians were even for expelling the Olynthian envoys from the city – though he did not say whether they actually suffered any more than the refusal of their request. For the Chalkidian League the issue was important. Although they can not yet have seen in Philip's Macedonia much more of a danger to themselves than it had been in the past, which was negligible, two of his activities must have given them cause for disquiet. His overtures to Athens, if successful, might well hem in the Chalkidian peninsula between a hostile Macedonian hinterland and an equally hostile Athenian sea. Further, if nothing more, the military reconstruction taking place across the frontier must already have thrown into jeopardy their important link with the silver-mines at Damastion, on which they had for decades been dependent for bullion.[28] Relations between Athens and Olynthos in the past decade had been unsurpassedly bad, and no doubt the former's unwillingness to accept the bona fides of so sudden a change of Chalkidian heart as well as the attraction of the new Macedonian king's overtures combined to produce the favourable Athenian response.

But their decision was not taken in ignorance and we err if we read it as the cynical hoodwinking of a naïve and gullible populace. Cynical it may have been and expedient it was, on Philip's part; on that of Athens it was no less so. In a costly war even a temporary advantage was worth pursuing, however little either side was likely to fall into the trap of guileless belief in the other's beneficence.

It is possible that we have part of an Athenian record of the preliminaries to the treaty in a few lines of an inscription apparently praising ambassadors from Macedon at a date early in Philip's reign, presumably in response to messages of goodwill.[29] As to the terms of the treaty itself[30] there is some doubt, hingeing largely on the meaning of Demosthenes' words: 'by saying that he would hand over Amphipolis and by cooking up that much bandied-about secret he won over our simple souls right at the beginning . . .'[31] It is most unlikely, as we have seen, that Philip straightforwardly recognized the Athenian claim to Amphipolis, for, whatever Demosthenes might assert here and elsewhere, the fact that Aischines failed to remind Philip of such a concession (or even to pretend later that he had done so), when he had no reason to suppress it and every reason, in support of the case he was making out, even to exaggerate,[32] must militate conclusively against it. But if Philip neither promised to hand over Amphipolis, because it was not within his power, nor acknowledged an Athenian right to it, he had, by his withdrawal, at least tacitly foreshadowed such recognition.[33] Probably some Athenians mistook the inference for the intention and very likely Philip carefully compounded their misapprehension with noncommittal encouragements. It is in any case unlikely, we may conclude, in spite of the vacillations of his predecessors on this subject, that Philip had to pay a high price for this peace; in a theatre where failure had followed failure the Athenians would find joy in any gain. All that was required of the Macedonian – and all, according to our best source, that he did – was to withdraw his military aid from the city and to affirm its independence of him.[34]

THE ARMY

The peace established, Philip was sufficiently relieved of external pressures in the late summer of 359 to devote his energies to border problems and perhaps to continue the military build-up he had certainly already begun. Ephoros' account (in Diodoros) of the first months of the reign lays heavy stress on the action taken by the king to reorganize, arm and train the Macedonian armed forces. In particular he singles out the infantry for mention.[35] We need not imagine that the evident transformation of Macedonian military capacities was anything but an arduous, expensive and protracted process; and it certainly took place over a good many years. But in view of the massive blow to manpower and morale suffered so recently, it is very likely that Philip gave much of his time at this stage to military matters. This is, therefore, an appropriate point to look briefly at some aspects of the subject. Although we are moderately well informed of the characteristics of Alexander the Great's army and are often justified in assuming that these were fundamentally the king's legacy from his father, we are on much shakier ground when we arrive at the task of assessing whether

Philip's responsibility for them was as innovator, reformer or merely transmitter. Just as, to the Athenians, practically every decree enacted outside living memory had to be Solonian, so there has been a tendency among modern as much as ancient authors to attach every pre-Alexandrian military feature to Philip.

The first clear achievement of Philip in this area was his very substantial expansion of the army. In part this was no doubt made possible by an increase in population, itself a product of the stability and security of Philip's reign, but in large measure it must have amounted to a realization of the hitherto little-tapped potential of the kingdom. Little is known of the army, especially of the infantry, before 359. The *pezetairoi*, according to Anaximenes (a contemporary, who should have known the current version), had been founded by Alexander I, a king whose expansive military efforts were by no means negligible.[36] In the century following his reign, however, not only does their title appear in no source but (and this may be the explanation) the only surviving references to infantry suggest that this first act of organization turned out, in the longer term, ineffective. The infantry remained a virtual nonentity. Nevertheless it was possible for Philip in 358 to levy 10,000 foot under difficult circumstances, and Perdikkas had presumably led as many against the same foe eighteen months earlier. When Philip is credited, therefore, with the virtual creation of the Macedonian phalanx[37] we are presumably to take this as an allusion to remarkable advances in size, training and technical sophistication – but not, even mistakenly, to the foundation of the *pezetairoi* themselves.

The *hypaspistai* are equally unknown to our pre-Alexander sources. Theopompos, writing during Philip's reign, seems aware of their function but – if so – misnames them *pezetairoi*.[38] But in spite of their late emergence into Greek awareness they were probably an ancient institution.[39] Originally, it is clear, they were a small foot-guard of the king; hence their occasional name, *somatophylakes* (bodyguards), which reminds us of their proper function.[40] They were a specially recruited force – distinct from the territorial levies of the Foot-Companions – chosen evidently (since their pay was higher) for their quality, and serving as the king's personal guard. By 334 they were 3000-strong, arranged in three chiliarchies, distinguished from the phalanx proper by their separate origin and recruitment rather than by any variation in armament,[41] and trained to serve in the new army, because of their smaller size, in a number of more mobile capacities.[42] As with their numerous fellows of the phalanx, they were not originated by Philip; but they were probably expanded in a similar way by him and trained in a new tactical use as the connecting link between phalanx and cavalry.

In 358 Philip raised 10,000 infantry and 600 cavalry to defeat Bardylis.[43] In 334 the grand total of Macedonians under arms was in the order of 35,000 with over 30,000 foot and 4000 horse.[44] Although the former figure was drawn from a smaller Macedonia than the latter it will presumably have represented, unlike that for 334, the heaviest levy the population could bear in the circumstances. So that, although certainties are out of the question, it is clear that over the period of Philip's reign a very substantial expansion of military resources had been effected. During Alexander's reign it was possible to spare substantial reinforcements for the expeditionary army without noticeably affecting the capabilities of the home guard under Antipatros.

High in the priorities of Philip's military programme must have been the provision of incentives and rewards at all levels. Most striking are the twin positions of the Companion Cavalry and the ('Companion') Hypaspists.[45] Both were élite corps in a special relationship with the king. Both could be regarded as royal. The Hypaspists' recruitment was presumably on the basis of excellence[46] – which is to say that their existence was an incentive to good service on the part of the *pezatairos* and a reward for his achievement. The same may have been true of the Companion Cavalry at a different level. Whether a high standard of service on the part of a light horseman could advance him to the *hetairoi* we cannot say. But Theopompos observed with surprise that the latter class (meaning the noble landowners) comprised not only Macedonians but Thessalians and other Greeks,[47] which means that Philip (that is, presumably he and not earlier kings) must have ennobled some of them. At this level, then, elevation was possible – even to the *hetaireia* – for the outstanding. The Companions, certainly, were levied by districts, but since these apparently depended on the location of the nobles' estates and those were granted (at least to new *hetairoi*) by the king, presumably as a concomitant of ennoblement,[48] this is no bar to our regarding the Companion Cavalry, like the Hypaspists, as an élite body to which access was possible from outside.

More usual inducements applied throughout the army, although our evidence for them relates only to the infantry. Arrian writes of 'double-pay men' (*dimoiritai*) and 'ten-stater men' (*dekastateroi*): 'the latter so called from their pay, which is lower than that of the *dimoiritai* but above that of the undifferentiated common soldiers'.[49] The pay-differentials arising from this passage and from an inscription-fragment probably of 336/5[50] (in which Hypaspist-pay is set at one drachma per day) appear to relate to three basic variations on standard infantry (*i.e.* *pezetairos*, presumably dr. 25 per month) wages: the Hypaspist rate at 30 per month, the ten-stater men at 40 and the double-pay men at

50.[51] These differentials were not for separate ranks; the lowest level of NCOs, the *dekadarchai* were superior to all of them (so Arrian). Apart from the prospect of advancement through the ranks, then, regular financial and status inducements were offered to the Macedonian soldier, in addition to the irregular emoluments of special bonuses and booty, such as Alexander later distributed.

These rates of pay are not Philip's, but presumably the status-differentials they reinforce were used by him. It has been urged that he had little need to spend money on his own soldiers, who were in any case obliged to serve him and might need sustenance only on longer and more distant campaigns.[52] And, if it is correct to assume that the Macedonian army down to the infantry class comprised landowners, large down to small, then the soldiery was in any case to some extent self-supporting.

But even with the use of mercenaries in later years to ease the burden of citizen-service[53] and allowing for the probability that Philip avoided heavier levies than necessary of the military classes,[54] still an appreciable call for service must have been made on the smaller farmer, who could less afford it. Yet only once do we hear of dissatisfaction among Philip's troops (although, had it been known to exist, Demosthenes would surely have delighted in reporting it)[55] and that was on account of a tactical blunder that cost unnecessary lives.[56] It seems justified, then, to conclude that the rewards for service under Philip, as under Alexander, were considerable. Macedonia's revenues were large and they were utilized to the full.[57]

We have noticed that land-grants were made to those elevated to the *hetaireia* and probably also to existing Companions.[58] The same benefits, it seems possible, were conferred on ordinary Macedonians, as Diodoros suggests when speaking of the division of Methonaian territory 'among the Macedonians' in 354.[59] To confer land on citizens was in some societies the best way of creating eligibility for military service, and this may well have been the king's aim; when it is remembered that the case for land-grants to *hetairoi* rests largely on a fortuitous fragment of Theopompos and on our knowledge of the areas represented by cavalry-squadrons,[60] it may be deemed a simple misfortune that, where the infantry are concerned, our sources mention (from a total of 12 to 14 recruitment districts) only three, and these by chance from Upper Macedonia. A fuller list might have allowed conclusions as to land-grants to the common Macedonians similar to those possible regarding *hetairoi*.

The inducements to wholehearted and efficient service were therefore very considerable and must have justified in the mind of soldier and officer alike the firm discipline and constant training and service demanded.[61] They served to bind the forces as a unit with its allegiance to its king-commander. In such ways an army was created that functions as a highly efficient and unified body. Developments made in the area of armaments were probably peripheral. Philip is said to have introduced the *sarissa*, a longer stabbing-spear. But on the whole his foot-soldiers were more lightly armed than the Greek hoplite, more akin to the Thracian peltast.[62] The heavy cavalryman carried a short sword, but his main weapon was a stout, iron-tipped stabbing-spear of cornel wood perhaps two metres long.[63] His armour, comprising iron helmet, some form of breastplate and protective padding (of bronze or leather) for the shoulders, neck and hips, and a smallish shield,[64] was much the same as that of the foot-soldier (except for the breastplate, which the latter did not wear). Although the bridle was in use, saddles and stirrups were not, so that fighting on horseback was a matter first of using the animal's weight and speed and then, once in contact, of the cut and thrust of hand-to-hand combat – rather than the armoured clash of mediaeval knights.

It was the use to which the heavy cavalry was put that distinguished Philip's army, especially in the eyes of most Greeks, to whom the horseman was an expensive luxury. The equestrian skill of the Macedonian troopers combined with the highly trained, relentless phalanx allowed the use of the latter as a base or pivot for all-out attack by the former, the striking arm. The Greek army, with its heavy, cumbersome line of hoplites, was no match for the variety of tactics open to Philip and his successors, although these are seen only in glimpses during Philip's reign itself, for the sources allow no more, but are clearly evident during that of Alexander.

PAIONIA AND ILLYRIA

In 359 much of this lay in the future and, in any case, probably counted in the end for less than the sheer confidence that flowed from victory after victory. As he prepared his forces to terminate the Paionian raids and for the important confrontation with the Illyrians of Bardylis, Philip knew that the most effective counter to the recent blow to the morale was a resounding triumph. When it came, at least, to the Illyrians, no quarter would be given and no prisoners taken.

The Paionian problem was not difficult and no doubt Philip tackled this first in order to train his soldiers against the easier opposition. There seems at no time to have been much interest among these inhabitants of the northern river-valleys in expansion southwards out of their fertile pockets.[65] Short-lived spells of military endeavour, brought about by the rise of an unusually strong chieftain, elevated by the zeal of his followers (and perhaps the ignorance of our Greek sources) to the status of king, could always be relied upon to subside into divided inactivity. Philip now availed himself of the death of one such leader, Agis, to launch an expedition to the north. Short and decisive it seems to have been, followed presumably by acknowledgements of allegiance by the defeated, recognition of frontiers and guarantees of military service when required. A small Paionian levy was taken to Asia by Alexander in 334, but we do not know when military service was first required of them. The Paiones, it is important to note, must inevitably play a significant role in Macedonian northern defences. Occupying especially the Axios valley, the main avenue of access to the Emathian Plain, these tribes represented a useful buffer on the fringes of Macedonian interest in that direction. Periodic demonstrations of military strength when necessary, but probably amicable relations on the whole, and the establishment of a string of fortresses at strategic points along the course of the Axios offered secure enough defence in that area, unless there should arise inordinate pressures from the populous Danube region beyond.

Either very late in this year or, more probably in the light of the harsh winter in this area, in the spring of 358,[66] Philip was able to reconsider his relationship with the Dardanian Illyrians with some degree of confidence in his rear. We have already had occasion to note the power of the kingdom of the Dardanoi, built up in the first four decades of the fourth century by Bardylis, now an old man of 90 years. The Dardanoi, one of the three most powerful Illyrian tribes (with the Autariatai and the Ardiaioi),[67] had been able through the weakness during this period of Macedonia and Epeiros to extend their influence southwards over Dassaretis and the important areas to the north of Lake Lychnitis, as well as westwards into Upper Macedonia and southwards into Epeiros – achievements sufficiently impressive to have attracted the alliance of Dionysios of Syracuse.[68]

Philip's preparations, his mustering of 10,000 foot and 600 horse, must have given some cause for concern to Bardylis, for the latter initiated negotiations apparently in the expectation of an easy settlement;[69] but his only proposal for maintaining the existing peace was that both sides should retain the territories they already held. The Macedonians, he proposed, should be content to continue to endure the occupation of their northwestern princedoms. Bardylis' mixture of mild misgiving and over-confidence, totally misguided as it turned out, should make it clear to us that to a contemporary outsider, at least, Macedonian military strength was far less daunting than we might anachronistically suppose it.

The offer failed. Philip, obliged to bargain from weakness in early 359 was now prepared to test and demonstrate his strength. The armies, equally balanced in numbers, met probably in the Erigon valley close to Herakleia Lynkestis (near modern Monastir), a likely location in view of the cavalry Philip took with him into this mostly mountainous area. Seeing that the Illyrian centre was strong, Philip placed his picked infantry on the right wing, then, using his horse to harass the enemy flanks and rear, thrust forward against its left. As this began to fold, Bardylis drew his flanks in and back into a defensive square, which held for a time but eventually broke, his ranks fleeing the pursuing Macedonians. The battle plan here is interesting in that it is in marked contrast with those of Philip's and then Alexander's later battles, according to which the cavalry served an offensive role, with the infantry primarily an anchor or pivot. Although it has been thought on this count that the plan was not Philip's at all but possibly that of one of his leading generals, Parmenion,[70] this conclusion is not at all necessary, depending, as it does, on the unlikely assumption that Philip had been able by this early date to effect in substance the military reforms whose results on tactics are later so marked. The army we see in action here, as regards its numbers and mode of fighting, was hardly different from its predecessors, although the confidence in his infantry implied by Philip's assignment to it of so central a role may lead us to believe that retraining had already begun.

CONSOLIDATION IN THE WEST

The victory, in the course of which 7000 Illyrians fell, was significant, although it was won far to the south of the central area of the Dardanian kingdom. Philip annexed the territory of Bardylis in Dassaretis as far as Lake Lychnitis, which at once gave him a more easily defensible frontier to his northwest and effectively impeded further Dardanian incursions southwards through the valley of the Drilon. In order to strengthen this line he began, probably at this time, the process of disentangling the population groups in western Macedonia, which probably for decades had seen the admixture of Macedonian and Illyrian stock.[71] The dispersed Macedonian mountain-groups were amalgamated into communities based on the small plains, superficially at least more akin to the Greek *poleis* than to the scattered pastoral groups whose movements followed the seasonal needs of their stock. Such a process must have involved some changes to the local economy, since the more settled life introduced to these areas implies an agrarian rather than pastoral system. This indeed is a feature of the speech attributed to Alexander at Opis three decades later:[72]

> Philip found you resourceless nomads, most of you dressed in sheepskin, pasturing a few sheep on the mountain slopes . . . he gave you cloaks instead of sheepskins, brought you down from the mountains to the plains . . . and made you dwellers of cities . . .

Transhumance of flocks, however, must have continued side by side with the new life, as it does to this day. Probably now too fortresses were dotted along the strategic passes to the northwest.

The Macedonians will hardly have believed that such measures would settle their problems finally on these frontiers; some resurgence of Illyrian and Paionian ambitions was to be expected, though it was perhaps unlikely to be so well concerted that periodic demonstrations of military superiority would fail to control it. However, some of the benefits were immediate. The most urgent requirement in the northwest and the west generally was for the reorganization of Upper Macedonia, and the relief of pressure won by these victories allowed that to be effected. The process has been regarded by some as an annexation, and in a sense this is so. But, as we have seen, the Upper Macedonian kingdoms had long been regarded as Macedonian and Philip will have been able to pose, with some justification, as the deliverer of his own people. The local princely houses and nobility had much to lose and some may have offered opposition. It may, for example, have been at this time (rather than before Philip's accession) that Derdas, probably an Elimiote prince, left the country; his appearance on the Olynthian side in 348 does not oblige us to suppose that his flight from Macedonia had taken him directly to that city.[73] In an inscription of 362,[74] a Menelaos the Pelagonian was named benefactor of Athens for his assistance rendered to Timotheos in the war against the Chalkidians and Amphipolis; he served, that is, on the side opposing his king, Perdikkas. Not long afterwards the same man was honoured by the city of Ilion in Aiolia as Menelaos, son of Arabaios, the *Athenian*.[75] It is possible, therefore, that this man (who may once have been Pelagonian king, but was certainly no longer so),[76] his period of antagonism terminated by Philip's annexation of the uplands, fled from Macedonia to receive Athenian citizenship.[77] The inscription from Ilion is not precisely datable, so that no certainty is possible, but since Philip could have expelled him before 358 and since Demosthenes' account of the matters appears to assign Menelaos' activities in Asia Minor to 359 at the latest, it seems more likely that he left Macedonia either voluntarily or as the result of pressure by the Pelagonian king[78] or, most likely, because he was driven out by the Argead king Perdikkas III, as the latter prepared for his campaign against Bardylis – a campaign intended *inter alia* to establish central control in the western uplands.[79]

The evidence for Upper Macedonian resistance, then, is far from certain. In the main, the few indirect indications we do have suggest that the local nobility, faced by superior power, took the line of least resistance and acquiesced in the annexation in return for recognized status in the enlarged kingdom – and perhaps, with it, a better vantage point from which the situation might be redressed in the future. Parmenion, who had possibly been king of the Pelagonians at Philip's accession, cast in his lot with Philip.[80] He is soon found commanding part of the royal army in his own area against Illyrians (356), and his status and influence throughout the reign are never in doubt. Three brothers from Lynkos – Alexandros, Heromenes and Arrhabaios, the sons of Aeropos – although they do not appear in the sources in the intervening years, are clearly powerful and influential men at the time of Philip's death; one, Alexandros, was by 336 married to a daughter of Antipatros and was a suitable appointee to the military governorship of Thrace.[81] The Perdikkas who became one of Alexander the Great's leading commanders and co-regent after his death was of the royal family of Orestis,[82] whence also came Pausanias, the member of Philip's bodyguard who stabbed him to death in 336.[83] The nephews of Derdas and sons of Machatas – Harpalos and probably Philippos and Tauron – who also occupied positions of stature in Alexander's army and administration, were probably from the royal house of Elimeia.[84]

But although this must have been a period of carefully planned activity – and the priority given it above other pressing problems accentuates its importance – it is likely that after the initial battle with the Dardanians large troop concentrations were unnecessary. And, in view of the inevitable trials of strength to follow, much of Philip's attention must have been given to the military build-up whose effects begin to appear within the next few years; in 356, for example, the army was to be capable of subdivision and simultaneous use on two different and distant fronts. Some reaction was to be expected from the Paiones and Illyrioi. From the Olynthians too, with Chalkidian access to the silver of the Damastinoi now closed off by central Macedonian control of the passes of Lynkos, reaction was likely. The mines of Damastion had now fallen under Philip's control and, although he allowed minting to continue there throughout his reign, new coin types reflect the change in ownership by the replacement of the ethnic by the names of two men, presumably administrative officials.[85] The eastern frontier at the Strymon was vulnerable to Thracian incursion –

a danger that could be considered no more than temporarily averted as a result of the division of territory and power within Thrace following the death of Kotys in 359.

THESSALIAN CONTACTS

Therefore, probably in late 358, Philip embarked on a flurry of diplomatic and other moves that were to complement the alignment with Athens already serving his interests. It is clear, although our sources give us little more than hints of its extent, that for decades there had been some understanding between the Macedonian Argeadai and the leading noble family of northern Thessaly, the Aleuadai of Larisa.[86] No doubt this link had been strained when Philip's eldest brother had attempted in 369/8 to retain under his own control the two cities he had delivered from the tyrant of Pherai,[87] but when an appeal came from the Aleuadai in 358 for assistance against the same enemy[88] this was the perfect complement to the aid certain Thessalians, probably they, had successfully advanced to Amyntas III, when in 392 he was temporarily driven from his country by Illyrian invasions.[89] Between the end of Philip's Illyrian campaign and his first-known contacts with Epeiros, that is in either late 358 or early 357, Philip accepted this plea and formed an alliance to resist the power of Pherai. Since our sources confuse this initial involvement in Thessaly with the definitive interventions of 353 and 352, we cannot be sure what commitments he contracted or actually fulfilled, though, in spite of his more immediate problems, he does appear to have supplied troops to his new ally.[90]

In keeping with what one source elevates to the level of policy, Philip cemented his treaty with the cities of the Thessalian League by marrying a woman of Larisa, probably a member of the Aleuad family.

OLYMPIAS

Then, at some time in 357, Philip contracted what was to become the most significant of his marriages, that to Olympias, who was a daughter of the late Molossian king in Epeiros, Neoptolemos. This arrangement, a natural enough link between the related Epeirote and Macedonian tribes, represented a successful intrusion into an alignment of some standing between the Molossians and Athens, and was to survive the disintegration of the latter's own treaty with Philip soon afterwards. In the 370s, Alketas, then king of Molossia in central Epeiros and educated in Athens, had entered the second Athenian alliance together with his son Neoptolemos.[91] On the former's death, the accession had been disputed, the army – which probably had the same powers in this regard as its Macedonian counterpart – placing both Neoptolemos and a younger brother, Arybbas, on the throne. By 357 Neoptolemos had died, leaving Arybbas king and guardian of his five-year-old nephew Alexandros.[92] Neoptolemos was also survived by two daughters, the elder, Troas, now wife of the ruler, and the younger, Olympias, probably in her middle to late teenage, now marriageable.

Although the marriage is represented in the sources as an *affaire de coeur*,[93] it was a bond expedient for both parties. Threatened and damaged, like their Macedonian kinsmen, by the expansion of the Dardanoi of Bardylis,[94] the Molossian overlords of Epeiros were impressed by Philip's great Illyrian victory and by the new treaty in force between their Athenian allies and the Macedonian king, and Arybbas was now content to ally himself also to the latter. For Philip too, during this time of reorganization in Upper Macedonia, the prospect was attractive, assisting, as it must have done, in the proper definition of the common frontier of the two states, at least by mutual agreement over the proper allegiance of the tribes occupying the Pindos slopes – though six years later this issue seems to have led to a serious dispute.

The Epeirote princess thus moved to the Macedonian court, at the latest towards the end of 357. In a polygamous situation there is no need to assume that she replaced Philip's existing wives, Phila, Audata and Philinna; neither the morality nor the politics of the occasion demanded it. Philip may have 'waged war by marriage',[95] but the wives he thus marshalled were not, as it happened, to be remarkable for their fecundity; Philip himself was to be deficient in the production of male heirs. Only two wives, Philinna and Olympias, bore sons, one each, to Philip, but that of the former was evidently mentally deficient[96] – and it is for that reason rather than out of diplomatic expediency that Olympias was later to enjoy the superior status accorded the mother of the heir apparent. It may have been that by this time neither of the first two wives remained on the scene. But whatever, if anything, had happened to Phila (and her crime, to judge by the silence of the sources, was that she was barren), and even if the Illyrian treaty sealed by Audata's marriage had been superseded, at least the latter's daughter remained at court to be married later to her cousin, Amyntas.[97] It is clear that, although among Macedonian royalty influential women were sometimes able to exercise power to an extent unusual in the Greek world,[98] the sins or deficiencies of the mother were not visited upon the children. (Rather, in reverse, the deviation of the offspring was likely to damage the parent.)

ATHENS' SOCIAL WAR

Meanwhile, outside Macedonia the Aegean power balance was in flux. It was apparent, following her recapture of Euboia from Boiotian hands in the summer of 357, that Athens, although in purely territorial terms her naval domination appeared impressive, was badly over-extended financially.[99] With the prospects of allied revolt looming, the Athenians took steps to safeguard their weak point at the entrance to the Black Sea by an alliance with the three kings of Thrace, Berisades, Amadokos and Kersebleptes.[100] But her actions of late had become increasingly reminiscent of her great imperialistic days of the fifth century, and, in the autumn, three of her more powerful allies seceded from her alliance. Joined shortly afterwards by Kos and with open aid and encouragement from the Karian dynast, Mausolos, the recalcitrants began to marshal their combined fleet at Chios.[101] After the heady success of their Euboian campaign,[102] the Athenians were quick to meet the challenge. However stretched their finances, this crisis faced them with the alternative prospects of seeing their whole alliance crumble before their eyes or of reconstructing the league convincingly enough to allow the reconstitution of its finances on a basis more favourable to themselves. For Athens the issue was crucial, and her attention and efforts must be wholeheartedly concentrated on it. Her northern and other interests, in so far as they were not involved directly in the allies' activities, would need to be pushed aside for the time being, for, dangerous as that might be, too much would hang on the outcome of the immediate war to allow any distraction from the achievement of her aims in it.

THE CAPTURE OF AMPHIPOLIS

If Athens' vital stake in the new conflict was not immediately realized, it was at any rate soon to become clear to the Greek world. Shortly after the return of the Euboian expedition, two Amphipolitans, Hierax and Stratokles, presented themselves in Athens before the *demos* with a plea 'to sail and take over the city' (as Demosthenes was to express it).[103] For such a course of action to have been even remotely plausible, the city must still have been free from Philip, but there must nevertheless be more than a little doubt over the orator's confidence that the Athenians, had they seized their opportunity, could simply have assumed control of Amphipolis there and then. The verb Demosthenes uses (*paralambanein*, translated above 'take over') is too indefinite in meaning to tell us, if we were prepared to believe him, whether an Athenian force would need to fight the inhabitants for possession (as they had already done in vain during six decades) or might simply accept it as a gift – though on grounds of sheer improbability the latter possibility should be dismissed, even if it is the orator's clear implication. It was to his advantage to parade this occasion as a simple opportunity missed. Demosthenes, as a matter of interest, did not call Hierax and Stratokles *envoys* (though Theopompos did).[104] But if they were officially commissioned and dispatched by the Amphipolitan *demos*, they were at any rate not *merely* envoys, for at least one of them was later to be among those exiled and outlawed after the fall of the city to Philip,[105] who is unlikely to have courted unnecessary unpopularity[106] or to have wasted his time by punishing mere instruments of the popular will. Hierax, Stratokles and presumably Philon and others must have represented a pro-Athenian or anti-Macedonian faction that feared Philip's growing strength more than distant Athens; but we must remain uncertain whether such a view was shared by the bulk of the Amphipolitans. This would presuppose a remarkably abrupt swing of opinion away from that which had welcomed the loan of King Perdikkas' troops[107] and which had fortified Amphipolis against Athenian designs for nearly two-thirds of a century.

No Athenian expedition was sent, by way either of pre-emption or, later, when the siege began, of assistance. On this count the case for acceptance of Diodoros' word in placing this appeal just after the outbreak of the Social War is strengthened.[108] The appeal, itself perhaps a desperate attempt to forestall any move by Philip to capitalize on Athens' new preoccupation, was unsuccessful because it was too late. Philip then struck, still reassuring the Athenians of his good intentions, but able now to choose the moment to preclude all chance of intervention; this campaign belongs in the autumn of 357, when the Etesian Wind (the Meltemi) will have made navigation at least problematical, or (more probably) in the ensuing winter, when it will have been impossible.

For Philip this heralded a substantial change in alignment, though it may be doubted whether he had wished it so. Over the past two or three years he had assiduously begun the task of creating a ring of buffers round the Macedonian kingdom. With Epeiros and the Thessalian League, with their developed (if, in the latter case, hard pressed) internal organization, he had established the beginnings of close ties. With the Illyrians and Paionians, both of which demanded military intervention, a firm definition of frontiers and establishment of military outposts, he had taken at least the first steps towards establishing Macedonian superiority. With Thrace, after buying off Kotys' support for the pretender Pausanias, he had as yet had no further need of dealing; the partition of the kingdom had temporarily removed any pressure on that front. The Athenian treaty of mid-359 had served to counterbalance, for the time, any threat from his naval neighbours of the Chalkidian peninsula.

Patently, no long-term and realistic Macedonian policy could be developed without taking account of Athens and the Chalkidian League. Athens' economic interests had involved her for more than a century on the coastline of the northern Aegean. With the Chersonesos and the Hellespont she must be concerned; and with the northern coasts, for reasons of trade and, in the end more vitally, for the security of her corn-route from the Black Sea, preferably so. But even though she excelled in that military area in which Macedonia was most deficient, the enmity of Athens alone was not an immediately serious threat to Macedonian security – unless her navy work in combination with Chalkidian wealth, harbours and hoplite manpower.[109] Philip's overriding need, then, where these two powers were concerned, would always be to prevent their collusion against him. In 359, the attempt of Argaios, and the determination implied in her backing of him, had driven Philip into the arms of the Athenians and the antagonism between the latter and the Chalkidians had left his neighbours antagonistic but temporarily alone.

However, the outbreak of the Social War drastically altered things. For although it is true, as many have seen, that this war was to provide substantial opportunities for expansion and consolidation for Philip, its initial impact was to deprive him of his most effective counter to Olynthian interests. Athens, whatever he might have wished, was no longer of use to him. Further, lest Athens should successfully re-order her allies and build for herself a new empire, he would need to act quickly in order to remove the bases she would then be in a position to use effectively in the furtherance of her interests and, inevitably, to the detriment of his own. From all points of view, then, the *entente* with Athens was finished. It is worth stressing, against the anachronistic view that Philip's intention from the outset was to increase his power progressively, step by step, until he stood at the head of the Greek world, that the initiation of this new alignment, which might be thought of as the second phase of his foreign policy, was brought on by the collapse of one of the major props of the first phase.

CHAPTER III

357–351
THE CHALKIDIAN ALIGNMENT

WAR WITH ATHENS

AMPHIPOLIS FELL BY STORM. After a series of assaults a section of the wall was breached and the Macedonians pressed through the gap amidst fierce fighting, during which many defenders were killed, until the last resistance subsided. This victory, with siege-machinery playing a significant role in its achievement,[1] marks the beginning of a long and successful Macedonian tradition; with the increasing sophistication of siege-equipment it became no longer exceptional that walled cities fell by direct assault.

Shortly afterwards the Amphipolitan *demos* issued a decree proclaiming the banishment and outlawry of Stratokles and Philon.[2] Ephoros, in a reference to the exile of Philip's opponents there,[3] claims that he treated the rest of the inhabitants considerately, suggesting, without actually saying so, that Amphipolis retained some of the forms of autonomy. This we might expect, since the Chalkidians had to be convinced of Philip's benevolence towards those who supported him; the form of the decree – a decision of the *demos* and not an executive order by the conqueror – reflects this, whether or not the assertion of autonomy was much more than a charade. At some time afterwards, Amphipolis was annexed and its territory ceded to Macedonians.[4] So, for example, by the end of Philip's reign the district served as a recruitment area for the Companion Cavalry. But the date of annexation is unknown, beyond that it took place before 336 and probably at some time after the conclusion in 356 of the Macedonian/Chalkidian alliance.

The Athenian declaration of war over Amphipolis followed immediately, but it was an empty gesture (especially since it must have coincided approximately with their defeat at Chios) and it was understandably ignored by Philip. He switched his attention to the coastal plain of Pieria and took the pro-Athenian town of Pydna. According to Demosthenes[5] the victories both at Amphipolis and at Pydna were won through the assistance of supporters within the walls. Pydna, like

Methone, was in origin a Greek colony[6] but, especially since its refoundation by Archelaos a half-century before, it may have contained a Macedonian element; but, even if not, there must have been those in the city who saw their safest course in maintaining at least a working relationship with the Argead monarchy, particularly now that its power was beginning again to look more firmly based. Treachery within Amphipolis too may have played a part in its fall, for the long and effective anti-Athenian tradition there must easily have conduced to pro-Macedonian sentiment. But, although we know no details of the means by which Pydna was taken, Ephoros, as we have noticed, is explicit in attributing the capture of Amphipolis to success in breaching its walls.

NORTHERN REALIGNMENTS

When Philip had needed alliance with Athens in 359 he had naturally given every impression of benevolence towards it; his actions at the end of 357, representing the transition to a new alignment, were similarly directed towards winning the confidence of his powerful Chalkidian neighbours. Some such reassurance was necessary, for the assault on Amphipolis had provoked a good deal of disquiet in near-by areas. The kings of Thrace, particularly, in the western region, Berisades and the sons who succeeded him at his death in the same year (357/6), saw it as a direct threat to their sovereignty. The Illyrian Grabos, ruler possibly of the Grabaioi, a tribe to the northwest which had apparently been able to expand to the Macedonian borders after the defeat of Bardylis' Dardanians,[7] was in communication at about this time with the Chalkidians, who agreed to form an alliance with him probably with the primary aim of recovering their connection with the silver mines of the Damastinoi. Negotiations, however, seem to have been broken off at a later stage[8] when it became apparent that Philip was prepared to bid high for Chalkidian friendship. Nearly three years before, Philip had ordered the abandonment by the Macedonian mint of the Persic coin-standard adopted by Archelaos and the reversion to the earlier Phoenician or Thraco-Macedonian standard in use among the members of the Chalkidian League.[9] This action, combined now with motions towards friendship, will have been taken to presage the restoration of Olynthian trading privileges within Macedonia, including those with Damastion.

Either in late 357 or early in the next year Philip stepped up his overtures to his neighbours, offering them alliance. Their doubts possibly already assuaged to some extent by the treatment of Amphipolis and the new enmity between Philip and the Athenians, their commercial magnates undoubtedly attracted by the new trading opportunities, the Chalkidians were won over by two additional undertakings: that Philip would assist them to take Poteidaia, which he acknowledged as the property of the league, and that he would cede Anthemous to them.[10] Poteidaia, anti-Olynthian, lapsed member of her league and stiffened in its opposition in 361 by the reception of a contingent of Athenian cleruchs,[11] was the most immediate source of discomfort to Olynthos; Anthemous, a Macedonian territory since the 470s but a source of dispute from time to time between its kings and their southern neighbours, lay to the immediate north of the Chalkidike, a rich and fertile river valley opening on to the Thermaic Gulf. They terminated their negotiations with Grabos the Illyrian and accepted Philip's terms. The arrangement is preserved, though without detail, in the fragment of an inscription set up in the Temple of Artemis at Olynthos and found there nearly forty years ago.[12]

PHILIPPOI

With this powerful alliance safeguarding his southern frontier, Philip was able to put into effect a strategy which aimed at the gradual elimination of the Athenian presence on the seaboard of Macedonia and Thrace. But the immediate initiative came from elsewhere, in the form of a request for aid from Krenides. Founded by islanders of Thasos in late 360 just to the northwest of the older Datos at the head of the Angites valley, eastern tributary of the Strymon, it was a base for the exploitation of the rich gold- and silver-bearing ores of the vicinity; this is reflected in the gold and silver coinage issued soon afterwards bearing the reverse legend 'Of the Mainland Thasians'. Such a wording indicates that the name Krenides had not been officially adopted; the foundation was initially no more than a collection of mining settlements. At the same time, the separate issue, distinct from that of the island Thasian coins, advertises the importance attached by its initiators to their new venture.[13]

In about May 356 the eastern Thracian king Kersebleptes seized the opportunity offered by the new military involvements of his ally Athens to trample on the agreement he had been obliged to sign in the previous summer with her and with Berisades and Amadokos.[14] Moving into the territory of the western ruler Ketriporis, son of Berisades,[15] he prepared to attack the Krenidean mining settlements.[16] Whether he was simply eager to re-unify for himself the kingdom his father had ruled or, perceiving that Macedonian sway now extended across the Strymon to Amphipolis, was acting to pre-empt any further move from that quarter we can only speculate. At any rate his action failed, merely providing an opportunity for Macedonian intervention. The Krenideans, finding themselves isolated among the weak and the unwilling, discovered in Philip a ready ally.

For the Macedonians this was a stroke of fortune. Krenides was located in a commanding position in the Angites valley, a mere 12–15 kilometres from the Athenian ally Neapolis (modern Kavala), though separated from it by the narrow range of hills running along the coast eastwards from Mt Symbolon. The area was well known to be rich in silver and gold and was capable of much more concentrated mining than had yet been devoted to it. The aid was given no doubt under the terms of a hastily concluded alliance[17] and it was successful. Afterwards the several communities, representing an ideal advance-post of Macedonian influence and defence, were drawn into one, renamed Philippoi (the plural form of the name, like the earlier, 'Krenides', probably indicating its originally scattered nature – and the allusion to the king who founded it setting a precedent for his successors) and heavily fortified with walls and towers. A large number of Macedonian colonists were settled there in order to stock a self-sufficient and defensible *polis*; apart from anything else, it might be some time before the surrounding territory would be secure.[18]

From the precious ores and, in particular, from the rich Asyla mines just to the east of the new colony, Philip was able by dint of more efficient extraction than before to draw annual revenues of more than 1000 talents. (It has been suggested that the increased productivity was due, at least in part, to the abandonment of tray-panning in favour of the use of long wooden flues with ribbed floors, into which the ore was shovelled after crushing by hammering. A water flow through the flues removed the lighter ore, leaving the heavy metal caught between the ribs.)[19] Whether this large revenue derived from outright ownership of the mines or from their lease is unclear.[20] Then, for the same reason as in the western uplands and elsewhere in Macedonia, possibly on the Emathian Plain itself, Philip made arrangements to stabilize the economy of the Angites valley (later known as the Plain of Philippoi) by the clearing of forests and the draining of the land. When the Thracians had occupied it, says Theophrastos, who may himself have visited it in the 340s, the plain had been full of forests and swamps, but now it was rendered cultivable; no doubt it was to till the soil that some of the Macedonian colonists were sent to the new city.[21]

The foundation of a colony was for Macedonia a new venture, one which however set the precedent for a long series under Philip and his successors. How many Philip established we do not know, but, as we shall see, at least one and probably several in Thessaly were to follow, and, in the late 340s, a number in Thrace. In immediate terms it was an invaluable source of revenue as well as an outpost against the Thracian kingdoms – those of Ketriporis and Amadokos as well as that of Kersebleptes. A new coinage with denominations in gold, silver and bronze, was issued by Philippoi under its new name, although its obverse and reverse types otherwise remained the same as before. It is generally believed that this autonomous coinage of Philippoi lasted only about a decade and a half,[22] but recent studies show that the mint continued to strike under its own name throughout Philip's reign and well into that of Alexander.[23] Since, by the time another decade had passed, all Thracian territory as far east as the Nestos had been annexed to Macedonia, such treatment of this one city is intriguing, representing the creation of a true colony and perhaps something of a showpiece. And, although it later emerged that its foundation had been a step towards the annexation of the whole area between the Strymon and the Nestos, the continuing colonial status of Philippoi is a useful warning against the unquestioning assumption that Philip's initial intentions coincided with his later achievements. In 356, it is clear, the most serious dangers facing the kingdom obliged Philip to concentrate internally on the unification of his diverse population-groups and externally on the fairly immediate safeguarding of its security by the formation of alliances with his neighbours. Philippoi formed a part of this pattern, in that it was akin to the forging of the Chalkidian, Thessalian and Epeirote links, an expansion of Macedonian influence beyond her own borders to establish buffers against more distant threats – particularly, in the longer term, against Athens.[24]

THE NORTHERN COALITION, RISE AND FALL

Such a step could not be taken, however, without immediate consequence. During probably the summer of 356 the initiative was seized by Ketriporis (the son of Berisades) in the negotiation of an alliance in opposition to Philip. He and his brothers won the support of Lyppeios, the Paionian successor to Agis, and of Grabos, whose Illyrian tribe[25] appears to have become stronger and more aggressive after the defeat of Bardylis in 358. These in turn were joined in July by Athens[26] in what, on the latter's part, could be no more than a display of sentiment, for by now she was pressed hard by her renegade allies and was in no position to honour new commitments. (By this time the rebels held Samos under siege. Soon afterwards, in the autumn, Athens was to transfer the action to the Hellespontine area, but this was born not out of success but out of a desperate need to distract her enemies from their Samian blockade.)[27] The strength of an enemy alliance of kingdoms to their northwest, north and east would have been very dangerous to the Macedonians, but the union of allies was not yet achieved and Philip moved quickly before their actions could be coordinated and their forces combined. Diodoros, in a brief notice of the campaign,[28] fails to mention Athens at all, either because he is referring only to the initial coalition before Athens joined it or because Athens played no part in its abortive activities. According to Diodoros' version Philip attacked the forces individually, terrified them and compelled them to join him. Plutarch,[29] in a tendentious context, mentions only the defeat of Grabos' Illyrians, which he attributes to a military victory by Parmenion. News of the victory – that is, its arrival at Poteidaia – he synchronizes with Philip's capture of the latter, with the success of the king's horse at the Olympic Games and with the birth of Alexander. Since the last is dated to July and the Olympics will have been held, as usual, in August or even September, clearly we must assume either that there were inexplicable delays in communication or (more likely) that later chronographers took liberties with their dates in order to manufacture an appropriately portentous context for the birth of Philip's successor. (Indeed Philip himself, or Alexander, may have first circulated the story.)

POTEIDAIA

Probably in about July Philip and his Chalkidian allies pinned down the Poteidaians under siege. (With no actual harbour but only a roadstead the city was vulnerable by land rather than by sea.) In spite of their other preoccupations the Athenians voted to launch a relief expedition but, as on several later occasions, the aid was too late; at this time of year the Etesian winds, as well as Athenian indecisiveness, may have been responsible.[30] The siege was soon successful and Poteidaia capitulated.[31] Although nominally autonomous[32] the city was completely dependent on Athens; it had been strengthened, as we have noticed, by the establishment there of cleruchs in 361.[33] At its fall these Athenians were allowed to leave and return to their own city without ransom. They were neither indigenes nor colonists but merely, as one orator was to say 'Athenians dwelling in Poteidaia'.[34] The same author, Hegesippos, was to claim[35] – to substantiate an allegation of Macedonian illegality – that the cleruchs were at the time Philip's allies; but his claim is false, since, as Athenians, their voice was not distinct from that of the Athenian *demos*, which was at war with Philip. Neither can his charge be interpreted to signify that the native Poteidaians were the allies in question, for any possible agreement between them and the Macedonian will hardly have been permitted by the resident cleruchs to survive the Athenian (and therefore their own) declaration of war at the end of 357. Hegesippos was merely indulging in fantasy in failing to admit that Philip's treaty of 359 with the Athenians had now been discarded;[36] he was the ally no longer of either the cleruchs or the Poteidaians. The latter, as willing hosts of enemy soldiers, were sold into slavery and their land handed, as promised, to the Chalkidian League.[37]

EXPANSION IN WESTERN THRACE

The foundation of Philippoi, as we have seen, posed an immediate threat to Neapolis, less than a day's march distant on the coast. A loyal member of the second Athenian alliance (as of the Delian League), Neapolis was a useful base for Athenian ships. Although on occasions nowadays its harbour may be unsafe for vessels of far greater sea-worthiness than the ancient trireme (like most northern harbours and roadsteads it offered little protection against the strong winds that often blow up during the sailing season), it was at that time normal practice for vessels to be drawn up on the beach, so that such adverse conditions would only affect actual landings and departures.[38] The Macedonian presence at Amphipolis and Philippoi was shortly followed up by the destruction of Apollonia and Galepsos, both located on the coast at the eastern end of the Strymonic Gulf not far from Amphipolis, and by the establishment of a small Macedonian base, Emathia, on the site of Oisyme, only 20 km. west of Neapolis.[39] All three of these coastal towns were probably (Galepsos and Oisyme certainly) Thasian colonies in origin and at this time, as in the fifth century, found themselves, like their foundress, in alliance with Athens.

In the early summer of 355, according to an Athenian inscription, two Neapolitan envoys were received by the Athenian Boulē and commended to the assembly along with a bouleutic recommendation whose content is lost.[40] In spite of the disappearance of what may have been the most useful information on the stone it can hardly be doubted that the Neapolitans were reacting in alarm to the activities of Philip in their area over the past year. However, although their reception before the Boulē was clearly favourable, the envoys will have received little (if anything) other than expressions of sympathy. More than that the Athenians could as yet ill afford. The date of Neapolis' capture by Philip is unknown, but it may have been taken and garrisoned at some time between the end of Athens' Social War and early 353, only to be re-won temporarily by Chares near the latter date. It continued to issue its own coinage until nearly 340 – roughly the time at which Philip became master of Thrace – but if this was intended to imply autonomy it will have been a transparent farce after about 346 or even the late 350s. With the defeat of Ketriporis (along with Grabos and Lyppeios) in 356 the western realm of Thrace became, at the least, much more secure for the Macedonians and for their colonists at Philippoi, and, whenever Neapolis was actually annexed, the Neapolitans as well as the western Thracians will have found themselves thoroughly circumscribed by Macedonian influence by 350.[41]

THE END OF THE SOCIAL WAR

In the midsummer of the year 355, on the orders of the Persian King, Athens' Social War ended. The independence of Chios, Kos, Rhodos and Byzantion was recognized and the example of their secession was soon followed by the bulk of the remaining members, leaving only (of any note) the northern Aegean islands, Euboia and a few towns on the Thracian coast. The war, whose outbreak had obliged Philip to realign Macedonia with the Chalkidian League, had turned out well for him by engaging Athenian efforts elsewhere. There had been times during the previous two years when Athenian prospects had looked promising – when, for example, after her defeat off Chios her efforts had increased to a level at which she might well have defeated her recalcitrant allies and managed to convert her league, as almost exactly one hundred years before, into an empire. The immediate result of such a success would inevitably have been a complete reconstitution of the league's finances and an expansion of the imperialistic activities that had so concerned the Aegean states during the 360s.[42] Early in 355 Athenian hopes rose again after Chares' 'second Marathon' while in the service of the Phrygian Artabazos.[43] But in the summer, with the war ended, the Athenian cause abandoned and the bulk of the already inadequate *syntaxeis* lost, the Athenians were brought face to face with the reality of their exhaustion and their disastrous loss of prestige. The peace brought with it even greater encouragement to their enemies.[44]

ORIGINS OF THE SACRED WAR

Thebes, smarting over her defeat of 357 over Euboia, had seized the opportunity offered earlier by *stasis* in neighbouring Phokis to strengthen her position in central Greece, engineering the passage of two offensive decrees in the 356 spring meeting of the Amphiktyonic Council at Delphoi.[45] One was an ultimatum threatening holy war against Phokis if fines owed by certain individuals there, including leaders of the anti-Theban group, were not paid forthwith; the second censured all others owing debts to Apollo, these including the Spartans. If the intention was to encourage the Phokians, who had fought on the Boiotian side at Leuktra, to expel their anti-Theban element it backfired badly, producing the reverse effect of bringing that faction to the fore with apparently general support. One of them, Philomelos, was elected commander-in-chief of the army and, after receiving private assurances of money and mercenaries from Archidamos at Sparta, seized the sacred city of Delphoi in the summer of 356. During the following eighteen months, while Philomelos' troops consolidated their position and his envoys proclaimed the justice of the Phokian cause and renewed their ancient claim on the Delphic sanctuary, Thebes and Lokris took ineffective steps to dislodge the enemy from Delphoi, but were hampered by uncertainty over the Thessalian alignment from attempting to force the issue in the Amphiktyonic Council, where Thessaly could command a large majority of the votes. While the Thessalian *koinon* might normally be expected to vote against the Phokians, it was heavily preoccupied with the continuing struggle against the Pheraian tyrant house that had prompted it at least once already (in 358) to seek Philip's aid. During the last months of 356, moreover, Philomelos' diplomacy had won alliances with Athens, Sparta and some other Peloponnesian states, probably Argos, Sikyon and Korinth; with Athens' potential unclear the Thebans were unwilling to risk being caught between the other major powers.[46]

But with the close of the Social War the position suddenly altered. Thebes was left dominant in her area, allied to a Persian King whose apparent belligerence and whose successful determination of the Athenians' struggle counteracted the declining impact of his successive ultimatums since 387/6.[47] Athens was in confusion and unlikely to participate to any effect. In Thessaly too the situation changed. During 355, it seems likely, the struggle between the league and the tyrant house was active and perhaps prompted another appeal to Philip from his friends at Larisa.[48] The change of heart was thus possibly induced by a temporary settlement of the feud with (again, possibly) Philip's aid.

In autumn 355 the Amphiktyony declared holy war on the Phokians with probably the support of 18 or 20 of the total 24 votes.[49] In spite of the massive opposition, the position of Philomelos was strong. Ensconced at Delphoi and protected there by some of the more rugged terrain of the Greek peninsula he found his initially small resources now sufficiently augmented by funds from Apollo's treasury, enabling him to offer a mercenary wage half as high again as the normal,[50] so that he was able to go on to the offensive early in the following year (354).

METHONE

Encouraged by his successes of the previous two years beyond the Strymon and elsewhere, Philip too was able to take advantage of Athenian disillusionment, confident in his alliance with the Chalkidian cities. Very near to Emathia itself, between that plain and the conquered city of Pydna, lay Methone.[51] Any Macedonian communication between the heart of the kingdom and Pydna, the ancient towns of Dion and Herakleia in southern Pieria and, further south, Tempe and Thessaly must pass close by it or take the circuitous and difficult route through the mountains of the hinterland. Indeed it is difficult to understand how Philip had been able for so long to avoid facing the threat it posed; the answer must be sought partly in the seriousness of the succession of problems that had so far taken up his time and partly in the assumption that since 359, when they had played host to the Athenian force supporting Argaios, the people of Methone had lain low, relying ultimately on their fortifications to preserve them in case of attack. According to Diodoros[52] they were now permitting their city to become an enemy base, but he gives no indication of specific instances. However, the Athenians' decision ultimately, if too late, to send help to Methone suggests that they had hopes, possibly based on recent experience, of using it – and it guarantees that there was a substantial pro-Athenian group there. Further, that the siege of Methone drew Philip away from his campaigns against Athenian points in Thrace, to which he seems to have returned immediately afterwards, adds some strength to the supposition that the blockade was occasioned by a recent and specific instance of its danger to him.

In late 355 Macedonian forces were moved up to invest the city. Before the siege began Philip appears to have drawn up his forces near by and offered a delay during which the Methonaians might avert war by their surrender; in December honours were voted in Athens to one Lachares for his achievement in entering Methone,[53] which implies that the city was hard pressed but not yet under full siege. The length of the campaign, during which Philip lost his right eye to an arrow from the battlements, is unknown.[54] Athenian help was sent but arrived too late;[55] that it could be sent at all means that the spring (354) at least had arrived.[56] On their surrender the citizens were obliged to hand over their city and to depart, each with a single garment and no other possessions.[57] The walls and buildings were razed and the fertile land distributed among Macedonians.[58]

Meanwhile, during spring 354 Philomelos the Phokian had taken the offensive in central Greece, advancing into Lokris where he defeated in a cavalry engagement a combined force of Lokrians and Boiotians.[59] Six thousand 'Thessalians and their neighbouring allies',[60] presumably attempting to join forces with their Amphiktyonic colleagues, were cut off and defeated.[61] But the appearance in autumn of a large Boiotian force – the Amphiktyons now well outnumbering the Phokians, their mercenaries and allies, including new Peloponnesian reinforcements – forced Philomelos to a pitched battle at Neon in which his troops were badly defeated and he himself lost his life. His co-commander Onomarchos gathered up the survivors and led them back to Phokis.[62]

During these campaigns, probably early in their course, Methone fell. In what was apparently a related campaign another town, Pagai, which is otherwise unknown, was defeated and compelled to submit.[63]

ABDERA, MARONEIA AND NEAPOLIS

To Thrace Philip returned in summer or autumn 354, this time by sea, not to consolidate his hold on the western area but to press beyond the Nestos towards the wealthy coastal towns of Abdera and Maroneia, both, again, allies of Athens. Abdera, to judge by its tribute, had been the third wealthiest member of the Delian League and Maroneia was not far behind; both had acquired their wealth through trade with the Thracian hinterland. Typically for this area, these towns perched above the coast, the former on the bluff of Cape Baloustro, rising out of the marshy ground that extends eastward from the Nestos mouth and makes passage along or near the coast difficult or impossible, the latter on the stepped slopes of Mt Ismaros where it touches the shoreline at Cape Charalambos. The coast here and to the east where Mesymbria and Ainos lay was and is inhospitable, so that the most natural angle of attack was from the landward side; without control of the approaches this was however not possible for Philip without first moving his troops and equipment into the general area by sea. The date of this campaign is admittedly conjectural.[64] But Polyainos groups together the fall of Abdera with that of Maroneia, and Demosthenes refers (admittedly inconclusively) to Philip's having landed at the latter before 352; the date adopted here is the latest at which Philip is known to have been in Thrace before that time.[65] Maroneia and probably Abdera lay within the realm of King Amadokos of central Thrace, who in this his first known contact with Philip barred the Macedonian's way inland

and further east. It seems likely that the Thracian was acutely conscious of the danger to his own kingdom should the forces of Philip join those of his neighbour Kersebleptes, whose territory extended from the Hebros to the area of Perinthos and Byzantion.[66]

Philip was not prepared to press the issue. Neither of the two towns he had just taken was vital to any conceivable Macedonian expansionist interests in Thrace; the natural east-west route by-passed both by some distance inland. Their significance for him lay purely in their relationship with Athens. To have pushed onwards against Amadokos would have left him with a tenuous line of naval communication depending on a small fleet and, at the Thracian end, a poor harbour; by land he was isolated. In any case he achieved some agreement with Kersebleptes without actually making contact with him. Demosthenes refers to a pact arranged here, in which the Theban Pammenes played a role.[67] For, following the Amphiktyonic victory at Neon, the Thebans, in near fatal overconfidence but eager for the financial rewards,[68] despatched this general with 5000 troops to the aid of the Phrygian Artabazos in his continuing revolt against the Persian monarch (winter 354/3).[69] His assistance at Maroneia was no doubt rendered as the *xenos* of Philip.[70] The truth of his assertion the orator supports with a letter from the Athenian general Chares, which is not extant but the fact of which is useful to us in putting him in the area at the time. We may well doubt, indeed, since Chares was near by, whether it was alone the interdiction of Amadokos that deterred Philip from going beyond Maroneia.

The pact sealed, Philip re-embarked the infantry and assault equipment in his small fleet and sailed for home. But at Neapolis Chares was lying in ambush for him with 20 ships beached there at the ready, and only by drawing the Athenians' pursuit with his four fastest ships was Philip able to slip past with his transports.[71] The lesson, however, was not lost on him; the policy of eradicating potential Athenian bases without first securing the communication lines by land was dangerous. Neapolis itself, clearly, was at this time free of Macedonian control, whether because it had not yet been taken or (more likely) because, once taken, it was re-won by Chares. More pressing matters might require Philip's immediate attention, but some rationalization of Macedonia's eastward interests could not long be delayed.

PHERAI AND PHOKIS

Meanwhile another appeal had arrived from the Thessalian *koinon*, which again sought aid in its resistance to the depredations of

Lykophron at Pherai. In Philip's absence in Thrace the Amphiktyons' position in central Greece had deteriorated. At the end of winter, in early 353, Onomarchos, a capable successor to Philomelos, had seized upon the absence of Pammenes and his troops to redouble the Phokian efforts. In the spring he convened what was recorded as a meeting of the Amphiktyonic Council; those represented were Athens, Lokris, Megara, Epidauros, Sparta and Korinth, as well as the hosts, Phokis and Delphoi.[72] With the blessing of his allies, Onomarchos made good the losses suffered by the army at Neon and embarked on a series of successful campaigns against neighbouring Lokris, taking near-by Amphissa (which was vital for control of the northward mountain-route by-passing Thermopylai into Malis) and Thronion, one of the three strategic towns controlling the southern road to Thermopylai itself (the others being Nikaia and Alponos). Turning south through Dorian territory, which he ravaged, he moved then westwards into Boiotia, there taking Orchomenos. But his ensuing blockade of Chaironeia was unsuccessful and a defeat at Theban hands decided him to return to Phokis.[73] In any case he had been summoned, probably by this time, into Thessaly by his brother Phayllos.

The movements of Onomarchos during these few months had been the easier not only for the absence of Pammenes and his 5000 but also for the failure of the Thessalians to support their allies. This is explained by Diodoros as the result of Phokian bribes – and such may have been offered and received. But more essentially the reason was that by the summer of 353 Philip's Thessalian allies were again hard pressed by Pherai – and, to judge by the easy collusion that follows between the tyrant and his Phokian friends, the two sets of affairs were related.[74] During the summer, then, Philip returned to Thessaly where he again took up the league's cudgels.[75] On this occasion, probably for the first time (at least since 358) he entered the fray in person – most probably as the ally of Thebes as well as Thessaly[76] and possibly as the elected archon of the *koinon* (see below).

The initial campaigning against Lykophron, of which we know no details, evidently went well for the league, for the tyrant turned for relief to Phokis, whence Phayllos was despatched with aid. But on entering Thessaly he was met, defeated and driven back out of the country by the Macedonian king.[77] This reverse probably contributed to Onomarchos' decision to abandon his Boiotian campaign and he now moved his entire force to the north, apparently hoping that a substantial success now would give him control of the whole of Thessaly.[78] His army outnumbered that of his opponents and he had with him field artillery that would increase his advantage if he could deploy it effectively. When the Macedonian and Thessalian forces went to meet him he inflicted two defeats on them.[79] The military writer Polyainos[80] describes an effective stratagem employed by the Phokian that must relate to one of these battles: allowing Philip to advance towards him he concealed infantry and catapults on the slopes of a semicircular range of hills; then he drew up his remaining units at the entrance to the valley below, into which, when the attack came, the Phokian troops were to feign retreat. The ploy was successful. It may not have been practical for Philip to send out light horsemen to scout the slopes ahead of him. At any rate, when the enemy fled before him he pursued them, as planned, until those on the slopes declared their presence with bursts of stone-shot from their catapults into the massed ranks below. Macedonian casualties in the fusillade and the ensuing infantry charge were heavy and, although the king himself escaped unscathed, it was to face desertions among his battered, demoralized troops. With difficulty he reasserted control and, opting for discretion, retired to winter at home – withdrawing, as he claimed, 'like a ram to butt the harder next time'.

This is the only known occasion on which Philip's relations with his subjects were put under strain. Although Demosthenes[81] was to claim only three years after this that the Macedonian people were exhausted by Philip's ambitions and tired of the demands he made upon them, he was unable on any occasion to cite any single example of such dissatisfaction. Significantly, the only occasion on which Philip appears to have lost control, if temporarily, this lapse was brought about by a remarkable military error on his part – something of which he was rarely, if ever guilty otherwise. Disillusionment of course was not new to the Macedonians, but one can well imagine the effect of this defeat when, after six years of unmitigated military success, it must have appeared at first that their buoyant new balloon had burst.

Bitter was the pill. But it was not without its lessons for the king. He had perhaps underestimated the strength of his opponents, for it was the first time he had faced a large, efficient and well equipped mercenary force supported by the newly developed and costly artillery now available to those states with the wealth to pay for it.[82] In his account of the campaign of 353 Diodoros does not mention the Pheraian forces; neither do they appear in his account of the famous battle fought in the following year. At that time, on the Crocus Field, Onomarchos is said to have had 20,000 foot and 500 horse, and Philip slightly above that in infantry as well as 3000 cavalry. Since Onomarchos is also said to have brought his entire military strength in 353 his numbers were presumably similar then, whereas Philip and the Thessalians were numerically inferior. The Macedonian king was to demonstrate often in his career a notable economy in his military actions; he avoided fighting when this was possible and, when it was unavoidable, did not use unnecessarily high levies.[83] On the other hand, neither did he again use inadequate forces. The role of Philip in the development of Greek artillery was to be an important one and he had perhaps already begun developing such weapons in Macedonia. Arrow-shooting catapults were to play a part in the capture of Olynthos in 348 (bolt-heads some three to four inches long and stamped 'Philip's' were found in the excavations there) and were to attract attention in the siege of Perinthos in 340,[84] but it is quite likely that the real impetus for such development came from the setback suffered at the hands of Onomarchos in 353.[85]

THRACIAN REVERSES

In Thrace the Athenian general Chares was quick to profit from Philip's involvement. He had been unsuccessful, as we have seen, in his attempted naval ambush of Philip's fleet on its return from Maroneia. But when the Macedonian forces immediately marched south into Thessaly Chares perceived the vulnerability of Philip's Thracian arrangements and he now took the opportunity to upset them. In the late spring or early summer of 353 he sailed to the Chersonesos where he captured Sestos, slaying its male citizens and enslaving the rest.[86] Such savage treatment was not implemented without a purpose. The key to Athenian control of this peninsula was Kersebleptes, whose territory bordered it and whose claim to ownership of it at this time was backed by his derivation of an annual revenue of 30 talents from its towns. In spite of his agreement of 357 with Athens the Thracian had since that time continually worked against Athenian interests in the furtherance of his own ambitions to re-create his father's kingdom. In reaction, his associate kings Berisades (and then Ketriporis) and Amadokos had faithfully served Athens; most recently, in early 353, the latter had opposed Philip's eastward movement from Maroneia, but he had not been able to prevent his reaching some agreement with Kersebleptes' envoy Apollonides. The Athenians thus found themselves in the unsatisfactory position of supporting two kings in whom they were only marginally interested against the one whose co-operation they most vitally required. In this context Chares' capture and brutal treatment of the Sestians may be seen as a powerful attempt to force Kersebleptes into line. He, seeing Philip defeated by Onomarchos in the late summer or autumn, took the only path open to him and accepted Chares' terms. (That this would and did inevitably drive Ketriporis and Amadokos towards Philip was of secondary importance to Athens, whose concern now was to win over the rest of the Chersonesan towns and to maintain Kersebleptes' allegiance.)[87] He undertook to support Athenian attempts on Amphipolis and renounced his rights over the Chersonesan towns (except Kardia, at the narrow neck of the peninsula) and their tribute. The Athenians promptly sent cleruchs to Sestos and elsewhere.[88]

THE THREAT OF DISINTEGRATION

A second and very serious consequence of Philip's defeat in Thessaly was a similar willingness on the part of the Chalkidian League, or at least of its leading city, to seek accommodation with Athens. The Olynthians declared their friendship for the Athenians and stated their willingness to negotiate an alliance.[89] There was evidently a growing anti-Macedonian group at Olynthos, possibly, as Demosthenes says, alarmed at the growing power of Philip's Macedonia, and this no doubt played a part in the overtures. But two things suggest that this was not the main stimulus to a change of heart.[90] In the first place, the Olynthian offer appears to have been made around the time (and therefore quite possibly because) of Philip's loss in Thessaly; that is to say it appears to have been an attempt to placate an increasingly energetic enemy when the signs were that their strongest ally was about to collapse. Secondly, the lack of response from Athens (there being still no alliance at the time of Demosthenes' first two *Olynthiacs* four years later) suggests that, at least in the Athenians' assessment, the offer was a mere expedient indicating no real change of heart. As was to emerge over the next few years, the anti-Macedonian group at Olynthos was growing in power; but we are not warranted in assuming that they were yet dominant in late 353.

These are the only specifically attested instances of breakdown in Philip's relations with his neighbours and they by themselves were serious enough; but there is reason for suspecting that his problems went further than this. Indirect evidence suggests that in Epeiros and possibly also in Paionia and Illyria the existing settlements began to crumble.[91]

In central Greece early in the new year (352) Onomarchos acted. Seeing the importance for Philip of the coming months and realizing that the Macedonian would be desperate to bring their conflict to a successful conclusion, he launched a quick campaign into Boiotia to neutralize her in the impending struggle. He took Koroneia and possibly Korsiai and Tilphosaion.[92]

VICTORY IN THESSALY

When Philip returned to Thessaly in the spring of 352 he was conscious that much depended on the issue of that year. Sinking morale among his own people and defections among his allies demanded a definitive and spectacular success, and even then he would need to follow it up quickly to recover his position among the buffer areas. In Thessaly he again commanded combined forces of the league and Macedon, numbering now more than 20,000 foot and 3000 horse. Receiving intelligence of this Lykophron of Pherai no doubt again sent word to Onomarchos, who prepared to bring his forces north. The Athenians, persuaded by Phokian funds[93] to man their fleet, agreed to provide naval support, with the aim first of preventing the loss of Pagasai to Philip. Chares was sent into the Gulf of Pagasai.

The Macedonian preparations are significant. According to Justin,[94] Philip instructed his forces to wear crowns of laurel, 'as if he were avenging not the Thebans but an act of sacrilege, and went into battle as if led by the god'. Some have doubted whether Philip fought here as the ally of Thebes, but even if this, the only explicit evidence, is rejected, such preparations – in effect, the assumption of the cause of Apollo – as well as the events following the battle, again with the emphasis on the religious motive, make it clear that the Macedonian king wished to be seen defending his Thessalian allies and additionally acting in the wider Amphiktyonic role on behalf of those who had lost Apollo's city to the Phokian commanders.

The first action of the campaign was Philip's attack on Pagasai.[95] It was probably this, if not his very arrival, that prompted the Pheraian appeal to Phokis, but by the time the latter forces were through Thermopylai on their way to Pagasai the port had fallen into Philip's hands and the Macedonian army was able to meet the Phokians on the Krokion Plain[96] ('Crocus Field') where the cavalry could be used to advantage. Chares also arrived too late to help Pagasai and sailed down the western side of the gulf to give whatever assistance he could, but, with Pagasai lost, there was little open to him.

Thus in spring or early summer 352 the two armies met. Little information survives on the course of the battle except for the comment in Diodoros that Philip's dominance in cavalry was the decisive factor.[97] In the course of the Macedonian victory many Phokians fled to the beaches where Chares' fleet was cruising offshore, and stripping off their armour attempted to swim to the ships. Among these was Onomarchos, on whose death however the tradition is confused; most likely he was killed or drowned in this last phase of the battle and Philip afterwards hanged or crucified his body as befitted the despoiler of the temple.[98] Six thousand Phokians and their mercenaries had been killed in the fighting and the three thousand captured were then drowned as temple robbers.[99] Lykophron of Pherai, now friendless and hard pressed, offered his city to Philip under truce; the latter, realizing that the Sacred War was no more finished than it had been after the death of Philomelos at Neon and that the time was now ripe to carry the fighting into central Greece, accepted the offer and allowed the tyrant family and two thousand of their mercenaries to depart; they promptly joined Phayllos, the brother of Onomarchos and successor to his Phokian command.[100]

After the victory, probably during the late spring and early summer of 352, Philip remained in Thessaly. He had learnt from the previous year's troubles in the north and northeast the danger of transferring his efforts to a new front when unfinished business lay behind him. So that, even though an immediate dash in pursuit of the battered survivors of Crocus Field might have taken him through Thermopylai before Phayllos could call up support from his allies, he first began the task of securing Thessaly. In a speech delivered around May or June 341 (the third *Philippic*) Demosthenes would date the beginning of Philip's rise to power in the Greek world from a point 'thirteen incomplete years' before that time, evidently somewhere within the year 354/3 – and, whether or not we incline to agree with him, the orator's definition of the achievement that began Philip's rise is important as a contemporary assessment. But it is difficult to identify what he had in mind.[101] The fall of Methone, since its capture secured the coastal route to Thessaly and eliminated the last non-Macedonian enclave from Macedonian soil, might well represent a suitable achievement; but it probably belongs late in the year 355/4 rather than in 354/3 (though the latter is possible)[102] and in any case relates much more naturally to the question of Macedonian sovereignty than to the growth of its influence beyond its borders. The activities in Thrace later in 354/3 were hardly definitive – indeed from the Athenian point of view any gains there were substantially vitiated by the end of 353 as a result of Chares' actions. The most likely candidate then is the Thessalian intervention beginning in the summer of 353, although it was not until the following year that success attended it. Arguably the catalyst out of which Philip's rise to Greek dominance was formed, in Demosthenes' view, was the close relationship that inspired and, more importantly, grew from Philip's co-operation with the Thessalian League.

At some time during 353 or – if not then – in the following year, the League elected Philip its archon, or *tagos*.[103] This was a constitutionally defined office, lifelong in tenure and presumably military, or largely so, in function – though the *auctoritas* of the appointee will in practice have given him wider influence over the league's affairs. What was unprecedented and altogether remarkable was its conferment on a foreigner. We can hardly be satisfied with the negative justification advanced by Justin;[104] Philip must have shown himself convincingly a friend of the league and an assiduous protector of its interests in the years between his accession and 353. The proceeds of the Thessalian harbour and market dues, again either before or in 352, were granted to the new archon, perhaps as a normal accompaniment to the office – though possibly as a separate act, since an assembly of the league could allegedly contemplate at a later date the withdrawal of these revenues from the archon's control.[105] The purpose of the grant was clearly to finance what military schemes the commander-in-chief was called upon or decided to perform – although Demosthenes, very likely out of ignorance, was to put it more broadly: 'the Thessalian League should be administered from these revenues and they should not go into Philip's own pocket'.[106] Together with this grant went the cession of Thessaly's main harbour, Pagasai, controlled for the previous 50 years by the tyrant house at near-by Pherai. It is an excellent port, the only one to speak of on the Thessalian coastline (it lies very near modern Volos) and its acquisition by Philip is probably to be interpreted partly in financial terms (since it will have been the main – virtually the only – source of harbour dues) and partly with the intention of preventing Athenian interference in Thessaly – rather than with a view to its offensive naval use on any scale. It is likely, however, that the occasional small raids made southwards to the Athenian area by Philip's small fleet will have been launched from here. By the end of 351 he had made at least two such sorties, one to Geraistos where, so Demosthenes claimed, he seized the Athenian merchant fleet and one a landing at Marathon where he captured the Paralos, one of Athens' sacred triremes.[107] With Pagasai for a base surprise attacks would be the more effective, escape from superior fleets quicker and easier and the perils of open-sea sailing might be largely avoided.

The cession of Pagasai was made at the expense of Pherai but Philip's settlement with the latter city was in the main directed at winning friendships, not prolonging enmities. After the departure of the tyrants and their mercenaries he organized a personal settlement with the inhabitants. He married a woman of Pherai, Nikesipolis, whose daughter, in recognition of the victory of 352, was to be named Thessalonike.[108] This marriage we must take as a sign that Philip wished to draw a distinction in his treatment of the Pheraians between the tyrants and their adherents on the one hand and their innocent subjects on the other

– a policy he was to attempt to repeat six years later in Phokis, but in that case without success. In Pherai, if he hoped by adopting this line to make of the people his reliable supporters, he was however to be disillusioned before long. Whether this settlement was ordained by the king of the Macedonians or by the archon of the Thessalian League we cannot tell; if Nikesipolis became his wife on the same terms as her predecessors and successors then the former is implied. In general terms we may only say that he should have conducted his negotiations in the same *persona* as that in which he had defeated the tyrants; but since that is unknown and was at least ambiguous (encompassing the roles certainly of foreign ally and possibly of Thessalian archon) the question cannot be answered.

When we discover what other territories were ceded to the Macedonian we begin to understand his immediate interest in Thessaly. He was already the ally of the league in a much more intimate sense than the usual, but he now began in addition to acquire control in the *perioikis*, the three neighbouring areas of Perrhaibia, Magnesia and Achaia-Phthiotis, all of which were of strategic value and all of which exercised votes in the Amphiktyonic Council. He now obtained at least parts of the first two of these territories.

Magnesia, to which Pagasai had once belonged and was now technically restored in accordance with Philip's promise,[108a] comprised for the most part the long range of mountains running north and south between the Thessalian plain and the Aegean coast, from the Pass of Tempe in the north to the far tip of the western arm of the Pagasitic Gulf; indeed Magnesia is little more than its mountains, Ossa and Pelion together with the lower Mavrovouni (its modern name) between them. Its coastline is difficult of access and contains no usable harbours. However, since Philip is said to have made plans to fortify some of its towns[109] it is evident that it must have been a more significant area than its topography might suggest; possibly he was interested mainly in its extreme north, where it terminates at Tempe, and at its extreme south, on the gulf.

The strategic importance of Perrhaibia is immediately plain. It controlled both means of southern access to Macedonia, either along the Peneios through Tempe or northwards to Oloosson (modern Elassona) and thence behind Olympos and through the mountain-passes into Elimeia. The Perrhaibians, although in theory autonomous (they, like the Magnesians, exercised two Amphiktyonic votes at Delphi), had in reality been subject to Larisa. Their tribute to the latter was now remitted instead to Philip.[110] This cession of the northern part of Perrhaibia[111] may be seen as a gesture of goodwill and gratitude on the part of the league or of its dominant city; as Philip had acted generously in devoting time and effort to the safeguarding of Thessalian security so the league now reciprocated in kind and to the same end.[112]

Perrhaibia, like Magnesia, was garrisoned and fortified at certain points. Gonnoi, the key to Tempe,[113] became in effect a colony, whose defence and administration were Macedonian-organized and whose population was heavily Macedonian in content – in the same way and for the same reasons as had Philippoi four years earlier.[114] No doubt Oloosson too received at least a garrison.

It may also have been in 353 or 352 that Philip intervened in a war being fought between the Hestiaiotian towns of Pelinna and Pharkadon. He captured and destroyed the latter and possibly near-by Trikka as well,[115] leaving Pelinna and Gomphoi dominant in the region, an area that again was important for its access to Epeiros, Athamania and Ambrakia. Gomphoi in particular seems to have been elevated from obscurity by Macedonian colonization under the name Philippoi or Philippopolis.[116] When these actions took place we cannot be absolutely certain – whether, for example, they were completed before Philip's departure from Thessaly or (more plausibly) were merely by then planned for later execution. The reasonable assumption though is that they were the actions of the archon following concessions by a grateful league. At any rate, when Philip withdrew from Thessaly in the middle of the year, his settlement there was to remain secure for some three years before any signs of strain showed, and these were to be removed quickly and with little apparent difficulty.

THERMOPYLAI

First, however, having secured his position there, the king turned to the task of pursuing the Phokians through Thermopylai. But Phayllos had not been idle in the months since his brother's death at Crocus Field. Turning again to the sacred treasures of Delphi he coined large amounts of silver and gold, prepared a large arsenal and attracted additional mercenaries with inflated wages. Three of his allies, the Achaians, Spartans and Athenians, supported him with forces and to these he was able to add the Pheraian exiles.[117] When Philip reached the northwestern entrance to the pass he was confronted by a large army comprising all these elements; for allies he had none but the Thessalians and he would certainly require help from the southern end of the narrow pass between cliffs and sea. This might have come from the Thebans and the Boiotian League, but so effective had been the precautions taken by Onomarchos between his Thessalian campaigns of

353 and 352 that these, finding the large enemy force[118] in control of Thermopylai and its approaches and with Phokian sympathizers holding Orchomenos, Koroneia and by now probably Korsiai and Tilphosaion, were not prepared to risk an attack on Phayllos' rear. Rather than waste time and men on a protracted assault or on a wearing march by the difficult alternative route through Doris, Philip retired, frustrated again by the now dead Onomarchos.

THE THRACIAN CAMPAIGN OF 352/351

But it was perhaps as well. Thracian affairs had gone unattended for too long and it was in this direction that Philip now turned his attention. Leaving Thermopylai around the middle of the summer and presumably picking up replacements and equipment en route at Pella, the Macedonian army by November of the same year was at Heraion, nearly 700 km. distant on the Propontine coast in close proximity to Perinthos.

When they had left Thrace only eighteen months before, in the spring of 353, it had been at the end of a successful (though hardly conclusive) campaign. In the interim, as we have seen, the skill of the Athenian Chares had wrought a drastic change for the worse.[119] The Chersonesos was now again Athenian, with her cleruchs firmly in control. Kersebleptes, forced to foreswear his short-lived Macedonian attachment,[120] had returned to his old policy of reconstructing his father's dismembered kingdom, now with the tacit approval of the Athenians. Philip, on his return, found the Thracian under attack over disputed territory from three of his disgruntled neighbours, the Byzantines, Perinthians and Amadokos, king of central Thrace.[121] His offer of assistance was accepted and it was as their ally that Philip invested the Heraion fortress. News travelled quickly to Athens. Confident from their recent gains in this area and at the general weakening of Philip's hold on the areas to his east, the assembly now saw its opportunity to defeat a foe fighting among his enemies and far from home. In a noisy assembly a force of 40 triremes was proposed and approved and arrangements made to call a levy of all those up to 45 years of age and to impose an *eisphora* to raise 60 talents.[122] But, probably very soon afterwards, there were second thoughts. For one thing, Kersebleptes was too undependable to entrust to his loyalty a substantial part of the male citizenry. More importantly, however, it was soon learnt that Philip was far from alone in this campaign, that he was acting in concert with three allies, at least one of which, Byzantion, had an impressive fleet. The excitement died and the expedition lapsed with it, before even reaching the water. All that was left for the Athenians was to await developments.

In Thrace the siege continued, while Philip, in addition, took measures to ensure for himself a degree of influence in Thracian internal matters – probably in eastern Thrace and with the support of his new ally Amadokos. He removed some local leaders from their positions and replaced them with others of his own choosing.[123] The year (352/1) passed with no further developments until, perhaps in July or August, rumours began reaching Athens to the effect that Philip was ill or even dead;[124] the former, it was to turn out, was the truth. To the Athenians it now seemed that the enemies of Kersebleptes might withdraw their forces from their dangerous proximity to the Chersonesos.[125] A small fleet was contemplated and, possibly at this point, established; it might be despatched from the city, once the fighting was known to have ceased, with the task of reconnoitring the effects of the campaign on Athenian interests. In September it set out. In the meantime Philip, recovered from his illness and with Heraion taken and handed back to its original owner (presumably Perinthos), began the march back to Pella.[126]

However, further unfinished business awaited him, in the Chalkidike, Epeiros and possibly Paionia and Illyria,[127] and he detoured into the territory of the first of these. As we have seen, the Olynthians at least, during his absence in Thessaly and probably at the time of his setback there in the 353 campaign, had in principle forsworn their agreement with him and were even seeking alliance with his Athenian enemy.[128] What action he now took is unclear. Although Demosthenes implies some sort of military venture his precise meaning is indistinct ('. . . he "made an attempt on" the Olynthians'). Theopompos, in what is apparently a reference to the same incident, has Philip (by implication at least) delivering a stern warning to the leaders of the Chalkidians.[129] It is impossible to choose between, on the one hand, an ambiguity and, on the other, a far from complete and certainly inexplicit piece of information; what does emerge is that Philip was not yet ready to seek a firm resolution of his relationship with this league. Very likely he recognized that a major factor in Olynthos' defection must have been its fear in 353 that the power of its ally was on the wane at the same time as its enemy, Athens, was recovering ground in the Thracian area; and this was a situation which was already beginning to improve. But, equally clearly, there was an influential anti-Macedonian faction at Olynthos, and to allow such a group unfettered freedom to oppose his interests was to invite trouble from a dangerous quarter. In 357 he had been prepared, with Athens weakened by war with her own allies, to surrender his alliance with her in exchange for one with his powerful neighbour. But now, in 351, although Athens was still relatively weak, her northern ambitions and interests were reviving, and this, combined with the rising influence of his enemies in the Chalkidike, augured ill for the future of his arrangements. The time had arrived for a reconsideration of the basis of Macedonian policy.

CHAPTER IV

351–346
TOWARDS A GREEK SETTLEMENT

KING ARYBBAS OF EPEIROS

Believing that he had settled the Chalkidian problem, at least for the time being, Philip turned to the reconstruction necessary on and beyond his northwestern and western frontiers. Some indications have already been noted that repercussions of the Macedonian setback of 353 had been felt in these areas also, and it is probably now, after his campaigns in the east and south of the kingdom, that Philip began to attend to difficulties with Illyrian and Paionian tribes and with King Arybbas of Epeiros. Of a Paionian campaign we know no detail, but it may be the action that led Isokrates to remark four years later that Philip had made subjects of them. Probably, from this time, Lyppeios (and later Patraos, who succeeded him, apparently in the late 330s)[1] paid a tribute to the Macedonian king and was liable to supply troops at his request.

In the same passage, Isokrates implies that a Macedonian expedition (probably in 351/0) was successful in establishing control over areas rendered unstable by the great Dardanian defeat of 358; one example of the same instability had already presented itself in the movement of the Grabaioi from the distant northwest to the very frontiers of the kingdom.[2] So far as we can tell, the Illyrian and Paionian campaigns were consistent with the general strategy Philip had adopted in dealing with these neighbours: one of pacification, where necessary reinforced by periodic demonstrations of Macedonian superiority. No Macedonian governors or military commanders appear to have been assigned to these areas, and, to our knowledge, there was no interference with their local government or organization. They were regarded as client-areas.

With Epeiros, on the other hand, the king was concerned to build a solid relationship that might guarantee him firm protection on his southwestern flank, as well as control over the alternative north/south passage, which ran from the northwestern Peloponnesos, across the Straits of Rhion, through Aitolia and Ambrakia to Epeiros. Some seven years earlier his marriage with Olympias, niece (and sister-in-law) of the reigning Arybbas, had had this end in view; its first product, Alexander, was now six years old. No more than twelve years of age was his namesake, the younger brother of Olympias, at present living in the Molossian court of Epeiros. In 350, war broke out between the two kingdoms – perhaps because Arybbas too had not hidden his disquiet over Philip's reverse of 353 and had sought support elsewhere; or perhaps simply because Philip had designs on certain Epeirote territory in the region of the Pindos range near the common frontier of the two states. Of the course of this struggle we know nothing, but of its issue some features are clear. The young Alexandros was removed from his uncle's court and taken to Pella, where Philip would arrange for his education and training until he was ready to instal him on the throne that had been his father's. This may have been inspired in part by Olympias, who must, like Philip, have recognized that the danger to her brother's life increased as he grew nearer the age at which he might occupy the throne. But, equally important, Philip had decided to bind the neighbouring kingdom to himself more closely than was possible with Arybbas on the throne.[3]

So it was that the status of King Arybbas underwent a change at the end of this campaign. Although, at the death of his predecessor, Neoptolemos, the latter's son would normally have inherited the throne, Alexandros was very young, and – his situation apparently being closely analogous to that of the young Amyntas on the death of Perdikkas III of Macedon – was evidently passed over for his uncle, whom our sources appear unanimously to regard as king. It seems likely that, as a complement to his plans to plant his brother-in-law on the Molossian throne, Philip at the same time forced Arybbas to regard himself for the time being as the boy's regent.[4] It was probably at this time that Tymphaia, Atintania and Paravaia were severed from Epeiros and annexed to the Macedonian kingdom; their addition completed Philip's hold on the Pindos range where it delimits the southwestern corner of Macedonia.[5]

If the dating of these three ventures – in Paionia, Illyria and Epeiros – is correct, then they will presumably have engaged Philip's attention through most of the year 350 and possibly in early 349. At any rate, nothing is known of other activities during that time.

ASIAN HORIZONS

When the Theban Pammenes had gone with 5000 infantry to Phrygia in early 353 to assist Artabazos in his revolt against the Great King, his success had been noteworthy, but he had then been dismissed by the satrap on suspicion of having plotted secretly with the king or his supporters. The loss of the Theban hoplite stiffening was fatal to the rebel cause and it collapsed soon afterwards. The satrap and his brother-in-law, the Rhodian Memnon, fled from the Persian domains (probably in late 353 or early 352) and successfully sought refuge at Pella.[6] There, for more than ten years, until their pardon and recall on the representations of Memnon's brother, Mentor, they and other refugees from the Persian yoke no doubt pressed for Philip's support against their erstwhile master. At some time before 346, and probably before his Chalkidian campaign began in 349, Philip seems to have decided to acquiesce in their wishes. There were many advantages to such plans. Ample wealth, especially by Greek standards, was to be found in Asia Minor, both in the Persian treasury at Sardis and in the tribute currently paid to the Persian realm, as well as in what booty might be won in the course of securing them. If he wished to win high prestige among the mainland Greeks, then he could do so by pushing the Persians out of the Greek-inhabited coastal satrapies of Asia Minor or out of Anatolia altogether. Perhaps more important, he was well aware of the political effects of the powerful military society he had built. Now, as never before, the bulk of Macedonian citizens must have had a heavy stake in military expansion. In military campaigning lay the *raison d'être* of the army – just as it provided the opportunities for the advancement and enrichment of its members. In Asia Minor suitable military goals might be found, which, for the indefinite future, offered fame and wealth as well as a means of absorbing the energies of his kingdom.

This idea now began to germinate. In the years that followed, as the impending break-down of relations with the Chalkidian cities became a reality, and as the king turned to a new alignment with the Athenians (those who had the greatest interest – an economic one – in the reopening of Asia Minor and its offshore islands to their trade), it seems to have governed his overall policy. Between 348 and 346 he would attempt to create a settlement of Greek affairs that would give him the co-operation of the Athenians in his venture and the stability of the Greek mainland behind his back.

PHOKIS AND PHERAI

Since the summer of 352, in Central Greece, Phokian fortunes under the new commander, Phayllos (and, after his death, Phalaikos, the son of Onomarchos) were very mixed. Although there were occasional successes on both sides, neither the Boiotian nor the Phokian forces were strong enough to bring an end to the Sacred War. The Phokians' policy continued in the cultivation of their allies, but, faced with an Athenian unwillingness to spend money on this war, they turned increasingly to their Peloponnesian friends, Sparta and Korinth, as well as other anti-Theban states, such as Epidauros, Phleios and perhaps others.[7] When war had broken out during 352/1 between Sparta and the Arkadians of Megalopolis (the allies of Thebes), the Phokians were quick to send 3000 infantry, who were accompanied by forces of the exiled Pheraian tyrants. In Athens, Demosthenes urged his fellows to add their support to Megalopolis, but to no avail. Returning successful from this campaign, a 4500-strong Boiotian army was able to eject Phalaikos from Chaironeia and to follow this with the devastation of much enemy territory. The exhaustion of the Phokians is reflected in their failure to continue the pretence of convening the rebel Amphiktyony after the spring meeting of 351; on the other hand, the Thebans, although readily furnished with cash by Artaxerxes Ochos, were unable to follow up their victory with more than minor skirmishes with their enemy.[8] The war had reached a stalemate, dragging through a series of desultory and indecisive engagements over the following years and resulting, in the early summer of 347, in the deposition of the hapless Phalaikos and, in reaction to the Phokian successes that ensued, a Theban appeal for Macedonian intervention.[9]

THE CHALKIDIAN CAMPAIGN

Meanwhile, by the middle of 349 events were moving in such a way as to bring Philip's Thessalian settlement under pressure. We know that mercenaries of the expelled Pheraian tyrants, Lykophron and Peitholaos, served in 351 on the Spartan side against the Arkadians and Thebans. The exiles had far from despaired of returning to their city and, perhaps at about the time that Philip began to move towards the Chalkidike, they were successful. Within a few months, Philip was to be obliged to give attention to Pherai, since it was thence, or from its port, Pagasai, that his major Thessalian revenues were derived.[10]

Precisely what brought the Macedonians and Chalkidians into conflict is not entirely clear. Perhaps, as most have thought, Philip had simply reached the stage at which he was ready to snatch this wealthy area for himself. But there may have been more to it. Soon after the warning issued to the Chalkidians in late 351 (possibly even immediately afterwards), the anti-Macedonian leader in Olynthos, one Apollonides, was banished. To the office of hipparch two pro-Macedonians were elected: Lasthenes and Euthykrates.[11] Demosthenes, who supplies the evidence for the expulsion, makes no mention of any direct (*i.e.*

military) pressure on Philip's part, but simply asserts that this was effected by Olynthians 'totally subservient to him', his partisans. Whatever the truth behind it, one thing is clear: that at that time Philip – if he was involved even indirectly – still hoped for a political solution to the problem of Chalkidian realignment. That this hope was vain is shown by the immediate pretext for the war eventually fought between the two states. Just before Olynthos was attacked in 348 (or before the general Chalkidian campaign began in autumn 349), Philip demanded that the Olynthians hand over to him two of his stepbrothers who were being harboured by the city. The inhabitants' refusal to do so was, according to one source, the cause of the war.[12]

There appear, at Philip's accession, to have been three members of this family: Archelaos, Menelaos and Aridaios, all older than the king himself, sons of his father by an earlier marriage.[13] Evidently, following the death of one of them, probably Archelaos, the two remaining brothers sought and found refuge in Olynthos. Since they are unlikely to have been given asylum before *c.*350 (for, if they had, they would surely have been expelled at the same time as Apollonides), it is justifiable to assume that in the last year before the Macedonian campaign against the Chalkidian cities there had been further signs of rift between the allies. By granting refuge and protection the Olynthians, presumably, were not acting out of humanitarian motives. In seeking an explanation our eye is inevitably drawn to the situation in the mid-380s, when Olynthos had installed Argaios as rival to the crown of Amyntas III. Presumably, in 350/49, this city had again evolved plans for advancing the claims of a pretender. Such a threat may well have given rise to the warning Philip is said to have delivered to his enemies as he advanced on their city. One of two things must happen: either they, the Olynthians, must abandon Olynthos, or he Macedonia[14] He appears to have grasped (what he failed to understand in 351/0) that the policies of Apollonides had been no temporary vacillation on his ally's part but were symptomatic of a revival of Olynthian ambitions, relatively dormant since 379. There was no room at close quarters for two such powers.

In early autumn of 349 he marched his forces across the frontier near Lake Bolbe and laid siege to the northeastern town of Stageira.[15] Occupying an important position quite close to the route (which ran north of the lake) between central Macedonia and Amphipolis, and, more importantly, commanding the best access from the eastern coastline to central and western Chalkidike, its fate was to sound a warning to the other communities of the peninsula. When it capitulated it was razed to the ground. Further towns, probably in the same area (certainly Stratonikeia and most likely Akanthos, Arethousa and perhaps even Apollonia),[16] capitulated without battle; Philip might now prevent the movement of enemy troops eastward towards Olynthos from the Strymonic Gulf coastline.

As soon as Macedonian intentions had become clear, Olynthian envoys travelled to Athens, renewing their past avowals of peace and goodwill and now asking urgently for alliance.[17] Their reception was not as they might have hoped. How much sympathy for their cause already existed among the Athenians we cannot be sure, but Demosthenes, for one, was prompted to deliver two separate speeches in their support and in both clearly implied that the opposition against which he argued was strong. In the second he professes himself puzzled that his fellows do not make an immediate decision and back it up forthwith by mounting an expedition.[18] Eventually, swallowing their suspicion of the petitioners and willing to see Philip thwarted, provided it was not substantially at their own cost, the assembly voted for alliance. The debate continued. Professions of alliance were no substitute for military aid and it was not very long before Demosthenes again rose to deliver the third of his speeches on the subject, urging the despatch of immediate and effective help in accordance with the new obligation. As a result – of the deliberations and not necessarily of this speech – a small force was detailed, comprising 30 ships (probably those on regular station in the north) with 2000 peltast mercenaries and an additional eight ships, the last apparently being launched as the result of an appeal for voluntary trierarchs.[19] Nothing is known of the activities of this force in the Chalkidike – very probably because no actual fighting was in progress at the time.

DISTRACTIONS IN THESSALY AND EUBOIA

It may have been that Philip wished to let the lesson of Stageira sink in before pressing eastwards against the more powerful members of the Chalkidian League. But, more certainly, he was forced to give attention to serious trouble in Thessaly. In the first of his speeches on Olynthos, Demosthenes had stated that 'the Thessalians' had voted to demand restoration of Pagasai and 'to make representations over Magnesia'.[20] In the second, delivered perhaps only days later, he had again alluded to the demand over Pagasai, noted that 'the Thessalians' had actually prevented Philip from fortifying Magnesia. He then produced a new datum recently come to his notice, that the revenues granted to the archon from harbour and market dues were to be cut off, since they were being spent on Macedonian and not Thessalian interests.[21] What appears to have transpired is that there had been a revival of Pheraian power under Peitholaos, which, combined (perhaps)[22] with dissatisfaction among other Thessalians over Philip's continuing failure to carry out his promises regarding the Phokian war, successfully produced a series of votes by the Thessalian *koinon* in favour of withdrawing his privileges – though not, it seems, of removing him from office. However, it is worth noting that the actions represented here by the orator as arising from the grievances of the Thessalian League accord closely with the inevitable effects of a *Pheraian* resurgence. Both Pagasai and Magnesia had been under Pheraian control until 352 and would have been among the first areas to fall under the control of the revived tyranny. Since Pagasai must have been a major source of at least the archon's customs dues, its seizure by Peitholaos would by itself remove a portion of this revenue from Philip's control. It is possible, that is, since we know independently of an intervention by Philip against Pherai at this time,[23] that Demosthenes, in order to lend courage to his fellows to challenge Philip in the north, was manufacturing a rift with the Thessalian League out of local difficulties in the region of Pherai.

By the time he came to deliver the third *Olynthiac* Demosthenes had nothing to say about affairs in Thessaly. Perhaps this was because he was concerned in that speech with the Athenian contribution to the defence of Olynthos, but it nevertheless implies (since the recent situation, if as serious as he had painted it, would have seriously affected Philip's ability to fight effectively) that the difficulty had been resolved in the interim. It is unlikely that Philip travelled in person to Thessaly; had he appeared so close to central Greece we should expect to hear of it. More probably, troops remaining nearby (at Gonnoi or elsewhere in northern Magnesia or in Perrhaibia) were detailed to perform the task, possibly with Thessalian assistance, while Philip and his main force prepared to resume the Chalkidian campaign during the next spring.

But, as Philip had to contend with his distractions, so, at the end of the winter, did the Athenian people – their decision to commit troops to Euboia, while diplomatically disastrous, serving to indicate to friend and enemy alike the main line of current Athenian policy. In 357 it had been clear, when their forces easily expelled a powerful Theban force from the island, that the key to influence over the Euboians was majority support among the islanders.[24] But this was a lesson the Athenians were quick to forget. By 349, Eretria lay under the hand of the tyrant Ploutarchos and his mercenaries, clearly with at least tacit Athenian approval. But when the tyrant, faced with internal revolt, appealed for aid, at which point the Athenians should have reconsidered their stance, they were persuaded to send a small force under Phokion, expecting (on what grounds remains incomprehensible, but presumably the assurance of Ploutarchos combined with blissful memories of the episode of 357) general support on the island. Phokion quickly realized the error and, fighting his way out of a tight corner, did his best to retrieve the situation;[25] but, in spite of the circumstances there, which evidently remained grim, he was recalled on other business.[26] On his departure the situation deteriorated disastrously, the Athenians were defeated, their relief commander captured and the *demos* was obliged to accept a few months later a settlement involving a large ransom and guaranteeing the independence of the Euboians. Only Karystos, on the southern tip of the island, retained its alliance with Athens.[27]

The affair obviously had been a serious miscalculation, but the motive behind it illustrates equally clearly what it was that might stir to action the *demos* that took such hesitant and half-hearted measures with regard to Olynthos. The Athenian people felt their primary loyalty to lie in protecting their immediate interests rather than in committing themselves to more distant (and therefore expensive) campaigns. The outcome of the Social War had produced this attitude; then the influence and conservative legislation of Euboulos had elevated it into policy.[28]

The converse is seen in the disparity between what aid Demosthenes urged must be given to the Olythians and the expeditions the Athenian *demos* actually sent. But, in any case, we must beware of elevating Demosthenes so early as this into a leading Athenian statesman – as also of believing his fellow citizens so gullible as to commit substantial forces to a distant zone in support of an ally whose bona fides was at least suspect, on the basis of past actions, and might evaporate at any time if Philip should offer sufficient inducement. It was at about this time that Aristotle, the man destined to be Stageira's greatest son and Plato's greatest pupil, left Athens and emigrated to the territory of the tyrant Hermias. Hermias, ex-slave and *castrato* by repute (but perhaps only out of the mouths of his enemies), had succeeded during the years of Persian impotence in Asia Minor in carving out for himself a thriving little princedom among the mountain-villages of the Troad and around the coastline opposite Lesbos between his seat of Atarneus and Assos. Wealthy and well furnished with mercenaries, he was recognized by a preoccupied Persia. With the Platonists Erastos and Koriskos from near-by Skepsis he formed with Plato's blessing a curious *amicitia*, establishing them as his 'companions' and advisers in Assos; their influence is said to have mellowed his rule.[29] Aristotle joined the 'companions' at Assos, where he passed three years combining study, teaching and political counselling in congenial company.

But there was more to it than this. Although it is impossible to sift facts from propaganda, there is not much doubt that Aristotle was no mere itinerant scholar and teacher. He was son of the Stageirite Nikomachos, who several decades earlier had been personal physician to Amyntas III, Philip's father. It is said that his departure from Athens (he had arrived there in 367) was occasioned by the death of Plato and the elevation of Speusippos, but he was also perhaps associated with Philip too closely for comfort in a city seething with news and rumour from the Chalkidike.[30] Travelling to Atarneus apparently by way of Macedonia he probably negotiated at this time an entente between Philip and Hermias, both of whom saw profit in an arrangement that promised for the former an Anatolian bridgehead and for the latter a stronger guarantee of independence from the clutches of Artaxerxes Ochos. With this preliminary step taken, Philip was now ready to set in train his plans for a Greek settlement which would allow him to turn with his new ally and an enthusiastic army towards the much greener pastures across the Aegean.[31]

THE FALL OF OLYNTHOS

In about March 348 he had returned to the attack in the Chalkidike, beginning a drive down the peninsula west of Olynthos to the areas of Bottiaia and Pallene (the westernmost peninsula), at least some major communities (perhaps all) submitting to him without battle.[32] A second Olynthian appeal to the Athenians elicited a response similar to the first. Charidemos, the general holding the regular command at the Hellespont, was ordered to Olynthos with 18 triremes (probably the ten he had taken in late 351,[33] augmented by the eight volunteers raised for the previous Olynthian expedition), 4000 peltast mercenaries and 150 horse.[34] Olynthos at this time (between March and May) was not yet under attack, for the Olynthians were able to combine with Charidemos in destructive raids in the areas recently fallen into Philip's hands.[35] How effective these were we do not know, but what was decisive – in late spring or early summer – was the capitulation to the Macedonian King of Mekyberna (the port of Olynthos) and Torone, by holding which Philip was able to cut off the Olynthians from the sea. The defenders brought up their forces but were defeated in two battles and confined to their walls. Under siege, they despatched, around the middle of the year, a third, desperate appeal for Athenian assistance further to what was there already.[36] From Athens 17 triremes, with 2000 hoplites and 300 cavalry in transport, set sail for the north under Chares' command.[37]

But Philip had timed his campaign well and bad weather (perhaps the northerly Etesian winds) hampered the contingent's voyage; it was not to reach Olynthos until after the city had fallen.[38] In fact, at about the time of its departure, quite possibly even before it had sailed, news was received in Athens that was calculated to cause confusion. A group of Euboian envoys, come to discuss terms relating to the recent Athenian campaign on the island,[39] brought the tidings that Philip no longer wished to be at war with the Athenians. This was only the first of a number of Macedonian overtures, which led eventually to the Peace of Philokrates. But the timing of this initiative, at about the time of the investment of the city of Olynthos itself, was probably designed to weaken the Athenian will to assist its ally. The reaction of the *demos* is not recorded, but it was probably unfavourable; the majority, like Demosthenes, had committed itself (however half-heartedly) to the northern alliance and was not interested in peace.[40]

Before very long – probably in August or September – the Olynthian siege was over. Philip's partisans in the beleaguered city played their role. Two of them, the hipparchs Lasthenes and Euthykrates, surrendered 500 cavalry to him and soon afterwards the city fell.[41] After plundering it and enslaving the inhabitants, says Diodoros, he sold everything as booty. The Olynthians themselves were in fact probably treated according to their political alignments, although most of our sources appear to believe that all suffered the same fate.[42] Chalkidian territory (or some of it) was allotted to Macedonians – at least to members of the *hetairos*-class, who appear later in Alexander's cavalry as the squadrons from Apollonia and Anthemous.[43] Athenian citizens captured during the campaign were transported to Pella and held there; Philip had other plans for them. In Athens itself, the Assembly could do no more than grant refuge and citizenship to the Olynthians who had escaped, pass condemnatory motions against their betrayers and engage in recriminations against their own generals.[44]

PEACE-MOVES

Such a brave show however could not hide the gloomy prospect facing the city. When news of Philip's unqualified victory was received they knew too that, with the allies of Thebes disillusioned by their failure to finish off an equally depressed Phokis, it was only a matter of time before the victor at Olynthos was invited into central Greece. Then, as the ally of the Phokians and the enemy of Thebes, Athens was in grave danger of direct attack. It was therefore with a sense of relief and jubilation that the Athenians received a second message from Philip, sent to capitalize upon their depression.

Shortly before the fall of Olynthos, during the Olympic truce of 348 (so probably in July) an Athenian, Phrynon of Rhamnous, had been captured by pirates who were apparently Macedonian or at least operating out of some part of the Macedonian realm. When he had arranged his own ransom, Phrynon presented himself before the *demos*, requesting the despatch to Philip of an official envoy to complain of this violation of the sacred truce and to ask recompense of his costs. Ktesiphon was sent, returning – by now certainly after the fall of Olynthos – with news of Philip's goodwill towards the Athenians and his assurance that, having entered the war with them in the first place against his wishes, he was eager even after his recent success to be quit of it. Although they may have doubted his avowals, they eagerly received Ktesiphon's report and conferred upon him an official vote of praise.[45] Philokrates, demesman of Hagnous and associate of Demosthenes,[46] rose to move that Philip be invited to send envoys to discuss terms; the assembly affirmed the proposal to a man.[47] The motion, however popular, was technically illegal, probably because a clause in the Athenian/Olynthian alliance will have forbidden any negotiations with the enemy by either party without the prior assent of the other.[48] When the case came to trial Demosthenes spoke in Philokrates' defence and won such an overwhelming victory that the plaintiff was fined and lost his right in the future to prosecute such a suit.[49]

THE DECREE OF EUBOULOS

While it is clear that the immediate reaction of most Athenians to the signs that Philip would not immediately march south with his Thessalian and Boiotian allies to crush all who stood against him was one of relief and even pleasure, it is equally clear that Philip had as yet no cause for complacency. While the Athenian people were happy to play the jade to Philip's advances, they were equally prepared to see what resistance could be organized among the Greek states to crush him, or at least to defend Thermopylai against him. Within a short time of the fall of Olynthos, Euboulos persuaded the very *demos* that had recently welcomed Philip's friendliness to despatch a number of embassies to the Greek states – 'almost as far as the Red Sea', as Demosthenes ironically remarked[50] – with a view to inviting them to make war in common against Philip. It was Euboulos' decree, but he had been greatly assisted in its passage by the appearance of his younger colleague, the actor Aischines, who dramatically introduced Ischandros the Arkadian as 'the representative of the friends of Athens in Arkadia'. Philip, they claimed, was building up support for himself among the Greeks, even in the Peloponnesos. Ischandros added his personal testimony of Macedonian-subsidized corruption in high Arkadian places. It is not difficult to imagine the sort of argument the *demos* was prepared to accept and act upon: peace with Philip was all very well if that was the only way they could protect themselves against his entry into central Greece, but if the Greek states could be induced to deny him entry, then so much the better. If the Athenians suspected Philip of talking peace while he plotted war, they were not averse to repaying him in the same coin. Although no evidence survives, it is unlikely that Demosthenes publicly opposed this scheme. He had decided that peace with Philip was both expedient and unavoidable, but no doubt was obliged to act circumspectly so as to avoid misunderstanding. But he had no hopes of Euboulos' success and is unlikely to have been enthusiastic.[51]

Among those commissioned was Aischines himself, who was sent to the Peloponnesos; unfortunately the Arkadian reaction to his visit is the only one on which information happens to survive. But it is clear from his report on his return that he had achieved little, if anything; for all his enthusiasm, all he could propose was that further envoys should be sent to denounce the pro-Macedonians. In general, the decree had merely served to show Philip where his difficulties lay.

PLANS FOR A SETTLEMENT

At this point it becomes important to determine what Philip did intend to achieve through the friendship and peace he claimed to want with the Athenians. As we have seen, pressure will already have been exerted upon him at the least to lend assistance to those with an interest in challenging the Persian King's dominion over Asia Minor. At about the time that this subject must have been broached he had in any case been forced to look beyond his Chalkidian alignment and had turned towards rapprochement with Athens. But there was more. First, Macedonia was vulnerable by land rather than by sea; Demosthenes might proclaim the desirability of assigning the Athenian fleet to raids on the Macedonian coasts, patrols along her shoreline and blockades of her harbours,[52] but he probably misled few of those who heard him. However, what did constitute a most serious threat to Macedonia was the possibility of a combination of both Athens and Thebes.[53] In the negotiations which now follow, and in the Peace of Philokrates itself, this is clearly the foremost factor. The second, of lesser importance in the long term, was the question of the role Thrace was to play in the settlement. To put it in Athenian terms: was Athens to be compelled to surrender her own gains in the area, especially those with Kersebleptes, or was she to be obliged – with neither bases nor (except through alliance with Philip himself) allies – to pursue her economic and strategic interests only by the grace and with the permission of the Macedonian king? That both of these factors were clearly recognized in Athens and Pella soon became obvious.

For Philip the climactic point in his dealing with his existing allies and in his longer term intentions regarding the Greek states and (by now) Asia Minor was fast approaching. Whether or not he wished it, he could not avoid intervening in central Greece; his Thessalian alliance depended on it. But to finish off the Phokians' resistance and to deprive them of the will and the ability to resist Boiotian domination in central Greece was to restore Thebes to a level of power from which she had declined only through their efforts and to drive Athens into peace and alliance with her – the combination he had most to avoid. The action he was to take, therefore, whatever fate the Phokians were to suffer, must leave Thebes too weak to damage him. This might come as a surprise to his ally and hers, the Thessalian *koinon*, but he could confidently expect to make the prospect appealing to a Thessaly which would be, as a result, dominant in the Amphiktyonic League. The Athenians, too, ought to find it attractive: their border-town Oropos would be returned to them and Thebes would no longer stand in the way of their influence in Euboia.

The supreme difficulty confronting this plan was that for the moment Thebes was and must remain his ally at least until alliance with Athens instead was assured. So that negotiations with the latter (and probably with Phokis) would have to be carried out without arousing Theban suspicions to a critical level. Provided that there remained no other safeguard open to the Athenians, the king knew by now that they would agree to peace; he knew too that, if he were to insist that he would not have peace without alliance, then they would agree to peace and alliance. The terms, combined with his holding of the Athenian prisoners from Olynthos, should give him the lever he might need to bring Athenian hoplites into play, if necessary, when the Thebans saw what was happening. It was inevitable, that is, that during the coming negotiations Philip would need to emphasize heavily the advantages accruing to Athens from his planned finesse – but without being publicly specific as to how they were to be attained.

The embassies commissioned under the decree of Euboulos, then, represented a setback to his plans – not because they were likely to raise a serious coalition against Macedon in the Peloponnesos or elsewhere, but rather because they indicated that the Athenians were not yet fully convinced that peace with Philip was expedient. In fact, some sixteen months would elapse between their enthusiastic approval for Philokrates' motion and their eventual decision (on the proposal of the same man) to despatch an embassy to learn Philip's terms.

CENTRAL GREECE: THE FIRST INTERVENTION

Since 351 the level of activity in the Sacred War had subsided almost to nothing. The Phokian will to fight seems to have been broken and Thebes was content to let sleeping dogs lie. The meetings of the rebel Amphiktyony had ceased and the leading Phokian allies, Athens and Sparta, had lost interest in a state that no longer offered them a weapon against Thebes. Phalaikos, no longer bothering to maintain the Phokian role of wronged innocence (and, besides, needing the money), cynically plundered the Delphic treasuries. During the spring or early summer of 347, after a series of skirmishes with Boiotian forces, he was removed from office, charged with embezzlement of sacred funds and replaced by a triumvirate of commanders, Deinokrates, Kallias and Sophanes. In the ensuing investigations the blame fell upon his administrator of sacred properties, one Philon.[54] From their three fortresses in Boiotia, Orchomenos, Koroneia and Korsiai,[55] the new leaders engaged upon so successful a campaign that, its territory ravaged, and unable to withstand the Phokian mercenary forces, the Boiotian League appealed to Philip.

For him the situation was difficult. While, no doubt, he would be better able to find support for his plans in the disgruntled Phalaikos, and consequently welcomed his demotion, he had also to keep some sort of faith with his Theban ally. On the other hand, he could hardly intervene definitively in central Greece until he had alliance with Athens. His sole alternative, therefore, was to commit only a few troops in answer to the appeal, enough to avoid losing his allies, but not enough to finish the war before he was ready to end it on his own terms. He was, as Diodoros says, delighted at the Theban plight and disposed to see them humiliated. But for the moment they must be kept guessing.[56] The leader of the Macedonian force was probably Parmenion (Antipatros being, at this time or shortly afterwards, in Thrace), who was a few months later (perhaps on his return from Boiotia) to lead the siege of Halos which was in progress by the end of the following winter.

The Phokians were currently attempting to establish a fortress near Abai, a town on the Phokian border opposite Orchomenos and Tegyra. Attacking the enemy there, the Boiotians, with their Macedonian support, won a victory but made no attempt to go farther.[57]

ATHENIAN COUNTER-MEASURES

So half-hearted an intervention may not in itself have impressed a sense of urgency upon the anti-Macedonians of Athens; but what it presaged clearly did. They could no longer doubt that the Thebans would call for larger efforts by Philip and would, if necessary, assist in his passage through Thermopylai. It was only a matter of time. As Aischines later said, it was by now, when the envoys despatched by the decree of Euboulos half a year or more ago had returned without a shadow of support, that he and others like him began thinking in terms of peace.[58] But, first, steps must be taken quickly to ensure that Athens was able to bargain from strength. Demosthenes too, who procured for himself membership of the Boulē at about this time,[59] perceived the urgency of the situation and spoke of a plan 'to protect the islanders and the Hellespontine cities'. Philip, these people saw, would wish to complete the eradication of Athenian influence in Thrace before the terms of peace could restrain him. Resolutions were moved by Euboulos, Aristophon and Diopeithes and a force was sent out, probably under Chares, to the Chersonesos. Here contact was made with Kersebleptes and the combined forces established a number of garrisons along the Propontid and Aegean coasts.[60] Myrtenon was fortified, and Doriskos, just to the west of the Hebros mouth (in Amadokos' territory), as also were Ergiske and Serrion, the latter a promontory near Doriskos. On the Propontis, Ganos was taken and nearby Hieron Oros. It is not clear whether any Athenian soldiers were left to man these outposts; on the whole it is more likely that their ally Kersebleptes maintained them.[61]

This was a disquieting setback to the progress of Philip's peace-negotiations. The garrisons themselves evidently presented no serious military problem (they were quickly and easily overturned six or eight months later), and for the moment he was content to order Antipatros into the area of Hieron Oros with orders to secure a base for later operations.[62] More worrying was the prospect that any Athenian gains would inevitably delay – even prevent – the opening of negotiations.

Encouraged by this success the Athenians turned to Thermopylai, whence Philip must come. If he were to be stopped then this would be only with Phokian help. In very late 347, the new Phokian commanders, chastened by the recent first appearance of Macedonian troops in central Greece, began to cast about for assistance and, in particular, for a means of inducing the Athenians and Spartans to abandon their movement towards the Macedonian camp. To both cities they sent envoys, offering to hand over the strategic towns of Alponos, Thronion and Nikaia, which commanded the central Greek approaches to Thermopylai. Both allies accepted. The Athenians decreed that these towns be taken over by the general Proxenos, that 50 triremes should be launched and that all able-bodied men up to the age of 40 should serve in the expedition.[63] In the southern Thessalian pericecic state of Phthiotis, trouble was flaring which might also be exploited to Philip's disadvantage. Halos, a pro-Athenian coastal town at the southern edge of the Krokion Plain (Crocus Field) and on the main route south from Larisa, Pherai and Pagasai, was at loggerheads with Pharsalos, some 40–50 kilometres to the northwest. Since Halos could be supplied and relieved from the sea, the Athenians could assist in its cause.[64] The Thracian campaign had been a success and the Halian resistance was at the least a useful diversion; all that remained was to take possession of the Pass of Thermopylai. At the end of 347, then, the Athenian position looked strong; and if negotiations could be delayed a little longer the peace might even prove dispensable.

Therefore, probably in December 347 or January 346, a new decree was passed despatching envoys to all the Hellenes to invite them to Athens.[65] This was significantly different from the decree of Euboulos more than a year before, in that the earlier decision had represented the attempt of the Athenians to organize a large-scale effort to meet Philip's advance with military strength, whereas the present measure was an invitation to deliberate on war, if that were necessary, or on peace if that were considered the better course.[66] This more realistic effort clearly belongs in the context of recent Athenian successes. The first steps had been taken towards a massive show of resistance to Philip. If enough other states were interested this might be proceeded with; otherwise they might all share in the peace, the terms of which would consequently be much less favourable to Philip.

STAMPEDE FOR PEACE

By mid winter, Philip's plans for his central Greek intervention were in severe jeopardy. He would need to erase the new Athenian advantage in coastal Thrace, but, more pressingly, he could secure his path to Thermopylai only by taking up the Pharsalian cause. Accordingly he ordered Parmenion (whose small command in Boiotia may recently have ended) to invest Halos and bring it to heel. At the same time he might test the Phokian wind to see whether he could forestall Athenian expectations there. Envoys were sent in secret to treat with Phalaikos and probably to persuade other influential Phokians (and perhaps, by attractive bribes, their mercenaries) to support the reinstatement of their demoted commander.[67]

Tension was high among the Athenians, for whom precise timing was now as important as it was for Philip. There had been no rejection of Philip's peace-offers, but as yet they had been unprepared to take the actual decision to negotiate. Once they and their allies took possession of Thermopylai and once the other Greek states indicated their support either for war or for an Athenian-dominated peace, then would be the time to act. Probably for some time now representations had been made, at least by the families concerned, for the release by Philip of the Athenians he had taken prisoner at Olynthos. In addition, if their release could be effected before peace-negotiations began, a powerful Macedonian advantage would be removed. By the beginning of winter the matter had been taken up officially by Philokrates and Demosthenes, with the result that Aristodemos, a friend of the king and member of the acting profession (whose itinerant and somewhat privileged existence made it suitable for such missions),[68] was instructed to sound out Philip on the question of the prisoners' release and to report to the *demos*. On his return to Athens there was a delay. He was not summoned to the Boulē to make his report. On the flimsiest of excuses – his alleged preoccupation with private business – so important a matter was temporarily suppressed.[69] Philip, seeing that the Athenian *demos* might be made to work on his behalf against its own leaders, took the initiative of releasing one prisoner, Iatrokles, who returned home in late Gamelion or at the beginning of Anthesterion (late January or early February) to report that Philip wanted peace.

Events quickly followed the course for which Philip had hoped. Angry at having been denied Aristodemos' report, many people pressed for his summons before the Boulē. On the demand of Demokrates of Aphidna the order was given and the envoy appeared, conveying Philip's great friendship towards the city and adding (for the first time, to our knowledge, that this was made explicit) that the king was eager not only for peace but also for alliance. At the assembly at which these tidings were reported, in the first days of Anthesterion, a second bombshell shattered the expectations of those who hoped that the new Athenian initiatives could reduce or erase Philip's bargaining strength. Shortly after the Phokian triumvirate's offer of Thermopylai, it had become known that Phalaikos had returned to the Phokian command. Proxenos had been sent to him to discover whether the agreement with his predecessors still stood, but he had been utterly rebuffed. His letter containing this information, as well as a report by the sacred heralds that the Phokians had refused to accept the truce for the Lesser Mysteries, were both received by this same meeting of the Assembly.[70] The timing was masterly. The *demos*, now eager for peace, was jubilant, and the most powerful ammunition of those who counselled delay was destroyed. Demosthenes, with the horse gone, wasted no time in trying to bolt the stable door; he stood and proposed a motion to confer a crown on Aristodemos for his efforts. It would thereafter be difficult, because of this promptitude, to accuse him of any connection with the delay – although his motion (as he perhaps did not foresee or was prepared to rationalize at another time) was to prove a source of embarrassment in the days after the *demos* turned against the peace.[71]

No further delay was possible. Philokrates, realizing that speed was now of the essence, that the earlier agreement could be reached, the sooner the present Thracian possessions of each side might be guaranteed them by its terms, moved the immediate establishment of an embassy of ten to learn Philip's conditions.[72] The Macedonian manoeuvres were thus successful. The Athenians were galloping headlong down the road to peace, out of the control of their leaders, who could do little but attempt to preserve what little initiative was left to them.

The effect on the uncommitted states may be imagined. More than two months later, by mid-Elaphebolion, no Greek states had responded to the Athenian invitation to discuss war or peace. Whether or not the Hellenes might have reacted differently had the Athenians not taken unilateral action in the meantime we cannot tell. But, whatever the result might have been, no envoys would ever come now.[73] Philip knew he had won the first round – provided, at least, that he could re-take coastal Thrace and subordinate Kersebleptes. The second round – to persuade the Athenian to join him in an assault on Theban power – had yet to be fought.

THE FIRST EMBASSY

The envoys left Attica by sea, probably from the region of Marathon or Rhamnous on the northwestern coast, crossed to Euboia, to avoid Boiotia, and travelled north to Oreos at its northern tip. A herald with authority to escort them thence to Pella had not yet arrived so, rather than delay, they crossed without him to Halos, still under siege but open by sea to the Athenian fleet. After making contact with Parmenion, who no doubt provided them with some form of safe conduct, they lost no time in pushing northwards across the Krokion Plain and through Pagasai and Pherai to Larisa, where the official escort met them for the remaining 150 km. to Pella. The journey will have taken them perhaps a week.[74]

Around the middle of Anthesterion (*c.* 12 March) this first Athenian embassy arrived in Pella 'to discuss with Philip the matter of peace and the common interests of the Athenians and Philip'.[75] Summoned to an audience with the king the envoys delivered one by one, from oldest to youngest, the speeches they had prepared. Undoubtedly the most significant were those of men with the stature of Nausikles (the commander of the Athenian force at Thermopylai in 352) and Philokrates. But nothing is known of their submissions. In the trial of Aischines three years later, without which we should have had no information at all on the matter, a summary of Aischines' speech alone survives. It is no more – if genuine – than a rhetorical display-piece on the subject of Amphipolis, though perhaps appropriate enough in the mouth of the next-to-youngest ambassador (Demosthenes being the most junior), who therefore spoke second-last, when all the important subjects had been exhausted by others.[76] Demosthenes, in the concluding address, was – so Aischines claimed – badly affected by nervousness and was unable to complete his piece.[77]

Aischines' topic will no doubt have appealed to the Athenian audience, who got it second-hand, but few of the more astute will have imagined that Philip accorded it any serious attention. Four subjects however, probably treated by the most senior speakers, must have been taken seriously. Two of them, so events were to show, and as he no doubt rejoindered, were not regarded by the king as negotiable: the independence of the Thracian coastal forts and the matter of the naval assistance Athens was giving to Halos. As regards the latter there was simply nothing to be discussed; whether or not Athenian aid before this point had been official, it will now have been terminated and there is no suggestion among the few references to the subsequent fate of Halos that it was an Athenian military loss. When it was delivered at a second audience, the king's answer to the question of the Thracian forts will have been equally unequivocal. As the envoys could well see, his preparations for a Thracian campaign were complete. He would not tolerate the presence of bases that interfered with the sovereignty of his Byzantian, Perinthian and Thracian allies; nor would he leave unpunished a Thracian ruler who, the ally of Macedon, had turned to peace with the Athenians when they were his enemies and, since that time, had acknowledged Athens' claim to the Macedonian town of Amphipolis and had been guilty of territorial crimes against the allies of Philip.[78]

However, to say this was not to deny that the Athenians were legitimately concerned with the passageway to the Black Sea. Philip would not dispute their claim to the Chersonesos; he promised that he would not take his army there while deliberations were in progress and, in accordance with the terms he was proposing, the peace itself would guarantee its subsequent security, for each party would by right retain the territories it then possessed.[79]

The fourth vital subject must have been the Phokian war. Philip's own intentions for its settlement and his need, in the meantime, to retain his Boiotian allies prevented him from being completely open with the envoys, at least in public, and certainly prohibited his committing anything on the matter to writing. He may have gone so far as to point out that, once it was possible to do so and provided that he had the support of Athens in full alliance, he would view the relative claims of Phokis and Thebes in much the same way as did the Athenians, to judge by their support for the former over the years of the Sacred War; until then, of course, the Phokians must be excluded from the treaty.[80] Above all he will have stressed that he must have alliance as well as peace.[81]

There must have been some discussion on the subject of the Athenian prisoners taken at Olynthos, although this is not specifically attested until the visit of the second embassy.[82] At this stage, no doubt, he pointed out (what he must already have told Aristodemos) that he would consider neither holding nor demanding payment for his own allies; their release was therefore in the Athenians' own hands. He will also have added the several inducements he was reported to have promised (but which, when the alliance neither operated as he had hoped nor showed any signs of permanency, he was unable to realise): Athenian influence would be restored in Euboia; Oropos would be restored to her; the Boiotian towns, Thespiai and Plataia, would be repopulated; and Philip would cut a channel across the narrow neck of the Chersonesos, severing it from the mainland.[83] None of these offers represented any loss to him and all should have been welcome to Athens. The first three would be both instruments and consequences of his planned circumscription of Theban power; but, as such, they would also be dependent on it. The fourth, although it may have removed a minor naval hazard facing the Athenian corn-fleet, was also complementary to his guarantee not to interfere in the Chersonesos; he would render the Athenian territory more easily defensible against assault from the Thracian mainland.

Now Philip well realized how much would depend on the ten men who were to return to their fellows with his terms. He would send back a letter with them pointing out that he was in a position to confer great benefits upon the *demos*, but he must remain vague once it came to details.[84] It would be the envoys themselves who conveyed, at least in general terms, the real import of this alliance.

THE THRACIAN CAMPAIGN OF SPRING 346

As they left Pella, around 20 Anthesterion (= *c.* 18 March), Philip also left, bound for Thrace. Kersebleptes had – until the time of his co-operation with the Athenians in establishing their coastal forts – lain quiet since his defeat by Philip and the latter's Perinthian, Byzantian and central Thracian allies in 351. It may have been that at that time his son had been taken hostage and remained in Pella,[85] which, if so, may provide us with the explanation. In the campaign that now follows, which lasted only three months, there appear to have been only two aims: to defeat Kersebleptes and subordinate him to Macedonian interests and to remove the newly planted bases on the coasts. The first of these objects was achieved in about a month, by 23 Elaphebolion (= *c.* 20 April). Philip pushed eastwards directly to the Propontis, perhaps to a base at Apros secured for him several months before by Antipatros, and there defeated the Thracian forces at the Hieron Oros stronghold. Not until *c.* 23 Thargelion (= *c.* 18 June), however, did he return to Pella,[86] and we must take it that, on completing his arrangements with Kersebleptes, he proceeded to pick off the remaining hostile bases – a task that was in all probability fairly straightforward, since word reaching their defenders (if any remained) must have made it quite clear to them that they would certainly be given no support.[87]

During the Thracian campaign of 352/1, during which he had fought in alliance with, among others, Amadokos of central Thrace, it may be that he had annexed the western Thracian area previously held by the sons of Berisades.[88] But, if not in 351, then certainly in 346, the eastern frontier of Macedonia must have been extended to the Nestos. Of Amadokos, in whose kingdom Doriskos and Serrion (and perhaps Myrtenon and Ergiske) lay, nothing is known after his participation in the campaign five years earlier. He had been by then, it seems, a very old man[89] and was most probably dead by 346. His successor was evidently a certain Teres, who fought, as the inheritor of his Macedonian alliance, alongside Philip.[90] Kersebleptes was not removed from his throne, which he still occupied four years later. But it is likely that he was obliged at the very least to renew his violated alliance with Philip.

Before leaving Pella on this campaign Philip had given orders to three of his most senior commanders, Antipatros, Parmenion and

Eurylochos,[91] to act on his behalf in Athens and, provided its Assembly accepted his terms, to receive the oaths of ratification from the proper magistrates.

THE PEACE OF PHILOKRATES

The Athenian ambassadors arrived home in the last days of Anthesterion, probably by the 27th (= *c.* 25 March), where they made their reports to the Council and to the Assembly. On the motion of Demosthenes, it was resolved that, when the Macedonian envoys arrived, the mandatory two consecutive days should be set for assembly-meetings. By the time they did arrive – and perhaps they delayed intentionally to just this end – the city Dionysia, which would prevent the transaction of non-festival business for its duration (9–13 Elaphebolion), was too near, and the 18th and 19th were set.[92]

We should recognize the difficult situation in which the Athenian ambassadors found themselves on their return. They, like most of the *demos*, were – now if not before – in favour of a peace;[93] but they alone knew the terms under which Philip was prepared to concede it. From the popular reaction on the first day of debate to Philokrates' motion (which was undoubtedly formulated in the terms Philip had dictated), it is clear, however, that the envoys had not given proper emphasis in their report to some of the conditions on which Philip insisted, notably the exclusion from the treaty of the Phokians, the Halians and Kersebleptes. Again, although we know almost nothing of the role played in the debate by any envoys other than Philokrates, Demosthenes and Aischines, it appears that, at least of these three, only Philokrates exhibited the moral courage to stand by the only terms Philip would accept. This was an unpleasant task that most were evidently prepared to leave to Philokrates and to Philip's own envoys.

When the *demos* assembled on 18 Elaphebolion (= *c.* 15 April) and other, minor matters had been dealt with,[94] it had before it not one motion but two. The first was Philokrates' in the form of a *probouleuma*, containing the proposal of peace and alliance on Philip's terms, a treaty open to Philip and his allies on the one side and Athens and the remnants of her naval league on the other, and with the specific exclusions already noted. Both parties were to retain what possessions they had at the date of ratification.[95] The *demos*, taken by surprise, reacted strongly against the motion, supporting overwhelmingly the alternative proposal, a *dogma* of their allied synod which recommended that no decision should be taken in the absence of the Athenian embassies to the Hellenes, but that on their return the question of peace (without alliance) again be debated. This was a proposal for Common Peace, in which all Greeks would be free to take part, if they so desired, at any time within three months of its establishment.[96]

All speakers (who certainly included Aischines and Demosthenes but not, presumably, Philokrates) gave support to the allied motion[97] – and, in so doing, these men who knew Philip's intentions were at best hypocritical. Since debate on the peace had been confined by Demosthenes' earlier procedural motion to the first day, allowing on the 19th only the actual vote, it was clear that the *demos* was unwittingly pursuing a line that would destroy all hope of peace. Demosthenes with his own procedural motion in mind, moved that the Macedonian envoys be summoned before the assembly, ready – now that his own (false) stance had been sufficiently demonstrated – to fasten on Philip himself the responsibility for Philokrates' peace. Aischines, apparently feeling that it would be better to leave this to the following day, when the procedural block on further debate could be rescinded, successfully adjourned discussion until the morning.[98]

On the morning of the 19th, Demosthenes rose and – no doubt still professing support for the allied motion – announced that the previous day's discussion was worthless unless Philip would agree to its terms. Calling Antipatros to the platform, he put to him the question whether the king would accept Common Peace without alliance. As the envoys all knew, he would not.[99] Thus, when the prohibition against further debate had been lifted,[100] discussion was resumed. If Demosthenes spoke at all – which seems unlikely – it cannot have been in favour of Philokrates' *probouleuma*.[101] The task of winning over the *demos* was left to others, Aischines, Euboulos and Kephisophon, against opposition from Aristophon and others.[102] Perhaps what swung the balance in the end was the blunt warning of Euboulos: either Athens must mobilize immediately for war and make the requisite arrangements to pay for it; or she must accept Philokrates' (Philip's) peace. The motion was carried, but not without amendment, for the clause excluding Phokis, Halos and Kersebleptes was struck from the text.[103] Demosthenes, like the others, knew this would be unacceptable to Philip, but decided that it was a fault that could be remedied later.

When the assembly dissolved, the Boulē met and set a date (the 24th) for another special meeting of the people at which a decision was to be made on the question how the Athenians' allies were to give their oaths to Philip. In preparation for this meeting both Demosthenes and Philokrates moved a *probouleuma* that 'the synod-representatives of the allies this day give their oaths to the envoys from Philip';[104] the synod contained no representatives of Phokis, Halos or Kersebleptes. On the appointed day, Demosthenes, who happened to be president of the assembly, put the *probouleuma* to the vote and it was carried. (We must assume that, since the decree in this form vitiated the refusal of the *demos* five days earlier to accept Philokrates' exclusion-clause, much lobbying had been done in the meantime. According to normal procedure, five days' notice of a special assembly had to be given,[105] so that the Boulē at which this assembly was set was probably held on 19 Elaphebolion. That is, the very day on which the Assembly amended Philokrates' motion had also seen the Council planning *in effect* to replace the expunged clause.) A last-ditch attempt by Kritoboulos of Lampsakos, representing Kersebleptes, to include the Thracian in the peace as an ally of Athens failed.[106] The decree of Philokrates, stormy though its passage had been, had come through unscathed. The Macedonian envoys received the oaths of peace and alliance from the Athenians and their allies and set out for home – significantly by way of Thebes,[107] for they doubtless felt the need to reassure their ally (falsely) that the rumours and reports of Philip's intention to favour the Phokians and Athenians at their expense were groundless.

THE SECOND EMBASSY

After a week's delay a bouleutic resolution (moved by Demosthenes) despatched the second Athenian embassy from the city. They might have gone straight to Philip in Thrace, provided they could find him, but that would have been at best pointless and quite possibly (had they attempted to hinder his campaign) destructive of the peace.[108] In any event, knowing that Philip was still in Thrace, the members of the second embassy made no haste on their journey to Pella. On arrival, they were obliged to wait a further three or more weeks for the king's return.[109]

Philip returned around 22 Thargelion (= *c.* 17 June), by Demosthenes' reckoning, to meet the Athenians, as well as envoys from several other Greek states, at least from Thebes, Sparta and Thessaly. These will have been pressing for his attention, but, in keeping with his current general policy towards Thebes, it was to his advantage to keep them guessing a little longer. When he met with the Athenians it must have been with satisfaction that he greeted them, not only for their successful transmission of his terms but for their skilful outmanoeuvring of those elements which had persuaded the *demos* to expunge his exclusion-clause. This, he knew, had not been reinstated, but the passage of Philokrates' motion on 24 Elaphebolion had achieved the same result. (When Demosthenes later charged that these envoys had, contrary to popular will and in collaboration with Philip, restored the clause deleted by the Athenian assembly he was lying. Those Philip wished excluded were neither signatories on his side, nor had been allowed by the Athenians to sign on their side; therefore they were excluded *de facto*.)[110] This had been achieved not by Philip's orders nor by the envoys' dereliction of their duty, but (best of all, from the king's point of view) by the vote of the Athenian assembly. If his hospitality to the embassy surpassed normal expectations, it is hardly surprising.[111]

What Philip now wished was to discuss with them the prospects of bringing the Sacred War to a successful conclusion in the way he had already intimated. But Demosthenes had other ideas. He had come prepared to bargain for the immediate release of the Athenian prisoners.[112] He well understood, of course, the point of Philip's promise to return them without ransom by the Panathenaia. By the time of that festival, just over two months away, Philip's plans for the Phokian settlement would have been realized. But now the king was faced with two unsatisfactory alternatives. Either he would release the prisoners immediately (and Demosthenes, to strengthen his own hand, had brought with him a token amount of money to offer as ransom), which would be to surrender a useful means of persuading the Athenian *demos* to comply with his requests; or, if he were to refuse, he would provide his opponents in Athens with ammunition for a charge of bad faith. In choosing the latter course he took the step that, more than any other, destroyed the peace at which he was aiming. At this point he cannot have fully realized its implications – as Demosthenes certainly did.

Much of what was then discussed by the envoys and Philip is lost to us. But it is likely that, in the speech Aischines later summarized in his report to the Athenian people, we have the main points.[113] In this speech the orator claimed to have urged Philip to give thought to the history of the Amphiktyonic League – or to two aspects of it: that all Amphiktyons were sworn to consider inviolate the cities of their co-members and to punish any who acted in a contrary way; and that they were equally bound to punish any who should violate the shrine of Apollo at Delphoi. In this way Aischines was clearly making the point that the transgressors against sacred law were not only the Phokians; for, while the cities which had suffered violation were indeed Boiotian, the transgressor in at least some of their cases had been Thebes,[114] which had razed their walls in order to enforce their subjection to her in the Boiotian League. Further, as regards the crime of the Phokians, Aischines distinguished very carefully between the individuals responsible for the sacrilege and the blameless inhabitants of their country, who had only to hand over the guilty for punishment to establish their own innocence. The message is unequivocal and is entirely consistent with what we can determine of Philip's own intentions; indeed, it is likely, whether or not Aischines did raise these specific points in Pella, that in his report to the assembly he was carefully aligning himself with the actions he knew Philip planned to take. The settlement of the Sacred War would achieve two ends: to punish both the Phokian military leadership and their mercenary soldiers, and Thebes.

To combine the public maintenance of one policy with the semi-private pursuit of a quite different one was bound to create confusion, especially when the difference between the two so profoundly affected two of Philip's major allies. Thus we are not at all surprised to find Theban and Thessalian embassies (as well, probably, as Phokians)[115] also present in Pella at this time. They wished to know what foundation there was to the intelligence they must have been receiving constantly to the effect that Philip was, at least in the Theban case, about to turn upon them. But these were not the only other embassies in Pella, and the presence of the Spartans – understandably at loggerheads with the Thebans – is very significant. They indeed participated with Philip and the Athenians in some negotiations and even came into open collision with the Theban envoys – to the consternation of the latter, who only too clearly saw what such actions might signify.[116]

So far we have considered the effects of Philip's real plan for the settlement of the Sacred War only in so far as they bear on central Greece. The Spartans were admittedly to play their role in this area.[117] But the ramifications of their participation were much wider, relating to the whole area of Theban influence in the Peloponnesos – and for this reason it is likely that a good many other embassies were present.[118] With the Peloponnesos divided, like central Greece, into two opposing camps, dependent respectively upon Sparta and Thebes,[119] the dilemma for all amounted to this: would Philip – in concert with Thessaly, Thebes and the latter's Peloponnesian dependants, Messenia, Megalopolis and Argos,[120] and now with the agreement of Athens – crush Phokis and, in effect, confirm Theban dominance in central Greece and the Peloponnesos? Or would he abandon his existing commitment and join with Phokis, Athens and Sparta (and, again, the Thessalians) in bringing Theban power to an end? All indications pointed to the latter. The Athenians, although they had excluded Phokis from the alliance with Philip, had not been asked to repudiate their treaty with the Phokians. The secret parleys in Pella between Macedonian, Athenian and Spartan envoys – with the Thebans excluded – and the confident belligerence of the Spartans gave promise of it. And as the envoys, in company with Philip and his army, left Pella and took the road south to Thermopylai, the same confidence and fears were as much in evidence. Phokian envoys were treated as though Philip were already their ally.[121] The Athenians and Spartans were assured by senior *hetairoi* of Philip that the independence of the Boiotian cities was about to be restored. So apprehensive were the Thebans that, at this time, or shortly afterwards, a full levy of their army was ordered out.[122]

THE OCCUPATION OF THERMOPYLAI

At Pherai the cavalcade stopped. The point of no return had been reached. With only two days' march to Thermopylai, it was clear that nothing could prevent Philip's gaining control of the pass. He was now ready to deliver the requisite oaths and signatures to the Athenian delegation.

In most respects this was entirely straightforward. But although we do not know which of his allies did sign, it is clear that not all did; Philip selected from among his total number of allies those who were to participate, and the Athenian envoys administered the oaths only to these.[123] It is likely that the most obvious omission was the Thebans, but there may have been others.[124] Kersebleptes, the Halians and the Phokians did not require mention, for Philip had only to swear his oath in terms reciprocal to those enshrined in the executive decree of Philokrates on 24 Elaphebolion.[125] Probably the main reason for Philip's selectivity among his allies in this matter was that he could not be certain of the results on his existing alignments once his secret plan became public. He did not know, for example, just how the Euboian cities would react.[126] So, with the intention of keeping everything as fluid as possible for a few more days, he sidetracked the Athenian delegates from visiting others of his allies for their oaths by urging them to mediate (as allies of *both* sides now) in the dispute between Halos and Pharsalos with which he was involved.[127] During the delay, Demosthenes made two attempts, one by letter and one in person, to influence Athens against Philip's plan before the arrival of his co-envoys, who would report in strong favour of it. In both attempts he was foiled, the envoys overruling the despatch of his letter and Philip himself preventing his departure by ship.[128] When the delegation left for Athens, Philip led his army to Thermopylai. By the time they arrived in Athens on 13 Skirophorion (= *c.* 7 July) he was in central Greece.[129]

Once through the pass, pitching camp probably at Thermopylai itself, he began to put his plan into effect.[130] The stage was now fully set for the action; all now depended on the presence of the other leading player, Athens. On the 17th or 18th of the month (*c.*11/12 July) he sent a request to Athens for the immediate despatch of hoplites to his base at Thermopylai.[131]

SABOTAGE

But by that time in Athens Philip's enemies were at work. On the return of the embassy things had initially gone relatively smoothly, although Demosthenes had successfully begun his task of discrediting Philip and his fellow-envoys. When the ambassadors reported on their mission to the Boulē shortly after their return, Demosthenes (whose influence on this body was clearly considerable) drew attention to the discrepancies between the instructions the embassy had been given and the way in which they had been carried out. He was evidently able to distract attention from the fact that they had achieved the most important aims of their commission by pointing to their failure to travel first of all to Thrace, to negotiate earnestly for the release of the prisoners, to obtain the oaths of allegiance at Pella, and to obtain, finally, the signatures of 'all the cities'.[132] However, by the time the matter reached the assembly on 16 Skirophorion (= *c.* 10 July), it was known that Philip had passed through Thermopylai and Demosthenes could not prevail against the support enjoyed by Aischines, Philokrates and the other envoys; the *demos* voted – exactly as Philip wished – to ratify the peace and alliance and to extend it in perpetuity to the king's descendants; the motion expressed appreciation of Philip's promise of 'just action' – that is, of his foreshadowed treatment of the Phokians and Thebans – and concluded with a clause providing that 'if the Phokians do not act correctly and surrender the temple to the Amphiktyons, the Athenian *demos* shall send aid to achieve this against *those who prevent it.*'[133]

To judge by the arrangements already foreshadowed at Pella and Pherai, it appears that in this decree the intention was that the decision as to which were the 'true' Amphiktyons should be made by Philip and those of his Amphiktyonic allies who supported the arrangements made between the king and the Athenians. The latter, it proposed, would be present at the time, to provide military backing to the decision; but more important than Athens' military role was the appearance she would give to the proceedings that Philip was merely assisting the right-minded members to separate out and punish their criminous colleagues, the Phokian leadership and the Thebans. The ground was now prepared. The Spartans, following the arrangements made recently in Pella, had already sent a force to the area of Thermopylai and stood ready to assist.[134] Everything now depended on successfully implementing Philokrates' motion; that, in turn, must necessarily follow an official request for aid in accordance with its terms. It is likely that unofficial word of the decree was carried immediately to the king, who should have been informed by late on the following day, 17 Skirophonion (= *c.* 11 July). Accordingly he sent his messenger, who will have left Thermopylai either late on the 17th or early on the 18th, with an official request for hoplites.

In the Athenian assembly on the 16th, following the passage of Philokrates' decree, most members of the first and second embassies were reappointed to a third with orders to convey the decision of the *demos* officially to Philip.[135] Demosthenes, however, refused to accept nomination, declaring that he would not leave the city. When the assembly adjourned, the other envoys met in consternation. It would be dangerous, even disastrous, to leave Demosthenes behind. At Pherai he had shown how much he wished to exert his influence on the Athenian people in the absence of his fellow-envoys. Thwarted at that time, he had worked assiduously in the meantime to discredit them. And now he had manoeuvred himself into a position in which he alone of the envoys would be present when Philip's expected letter arrived. They were justifiably afraid (as Demosthenes later exulted) that he might succeed in convening a special assembly and persuade the *demos* to rescind its decree or, in some other way, reverse its intention. Aischines, it was decided, must remain as watchdog. He arranged for his brother and a physician to declare before the Boulē that he was unfit to serve. The excuse was accepted.[136] Receiving its formal commission, the third embassy departed, probably on the 17th, travelling again by way of Euboia.[137]

But, in fact, their mission was quite unimportant. By the time they had travelled far through Euboia, they knew, Philip would have heard the results of the debate on the 16th. Armed with that intelligence he would then send an official request for aid. It was the response to that call that would govern the settlement, not the news they were carrying. There was indeed more than a little risk in their task, for, by the time they reached Thermopylai, Philip (whose horse-borne messengers would travel by the most direct route through Boiotia) would already know the result of his request; and, if Demosthenes had meanwhile succeeded in turning the *demos* against the plan, then their own position at the pass would be extremely embarrassing, not to say dangerous. So, when they reached Chalkis, they decided to remain there until news should arrive of the outcome.

Philip's request must have reached the city on 18 or 19 Skirophorion and the assembly will have been convened on or about the 20th, three days after the departure of the third embassy. By this time things had gone badly wrong. Already on the 16th, after the assembly-meeting of that day, everything (as Demosthenes was to remark) was unsettled; groups were forming and re-forming in the Agora to discuss the situation.[138] To those citizens who comprehended and accepted Philip's assurance it was clear that, with the best Athenian will in the world, the king had yet to effect an extremely tricky finesse at the expense of a powerful ally. At the same time, the pro-Thebans of the city concentrated their efforts on arousing fear and suspicion of Philip among their fellows. Philip, they pointed out, had forced the Athenian people into peace and alliance on his own terms, but now claimed to be acting in their interests. But was not the true indication of his trustworthiness to be seen in his failure to release those citizens of his new ally interned in Macedonia now for more than eighteen months? If the Athenians were to send out their hoplite force, was it not likely that, rather than using them as he was alleged to have promised (and that never in writing), he would use his Amphiktyonic allies to capture them and hold them too as hostages?[139] The lobbying was successful. When the assembly met to consider the summons to action, it was persuaded to reject it.

THE ALTERNATIVE SETTLEMENT

At Thermopylai, as his herald sped back from Athens with the answer, Philip found himself in an increasingly difficult position. As we have seen, he had – up to this point – the support of at least the Spartans; probably the Thessalian League too, well aware of the increased role it could play in Amphiktyony with Theban power diminished, and certainly some among the smaller states of the league were behind him.[140] His own troops were perhaps stationed in the pass itself, probably deliberately so, since he wished to enter central Greece not as an intruder but as the agent of a willing Amphiktyonic League reconstituted so as to restrict Theban influence and to restore the Phokian people to their proper position in it. Behind him the Thessalian cavalry was camped and ahead of him were the Theban hoplites. By 22 Skirophorion (= *c.* 16 July) they had been in this position for more than a week – while only a few kilometres distant were Phalaikos and his forces at Nikaia. During this time embassies had been passing between the tyrant and the Macedonian king.[141] Such a situation was bound to arouse the suspicions of his allies and Philip found that the Thessalians, who stood to gain by the Macedonian settlement of the war in whichever way it was achieved, were pressing him to take action without waiting on the Athenians and without risking, at the same time, a major battle with the Thebans.[142] In the absence of the Athenian hoplites, Philip found himself without support for his plan, except from the Boiotian cities that had been under Phokian control and now feared heavy Theban retribution.[143] But their help counted for nothing against the odds lining up in favour of immediate resolution.[144]

In a situation rapidly becoming impossible, a constant factor in Philip's thinking appears to have been his concern for the ordinary Phokians – his unwillingness to be associated with the mass slaughter and looting that would inevitably accompany and follow a battle in which the major Amphiktyons overran the forces of Phalaikos. If it came to armed struggle there was no way of controlling such injustice and excess. More pragmatically, the king had no wish to see the obliteration of so useful an anti-Theban force as the Phokians represented. His plan provided the opportunity for the people to dissociate themselves from the actions of Phalaikos and his mercenaries; the battle (if battle were necessary) would be only against them and possibly the Thebans. But as the king became more strongly aware of the possibility that his plan had failed, he was obliged to salvage what he could of his hopes. By honouring his agreement with Phalaikos, he could prevent the indiscriminate slaughter of the Phokians,[145] even though it meant their leadership would go unpunished.

Thus it happened when his messenger returned (on the 22nd or 23rd) from Athens with the news of his ally's delinquency. First he proclaimed the 'Convention between Philip and the Phokians', by which he allowed Phalaikos and his mercenaries to surrender their fortresses in Phokis and Boiotia and to depart immediately; and he accepted the surrender of the Phokian people. Then, assuring the latter that he would use his influence to moderate the vengeance of Thebes, he asked for the convention of the Amphiktyonic Council.[146]

AMPHIKTYONIC DECISIONS

Since it would not have been clear what delegates would be admitted to this meeting, which must have fallen early in Hekatombaion (= late July/early August), no doubt all regular Amphiktyons, with the exception of the Phokians, sent embassies seeking authority to seat their representatives (*hieromnemones*). The meeting was probably held at Thermopylai.[147] We cannot be certain which were accorded membership (although we are better informed when it comes to the next regular meeting of the Council). When Demosthenes speaks as though only Thebans and Thessalians were present, he is at best indicating where the strength lay,[148] and we should expect that Philip (at least) wished the roll of *hieromnemones* to be complete, so as to continue to avoid the impression of irregularity. Apart from the Boiotians (meaning at least one Theban delegate but possibly one from a safely subservient town)[149] and Thessalians, there were delegates from Lokris, Oitaia, the latter participating in the Ainianian vote, and Dolopia,[150] and certainly from such other areas under Macedonian influence as Perrhaibia, Magnesia, Phthiotis and Malis. The Dorian votes were probably controlled by Metropolis (in Doris) and Argos, and the Ionian by representatives of Euboian cities.[151]

The first item of business will have been the reorganization of membership consequent upon the outcome of the war and the division of loyalties during its course. The Phokians were debarred from the shrine of Apollo and deprived of their place in the Council, their votes conferred upon Philip – appropriately, since technically Phokis was his by surrender, and he will now have officially handed it over to the Amphiktyons.[152] With the freedom of Delphoi now restored, attention was given to its status within the Council; for the first time the Delphians were given full voting status, receiving two votes removed, one each, from the Perrhaibians and Dolopians. And, since these were both areas either directly or indirectly accessible to Philip's influence, it is clear that the action was taken with his support and most likely on his motion. One may only speculate over his intentions, but the existence of an extremely laudatory decree passed in his favour by the Delphians[153] suggests that the king stood very high in their favour and so could feel that at least he would lose no influence on the Council in this way. More positively, although this may not have been apparent at the time, a likely result (and therefore a *possible* aim) was that Delphoi would become legally subject as never before to an Amphiktyonic majority. In other areas of action at this time, Philip showed himself to be seriously concerned with observing the traditional proprieties, especially those concerning the Amphiktyony and the Delphic sanctuary.[154]

But, while he was eager thus to enlist the support of Apollo for himself and to avail himself of the consequent opportunities for panhellenic propaganda, this was a matter he would not leave in the hands of fortune. Through his own votes and those of the Thessalians and their periœci (not to mention those of other members currently well disposed towards him), he could reasonably expect for the foreseeable future to carry what decisions he wished in the Council; if Delphoi should turn against him, it would simply be outvoted and, if it continued to resist, it would be in violation of the Amphiktyonic law to which – through its membership – it subscribed. The effect, we may speculate, is that matters previously decided by Delphoi alone tended henceforward to move into the wider province of the Council as a whole, with a consequent gain in influence of him who could dominate the Amphiktyony.

The main item of business before the Amphiktyons concerned the punishment to be imposed on the Phokians and it was here that the moderating influence not only of Philip but also, perhaps, of Aischines had its effect. For when news of the capitulation had reached Athens, after taking certain defensive measures dictated by panic at the thought that Philip might treat the alliance with the Athenians as casually as he appeared to have treated his earlier professions of goodwill, the Assembly elected a fourth embassy. This was commissioned to represent Athenian interests at Delphoi and, in particular, to urge moderation and humanity upon the allies over the punishment of the vanquished and over the treatment of the Boiotian towns, which, it appears, had preferred Phokian occupation to subjection by Thebes. The role of Aischines on this embassy was a noble one. His efforts to effect a settlement favourable to the Phokians had, as we have seen, crashed in ruins, but his subsequent devotion to their preservation continued. Demosthenes, on the other hand, stands indicted in perpetuity for his actions. His role in preventing the despatch of the hoplites had firstly condemned the Phokian people to the judgement of their enemies. That, of course, was the unavoidable consequence of his desire to save Thebes. But in refusing nomination to this embassy too, he declined to add his voice to the moral pressure on which Philip must rely if he were to withstand on the Phokian behalf the pressure of a hung jury at Thermopylai.[155]

How dire a fate the Phokians and their allies might have suffered had it not been for Philip's influence is a matter for conjecture. The Oitaians, we are told, demanded that all adult Phokian males be thrown from the cliffs (probably the Phaidriades rising sheer above Delphoi), the standard penalty for despoliation of the temple.[156] It is also very likely that Thebes wished to acquire Phokian territory in compensation for the costs and losses of the past decade. The Lokrians, for the same reason, will hardly have been surpassed in their vindictiveness. Evidently, too, there were appeals for the expulsion of Sparta, Korinth and Athens.[157] But the terms that emerged were remarkably moderate.[158]

Phokian territory was neither confiscated nor ravaged; its population was neither enslaved nor slaughtered. Those among the Phokians themselves who fled the country and those suspected of complicity in

YEAR	ARCHON	NUMBER AND AMOUNT OF PAYMENT		DOCUMENTS
		autumn	*spring*	
343/2	Kleon	(1)–(30)	2 – 30	*FD* 14 I.12ff.
342/1	Chairolas	(3)–(30)	4 – 30	*FD* 14 II.1ff. (= Tod ii 172B)
341/0	Peithagoras		5 – 30	*FD* 14 II.20ff.
340/39	Aristonymos		(6)–(30)	
339/8	?		(7)–(30)	
338/7	no meeting held			
337/6	Palaios		(8)–30	*SIG* 232
336/5	Dion		(9)–(10/30?)	
335/4	?		(10)–(10/30?)	
334/3	Damochares		11 – 10	*FD* 48 II.37ff.
333/2	Damokrates		(12)–(10)	
332/1	?		(13)–(10)	
331/0	[Thy]meas		(14)–(10)	
330/29	Lykinos		(15)–(10)	
329/8	Bathyllos		(16)–(10)	
328/7	Theolytos		(17)–(10)	
327/6	Kaphis		18 – 10	*FD* 58.69ff.
Between 323/2 & 316/5				
	Eribas		(?)–(10?)	*SIG* 235A

Table 2: Phokian Reparations

the pillaging of the shrine were anathematized and rendered liable to arrest – but not summary execution – wherever they might be found. But such seizure, since it naturally depended on the sympathies of the state in which they sought sanctuary, was in the nature more of fulmination than of warranty; thus those who reached Athens were harboured in spite of the demands of other Amphiktyons.[159] A value was put on the treasures taken by successive commanders (perhaps the 10,000 talents mentioned by Diodoros)[160] and large reparations of 60 talents per annum were imposed on the whole state. (However, a moratorium was allowed and the payments did not begin until 343; two years later they were halved, and, several years after that – between autumn 337 and autumn 334 – were further reduced to 10 talents annually).[161] Until the designated amount was repaid (and it is noteworthy that the compensation was due only to Apollo's sanctuary; there was none required for the combatant states of the opposing side in the war) the Phokians, it was decreed, were to own neither horses nor weapons, those found there in 346 being respectively sold or destroyed. All Phokian towns except for Abai – over 20 of them – were to be razed and the population resettled in small villages each no closer than a furlong from its neighbours and containing no more than 50 dwellings. This was the aspect of the punishment most dangerous to the welfare of the Phokian people, because it was the most open to abuse by the soldiers charged with the task, and it is thus interesting to note that, although Thebans participated in it, this was only in the company of Macedonian troops.

Philip may not have wished and perhaps could not afford to be associated with mass atrocities enacted by vindictive victors; and, in any case, although his plans for limiting Theban power had had, for the time, to be abandoned, he had no desire to benefit the Thebans more than was unavoidable nor to weaken the vanquished more than was inevitable. So that we may assume that the Macedonian soldiers, to whom Phokis had been surrendered in the first instance, remained there in order to limit the excesses of the Amphiktyons.[162]

The Council meeting closed[163] on a note of celebration, with the Amphiktyons appointing Philip president of the coming Pythia, due to be held in the autumn – the first festival of Apollo at Delphoi for twelve years There were inevitably undercurrents of resentment among the successful allies; the tensions created over the past few weeks must have left their mark. (Thus Demosthenes very soon afterwards is able to imply that the Thessalians and especially the Thebans are less than fully satisfied with the resolution of the troubles in central Greece.)[164] Such were inevitable. But it is also clear that in general, and certainly so far as appearances were concerned, Philip's success and his moderation in victory were widely acclaimed; his presidency of the Pythia, a singular honour normally reserved for the Dorian tribe,[165] is a measure of this approbation, and was only one of the honours conferred upon him by the Amphiktyons and by a grateful Delphoi.[166]

CHAPTER V

346–342
THE UNEASY PEACE

'THE PEACE OF DEMOSTHENES'

IT HAS BEEN OBSERVED in a recent discussion of the Peace of Philokrates[1] that the role of Demosthenes as 'the real patron of the peace' would justify our regarding it more properly as 'The Peace of Demosthenes'; his procedural motions of early Elaphebolion, his solicitous treatment of the visiting Macedonian ambassadors and his successful piloting of Philokrates' motion through the assembly on the 18th and 19th of the same month were vital to the architecture of the peace. But, as we have seen, the terms approved during Elaphebolion – and, we may include, the *de facto* reinstatement of the exclusion clause, again, significantly, the work of Demosthenes[2] – did not by themselves represent the whole of the settlement Philip had envisaged or intended; the Athenian envoys knew his plans went further and the Athenian *demos* had been promised more. Philokrates' motion of 16 Skirophorion, carefully designed to allow Philip the use of the Athenian hoplites, was the keystone in the construction that Philip set out in his discussions with the Athenian ambassadors. What is common to each and every stage of the negotiations is, first, that the terms were Philip's own and, second, that although it was Philokrates who translated them into the form of decrees it was Demosthenes who made himself instrumental in their acceptance by the Athenian people. But although the latter's role was important he made it so only because he realized – as did most of his fellows – that peace was expedient for Athens and that only a peace on Philip's terms was possible. The peace-that-might-have-been, that is to say, would properly have been known either as the Peace of Philip, its architect, or (from the Athenian viewpoint) the Peace of Philokrates, its engineer, the man whose decrees shaped it into the form intended by the designer. But that peace was not to be – and the man most responsible for its failure, through his campaign of sabotage between 17 and 20 Skirophorion, was Demosthenes. It was his success in so terrifying his fellow Athenians as to Philip's alleged intention to kidnap the hoplite force that when it came to the point they refused to give the order to march, that destroyed the treaty Philip and Philokrates intended.[3] The peace that did come about was indeed the Peace of Demosthenes but it became so only on or about 20 Skirophorion.

Once the peace was in force Demosthenes was freed of most restraints upon his real intentions. His final double-cross had achieved for him two outstanding advantages. In the first place, at the cost of the benefits Philip had promised to Athens at Theban expense, he had preserved the Thebans against the attenuation of their power intended by the king and left them a strong potential ally of the Athenians. As soon as Philip should move to achieve his original end at a later point, Thebes must almost automatically turn for alliance with Athens against the Macedonians. In the second place, Demosthenes had successfully captured for himself the initiative in Athenian foreign policy. Had the intended peace come about, Philokrates, Aischines and others would have shared the credit and their standing in Athens would increase with every bounty procured for their city by a generous Macedonian king who had no wish for naval empire but whose interests would be well served by a co-operative Athenian fleet in the Aegean and perhaps beyond. The peace of Demosthenes, on the other hand, prevented Philip from realizing his promises (with which the reduction of Theban power was co-requisite), a failure which, while the treaty represented a shield behind which efforts to overthrow the king might be renewed, rendered the Macedonian's goodwill suspect from the very beginning and provided a fertile soil in which Demosthenes could take the initiative in sowing further seeds of suspicion and distrust.

However, Philip quickly recognized that the advantages he had gained were very tangible; indeed since he had begun to prepare his attempted finesse he must have known that it might fail and that, even so, the security of his kingdom would be greatly enhanced by his reception into the old and respected Council of the Amphiktyons. His bloodless success, while it failed to remove the most serious Greek threat – that of a combined Athenian/Theban assault on Macedonia, had heaped upon him unprecedented honours as the saviour of Apollo and gave him an influential voice in an ancient Hellenic institution. The frustration of Athenian and especially Spartan hopes, combined with his success at least in preventing Theban aggrandizement at Phokian expense, gave promise to the smaller states of the Peloponnesos and central Greece that they had found a champion able to give them support against the rapacity of their imperialistic neighbours. At the very least, that is, he had achieved a panhellenic settlement in embryo, one which might be expanded by skilful diplomacy to the point where the power re-alignments he had hoped for in 346 might be attainable by other means. Meanwhile, so far as the bulk of the Greek peninsula was concerned, he had no immediate demands for military engagement and could return to his kingdom to prepare it for the longer-term Asian plans. He accordingly let it be known that these were indeed his aims[4] – not, perhaps, because such an object was practical in the short term, for it could not be ventured until Athenian co-operation was assured, but rather because the very knowledge of his objectives might serve to assuage the doubts of those who feared that he had imperial ambitions on the mainland. It was in accordance with such hopes that he did not himself so much as set foot south of Thermopylai during the next seven years, that, until it had become obvious that the Peace of Philokrates had irreparably broken down, he committed no troops for any reason to central Greece or the Peloponnesos, and that in his dealings especially with Athens he demonstrated a generosity and a readiness to compromise that took all the rhetoric of Demosthenes and his colleagues to disparage and distort.

ATHENIAN RESENTMENTS

In time for the Panathenia in late Hekatombaion (*c.* mid-August) the Athenian prisoners were released.[5] At about the same time Philip sent a letter aimed at reassuring his ally that her fears were unjustified.[6] But the majority of the Athenians were as yet in no mood for soft talk, and, at the time of the Pythian festival at Delphoi in early autumn, the Assembly refused to make the normal arrangements for the city's participation, and gave promise of withdrawing altogether from the Amphiktyony in repudiation of its Phokian settlement.[7] This in fact turned out to be no more than a gesture, for not only was opinion more bitterly divided than the decision would imply, but enough leaders among the Athenians realized that to act in this way was extremely dangerous. Aischines and others continued to urge their fellows to acknowledge the peace as the vehicle of Philip's potential benefactions to their *polis*,[8] while the colleagues of Demosthenes, carrying the majority with them, pointed to Philip's failed promises, to the Delphic *promanteia* he now enjoyed in their place, to the reconstructed Amphiktyony and his role in it as the signs of his duplicity.[9] However, for all his different motives, Demosthenes too wished to see the peace of Philokrates remain in force; so, when an Amphiktyonic embassy arrived in Athens asking the people to reverse its decision, he gave guarded support.[10] His line – probably the view most acceptable to and finally adopted by the Assembly – was that the peace was a bad one but it gave protection to the city against the Amphiktyons, who needed little excuse to declare sacred war against it. The peace – and therefore the settlement – must not be rejected; rather, under its protection the Athenians might prepare themselves and their allies, existing and potential, for war against Philip – but a war that would be fought over some issue that did not – like the present one – align all the Amphiktyons on the Macedonian side.[11] The Assembly agreed and the embassy withdrew to Delphoi.[12]

To recognize the Athenian disgruntlement over recent events is not, however, to imply that they fastened the blame for their humiliation on Aischines, or even (yet) on Philokrates. Although, according to Demosthenes, the former had been shouted down when he rose to support the Amphiktyonic request,[13] and although the city continued to harbour Phokian refugees in contravention of the new regulation,[14] Aischines was successful during the winter of 346/5 in his prosecution of Timarchos, a trial which, although ostensibly directed against the latter's morals, was anchored firmly in the current political situation.[15] Demosthenes, who had organized Timarchos' defence, may have written a speech for him but did not appear on his behalf.[16] The original charge against Aischines was not to be pressed until three years later.

On the other hand, suspicion and fear of Philip remained. At the beginning of the Attic year, that is, in Hekatombaion (late July or August), a revision of the citizen register had taken place, resulting in the removal of, among others, one Antiphon, who left Athens. Not long afterwards, probably in autumn or early winter 346, he returned after promising Philip – so says Demosthenes – to burn the Athenian dockyards. According to the orator, he was found in Peiraieus and brought to trial but acquitted. However, on Demosthenes' instigation, the Council of the Areiopagos re-arrested him and had him re-tried and condemned. After torture he was executed.[17]

ISOKRATES AND THE ASIAN PLANS

A third viewpoint – represented by Isokrates – emerged at this time, and now needs to be taken into account. We shall have further occasion to examine his proposals insofar as they are concerned with Philip's Asian plans, but at this point two aspects of the argument he addressed to Philip in summer 346[18] are of particular importance. Firstly, whatever criticisms may be levelled against his patriotism or his pragmatism,[19] his attitude to Philip coincides neither with that of Aischines and others, who urged that the Peace of Philokrates be observed in letter and spirit with a view to extracting from it the benefits it was originally intended to confer on Athens, nor with that of Demosthenes and his associates, whose distrust of Philip allowed them no confidence in the peace except as a licence for their own attempts to overthrow the king. Secondly, it contains important contemporary comment on the interests of the Greek states in mid-346 which may enable us the better to comprehend both the events of the following six years and the hopes of Philip that the general intention of the peace might yet be realized by other means.

In one sense at least, Isokrates was more of a hard-headed realist than either Demosthenes or Aischines. Much as one might approve in theoretical terms of the stand taken by the anti-Macedonians,[20] one cannot deny that in the event they were wrong – at least to the extent that the panhellenic alliance they sought so assiduously between 346 and 338 (and even earlier) was not attained (and was perhaps unattainable); in the end, insufficient allies stood together to confront the giant they had provoked into action. On the other hand, although one might incline to the view that Philip in fact wanted not a Hellenic empire, but merely Hellenic co-operation in an Asian empire, such an interpretation cannot be said to have been clear beyond reasonable doubt by this time. Indeed there had not yet been much opportunity for Philip to make this clear and it was one of his major preoccupations over the succeeding three years or so. This being the case, Aischines, in his belief in the genuiness of Philip's stated aims, was arguably prepared to run too great a risk; lest Philip spoke with a forked tongue Aischines ought to have adopted at least a more wary stance. On the one hand, there was an unrealistic and dangerous policy of provocation; on the other, a hazardous acceptance of Philip's good intentions at face value.

Isokrates, so he said, was strongly in favour of the Peace of Philokrates, but even before it was finally ratified and before the decision of late Skirophorion reversed its intended effects, he was already deeply concerned that influential elements among his fellow-Athenians would agree to adhere to it for only so long as they found it immediately expedient. This was the first threat to lasting peace. But he was equally concerned that Philip himself was not entirely a free agent. It was not only that there were those about the king advising him to press onwards towards domination of the Hellenic peninsula. In Greece itself, existing social and political conflicts were rife and made the possibility and the opportunity for intervention very much more attractive. Large numbers of impoverished and unsettled men were a threat to social and economic stability. Their availability for mercenary service had not only inspired petty tyrants, as in Pherai and Phokis, to pursue their inflated ambitions, but had ensured that, granted only a ready supply of funds, they were assured of a considerable degree of success.[21] In the Peloponnesos, hatred and fear of Sparta stood at so high a level that large numbers of Peloponnesians would be willing to press for the entry of the king. The Thebans had incurred the hatred of most of Hellas during their military hegemony in the 370s and 360s.[22] Under such conditions the pressures upon Philip would inevitably be strong. It was therefore essential, since Macedonian military imperialism seemed inevitable, to channel it away from the Greek mainland.[23]

Isokrates doubtless knew of the Persian refugees harboured in Pella now for several years – just as he knew something of the activities of Aristotle, who, on leaving Athens two years before, had, after briefly serving his Macedonian patron, made his way to the court of Hermias in northwestern Asia Minor.[24] The king must, he realized, have considered the possibility of extending his interests to Asia Minor; and the activities of Aristotle gave promise that Macedonian military energies might soon be directed thither. When Isokrates urged Philip, therefore, to organize and lead a panhellenic crusade against the Persian King, he had in mind not only the welfare of the Greek states, who might find a new unity in the venture. It seems likely that he chose this king as the recipient of his plea not only because Macedonian resources were adequate to the task or because these resources posed a serious threat to Greece if they were not directed elsewhere, but also because, perceiving that the military society Philip had created needed objects on which to expend its energies, and believing that Philip already gave promise of interest in eastern campaigns, he decided to sow the seeds of his encouragement on what *already* appeared to be fertile ground.

THE COURTING OF ATHENS

However, the Peace of Philokrates had not fulfilled the purpose intended for it. In particular, with Theban power undiminished and Athens suspicious and mistrustful, some of the most fundamental tensions existing in the mainland remained. As Philip repaired to Pella after the autumn Pylaia of 346 he well knew that, although he might continue long-term preparations for an Asian campaign, he was not yet within distance of turning his back on a Hellas that promised so much dissension to come.

For the peace to survive at all, he knew that it would be necessary ultimately to reverse the effects of the Phokian settlement. In the meantime he would need to work on Athenian public opinion to counteract the effects of her disappointment and humiliation. In early 345 the Delians took the opportunity now offered by the restoration of

Amphiktyonic control over Delphoi to lodge an appeal before the Council, though not a member, against Athenian control of the Temple of Apollo on the island. Their reasoning is obvious. There was no love among the Amphiktyonic majority for the defendants, and at least the moral backing of the Council could be expected for the Delian cause. The issue – though this has often been overlooked – was crucial to the relationship for the future between Athens and the Amphiktyony. To have a new injury added to the humiliation of the previous summer would possibly detach Athens from the Council altogether and at least produce such disillusionment with this body among the *demos* that it could no longer conceivably be hoped to serve as an instrument of reconciliation. Determined to oppose the claim, the Assembly elected Aischines to present the Athenian case at Delphoi; the Areiopagos, authorized to vet the appointment, promptly replaced him with Hypereides.[25] At the spring Pylaia, 345, Hypereides' arguments were accepted, for control of the temple continued in Athenian hands. The Amphiktyons' decision is of course most revealing: the vote must more naturally have gone in the opposite direction and it is clearly the recommendation of Philip's representatives that carried the day for Athens. Equally interesting is the question of the termination of Aischines' appointment. He had presumably been selected in the belief that he was more likely than most Athenians to receive a sympathetic hearing from the influential Macedonian representatives; it shows that he was both relatively unscathed by his role in the peace-negotiations and yet more closely associated with Philip in the public mind than were Demosthenes and his partisans, who had much earlier than Aischines supported the movement towards peace. The action of the Areiopagos Council in overriding his appointment, however, needs closer examination than it has usually been given. It *may* be interpreted as stemming from the sort of extremely conservative anti-Macedonianism implied by its prosecution of Antiphon, as many scholars have thought; but such a view depends rather too heavily on the assumption that this Council would allow important international issues to be determined by childish petulance. It is probable that its reasoning was far more pragmatic. Tactically, the Assembly's choice had been a poor one for an obvious reason. The outstanding feature of the reconstructed Amphiktyony was the triumph of the anti-Phokian elements. To send as emissary the man who more than any other Athenian had associated himself with the attempts to confine the Phokians' punishment to their leaders alone was not the way to obtain a favourable judgement. It was this error that the Areiopagos corrected by cancelling Aischines' appointment. Philip himself would not alter

	KLEON (archon) *autumn 343*	*spring 342*	CHAIROLAS (archon) *spring 341*	PEITHAGORAS (archon) *autumn 340*	ARISTONYMOS (archon) *autumn 339*
THESSALIANS	[Kottyphos]	id.	[id.]	id.	id.
	[Kolosimmos]	id.	id.	id.	id.
Those from PHILIP (or ALEXANDER)	——	Eurylochos	[Euryloch]os or [Kleandr]os	Theodoros	Kallikles
	——	Kleandros	Akron	id.	Eperatos
DELPHIANS	[Damon]	id.	id.	Alkimachos	Phil——
	[Mnasidamos]	id.	——	Theolytos	Akanthios
DORIANS	Nikon	id. Metropolis	——	——	Eukleidas Erineos
		Deinomenes Argos	——	—— *spring 340*	Lysias Megara
IONIANS	—— Histiaia	Timondas	——	——	Diognetos Athens
	Mnesilochos Athens	id. Athens	Polykritos	——	Agorakritos Chalkis
PERRHAIBIANS & DOLOPIANS	Asandros	id.	[id.]	[id.]	id.
	Phaikos	id.	[id.]	[id.]	id.
BOIOTIANS	Dionysos	Datadas	Damoxenes	[Ismenias]	id.
	——	Olympion	[Olympi]on?	[Stilbond]as	id.
LOKRIANS	Charinos	Pleistea(s?)	——	Smenos	id. Opountis
	——	Theomnastos	Echesthenes	Kallikron	id. Amphissa
ACHAIANS	Pythodoros	id.	Onomastos	id.	id.
	Agasikrates	id.	id.	Eunomos	Kertomos
MAGNETES	Hagesipolis	Epikratidas	id.	id.	id.
	Philonautas	id.	id.	id.	id.
AINIANES	Agelaos	id.	[id.]	id.	id.
	Kleomenes	id.	Eubios?	Echekrates	Agasikles
MALIANS	Psaidaros Herakleia	Antimachos Herakleia	—— Herakleia	—— [Herakleia]	Phyros Herakleia
	Sthenedamos Lamia	Demokrates Lamia	Theomnastos [Lamia]	Kottyphos Lamia	Phe—— Lamia

Table 3: Members of Amphiktyoic Council 343–336, 335 and 326

spring 339	? *spring 338*	PALAIOS (archon) *autumn 337*	*spring 336*	DION (archon) *spring 335*	KAPHIS (archon) *spring 326*
id.	[id.]	id.	Daochos	id.	Politas Pharsalos
id.	[id.]	id.	Thrasydaios	id.	[Nikasipos] Pelinna
Theodoros	[id?]	[The]o[doros]?	Euthykrates?	id.	——
Nikanor	[id.]	id.	id.	Philoxenos	Archepolis
id.	Philistion? (Melission?)	——	——	Chairolas	Deinomachos
id.	——	——	——	Philoxenos	Pleiston
id. Metropolis	——	—— Metropolis	—— Metropolis	Nikaios Metropolis	Kleonymos Metropolis
Polyainos Peloponnesos	——	——	——	Phantos Peloponnesos	—— Peloponnesos
[id.]	——	—— Athens	—— Athens	Archidemos? Athens	Apemantos Athens
Dorixenos Euboia	Protarchos	—— Chalkis	—— Euboia	Philistides Euboia	Timokrates [Eretria?]
Megakles Perrhaibia	[Asandros?	[id.?]	——	——	Aristolaos Phalanna
[id.] Dolopia	id.	[id.]	id.	id.	Hellanokrates Dolopia
Eunostos	——	——	—— Tanagra	Opheliades	Pheres Tanagra
Asopodoros	——	—— Orchomenos	—— Orchomenos	Kallion	Phillis Orchomenos
Kleomachos	——	Agathon?	[id.?] Opountis	Nikasidamos Opountis	Polykles Opountis
[id.?]	——	—— Amphissa	—— Amphissa	—— West. Lokris	Eudikos Amphissa
id.	id.	[id.] Larisa	[id.?] Larisa	id.? Larisa	Euxenes Larisa
id.	[id.?]	[id.] Melitaia	[id.?] Melitaia	id. Melitaia	Episthenes Melitaia
Menoitas	——	Philonautas Methone	id. Methone	——	Pausanias Methone
Hagesipolis	——	[Ainesida]mos Homolion	[id.?] Homolion	——	Simias Homolion
id.	——	Aristeas?	——	Aristeas	Kelon Korope
id.	——	——	——	——	Nikanor Phyragos
Bathias Herakleia	——	——	——	——	Lykophron Herakleia
Philippos Lamia	——	Mikon Lamia	——	——	Archippos Lamia

his judgement because Aischines, rather than someone else, pleaded the Athenian case; the new appointment was therefore irrelevant to the whole question of relations with Macedonia, but was directed at the feelings of the other Amphiktyons.[26]

Perhaps at the autumn Pylaia of the same year, another significant request was received by the Amphiktyons. In the College of Naopoioi in autumn 346, the Spartan membership of three had been well counterbalanced by the seats granted to her Peloponnesian allies: Argives four; Megara, Epidauros, Troizen and Phleios one each; two for Korinth, and one each for Sikyon and Aigina.[27] What precisely was the political significance of the *naopoioi* is uncertain – technically they were merely financial officials concerned largely with the rebuilding of the temple of Apollo – but the varying representation, which bears no relation to the two votes accorded each member-tribe in the Council proper, evidently reflects political strengths and expediencies within the Amphiktyony. In late 346, it was a college stacked against (among others) the Spartans – and it was no doubt this that led the Megalopolitans and the Messenians to request their own enrolment as Amphiktyons. Their plea was granted – as also, perhaps, was that of others.[28] The request and its approval belong in the general context not only of the Amphiktyonic reconstruction of 346 but also of the modifications made to its membership and to the relative strength of the member-tribes in the following years. For example, although the Spartans continued to occupy seats among the *naopoioi*, their role among the *hieromnemones*, those who comprised the Council itself, declined; for the Dorians one vote had traditionally been reserved for Metropolis and the other had since the fifth century been exercised on behalf of all Peloponnesians by the Spartans alone; but from 346 or shortly after we find Epidauros, Argos, Aigina, Megara and others in turn exercising the second Dorian voice on this body.[29] The admission of the Messenians and Megalopolitans may thus be seen as part of a policy by Philip, with the support at least (presumably) of the Thebans, to weaken the Spartan role, thus exhibiting a sympathy towards the anti-Spartan elements of the Peloponnesos that would encourage their growing tendency to look to him as the guarantor of their independence. Here, as in the matter of the Delian Apollo, we see Philip using the Amphiktyony as the benign instrument of his policy towards the Greeks.

THE ILLYRIAN CAMPAIGN OF 345

Between a garbled account of the end of the Sacred War and a brief reference to an Illyrian campaign (which has normally been dated to

		a. 346	s. 345	s. 344	a. 343	a. 341	a. 340	a. 337	s. 335	s. 334
			(no naopoioi-lists extant) prostatai and epimenioi							
Delphians		1	★	★	★	★	★	0	1	1
Thessalians	Gyrton	1		★				1	1	1
	Pharsalos	2	★					2	0	1
	Larisa	2			★	★		2	1	2
	Pherai	1		★				1	1	1
	Pelinna	1					★	0	1	0
	Krannon	1						1	1	1
Macedonians		2						0		1
Ionians	Athens	2			★	★		0		3
	Chalkis	1						0		0
	Histiaia	0						0		1
	Karystos	0						0		1
Boiotians	Thebes	3			★	★	★	1		0
	Tanagra	0						0	1	2
	Thespiai	0						0	1	1
	Plataia	0						0	1	0
Perraibians		1						1	1	1
Dorians	Lakedaimon	3					★	0	[1]	4
	Korinth	2		★	★			2	1	2
	Sikyon	1	★					1	3	1
	Argos	4						3	4	4
	Megara	1						0	1	1
	Epidauros	1						0		0
	Troizen	1						1	1	0
	Aigina	1			★			1		1
	Phleios	1	★					1		0
Lokrians	Amphissa	1						0		0
	West Lokris	0						1	1	0
	Opountis	1						0	1	1
	Thronion	1						0	1	0
	TOTAL	36						19	24 in-complete	31

Table 4: The Naopoioi at Delphoi (States known to be represented 346–336 and in 335 and 334.)

344), Justin describes in highly rhetorical terms the wholesale transfer of population-groups from one part of the Macedonian kingdom to another.[30] Although it is clear that Philip for social and strategic reasons took such action at several points in his reign, this placement of the passage implies that in 346/5 some particularly notable instances took place. Since we know, for example, that after the capture of the Chalkidian peninsula the land was annexed to the kingdom and at least some of it distributed among Macedonians, we may infer that this territory and some of its inhabitants – those not retained in their own area to work the land for their new masters – were among those dealt with at that time. Further activities of a similar nature may have taken place also on the Illyrian borders, for it was shortly afterwards, in 345, that Philip launched his campaign against the distant Ardiaioi; and the passes through Lynkos, through which he must have travelled, were appropriate for the establishment of military outposts. In explaining the sort of activity described by Justin we are reduced largely to guesswork, but it seems likely that Philip was aware of the benefits to be gained by manipulating his own population, especially in order to stiffen the frontiers, to guard communication-lines and simply to divide concentrations of subjects, especially in Upper Macedonia and in the annexed areas of western Thrace and the Chalkidike, where disaffection was possible or likely.[31]

In 345 Philip again turned his attention towards the northwest. The Ardiaioi, one of the three greatest of the Illyrian tribes, dominated the territory by the Rhizon Gulf on the Dalmatian coast, and it was probably against these and their chieftain, Pleuratos, that he now moved.[32] According to Diodoros, this war arose out of the irreconcilable enmity of Amyntas, the father of Philip, towards the Illyrians;[33] but such a reason is hardly convincing. Isokrates, who wrote to Philip during the war, was aware of no particular motive behind it.[34] But it was evidently a fiercely fought campaign, in the course of which Philip sustained his second serious battle-injury, a wound to the lower right leg.[35] The most likely explanation appears to be that Ardiaian influence had spread southwards into the vacuum left by the defeat of their southern neighbours in 358, 356 and 351/0, leaving Philip with the alternatives either of striking before their growing power could be consolidated or of delaying until it impinged more directly on the Macedonian sphere of interest – the decisive difficulty with the latter being that the matter might become pressing at a difficult time for Philip's Greek or Asian plans. It is quite likely that information on distant tribal movements was unknown to Isokrates. The campaign proved profitable and the Macedonians returned home victorious.

THE REORGANIZATION OF THESSALY

However, there was little time to waste, for there were serious indications of disruption in Thessaly. As we have seen, when Philip – already archon – had last been obliged to interfere there in the autumn of 349, his intervention had been provoked by rising dissatisfaction over several internal matters as well as by the return to Pherai of the expelled Peitholaos.[36] When re-expelling the tyrant he had evidently settled the other difficulties by reiterating his promise to settle the third Sacred War in the Thessalian interest. There being discontent over the status of Magnesia, parts of which he evidently planned or had begun to fortify, he promised to restore this area to its periœcic dependence on the *koinon*.[37] Since that time his successful resolution of the Phokian War had enabled him to realize these undertakings. He had handed over Magnesia and, by way of bonus, also the fortress Nikaia, just beyond the Pass of Thermopylai[38] – and indeed more decisive than the pass itself in the control of north-south movement. As archon of the Thessalian *koinon* he would exercise a decisive voice regarding such military colonies and in fact would retain the town virtually in his own hands but without inviting criticism by stationing Macedonian troops in central Greece. In the re-establishment of the Amphiktyony at Delphoi he had favoured Thessaly.[39] In the Council, the Thessalian *hieromnemones* retained their previous precedence, above even the two Macedonians, who in Amphiktyonic decrees were listed second. From autumn 346 until autumn 339 the Thessalians Kottyphos and Kolosimmos were unchanged and the former, a Pharsalian, may have presided permanently in the Council during his long term of office.[40] In the College of Naopoioi (which, while the lesser in function, better reflected by its varying composition the contemporary political balance), of a total of 36 seats, Thessalian towns in 346 filled a total of eight, two each for Larisa and Pharsalos and one each for Gyrton (only 8 kilometres north of Larisa), Pherai, Pelinna and Krannon.[41]

In spite of these beneficences – or perhaps precisely because they tended to strengthen the pro-Macedonian elements in the country – a reaction followed in some cities, notably Pherai and, more surprisingly, Larisa. In the latter, as the result of some unidentified political stasis, a 'mediating' magistrate, one Simos – apparently of the dominant aristocratic Aleuadai – was appointed with mercenary troops under his command. When with his supporters he began to abuse his position – for example, by striking coins in his own name – the situation began to deteriorate; and it was probably at this point that Philip intervened.[42] Stasis was not confined to Larisa, though we know no details of it anywhere else. It is possible that the personal successes of the archon

Map 3 Thessaly

were seen as a threat to such leading families as the Aleuadai of Larisa and that those outbreaks represented their efforts to counter the consequent successes of more openly pro-Macedonian elements.[43] During the summer of 344,[44] Philip entered Thessaly, expelled the Aleuadai from Larisa and after taking the city of Pherai – now for the third time – installed on its acropolis a Macedonian garrison. He appears to have taken similar action elsewhere.[45] Further, (probably) in Pherai, he judged it necessary to instal in place of the ousted rebels a board of ten governors – a dekadarchy.[46]

However, the existing Thessalian civil organization was evidently unsatisfactory for his purposes and he decided to take more drastic measures. In Thessaly – as in Macedonia, though to a lesser extent – the rivalry of notable families had seriously weakened the capacity of the country for unified action. In the seventh and sixth centuries, under strong central leadership in the military sphere, Thessalian power had been very considerable, rivalling that of Sparta.[47] Thessaly proper – the four tribal areas of Thessaliotis, Pelasgiotis, Hestiaiotis and Phthiotis, occupied by newcomers at the time of the Dorian invasion, who had subjected the indigenes (*penestai*) to their rule – was in form a feudal kingdom, whose monarch (his local title was *tagos*)[48] appears to have been elected. Each tribal area (tetrad) was headed by a tetrarch, whose main function was probably his command of the levy required from his region, but whose title was national not regional: 'Tetrarch of the Thessalians'.[49] For military and perhaps other purposes, the surrounding subject territories (the *perioikis:* Achaia, Magnesia and Perrhaibia) came directly under the *tagos'* control. This tetradic organization had been sufficiently strong to override – at least for military purposes – the clan rivalry that must have existed between the groups inhabiting the (in some cases) vast estates[50] of Thessaly.

During the fifth century, with the increasing importance and growth in power of the *poleis* in the society and economy, the central organization appears to have largely broken down (thus when coinage began soon after 500 BC, for example, it was minted by the cities),[51] and the influence of the major aristocratic factions reasserted itself through their control of these centres. The evidence is not plentiful enough to allow us any confident assertion, but it is likely that while the trappings of 'federal' organizations remained, real power now resided in the *poleis*; so, when the tyrant Jason (of Pherai) proclaimed himself *tagos* of Thessaly in 374, he levied his army by proclaiming to each *city* the size of its required contingent.[52] During the four short years until Jason's death (in 370), united Thessalian power again looked redoubtable, but then the authority of the *tageia* quickly dissolved in the less capable hands of his brothers.[53] In 369 and later, on the intervention of the Theban Pelopidas, some attempt was made to reinstate it.[54] The earlier tetradic organization was restored – at any rate for military purposes – with each division commanded by a polemarch, successor to the tetrarch, who was subordinate to the *tagos*. (The title *tagos*, probably at this time, gave way to that of archon.)[55] There is no evidence though of any real diminution of the powers of the cities and it is likely that the reform represented a compromise, whereby one tetrarchy represented a collection not of *kleroi* but of *polis*-territories.[56] However, although Pherai no longer had the power to unite Thessaly under it, it remained sufficiently strong, with the assistance of mercenary forces, to prevent any real possibility of the development of effective central government; thus the Aleuadai at Larisa, who had called in Macedonian aid in 369 and probably had called upon the Thebans when that aid became a Macedonian occupation,[57] also invited Philip to intervene one and more decades later.[58] During the late 360s, although the Thebans devoted sufficient time to Thessaly to prevent the re-establishment of Pheraian dominance, their actions had also contributed to the weakening of the *koinon*'s power; after two successful Theban interventions in 364, although these were fought on behalf of and in alliance with the League against Alexandros of Pherai, the Boiotians retained in their own league the periœcic territories of Achaia Phthiotis and parts of Magnesia, won from Pherai.[59] When their membership had lapsed after the battle of Mantineia, at least the latter and perhaps areas of the former had been re-won by Pherai.

It was into so badly divided a state that Philip had entered in the 350s, its federal organization artificially re-imposed from without on a social and economic system primarily *polis*-based and in any case unable to control (indeed under dire threat from) the Pheraian tyranny. Its two major cities, Larisa and Pharsalos, were under the control of major noble factions – respectively the Aleuadai and the Daochidai – which, while they might support Philip loyally during his expulsion of the tyranny at Pherai and of the mercenary regime at Delphoi, must now have reverted to the rivalry for power and office that only an outside threat had (apparently) been able to suppress. Pelopidas' reforms – except in the most superficial sense (for example, in the use of the titles, archon and polemarchos) – had utterly collapsed.

It was to this problem that Philip's energies were perforce directed in the summer and autumn of 344. The crises that had drawn him into Thessaly all apparently centred upon the cities and, having settled them by expulsions and, where necessary, by establishing garrisons, he was not disposed to retire before undertaking, as archon of the League, a more thorough overhaul of the whole administrative system. This of course was largely a matter of revival, for the forms of national, or federal, government were already there – if in bad disrepair and perhaps somewhat tarnished by their association with Pheraian abuse and Theban interference. It was perhaps for this latter reason that Philip, while presumably retaining the archon's title,[60] returned to the regional polemarchs their ancient Thessalian title of tetrarchs – a reform of the *koinon* by its own archon and not a foreign imposition.

What precisely the alterations comprised we do not know. Clearly, to destroy the corporate nature and the socio-economic role of the cities would be a damaging measure, so Philip will have made no attempt to return to the ancient *kleros* as the basis of the structure; the city with its surrounding territories, must have remained the basic unit.[61] In the College of the Naopoioi at Delphoi the representatives of the Thessalians continued to be styled by city and not by tetrad or nation. (In the Council of *hieromnemones*, on the other hand, with its fundamentally tribal membership, Kottyphos and Kolosimmos were styled 'Thessaloi'.)[62] But then a new tetrarch probably exercised a considerably greater power over his tetrad than had the polemarch before him; Theopompos refers to one (Thrasydaios) as 'tyrant' over the peoples of his tetrad.[63] It may be that the tetrarchic sphere of responsibility now extended beyond military matters to those of general and financial administration – since one of the weaknesses of the old system appears to have been that the prerogatives of the federal organization (especially after the rise of the *poleis* in the early fifth century) were virtually confined to military affairs. In time of peace – which Philip meant Thessaly to enjoy – *polis*-interests would have reasserted themselves.

Only two tetrarchs are known to us by name, Thrasydaios and Daochos. The latter was a Pharsalian and the former probably so.[64] The family-inscription commemorating the latter's office refers to him as 'Tetrarch of the *Thessalians*', indicating presumably that his election was the function not of the tetrad but of the *koinon*;[65] and it is for that reason possible to find (probably) two Pharsalians (that is, two men both from the tetrad of Thessaliotis) in control of different tetrads – though of which we do not know. While both are condemned by Demosthenes in his famous catalogue of traitors as sycophants who sold out their countries, we need not take him any more seriously than Polybios did.[66] In the spring of 336 both men became *hieromnemones* of the Thessalians at Delphoi.[67]

The most puzzling aspect of Philip's reorganization is to be found in its effect on Thessalian coinage. The conventional view of its general development is that it fell into three periods: *c*.480, or earlier, to 344 (with approximate subdivisions: *c*.480–400 and *c*.400–344), 302–286 and 196–146. In 344, at the end of the first group, 'the autonomous issues of the Thessalian cities come to an abrupt termination, and are supplanted by the regal money of Macedon'.[68] Surprisingly, however, Philip's coins appear in very few Thessalian hoards and then not before the late fourth century.[69] Then, with the discovery of the Thessaly hoard of 1938, the conventional view was cast into doubt. Of the 575 silver pieces discovered, approximately one half were drachms of Alexander the Great and his immediate successors (the successors' coins pointing to a rough burial-date of *c*.250 BC), but of the remaining pieces 155 were Larisaian drachms of a type usually dated (because the model for the female head on the obverse appears to have been late fifth-century Syracusan coins portraying Arethousa)[70] to the early fourth century. But since the hoard was buried so late and since the bulk of the coins represent Macedonian pieces of *c*.525 and onwards, as well as this large group of Larisaian drachms, it appears likely that – there being no coins present of Philip II or of the first decade of Alexander's reign – the group in question was the last autonomous Larisaian coinage before Macedonian regal issues took over and must therefore last into the early 320s.

A strong presumption is thus raised that Philip did not terminate the autonomous Thessalian issues. However, the answer cannot be so simple, for it seems *prima facie* unlikely that he should have allowed one city's autonomous issues to stand as the official currency of the reconstituted League. (It is, of course, possible that other cities may be found to have retained the right to strike autonomous silver; but, even if so, there is still the apparent incongruity of *polis*-coinages serving a federal state.) It has now been suggested that a group of bronze coins, bearing the name of the 'Petthaloi' (a dialect form, so it is now realized, of 'Thessaloi', or 'Thettaloi'), in fact represents federal issues of Thessaly in the time of Philip's, and then Alexander's early reign. There are serious difficulties in the way of this view – notably, that the coins have been assigned independently to the fifth century – but it is a promising lead. While much work remains to be done in the area, what has been proposed to date suggests the following hypothesis. It seems that Philip's concern in his reorganization of Thessaly was to promote a unity of administrative arrangements and of outlook within the Thessalian League. Since this was primarily an internal matter, he may have encouraged the institution of a federal coinage for smaller denominations (bronze); these would be the currency of day-to-day transactions within the country and would be the coins seen and used more exclusively by ordinary Thessalians. But, perhaps, as regards the currency of trade and of larger transactions in general, he was content to allow at least one (and possibly others) of the established mints to continue emissions under its own name – a policy followed evidently too by Alexander until after the middle of his reign.[71]

Such an interpretation, it is worth noting, is consistent with what appears to have been the general line adopted by Philip in his Thessalian organization. On the one hand, the revival of the tetrads as the components of the *koinon*, the increased powers given to their tetrarchs and the responsibility of the latter to the *koinon* or even the archon himself all suggest that the emphasis was on promoting a unity that would override the local *polis*-loyalties. On the other hand, as we have seen, the *poleis* continued to function as corporate identities and probably as basic units within the tetrarchies. Thus at Delphoi, in the College of the Naopoioi, Thessalian members, like those of most other member-tribes, were named by city and not tribe. Further, there is evidently no attempt to balance the selection of Naopoioi between the four tetrads: of those serving in autumn 346, no fewer than five of the eight were from towns in Pelasgiotis, two were from Phthiotis and one from Hestiaiotis. There was none from Thessaliotis.[72] Apparently while Philip sought to re-create a unity of outlook among Thessalians – and thus possibly authorized the emission of a federal coinage for low-denomination bronze issues, primarily for internal use – he was not so dogmatic as to attempt to eradicate the influence of cities which had become over 150 years the economic and religious centres; he allowed them to retain certain rights and powers, perhaps primarily those that related to established contacts in largely international spheres.

At this time, with his influence in Thessaly consolidated and with Pherai garrisoned by his troops, Philip found further support among the small states to the south of Thessaly: Achaia, the third of the periœcic states, entered into a direct relationship with him, together with some smaller states in the Spercheios valley and Aitolia and Dolopia.[73]

THE EMBASSY OF PYTHON

But in the meantime his prospects in Athens were not so happy. When Isokrates had written in 345 (perhaps in the late summer) to urge the king to avoid such risks as he had faced in the campaign against Pleuratos, the old man's concern was not only with Philip's health or even just with the danger of a Macedonian collapse should he fall in battle. A large part of his letter (*Ep.* 2) was directed to a problem Isokrates rightly saw as of overriding importance to Philip's success: the cultivation of Macedonian relations with Athens – and this is the ostensible theme of the second part of the letter. But alongside this lies another theme. Isokrates feared that the 'calumnies' directed against Philip by certain Athenians would not only have their effect on his own fellow-citizens and on the uncommitted among the Greek states, but that Philip too might grow to believe that the rapport he sought was unattainable. The advantages of a general concordia were so beneficial to the king, no less than to Athens, that this goal must not on any account be abandoned.

Towards the midsummer of 344, it became clear to Philip that Isokrates' fears were justified. Opposition, confined earlier to the domestic forum, was gaining momentum. So that when Demosthenes successfully proposed an Athenian embassy to the Peloponnesos, perhaps with the aim of resisting there the natural anti-Spartan movement towards Philip,[74] the king decided that the time had arrived when he must strive to construct by re-negotiation the state of affairs he had aimed at achieving by his attempted finesse of 346. He despatched to Athens his Byzantian friend Python with representatives of others of his allies, including Peloponnesians, bearing instructions to convey his offer to revise the existing peace.[75]

Before the Athenian people, Python began by registering a justified complaint against the activities of the anti-Macedonian element. Philip, after all, had committed himself to aiding Argos and Messene only if they should be attacked, as they feared, by Sparta – precisely as Athens had promised the Messenians a decade before.[76] The Athenian reaction to this was sympathetic, so much so that Demosthenes was sufficiently concerned to deliver, at some stage of the proceedings, a stern warning against what he saw as the naive willingness of his fellows to underrate Philip's growing influence in the Peloponnesos, a speech which amounted to a defence of his own provocative canvassing there. Messenians and Argives were among Philip's allies in Python's deputation and their presence gave added impact to his words.[77] The assembly was impressed by the main point made by Python. If the Athenians were disturbed at the inevitable tendency of many Peloponnesians to turn to Philip as the guarantor of their freedom, then the simple answer was to join him in extending the bilateral peace into a multilateral arrangement open to all who wished to participate. If the Athenians insisted upon interpreting Philip's attempts to preserve Peloponnesian peace as a conspiracy against herself, then she should in this way lend her own efforts to making general peace a reality. With this in mind Philip wished the Athenians to propose whatever amendments to the Peace of Philokrates they felt were desirable.[78]

In 346, Philip's primary aim had required a military alliance between himself and Athens, and his envoys on 19 Elaphebolion had had to insist that only this – and not a Common Peace open to all Greeks, as the allied synod had proposed – was acceptable. Since, however, his plan had failed, and in failing had severely set back his relationship with Athens, he had, as we have observed, devoted the following two years to attempts to allay the fears and suspicions of his new ally. Now, with the actions of a few threatening to destroy the relationship utterly, he brought into play his alternative plan. In 346, he had aimed at making a partner of Athens with two ends in view: first, the Athenians with their fleet and their merchant interests would provide him with suitable support for his planned foray into Asia Minor, with obvious benefits in booty and prestige, combined – for Athens – with expanded trade contacts; second, by elevating Athens to a hegemonial position over the central and southern Greek states (a hegemony that would, of course, depend upon his own co-operation and, if necessary, military support), he might with greater confidence embark upon his Anatolian campaign without fear of disastrous repercussions at his rear. That is to say, he had intended the Peace of Philokrates to be, not – as Demosthenes thought – a means of entry into Greece, but rather as a means of exit from it. But, that having come to nothing, he now pursued an alternative whose results would be similar, having – he hoped – cultivated enough sympathy among the Athenians to regain their co-operation. The establishment of a Common Peace was now not merely acceptable to Philip; it was his positive aim, and Python probably said as much.[79] This hope was not unrealistic, since such had been the overwhelming wish of the Athenians on 18 Elaphebolion 346, and the reality now lay open before them. The treaty, the assembly decided, should be extended to include all Greek states who so wished and should contain the standard guarantee by the collective group to protect the freedom and autonomy of any threatened member.

However (and here we may see an intrusion of the 'war-party' into the proceedings), unable to prevent – as Demosthenes had attempted to do – a favourable response by their fellow citizens, they now shrewdly proposed several additional amendments, ostensibly as mere responses to Philip's generosity but with the calculated intention of bringing the whole arrangement down in ruins. It was relatively easy – in view of Athenian irrationality over the claim on Amphipolis – to suggest that Philip be asked to amend the clause in the original treaty guaranteeing to each party 'what he possessed' to 'what was his own'. Two further requests were tacked on, probably by Hegesippos. The Thracian fortresses established by Kersebleptes and Chares in 347 might be recovered; they had been lost after the Athenians had decided upon peace and had sworn the requisite oaths (although before the king had reciprocated) and perhaps Philip, now clearly in a generous mood, might be persuaded to reconsider.[80] Further, since the peace, the small Athenian-controlled island of Halonnesos had been captured by pirates led by one Sostratos. Philip had expelled his band and could now be asked to restore the island to its rightful owners.[81]

It is to be presumed that, in view of the willingness of the Athenian citizens to respond to the king's offer, they did not fully realize the significance of the additional amendments submitted in their name. Python, as we should expect, was no more than an emissary and had no authority to accept any proposals without reference to Philip. Nevertheless, content that Common Peace was mutually acceptable, impressed by the atmosphere in which his speech was received and believing, presumably, that enough that was constructive had emerged from the debate to make the decisions worth carrying to Pella, and, this being so, that the unacceptable might be modified by further such amiable negotiation, he gave an impression of being satisfied with the proceedings and was entertained in a friendly manner before leaving Athens.[82]

Of course, to any who gave the matter much thought, it was obvious that more than minor negotiation was necessary; it is indeed not too much to say that application of the 'to each his own' principle (which in practice could only mean 'to each all to which he laid claim') was not only impossible for Philip to accept but, were it applied strictly, would be equally unacceptable to Thebes, Thessaly or Athens herself. That is to say, were Philip foolish enough to attempt to apply it, the immediate effect would be to set all of the major powers, potential members of the proposed Common Peace, at one another's throats. It would place under threat for Philip, Amphipolis and Kardia, the Chalkidian peninsula and more; for Thebes and Thessaly, the Phokian settlement of 346 (at least as it affected Nikaia, Koroneia and Orchomenos) and the Pheraian settlements of 352 and 344.[83] This amendment was a sham in two ways: first, in that it meant (at any rate to those who had proposed it) an attempted reversion to some past status quo, the possible definitions of which would be as numerous as there were cities in Greece;[84] second, in that its general application would automatically be opposed by some of the larger states without whose acquiescence no Common Peace was feasible. The ploy of Demosthenes and his colleagues, unable to prevent a favourable popular reaction to Philip's offer of Common Peace, was thus to discredit and negate it.[85] In so doing (and here we see the same successful strategy as was employed by Demosthenes in 346), they ensured a strong reaction against Philip, whose offer would thus be made to appear empty, and, at the same time, would prepare the way for prosecution of the proponents of the original peace, on whom the blame for this further disappointment could then be pinned. When Hegesippos was chosen to head an embassy to Pella to convey these decisions officially to the king he went therefore with no intention of negotiating a Common Peace – and Philip's disgust was all too apparent.[86] Nevertheless, perhaps, given time to realize what they had in fact been asking and presented with further tokens of his good faith, the Athenian people might yet come to realize the benefits of what he could offer; he therefore kept open the possibility of Common Peace.[87]

A further indication that at the time of Python's embassy the Athenian *demos* had swallowed some of its earlier doubts about Philip's intentions may be seen in its response to a Persian embassy in Athens at or about the same time.[88] In preparation for his huge campaign against Egypt, planned for the following year,[89] Artaxerxes III (Ochos) sent requests for military aid in an attempt to collect enough of the superior Greek forces to counteract those supporting the Egyptians. Thebes and Argos complied, as did some of the Greek cities of Asia

Minor, who had less choice.[90] In Athens, not only were the Persians rebuffed with a contemptuous answer, but a decree was passed calling upon 'Philip and the rest of the Greeks to make common cause against Ochos in case he attempted to interfere with them. Clearly there was some trepidation – and it was probably justified in the longer term – that the Great King, with his dominions again under control, might next turn to the west, at least with money, if not with men.[91] But it is striking that the Athenian *demos*, in the face of what was no more than a relatively distant possibility, were prepared to give Philip the satisfaction of an Athenian request to join the common Hellenic cause. The manner and terms of the decision reinforce what Hegesippos some 18 months later was to imply: that in summer 344, at the time of Python's embassy, Philip's attempts since 345 to revive in Athens the popularity he had enjoyed before the surrender of Phokis were taking effect.

Philip's anger with Hegesippos in Pella, probably in the last month or so of 344, then, was directed at one of the men who had combined to frustrate a genuine and positive attempt to give to Athens in effect what he had intended to give in 346 ,when there was every sign that the majority of the Athenians were receptive to his wishes, and had done so in such a way as to fasten the blame for this failure on Philip.

THEBAN DISQUIET

He was as yet, however, far from abandoning hope of success in his venture. But, for the present, a more immediate difficulty had to be faced. On the one hand, while the violently anti-Macedonian group in Athens continued to determine the Athenian response to his overtures, the prospect of the Athenian/Theban combination he most wished to avoid became more strongly possible. On the other hand, beyond acquiescing grudgingly in the bare minimum of Theban demands in the eventual settlement of the Sacred War, he had done little to give the Thebans any confidence in his intentions towards them. His pointed overtures to Athens over the past two years, combined with their memory of what they had (correctly) feared might happen in Skirophorion 346, must have deepened their suspicions of him, and indeed in 344 it was known, or suspected, in Athens that the Thebans were far from happy with their Macedonian ally.[92] This, to the king, had not been a matter of much concern, especially as (had the Athenians stepped into the role he had cast for them) the more violent Thebes' reaction the better justification he would have for cutting back her power decisively. But now the state of his relationship with Thebes was becoming serious, the more so with the recent reaffirmation of

Theban/Persian friendship. It is not overstating the case to suggest that he saw a growing possibility that an antagonistic Athens, a disenchanted Thebes and even the Persian King himself might combine to crush the Macedonian state.

Probably what rankled most in Thebes was that, two years after the Amphiktyons had watered down the extreme penalties demanded for Phokis by the Thebans and one or two others, one of the few impositions eventually agreed upon – repayment of the cost of the pillaged treasures of Apollo – had still not been applied (no doubt because to have enforced it would have made Philip's conciliation of the Athenians more difficult). So that now – although he intended to return to his wooing of Athens – he felt unable to delay any longer; probably at the spring Pylaia (*c.* April/May) of the Amphiktyons at Delphoi in 343 he put in hand arrangements for a decision ordering the Phokian reparations to begin.[93]

THE EXILE OF PHILOKRATES

On hearing of this resolution Athenian opinion inevitably polarized more strongly,[94] and shortly afterwards Hypereides impeached Philokrates. This prosecution, among others, had been foreshadowed by Demosthenes a year earlier when attempting to discredit Python's offer.[95] It is to be seen not so much as a 'test-case' prior to the prosecution of Aischines, but as complementary to it. Philokrates had assumed the responsibility among the peace-envoys of 346 for proposing the decisive decrees and so must, at this time of disenchantment with Philip, be more vulnerable to impeachment even than those others who continued to urge that the peace be observed. If the prosecution were successful then it would be an easier matter to procure condemnation of those also associated, though less directly so than he. When Demosthenes and Timarchos in Skirophorion 346 had lodged complaint against Aischines it may not have been with the intention of proceeding against him immediately and in any case his countercharge against Timarchos had successfully delayed it.[96] After the latter's condemnation in winter 346/5, the way had been open for Demosthenes, who seems to have tried to dissociate himself from his co-appellant at the time, to bring on his suit; and that he did not do so – nor Hypereides in the case of Philokrates – for more than two years indicates, first, caution over the association with Timarchos and, more importantly, that, when memories of this had faded, there was not yet a sufficiently decisive swing of opinion away from the Peace. Now, however, with the anti-Macedonians again successful in discrediting Philip's bona fides and with the consequent necessity upon him to appease Thebes over the Phokian reparations, they judged the time ripe for success.[97]

The charge brought by Hypereides was that Philokrates had 'made proposals contrary to the public good in response to bribery'. Unfortunately, Philokrates decided that, in the present atmosphere, his condemnation was certain and so fled from Athens; as a result not only was he condemned to death in his absence, but his opponents were enabled to say what they would of him without fear of denial. His supporters, those like Aischines who might have stood to refute the charges, could only conclude that, by the ignorant at least, his flight was taken for guilt and that their only safe course was to dissociate themselves, as far as possible, from their former colleague. Thus, while we know from our observations of Philokrates' role in 346 that there was no legal validity in the first part of the charge, beyond – at any rate – the later odium associated with a once-popular but now discredited policy, we have no means of assessing Demosthenes' imputations (during his prosecution of Aischines) not only of bribery but also of Philokrates' almost suicidal parading of its proceeds. The defendant on that occasion thought the matter too sensitive for any response at all, but confined himself (as he was to do 13 years later) to showing how closely Demosthenes himself had co-operated with Philokrates in the construction of the peace.[98]

During the one-sided trial Demosthenes rose to challenge the other envoys to declare their innocence in the matter by repudiating all connection with the absent accused. Evidently some produced excuses for not doing so, but, in the event, not one accepted this avenue of escape.[99] This is perhaps the most interesting aspect of the whole affair, and is certainly not to be written off, as Demosthenes hoped it would be, as a demonstration of Aischines' impudence as well as his guilt. Two explanations suggest themselves, either or both of which might explain such reticence. In the first place, there was probably a distinction in the public mind between the man who had agreed during the peace-negotiations to lend his name to the operative decrees and those who had carefully aligned themselves in the debate of 18 Elaphebolion with the contrary proposal of the allied synod. The latter group, at Philokrates' trial, although Demosthenes himself magnanimously offered to declare them innocent of Philokrates' 'crimes' were they to respond to his challenge, may well have preferred, in the event of their own impeachment at some time in the future, to rely upon their record on that day; to dissociate themselves from Philokrates' actions might be taken to imply that they had previously been associated with them, which would be a dangerous admission under the present circumstances.

In the second place, it is legitimate to distinguish at this time between, on the one hand, a positive Athenian disgruntlement over the peace and its formal architects, Macedonian and Athenian, and, on the other, a rather less positive suspicion of those who had gone along with peace-terms which were ultimately accepted by all because they were unavoidable and because they were accompanied by attractive promises. This distinction is also suggested by the contrasting responses of Philokrates and Aischines, respectively, when charges were brought against them, the one fleeing because, whether guilty or not, he foresaw the verdict, the other remaining to contest the issue successfully. It may also be observed that the refusal of these other envoys to repudiate Philokrates may have suggested to Philip that, while the original peace-terms were beyond resuscitation, Athenian public opinion – at least implicitly in the action of the majority of the envoys – might yet be favourable to a revised treaty provided he could make it sufficiently attractive.[100]

PELOPONNESIAN STASIS

We have already noticed that the new role of Philip in Greek affairs, as a result of his achievements of 346 and, in particular, his influence in the Council of the Amphiktyons, produced an immediate effect among especially the smaller states of the Peloponnesos and elsewhere. Most obviously, he was seen by some – for example, Argos and Messenia – as the guarantor of their independence from Sparta. But such alliances as were born out of these circumstances probably represent only a small part of the indirect effects of the new power-balance on the Greek mainland. Just as, during the fifth-century Athenian empire, the internal politics of member-states had inevitably produced a polarity of stances, democratic (usually taken to mean pro-Athenian) versus oligarchic (similarly anti-Athenian), which often poorly reflected either genuine ideological differences or even genuine foreign commitments, but rather served as convenient political catch-cries for internal use; and just as, in the immediate aftermath of the battle of Chaironeia in 338, in a large number of cities, political groups claiming to be pro-Macedonian swept into power, with no actual assistance from the benefactor whose sympathy they claimed, so, we must expect, after the settlement of the Phokian war, the internal politics of many states revolved around sympathy, or the lack of it, for Philip. It is thus heavily incumbent upon us, in taking account of the rather complicated events (especially in the Peloponnesos and Euboia) over the period 343–340, and especially so since it was in the political interest of our major source for these events,

Demosthenes, to implicate Philip as directly and literally as possible in all affairs causing discomfort to Athens, to attempt to distinguish between acts of intervention (whether direct or indirect) by Philip himself and internal disorders involving his partisans, real or self-proclaimed.[101]

In the summer of 343, before the trial of Aischines in the autumn of that year, there were instances of stasis in both Elis and Megara. In both cases, according to Demosthenes, the troubles were caused by aristocratic factions which laid claim to the friendship and support of Philip. In Megara, although the details are very obscure, there appears to have been a serious threat to the status quo, responsibility for which Demosthenes attempts to pin on an element that he characterizes as both oligarchic and pro-Macedonian. Evidently the threat was successfully resisted, although he curiously (and perhaps significantly) does not explain how.[102] Similarly, in Elis, an oligarchic group – perhaps that overthrown not long before – staged a successful counter-revolution; this group too, so Demosthenes alleges, were Philip's partisans.[103] In both cases, however, whatever allegiance or support was claimed by those involved, it is clear that there was certainly no direct and probably no indirect intervention by Philip. His offer to Athens to re-negotiate the peace remained open in spite of the initial rebuff. He might yet hope for a repetition of the situation in early Anthesterion 346, when popular sentiment over the Phokian rebuff and the report of Aristodemos had forced the hand of those who wished to delay or prevent peace, and he had no intention now of negating his own efforts.

THE ACQUITTAL OF AISCHINES

But, however little truth was contained in the allegations Demosthenes and his partisans were making, their constant iteration must have had noticeable effect and in the autumn they judged the time ripe for a legal attack on Aischines. In the case that ensued there was really one issue: whether sufficient disfavour now attached to the Peace of Philokrates to bring down those who continued, since the surrender of Phokis, to proclaim – if not its virtues – at least its potential; closely allied was the consequence that if this were so then the Peace might be violated almost with impunity – with only such restraint as was enjoined by strategic necessities. The charge itself, that Aischines had been guilty of serving the interests of Philip against those of his own city, and this as the result of bribery,[104] was a sham. While, in practice, the trial may have amounted to little more than a political popularity-poll, it was nevertheless something more than that; there will have been among the Athenians, and thus among the jurors, those who were not finally committed either way and would need persuasion. Some of these would presumably be informed persons, others not, and the arguments (as presumably in all similar trials, just as in the preliminaries to a modern election) were designed with a combination of motives – partly to confirm the prejudiced in their views and partly to win over the more neutral by whatever means necessary. On Demosthenes' part, the stated aim was to show that Aischines, from opposing Philip until 18 Elaphebolian 346, had reversed his policy on the following day (through what other than Philip's bribes?) and then had collaborated with the Macedonian king, firstly, in delaying the arrival in Pella of the second embassy, so as to allow Philip in the interim to take western Thrace under his control; secondly, in hoodwinking the *demos* on 16 Skirophorion, by either fabricating or at least relaying false promises as to Philip's intentions, into ratifying the treaty and extending it to the king's successors, so depriving the Phokian people of all hope of support and driving them into an abject surrender a week later. Had the accused been Philip's unwitting tool in all this, argued Demosthenes, he would have proved it by denouncing the failure of the promised benefits to materialize; since he had not done so, his treason was therefore calculated and obdurate.[105]

As we have seen from our examination of the events of 346, such a charge was a tissue of lies and distortions. Of this Demosthenes was well aware. And while, three years after the event, he may have hoped to dupe the ignorant and the forgetful among the jurors, his success, he knew, depended on three things. First: as we have seen, a proportion (perhaps a majority) of the votes were determined before the case began. Second: if he were to succeed in pairing Aischines closely with Philokrates, then the latter's flight a few weeks before and his subsequent condemnation *in absentia* might be sufficient to condemn Aischines by association. Third: he had to fabricate a plausible reconstruction of the events to the end of Elaphebolion 346 in such a way as to omit the centrality of his own role in achieving the peace, while emphasizing that of Aischines in making it palatable.[106]

As regards the second aim, Demosthenes was probably unsuccessful, for, although we know nothing of what passed through the jurors' minds, once it came to facts the defendant was able to point to the record of Demosthenes' own association with Philokrates and the peace until mid-Skirophorion. Indeed so clearly did the facts known to the jury refute his argument that the only specific accusation Demosthenes felt able to make was that Aischines and Philokrates had collaborated secretly during the actual course of the second embassy. But as regards his third aim Demosthenes may have been more successful. His arguments are still influential to this day, and fall only when seen in the light of a proper examination of Philip's interests and aims, an exercise probably beyond the ordinary Athenian citizen in the atmosphere of late 343.

The acquittal of Aischines, though by a mere thirty votes, was no doubt significant, but its precise import was difficult for Philip – as for us – to assess. It has been taken to indicate that Demosthenes had not yet reached a position of predominance in Athenian political life.[107] But it seems more likely that it indicates the contrary; for on the assumption that the political views of the jurors were already fairly evenly divided, but granted that in their essentials the charges were fairly easily refuted, the acquittal probably signifies that Demosthenes was already in the ascendant and that, had he been able to lay charges less transparently false, Aischines would surely have been condemned. To Philip this meant that success was fast receding; his offer to renegotiate the treaty remained open, but it had already been once rejected – and if that rejection was arguably not in accord with the public will at that time (mid- to late-summer 344) but largely the result of his opponents' tactical subterfuge, now, over a year later, he could no longer hope seriously that the *demos* would respond to those overtures. The time had come for the final attempt to salvage the plans of 346. If this failed, a new policy must be developed.

THE LAST BID FOR ATHENS

It is very likely that the recent events – however little understood and falsely portrayed at Athens – in Megara and Elis had had some influence (at least when added to the disappointment over the breakdown of the negotiations represented by the embassies of Python and Hegesippos) in turning the Athenian *demos* more decisively against any rapprochement with Macedon. In Euboia too, lost from Athenian to Macedonian influence by the ill-chosen intervention there in 349/8, the situation was far from reassuring to near-by Athens – at least when given the appropriate colouring. The anti-Athenian governments in the major Euboian democracies had their pro-Macedonian elements and these were probably dominant at the time. Indeed by now numbers of pro-Athenians had been expelled from Eretria and had probably taken refuge at the fortress of Porthmos, facing the Attic Diakria across the Euboic Gulf;[108] there it stood, a constant reminder of Athenian impotence in the island; at Oreos too the pro-Macedonians were in power. Most Euboians depended on Philip as their protector.[109]

Such indications of the body of support he enjoyed within some of the Greek states can hardly have displeased Philip, but at the present time their advantage was outweighed by the ammunition they provided to the opponents of the peace in Athens, the city with which he was prepared to go to the greatest lengths to preserve it. When, at the autumn Pylaia (343) of the Amphiktyony, the first semestrial repayment was handed over by the Phokians, he will have been aware of further loss of support in Athens.

With the prospects of a breakdown of the peace now appearing virtually inevitable, a new problem presented itself on a different and long-secure front. On only two known occasions hitherto had Philip felt the need to take any action regarding his Epeirote neighbours to the southwest. In 357 he had, by his marriage with Olympias, cemented an alliance with her uncle (and brother-in-law) Arybbas that had apparently continued without serious friction until the end of the decade, when firmer action had been called for. Removing to Pella Olympias' young brother, Alexandros, then only twelve years old, from the court of his uncle, where the regent's intentions will have become more suspect the closer the boy grew to an age at which he might assume the throne of his father Neoptolemos, he had additionally severed Tymphaia, Atintania and Paravaia from the Molossian-controlled kingdom.[110]

Towards the end of 343, in the late autumn or very early winter, Philip again turned to the southwest. A number of possible explanations may account for this move. With the breakdown of the Peace of Philokrates becoming more clearly imminent, it may be that Arybbas had given signs of reversion to the Athenian alignment enjoyed by the Molossian dynasty in the past;[111] the dispensation of *c.* 350 had been forced upon him and, as the young Alexandros approached an appropriate age to supplant him on the throne, his position became steadily weaker. No doubt Philip had been planning for some time the move he now put in train, but, in view of the complications likely to arise on its account in his last-ditch negotiations with Athens, it is unlikely that the initiative for intervention at this particular time came from him.[112]

However, if Epeiros compelled his attention, so did Athens and, at about the same time as he set out for the former, he despatched a letter with envoys to the Athenian Assembly. In the main, what it offered (in repetition of what Python had conveyed a year and a half earlier) was an extension of the existing treaty into a Common Peace, open to all states who wished to join.[113] Further, with respect to matters which had arisen either in the debate on Python's proposals or in the unhappy negotiations in Macedonia between Philip and the embassy of Hegesippos, a series of further concessions was proposed. In 344, Philip had offered to give Halonnesos to Athens; if not mentioned by Python, this was at least discussed at Pella. Negotiations had in any case broken down on that occasion, but, at this time, what had been unacceptable to the Athenian diehards and still remained so to Hegesippos was that Philip was content to give the island to Athens as if it were 'his own property' instead of restoring it to her as her own possession.[114]

Before we write off the king's action as unnecessary and, in the event, provocative hair-splitting over what was, when all is said, a singularly unattractive piece of real estate (of no value to anyone but a naval power, to which any possible landfall might be decisive in a storm), we ought to endeavour to discover why Philip should have failed simply to acquiesce in Athens' semantic preference when we would expect extreme benevolence to have governed his actions at this time. He might have expected, of course, that his expulsion of Sostratos' pirates would be welcomed at Athens as the removal of a threat to orderly trade in the area. It is unlikely that he contemplated using it himself. (Indeed, when Athens rejected his offer, settlers from Peparethos moved in.)[115] But in legal terms he was faced with a dilemma, for the real stake here was not Halonnesos itself but the relationship between conquest and ownership. Does capture by one party from a second override the prior claims of a third? To answer in the negative was to leave himself and some of his allies open to challenge regarding possession of several key cities or areas. Why then was he prepared now to submit the matter to independent arbitration? Probably because he was confident that Athens would not press this argument in such circumstances, since some of her own possessions were vulnerable to precisely the same principle.[116] Thus, while he was perfectly happy to allow Athenian possession of the island, he would not do so according to a prescription which, if applied selectively, would cast doubt on certain of his own possessions. The offer was in the event rejected, but it was made in good faith and in terms as generous as were practical. Athens was prepared to cut off her own nose to spite Philip's face.

As regards the Thracian fortresses, claimed by Hegesippos' embassy in 344, Philip now offered to submit this matter too to arbitration; there was no validity to the Athenian claim and, rather than giving offence by a direct refusal, the king could only hope that the authority of an independent adjudicator would settle the dispute, or that, acknowledging the folly of their claim, the Athenians would quietly drop the matter. Dissension having arisen over conflicting territorial claims between the Athenian cleruchs in the Chersonesos and the neighbouring Kardians, Philip's allies, he proposed arbitration.[117]

Such compromises, however reasonable, were not likely to win much support for a renewal and extension of the Peace of Philokrates; so, along with his repeated offer of its re-negotiation, Philip made two additional suggestions as to means by which the friendship between the two states might be cemented in practical terms. He had already sent envoys to discuss the establishment of an inter-state legal agreement, whereby Macedonians and Athenians respectively might obtain legal redress in cases of commercial dispute in the state of the defending party. The reiteration of this offer Hegesippos portrayed as a clandestine attempt to hoodwink the Athenians into surrendering any claims to Poteidaia and, in admonishing his fellows to reject it outright, attempted to infer from the form of the proposal (which was standard in any such dealings: that party A proposed and party B, if willing, accepted and then returned the agreement to the proposer for final ratification) that Philip had set himself up as 'a court of appeal from (the Athenian) decision'.[118] Such an agreement, if set up, would presumably be open to extension to cover all new members of the Common Peace. Even more important, and perhaps as an indication of the benefits for Athens in the adoption of Philip's general plans for peace, he proposed that a joint effort be mounted to clear the Aegean of pirates.[119] We know little of the magnitude of this pestilence at the time, but it is likely that, with the virtual collapse of the Athenian naval league in 355, piracy was on the increase. Apart from the band expelled from Halonnesos, it may be that there were others established on Thasos and other northern islands, which Philip offered to replace with Macedonian settlers. All this was evidently to be done at Macedonian expense, the Athenians supplying only their share of ships and crews.[120] By careful distortion of his intention, Hegesippos made it appear that Philip hoped his allies would co-operate in handing him control of the Aegean as a gift.

The ripostes offered by Hegesippos, for all their speciousness, carried the day. But perhaps more effective than his destructive rhetoric was the capital he was able to make out of Philip's current campaign in Epeiros. Just as Demosthenes in early 350 had found it easy to misrepresent the campaign of 352–351 as an attack 'against the Chersonesos', so now Hegesippos could call the intervention in Epeiros a campaign 'against Ambrakia', an allegation the Athenians took seriously enough to dispatch troops to the area shortly afterward.[121]

THE EPEIROTE CAMPAIGN OF 343/2

Late in the previous year but before the winter set in, virtually cutting off Epeiros from Macedonia and Thessaly, Philip had led his troops up the Haliakmon valley and through the mighty Pindos range to the southern edge of the populous plain of Ioannina and, a few miles farther southwest, the tiny plain of Dodona.[122] No source – even Justin, who deplores the ensuing action as a violation of the consanguinity of Philip and Arybbas – refers to any use of force and it therefore seems likely that the 'regent' capitulated without a blow on condition of a safe departure into exile.[123] Perhaps this was the result of pressure from the President and the Council of tribal representatives of the Molossian *koinon*, who will have had no wish to go into battle with the Macedonian army. He left for Athens where the citizenship held earlier by his father and grandfather (Alketas and Tharyps) was extended also to him and his sons.[124]

The significance of this move is probably twofold. Following a succession of successful Illyrian campaigns, the regulation of Thracian affairs at least as far as the Hebros and the new reorganization in Thessaly, the one remaining among the neighbouring states in which Macedonian influence was less than satisfactory was Epeiros to the southwest. In the long term, as we have already seen, Philip had given notice – by his raising of his young brother-in-law at the Macedonian court and by his insistence that the boy's uncle Arybbas regard himself as no more than regent – of his intention to contrive a continuing and substantial degree of patronage over the ruling Molossian family. With the young Alexandros now twenty years old the time was suitable for putting this plan into action – and although the timing of the intervention (vis-à-vis the progress of negotiations with Athens) was inappropriate, implying that Arybbas was known to be working in some way to circumvent the scheme, the action itself appears to have gone smoothly. The Molossian *koinon* perhaps evinced less concern at such a Macedonian intervention than they rejoiced at the prospect of a stronger front against future Illyrian movement. The Molossians saw too that a close alliance with the powerful Macedonians confirmed and strengthened their own dominance over the other Epeirote tribes, a prospect heightened further by Philip's promise to subordinate to them, when possible, the important southern areas of Epeiros on the Ambrakiote Gulf, presently controlled by the Ambrakians and the Greek cities of Kassopia. His claims to do so were tenuous, based on an incident in the life of the demi-god Herakles, who had allegedly entrusted Ambrakia to the care of others with the order to return this charge to his descendants (among whom the Argeadai numbered themselves).[125]

In the event, this promise was not to be fulfilled in its entirety for several years. But in 342, very early in the year, Philip forced the Kassopian towns – Elatreia, Boucheta and Pandosia (to which Theopompos adds a fourth, Bitia) – to enter the Molossian *koinon*.[126] The Ambrakiotes and their neighbouring island colleagues on Leukas, fearing for their safety, called upon their common founding-city, Korinth, which in turn appealed to Athens. At the time of Hegesippos' speech on Philip's offers to extend the peace, as we have seen, the king's activities in Epeiros and Kassopia were recognizable as a threat to Ambrakia, and Demosthenes now spearheaded a campaign to resist it. Athenian troops were despatched to the area, actually to Akarnania, together with embassies to stiffen the resolution of the Ambrakiotes and their southern neighbours (as far south as the Peloponnesian states, especially those of the northwest) to resist Philippic influence. It was seen, probably rightly, as the second aim of Philip's Epeirote campaign. to open a western communication-route southwards from his ally, past the Ambrakiote Gulf to the Gulf of Korinth, and thence across the straits of Rhion to Achaia;[127] but it is unlikely that at this time, with the Athenian decision on his peace-offer still pending, the king intended to push farther south than Epeiros itself. That, if ultimately inevitable, must wait until western Thrace was secure against both Athens and (with Egypt now recaptured) Persia.[128] But he does seem to have negotiated a treaty of some sort with the Aitolians, who occupied the important position on the northern coast of the entrance to the Korinthian Gulf. With their best port, Naupaktos, in Achaian hands, they were susceptible to Philip's promise to recover it for them, and it is likely that he did so in return for alliance. When the opportunity arose (after his capture of Amphissa in 338) he carried out this promise.[129]

THE UNBRIDGEABLE GULF

But less satisfactory to him were the successes scored by the Athenian embassies. By late 343, Argos, Messene and Megalopolis had been in alliance with Philip, whom they saw as the only effective guarantor of their independence from Sparta.[130] Although they did not forswear their agreements (there being no need, since Athens too was Philip's ally) they joined the Mantineians and their allies in northern Arkadia, as well as the Achaians (who, if for no other reason, will have acted out of resentment at the threat against Naupaktos), in concluding alliances with Athens.[131] But if these arrangements represented a setback to Philip, the gain to Athens was hardly more than a morale-booster. A year later, in his third *Philippic*, Demosthenes was to speak as though alliances between the Greeks did not exist.[132] That some did exist, however, is not to be doubted; what Demosthenes manifests is sufficient pragmatism to see that these were (for the most part, if not entirely) motivated not by opposition to Philip, which is what he would have wished, so much as by fear of Sparta and the desire to build as many defences as possible against any resurgence of Lakedaimonian influence in the Peloponnesos. That the Spartans too interpreted them thus is strongly suggested by the apparent abandonment at this time of their buffer-state policy of venerable antiquity and the despatch of King Archidamos with troops to assist in the defence of Tarentum against Lucanian attack.[133]

The failure to achieve all that he had intended, however, was not Philip's major concern. The Athenian military and diplomatic activity, while it achieved little of importance at this time (even Thessaly and Illyria were canvassed, but without noticeable effect),[134] gave unmistakable notice that his own overtures to the Athenians had finally failed. Whenever and in whatever form the refusal actually reached him it was now clear that the internal struggle between those for and those against extending – or even maintaining – the Peace of Philokrates had been not only resolved but translated into a definite foreign policy. Irritated as he may have been by his partial failure north and south of the Korinthian Gulf, Philip had nevertheless given a good measure of security to his western flanks, in the process strengthening his hold over the Thessalians, the Epeirotes' immediate western neighbours. Moreover, he saw little in the recent diplomatic successes of Athens to suggest that there was any real danger in the near future of a concerted Greek attack on his interests.[135]

CHAPTER VI

342–340
BREAKDOWN

ARISTOTLE, ALEXANDER AND THE ROYAL PAGES

As we have had cause to notice,[1] it is likely that since 348/7 Philip had been in contact with the Atarnian ruler Hermias, whose small principality on the Aiolian coast of Asia Minor, opposite Mytilene, offered an ideal advance-post in the planned, but now delayed, Asian campaign. The go-between in this arrangement appears to have been Aristotle and it is quite likely that he had negotiated an actual alliance, necessarily in secret. Hermias' position, always somewhat slippery in the longer prospect, had become far more precarious after Artaxerxes Ochos' successful re-conquests of Phoenicia, Cyprus and Egypt.[2] There was of course nothing Philip could do at this time to strengthen him; the recent events in Greece had made it abundantly clear that any plans to expose his back to the mainland could be reactivated only after the construction of a new settlement. He certainly could not afford to provoke Ochos into an alignment with an Athens now perhaps willing to seize the opportunity.

Aristotle himself, for reasons unknown but perhaps out of common interest with the Lesbian Theophrastos, had moved in 345/4 to Mytilene, taking with him his wife Pythias, the niece and adopted daughter of Hermias. There for two years he had worked on his *Historia Animalium* when an invitation arrived from the king of the Macedonians asking him to accept the post of tutor to the 13-year-old heir apparent Alexander.[3] The offer was bound to cause resentment among other contenders. Philip's connections with Plato's pupils was of long standing and Speusippos' fawning letter to the king only a few months before in recommendation of one Antipatros was no doubt aimed at securing the latter's appointment. Isokrates' pupil, Theopompos, evidently fancied his chances and composed an uncharacteristically charitable eulogy of Philip; disappointed, his admiration for the king suffered something of a decline.[4] The fee offered was attractive, but so was the honour, however the cultivated might sneer; and Aristotle's acceptance represents, moreover, the continuation of existing ties.[5]

Aristotle must have arrived at Pella shortly before the army started on its long campaign in Thrace, which began by June 342. To the southwest, in the Gardens of Midas on the cooler slopes of Mt Bermion, lay the city of Mieza and, a kilometre or two to its southeast on a most attractive site, a group of caves with shaded walks near by, known as the Nymphaion.[6] To this retreat Aristotle was despatched with his young charge and a number of other youths, probably including Hephaistion, Ptolemaios and some of the sons of Antipatros, who remained as regent during Philip's Thracian campaign and formed now, if not before, a friendship with the philosopher fourteen years his junior. (The former was now 56, the latter 42.)[7] The arrangements are significant in several ways. From childhood the young prince had been subjected to a number of conflicting influences: primarily the overwhelming ambition and dark mysticism of his mother Olympias, whose stern kinsman Leonidas had been his first tutor; the rough brilliance of a father much of whose life was spent away at war and in diplomatic intrigue; and the ambivalence of the Macedonian nobles of the court, men whose native vigour and bluntness was tempered by the Hellenic influences attracted to Pella (and, before that, to Aigai) by successive Argead rulers. Following Leonidas' 'Spartan' regime, Alexander was tutored by Lysimachos of Akarnania, to whom has been attributed the encouragement of the Homeric fantasies supposedly fostered in the prince by his mother.[8] Certain of these influences – perhaps in particular that of his mother – were becoming embarrassing at a time when the youth was approaching the age of responsibility and it was probably for this reason and to remove him from the intrigues of the nobility at Pella that Philip, who saw that his own absence in Thrace might well be lengthy, decided to establish Aristotle's school in surroundings more moderate in temperature and atmosphere than the steamy heat of lakeside Pella in summer.

The boys among whom Alexander studied were almost certainly no random selection of young nobles, but members of an élite group known as the Royal Pages, adolescent sons of the Macedonian nobility. These teenagers were taken from their fathers to the royal court, where they attended personally on the king and received an appropriate training for senior posts after graduation from page-status. They were educated at court, where the king supervised their schooling and selected their instructors.[9] The founder of the institution was Philip.[10]

We cannot say with much confidence where the *hetairoi* of the king passed their time when not on campaign. But, presumably, although Philip will have kept his inner Council close by him and was undoubtedly able to call upon at least some of his Companions (and his

Hypaspists) at short notice, the powerful nobles of the *hetairos*-class (probably most of them) must have spent time on their own estates in their own districts. Although Philip's military reconstruction of the kingdom had, as we have noticed,[11] applied a powerful unifying influence to the society, opportunities still abounded in especially the more inaccessible areas of Upper Macedonia for the spread of anti-Argead sentiment. But, while the king could not have the potential opponents among his nobles constantly under his eye, the institution of the Royal Pages allowed him to hold their sons. While, presumably, pageship was considered an honour, both for the royal associations and as a training-school for high office, it was also – and was no doubt intended to be – a benign form of hostageship. More positively, it provided the machinery for the instilling of national ideals into the young aristocracy. It has been convenient to look briefly at this institution at this point, when Alexander himself was of much the same age as the pages about him. But, in fact, we have no idea when Philip decided on the innovation.

Few of his pages are known. Alexander's childhood friends are almost certainly of this order; and, of those named, Harpalos was probably of Elimiote royal stock, Ptolemaios (son of Lagos) of Eordaian royalty, and Philotas was a son of Parmenion, who may have been royal Pelagonian.[12] By contrast, Nearchos and the brothers Erigyios and Laomedon appear to have been sons of non-Macedonian *hetairoi* ennobled by Philip.[13] Lack of evidence hampers our pursuit of this matter very far, for even under Alexander the origins of pages are seldom given by our sources.[14] We might attempt to extend our resources by considering young commanders appointed during Alexander's reign (such as Derdas from Elimeia, Leonnatos of Pella and Marsyas of Pella, among many other candidates);[15] these may well have been among the pages of Philip, but we have no way of being certain. It was probably with a selection of such youths that Alexander and Aristotle worked and played at Mieza.

EUBOIA

In the Pella of mid-342 preparations had been made for a major Thracian campaign. Gone now were the careful attempts of Philip to win Athenian friendship. Perhaps as long as a year before, Kallias of Chalkis had come to Macedonia seeking Philip's support for a Euboian League sufficiently powerful to withstand the respective ambitions of Athens and Thebes to reassert their lost influence in the island. Although the prospect must have been appealing, Philip had turned him down.

(Kallias had then found no support in Thebes either.)[16] Now, on the contrary, Euboia was shortly to become a pawn in the struggle against Athenian power. The velvet glove of Macedonian diplomacy had been removed, and, while it was not yet replaced by the mailed fist, Athens was now to be treated as a potential enemy. Thus at about the same time as Philip led his main army to the areas beyond the Nestos, other troops, probably mercenaries for the most part, were stationed in the south near the Gulfs of Pagasai and Malia opposite northern Euboia. Kallias' efforts had evidently caused alarm among the Euboian cities; and the Macedonians were now ready to capitalize on it, in part to preserve their own influence but also no doubt to create a diversion that would distract Athenian attention from the North.[17]

During the following few months no fewer than three Macedonian commanders serve on this island (Parmenion, Eurylochos and Hipponikos), while Antipatros during the autumn is also present in central Greece to represent the king at the Pythian Festival at Delphoi. Such a concentration of high-ranking officers calls for comment.

In the first place, it emphasizes the importance attached to Euboian affairs at this time, although we need hardly believe that three leading generals were assigned for so long to Euboia alone. As it was to happen, Philip would not return to Pella for more than three years. This was unforeseeable in 342 but, if Philip's achievements in that period were at all consonant with his intentions, he must have planned on being absent from the kingdom for well in excess of one year. Under such circumstances it is very difficult to doubt that the king appointed a deputy to supervise his Greek interests at closer range.[18] Two years later this was to be the 16-year-old Alexander's first (known) position of importance, terminating the final phase of his formal education under Aristotle. But in 342 it appears likely that Antipatros for the first (known) time held the office that he was to occupy again during Alexander's reign.[19] In this role he rode south to Delphoi in early autumn for the Pythia.[20] As for Parmenion and the others, it is not known where they were stationed. Parmenion was to appear twice or three times in Euboia during the summer and autumn of 342, and Eurylochos and Hipponikos respectively at least once, and it may be conjectured that they were stationed with troops at key points in Thessaly – perhaps, for example, at Pagasai and at some point on or near the Malian Gulf (probably at Echinos and Antron).[21] The absence of so many commanders from the force in Thrace is probably to be explained in terms of Philip's recognition of the critical point at which Greek affairs stood. At all costs now further efforts by Demosthenes to construct an anti-Macedonian alliance were to be resisted.

During 343, perhaps in the summer, the pro-Macedonian faction in Eretria – led by Kleitarchos, Hipparchos and Automedon – had successfully persuaded the *demos* to exile their opponents, who had probably taken refuge at Porthmos.[22] Similarly at Oreos (Histiaia), the pro-Philip group (among whom Demosthenes names Philistides, Menippos, Sokrates, Thoas and Agapaios) in summer 343 were sufficiently powerful to imprison Euphraios, the leader of the pro-Athenian group.[23] At that time, then, of the four major Euboian cities – Eretria, Oreos, Chalkis and Karystos, while the last remained favourable and allied to Athens, two were openly hostile and one (through Kallias) was actively bidding for Macedonian support.[24] For the rest of 343 and over the winter (until the time of the speech of Hegesippos *On Halonnesos*), apart from the rebuffs to Kallias in Pella and Thebes, little new had happened – and, as we have seen, this (in so far as he might easily have become involved) was probably out of deliberate abstention on Philip's part. But with his most generous offers rejected, he was no longer prepared to leave his Euboian partisans unsupported.

In the summer of 342, probably close to the time of the launching of the Thracian campaign, Hipponikos with 1000 mercenary troops crossed to the island and destroyed the walls of Porthmos, expelling the pro-Athenian Eretrians; where these went we do not know, but they were apparently unharmed.[25] This was clearly what we would regard as a 'pre-emptive strike', directed at removing a potential threat. Porthmos was a fortified place on the southern Euboic Gulf, well situated for an Athenian landing on the island. With this threat removed Hipponikos marched his mercenaries the 20 kilometres west to Eretria, where the dominance of Hipparchos, Automedon and Kleitarchos, established a year before with popular consent, may have been under challenge, and in some way confirmed the power of these three. The action on some occasions is referred to by Demosthenes as establishing a three-man 'tyranny'; on others Kleitarchos alone is called 'tyrant'. We are not informed as to the precise nature of the group's control, but should beware of according the slanders of their enemies too much weight.[26] All we may say with much confidence is that the three men *had* enjoyed popular support and that the control with which Hipponikos now supposedly invested them did not stop two further attempts at their dislodgement during the next few months. On both occasions Macedonian mercenaries, led respectively by Eurylochos and Parmenion, are said to have protected them by expelling their opponents.[27] It was perhaps at the time of his intervention (the third) at Eretria that Parmenion secured Oreos for the pro-Macedonian group. Crossing the Oreos Channel from Antron, probably in the autumn, he landed in the territory of the city, which controlled one quarter of the island.[28] In answer to the ensuing panic the commander proclaimed that he came in friendship towards the *demos* to assist in settling their internal problems, a plausible disclaimer in view of the *demos*' own actions regarding the predominance of the pro-Macedonian group. But many of the Oreitai were far from happy; while they had been prepared to pursue the Macedonian line as a useful defence against Athenian and Theban intervention, the appearance of even a 'friendly' army suggested something rather different. But in the end the dominant group won out and opened the gates, and Parmenion proceeded to take the necessary action to guarantee the authority of the 'Philippizers'.[29]

Behind this succession of Macedonian interventions in the island in 342 there was presumably some general plan on the part of Philip. But it is one which is made difficult, if not impossible for us to discern by the lack of contemporary references other than those of Demosthenes.[30] The strong impression conveyed by all his allusions is that the interventions represented no more than cynical attempts to elevate partisans to supreme power, and that the Macedonians, in so doing, acted in a provocative and distinctly anti-Athenian manner.[31] Possibly there is some truth in this. But, of all Euboian cities, probably the two with most strategic significance were Karystos (which was vital to the Athenian corn-route) and Chalkis. While the former of these was, to our knowledge, solidly pro-Athenian throughout this period,[32] there is no reason to assume that the latter did not contain a pro-Macedonian group; indeed Kallias himself, apparently the dominant political figure, had sought Macedonian aid, if in vain, a year earlier. Presumably we are to explain Philip's failure to order his generals to do for his Chalkian partisans what they did for those in Eretria and Oreos as the result of his recognition that the pro-Macedonian group in Chalkis was not sufficiently strong to be sustained in power without overt foreign support and a bloody purge of the opposition. It may be that the interventions that did occur contributed to an alienation of much Greek opinion hitherto relatively favourable towards Philip, or at least irresolute, and it is quite certain that the growth so close to home of Macedonian influence had a significant hardening effect on the Athenian outlook and aroused fears in an already apprehensive Thebes.[33] At the same time, however, the discrimination in Macedonian policy between Eretria and Oreos on the one hand and Karystos and Chalkis on the other suggests a miscalculation of public opinion on Philip's part rather than a policy of deliberate provocation. He was prepared, after the rejection of his peace-offer, to foster the growth of Macedonian centres of influence and thereby to put pressure on Athens; but he was as yet some distance from the point at which he would consider direct and unprovoked action against an Athenian ally or even install and support a minority regime where it was not vital to his interests. His policy, we might conclude, was both understandable, and from his own viewpoint, reasonable. Where he erred was in attaching insufficient weight to the capital that might be (and, in the event, was) made by such opponents as Demosthenes among the uncommitted and the wavering.

THE FINAL THRACIAN CAMPAIGN

In Thrace, by contrast, the Macedonian plans were so far progressing smoothly. They were evidently both ambitious and final. With a reconstituted Persian Empire looming as a potential ally for his Greek enemies, a tight Macedonian control as far as the straits was essential. Alliances of convenience or expedience, such as Kersebleptes had accepted to save his throne (or such as Amadokos had requested earlier for his own safety, but which his successor Teres now repudiated), were no longer sufficient in this key area, one supremely important for Macedonia both for its vast manpower and its strategic position athwart the land-communication route between West and East. In earlier years Philip had been able to rely upon a combination of such alliances, in view of the diverse, disunited nature of the Thracian tribes even when the dominance of the Odrysians was at its height.[34] But now his aim was twofold: to hold down the Thracians firmly and directly and to hem them around with a series of alliances designed to prevent their finding outside support in the future. Thus, during the first season of this campaign, Philip appears to have consolidated his influence on the southern coast of Thrace and developed new ties in the deep interior. According to the account given by Diodoros,[35] in fact, the move into Thrace was justified as having been designed to free the Greek (coastal) cities from the continuing depradations of Kersebleptes,[36] and two factors lend likelihood to this explanation. Firstly, it was a relatively acceptable motive for Philip to have proclaimed; he wished to have support – and to be seen to have it – in his final settlement of the interior. Secondly, it is clear that during the first part of the campaign (thus in late 342) he formed an alliance with Kothelas, king of the Getai, who occupied the area between Thrace and the Danube in the neighbourhood of the Schipka Pass.[37] Kothelas found himself under pressure from a Skythian southwestward movement under the dynast Ateas[38] (whom Philip in 339 would himself have to face) and was no doubt as glad to find a firm support at his rear as Philip was. Back to back the two could better face their respective enemies. The alliance was cemented by the marriage of Philip to Kothelas' daughter, Meda. Probably during the same period, late 342, Philip appears also to have visited some areas of southern coastal Thrace, at least Kardia and perhaps Ainos, the last of the Athenian bases on this coast to fall into Macedonian hands.[39]

The western and central Thracian kings Kersebleptes and Teres were therefore cordoned off completely by Macedonia and its allies by the time that the campaign proper began. Unfortunately we know little of its progress. When Demosthenes delivered his speech *On the Chersonesos* in the late spring of 341, Philip, he said, had been out of sight for ten months, hampered by illness, winter and war.[40] We are told of a number of battles, not all overwhelmingly successful,[41] but have no way of dating them. It seems likely, however, that the methodical weakening of the opposition and preparation of the country for Macedonian overlordship continued and it was perhaps during the first winter that the beginnings of a string of fortresses was established in the important Hebros valley. Following the capture of such backwoods outposts as Drongylos, Kabyle and Masteira, their fortification proceeded during the cold months. Macedonian garrisons were posted to them and were perhaps augmented by involuntary colonists from farther west, beyond the Nestos and in the Chalkidike.[42]

Colonization, though not on a vast scale, had earlier been a feature in Philip's reign. Indeed Philip's first and most outstanding colony, Philippoi, originally established as something of a showpiece, continued to flourish with its status apparently unchanged – even though, with the surrounding Thracian area between the Strymon and Nestos now annexed to Macedonia, its value as an outpost was, if not lost, at least diminished. Its impressive issues of gold, silver and bronze coinage continued to be struck, since soon after 348, on the 'Thraco-Macedonian' standard adopted by Philip for the Pella and Amphipolis mints in 359 and *c.*356 respectively.[43] Its type remained unchanged from that of the original coins struck by the Thasian colonists around 360. The purpose of Philippoi had not only been the establishment of an advanced military post beyond the then frontiers; it had also enabled the exploitation of the rich gold and silver mines in its vicinity.

In the Hebros valley, on the other hand (just as on the Illyrian and Paionian frontiers), the role of the colonies was probably in the first place military. The surrounding territory had first to be won and then protected not only against local revolt but also against southward movement down the valley from above the Rhodope massif. But there were also economic gains in prospect. A tribute of one-tenth of the land's produce was to be imposed on central and eastern Thrace and this revenue – in particular from agriculture and mining – needed collection. So that, difference in emphasis though there may have been, Philippoi served as a model for the less productive and more outlandish colonies beyond the Nestos and, in the longer term, for Alexander the Great's colonization. At some point in the process, the practice adopted in the original establishment of allowing an indigenous coinage to continue was dropped. It may be indeed that none but the first colony was granted this privilege – and at Philippoi it was not lost until more than halfway through Alexander's reign – but our knowledge of small inland Thracian coinages is hardly comprehensive enough to be certain.

Such colonies – like most Athenian cleruchies – were no doubt detested by the natives and, when we find them nicknamed 'Poneropolis' ('Roguesville' = Kabyle) or Moichopolis ('Sin City'? = Bine)[44] we need not assume that they were literally settled with criminals and adulterers, for such titles more probably reflect Thracian resentment at the colonists' local activities. The two most important establishments in the longest term were at Beroi, which has become the modern Stara Zagora, an administrative centre of importance in Bulgaria, and Philippopolis (Plovdiv) some eighty kilometres to its southwest on the right bank of the River Maritsa. Both have played a significant hellenizing role in the development of the fertile Maritsa (Hebros) Basin.

THE OPPOSITION GATHERS

From the more southern of these areas the war against Teres and Kersebleptes was fought. But by spring 341 new difficulties were arising. Apart from Philip's illness – we have no idea how serious it was or how long it lasted – he had received news, probably late in the preceding autumn, that the territorial dispute between the Athenian cleruchs of the Chersonesos and their Kardian neighbours had reached the point of violence. Our only information on the issue comes from the speech of Hegesippos in early 342, in which it is made clear that the cleruchs wished to confine the Kardians to the north shore of the peninsula overlooking the Gulf of Xeros; Agora and Paktye, which formed a close group with Kardia across the narrow neck, were to be regarded as separate from their more powerful neighbours and as part of the Athenian possessions, which would then crowd Kardia between them and the sea with no land approaches.[45] That the legal position of cleruchs in foreign territory must always be difficult is obvious enough; and the Kardians were even able to point to the existence of an Athenian statute that supported their position, at least in part. But we simply do not know the relative strength of the opposing claims, for although the Athenians had long grown used to excepting Kardia from the Chersonesos[46] – and there was no reversing that – clearly this was a dispute over the rightful extent of Kardian land; whether in fact Kardia was entitled to the whole width of the peninsula at its narrowest point. On this we have no information.

As soon as hostilities broke out, Philip and the Kardians again requested Athens to submit her claims to arbitration. Kardia appealed to Philip for assistance, but, preoccupied for the moment, he preferred to hope that Athens might at least delay to consider the plea.[47] Far from agreeing, the Athenians, or at least their cleruchs, with the assistance of their free-booting protector Diopeithes, went further. During the winter, a Macedonian herald, one Nikias, was kidnapped from Macedonian territory and taken to Athens, where his letters were read to the Assembly and their bearer imprisoned for 10 months.[48] Diopeithes and his mercenary troops then ventured into Thrace, attacked two towns and carried off the inhabitants as slaves, ravaging the surrounding countryside before retreating into the Chersonesos. When Philip despatched an envoy, Amphilochos (whether to Athens or to the Chersonesos is not clear), to treat for the release of the prisoners, Diopeithes held and tortured him and obtained a nine-talent ransom for his release. At the same time he held up merchant-ships, probably to raise money by extortion.[49]

In Athens itself there was a good deal of disquiet, which was shared by Byzantion and probably Perinthos. The latter two, both Philip's allies, were evidently beginning to doubt the king's intentions; such at least is later implied by Philip, although by late spring no sign of this was discerned by Demosthenes.[50] With his hands full in Thrace the king sent a small force, apparently of mercenaries, to assist Kardia. Simultaneously he sent back to Macedonia for reinforcements.[51] Evidently he could see that what he had intended to be the subjugation of Thrace showed signs of developing into something much bigger and that, with the possibility of actions on a number of fronts together, Thracian, Chersonesan and Byzantian, he needed more troops.[52]

Meanwhile, Demosthenes' anti-Macedonian policy bore a little fruit.[53] From Euboian Chalkis came three envoys sent to Athens by Kallias in spring or early summer 341[54] with the proposal that the two cities form a free alliance – not that Chalkis re-enter the Athenian naval league, but that Athens, as her ally, support Kallias' plans to establish a new league of the Euboian cities. As hegemon of the planned Euboian League, Chalkis, after the other cities had been brought to heel, would collect its own contributions (*syntaxeis*) and keep the whole island in close alliance with Athens, so assisting in her endeavours to build an anti-Macedonian coalition.[55] Demosthenes managed to have the scheme accepted by the *demos* – no doubt with some difficulty, since it entailed the substantial concession that these previously subject allies were now to be treated as equals.[56] The orator had the wisdom to accept Kallias' point. If Athens wanted to recover her lost influence in Euboia, she would have to modify her past stance so as to allow what passed for the legitimate expression of Euboian nationalism – even though in reality it may have been little more than the expansionism of Chalkis.

During the ensuing months, successful attacks were launched against Oreos and Eretria by the Athenian commanders Ktesiphon and Phokion, with assistance from Chalkis and Megara. Both cities were won for Athens, for the time being re-entering her league.[57] But, probably even before that, in order to hamper Macedonian communications between Thessaly and Euboia, Kallias, with assistance from his new ally, had launched a series of piratical raids on the coastal towns of the Gulf of Pagasai and on ships sailing north for Macedonia. When the Athenian people accordingly passed him a vote of thanks, this was nor just on account of his impudence towards Macedonian power – for these towns, as allies of Philip, were protected by the peace with Athens – but because his success was likely to create confidence in the other Euboian cities that it would be in league with Chalkis and alliance with Athens that Euboian interests could best be served.[58]

THE REORGANIZATION OF THRACE

But, during the same period, Philip's position in Thrace had also taken a turn for the better. Fortified with fresh troops, he pressed home the final attacks on Teres and Kersebleptes and, following their defeat perhaps in the summer, these two were removed from their thrones.[59] A Macedonian 'General of Thrace' was appointed, probably at this time, although we do not actually hear of the office before the events of 336/5, when the Lynkestian Alexandros, son-in-law of Antipatros, was allocated the post.[60] Such an appointment, while superficially innovatory, followed closely from Philip's growing experience of the difficulties of maintaining his control over extensive areas. In Thessaly, for example, whereas for a number of years after his appointment to the archonship he had been content to continue to wield his influence through this office, in 344 he had re-vamped the tetrarchic system to give himself control through favourable deputies. Similarly, in Macedonia itself, he had probably left Antipatros as regent during the Thracian campaign; later he gave his sixteen-year-old son the responsibility for the administration of the kingdom. In Thrace itself he had long realized the importance of control over the multifarious governing structures of the country. Since his earliest campaigns in western Thrace he had installed people he could trust in key positions in the local hierarchies.[61] Although now, at the end of the final overthrow of Thrace, there were some areas not firmly under control (so that both Parmenion and, apparently, Antipatros towards the end of 340, with the siege of Byzantion in progress, had to fight further campaigns in Thrace),[62] and some (perhaps many) in which no fundamental change was made to the structure of government,[63] it is likely that the Generalship over Thrace was established.[64]

The Thracians, as we have seen, were required to pay a tithe of their produce to Macedonia and no doubt were obliged to open their country to Macedonian trade and exploitation of their mines.[65] They had also to supply troops, which would serve as auxiliaries in the Macedonian army;[66] in Alexander's force they furnished both cavalry and infantry, the latter probably the typical Thracian javelin-slingers (*akontistai*) and peltasts, as well as ordinary infantry.[67]

THE OPPOSITION GROWS

Philip had been aware some months earlier of increasing strains in his relationship with Byzantion; at the same time, to Demosthenes it appeared from the outside to be as stable as before. But, following their victory in Thrace, the Macedonian forces marched north to the modern Bulgarian coastal district between the borders with Turkey to the south and the Romanian Dobrudja to the north. Nothing is known directly of this campaign, but, some twenty months later, Apollonia (Sozopol, at the southern end of the Gulf of Burgas) appears to have been already Philip's ally.[68] It is probable that, with this in mind, we should read Diodoros' reference to the Greek cities that allied themselves with Philip after his defeat of the Thracian kings as an allusion to these Black Sea colonies.[69] These were the entrepôts through which the Black Sea corn from the Maritsa and Danube Basins was extracted by the Greek merchant fleets, which would then sail via Byzantion for the Aegean with their precious cargoes. It was an area in which the Byzantian role had always been powerful but in which her merchants were now dependent on Philip's permission for its exploitation. So, when Demosthenes travelled in the autumn (341) to Byzantion, it was to exploit there the fears of the Byzantian merchants and their neighbours in Perinthos and Selymbria,[70] and when further embassies were despatched at the same time, apparently under Hypereides, to Chios and Rhodos, it was to exploit the relationship between these islanders and the

Byzantians, with whom they had fought in the Social War.[71] In none of these cases does an actual alliance seem to have resulted, but events to come would show that the Athenians were at least interpreting aright the sympathies of those they canvassed.

HERMIAS OF ATARNEUS

Beyond the Aegean, prospects looked even brighter. Only a few months before, during the early summer of 341, Demosthenes had exulted publicly that Hermias, the Atarnean dynast, had been kidnapped. Under torture, so it might be expected, he would reveal those of Philip's schemes to which he was privy. Now that Ochos would hear all of this from Philip's own 'agent', instead of in the form of Athenian complaints, it was the opportune time, the orator urged, for Athens to offer to act with the Persian King against their common enemy.[72] The Hermias affair had been an unsavoury business. The Rhodian mercenary commander Mentor, earning the Great King's gratitude for his service during the reconquest of Egypt, was entrusted with the task of strengthening the imperial hold over Asia Minor. Two relatives, his brother Memnon and brother-in-law Artabazos, both involved in earlier revolts against Persia, remained still in exile at Pella. Securing Artaxerxes' pardon for their actions, he invited them to join him in Asia Minor, where he no doubt hoped to learn something of the Asian intentions of Philip from them – although it is unlikely that they would have been allowed to leave so easily, accompanied by their large families, had they been in possession of anything very important. Indeed, at this point in Philip's reign, with the Thracian campaign still unfinished, with the Chersonesan problem barely touched and with new tensions developing between Macedonia and its Greek allies at the Hellespont, we may hardly expect that much more than hopes existed. At any rate, evidently finding no satisfaction in this direction Mentor turned to Hermias, from whom he might learn rather more of what Philip intended and, at the same time, recover for the King a thriving principality whose very existence had only come about as a result of the Persian troubles in recent decades.

Again putting his connections to work for himself, Mentor (who was the guest-friend of Hermias) promised the dynast to persuade Artaxerxes to pardon him too. Perhaps rather gullibly – although his position now looked decidedly shaky and he could expect no support from Philip for the time being – Hermias (forgetting the lesson of Xenophon) accepted the mercenary's invitation to meet in conference. He was arrested, his signet ring used to forge placatory letters to the cities under his rule and he was then delivered in chains to Artaxerxes himself. It was this news that had given Demosthenes such joy when he delivered his fourth *Philippic* in the first half of summer 341.[73]

Hermias failed to break under torture, so our tradition agrees. Allowed a statement before execution, he is reported to have asked that his friends and companions be told that he had done 'nothing weak or unworthy of Philosophy'.[74] It is unlikely, in any case, that he knew anything more than Memnon and Artabazos of Philip's plans.

DEMOSTHENES AND KALLIAS

It was in this context that another Athenian embassy visited the court of Artaxerxes Ochos. Here, as in Byzantion, Chios and Rhodos, the reception was guarded but encouraging and, while it could not reasonably be expected that any formal agreement would be reached,[75] the King was sufficiently concerned at the extension of Macedonian power virtually to the Hellespont to aid the opposing cause with money, both for the purchase of support and for the campaign at the Chersonesos.[76]

Following these successes during the autumn, and with Philip presumably still on the western Black Sea coast, Demosthenes' initiatives continued during the winter, aided by the assiduous campaigning of Kallias. When the two reported to the Athenian assembly late in winter, the Chalkian was able to assure the *demos* that the Achaians and Megarians would support a campaign against Philip and would undertake to furnish sixty talents towards the cost; the Euboian cities, he added, would provide another forty. The result of Demosthenes' mission was that all the Akarnanians were now united against Philip and that the Peloponnesos was solidly behind Athens (an exaggeration designed by Aischines, our sole source for this boast, to heighten the contrast between what his opponent promised and what eventuated) and was prepared to accept her hegemony. A meeting of delegates sent by all the interested cities was planned for 16 Anthesterion (February or March 340).[77] According to Aischines, this congress did not materialize, and there seems no good reason for disbelieving him, since such a lie, if that it was, would be easily refuted even a decade later. But no doubts as to the truth of the two reports disturbed the people's enthusiasm for their attainments, and it was an easy matter – although it took, Aischines says, a resolution 'longer than the *Iliad*' – for the triumphant Demosthenes to win the assent of the assembly for the motion he had brought with him. By its terms Chalkis was authorized to convene a *koinon* in the island of Euboia and to collect the *syntaxeis* there in Athens' stead.[78] The Euboian League now came into being – though not the Hellenic League of which Demosthenes and Kallias had given promise.[79]

PERINTHOS

His business north of Odrysian Thrace unfinished, but uncomfortably aware of the Hellespontine oppositions building up, Philip returned from the Pontic coast. Byzantion, he knew, was prepared to make a stand against him with Athenian encouragement and with indications of support from its neighbours, Perinthos and Selymbria, and from its Chian and Rhodian allies as well as from the Persian King himself. No further delay was possible. Any remaining settlement of the upland Thracian tribes, any military resistance to the southward movement of Ateas' Skythian tribes would have to wait until the Hellespont was settled. Philip prepared for action and in the spring of 340 advanced to Perinthos.[80]

What reasons he gave for this attack we are not told, nor why it was against Perinthos rather than the more crucial Byzantion that he launched the initial assault. The ancient fortifications of the latter have yet to be excavated, little having been carried out on the site which corresponds to the old city of modern Istanbul; but, in view of its wealth and of its strategic importance to all who exploited the rich Black Sea trade, it is probable that its walls were tall and thick. In fact Pausanias was to remark five centuries later that it was one of the best fortified cities he had seen in his wide travels.[81] Like Perinthos, Byzantion stood on a peninsula, almost an island. The taking of a walled city had never been an easy task in the ancient world, most falling because of starvation or treachery. It is only during Alexander's reign that this particular military exploit becomes more commonplace, and the reason is not hard to find. The development of the necessary technology was only now in train, in the 'Department of Mechanical Engineering'[82] set up by Philip under the supervision of the brilliant Thessalian engineer Polyeidos, whose apprentices Diades and Charias were to lead the vital team of technicians responsible for some of Alexander the Great's more notable successes.[83] Philip had taken a string of towns during his career. In some cases we know they fell because the gates were opened from within; in others they may have been forced into surrender by starvation. For most we have no details. But if, hand in hand with the development of torsion artillery, Macedonian siegecraft had been the subject of assiduous research and experiment from the late 350s onwards,[84] it will have been the Hellespontine campaign that offered the first major challenge to its capabilities. Good reason perhaps for choosing the less difficult (probably) of the two cities to be conquered. Perinthos in fact could be no easy task, but it was less impregnable than Byzantion.

It is easy to gather from our sources the impression that the war against Perinthos, Byzantion and Selymbria was unprovoked, brought about purely by Philip's ambition. There is of course little doubt that his longer term plans made it essential that the straits come under his control, and that he was unlikely to depend for Hellespontine security on the goodwill of these cities as his allies, without at least being very confident of their continuing support. But by this time it was clear that a rift had already opened between them and him, and it was better that the issue be fought to his time-table. In Demosthenes' mouth, the cause of the attack was Philip's desire, having failed in Euboia, to get at the Athenian corn-supply.[85] But this is not acceptable, for, beyond being more than a little Athenocentric, it ignores the effort and cost of the several months of warfare that preceded the passage of the great corn-fleet through the Propontis. This may be the reason why Athens ultimately dispensed with the pacific umbrella of the Peace of Philokrates and openly declared war, but it was only incidentally (and that particularly because of the belligerent role already played by the Athenians in Greece and at the Hellespont) Philip's motive. Philip himself, in his surviving letter of summer 340 ([Dem.] XII),[86] made no attempt to justify his action and, however easily he might pass it off as none of the Athenians' business, he would presumably have done so had there been a suitable pretext. The most reasonable comment therefore is that of Diodoros (once again, at this point, probably using the contemporary Ephoros as source), who simply remarks that Perinthos 'had opposed itself to Philip and inclined towards the Athenians'.[87] Whether or not the Perinthians had declared their change of allegiance openly, the king could not fail to have received the relevant information, as he must have known too of the Byzantian reception of Demosthenes' embassy during the previous autumn.

By this time Diopeithes was dead. Chares, transferred from a posting with mercenary forces based on Thasos, was now in charge of the Athenian effort in the Hellespontine region.[88] The additional ships and men he will have brought with him made the straits extremely dangerous for the small and unskilled Macedonian fleet, which accordingly kept its distance for the time being. (At about this time, under its commander Alkinos, it descended upon Peparethos and ravaged the island – partly, perhaps, in retaliation for the islanders' unauthorized occupation of Halonnesos, but no doubt also to discourage Athenian fleets from sailing north by the normal route, which passed close by.)[89]

Perinthos occupied an impressive site. Built on a high peninsula (that near modern Corlu) its houses rose up the slopes behind the walls like the tiers of a theatre. It could not be blocked off from the sea, so the Macedonian attack was not fully a siege.[90] All depended – and we see here, no doubt, a sign of Philip's confidence in his engineers – on opening a significant breach in the walls to enable a formation of attackers to burst through. The siege-towers, nearly 40 metres high and towering above the Perinthian parapets, were assembled and winched into place. In their outlooks artillerymen manned the new torsion catapults; the defenders had none. Philip divided his force into shifts and the attack began, continuing day and night, with a constant barrage of artillery taking a heavy toll of the defenders on the battlements, who desperately strove to hinder the sappers at work undermining the walls. Before long Perinthos was running low in manpower and arms, and appealed to Byzantion for assistance. Up to this point the Byzantians seem to have held back, possibly for fear that Philip was creating a diversion while he prepared to attack them; but they finally decided to send supplies of men, missiles and other equipment (including catapults, probably of the less efficient non-torsion type), which now made the task of the invaders' engineers, operating under artillery-fire, very much more difficult. The complexion of the battle began to change. When the Macedonians did break through, the Perinthians would block up the lanes between their houses and so create a new wall, each one higher than the last, the attackers constantly having to fight uphill.

PHILIP'S LETTER

By midsummer the situation had become impossible. The Perinthians were kept in supplies by Byzantian galleys, their deficiency in artillery (the prerogative at this time of the rich states) had been to some extent remedied and the walls could not be decisively breached. Dangerous as it might be, the only possible solution was to bring up the Macedonian fleet. In the days in which ships might be beached as soon as seaborne danger threatened, this was no insuperable problem, even when the straits were controlled by a hostile fleet – provided that a friendly coastline could be guaranteed. But in this case much of the nearer coastline was controlled by the Athenian cleruchs in the Chersonesos, so that the landfalls would be even more dangerous than Chares' fleet between them. This Philip had in mind from the outset or, presumably, he would have made earlier use of his fleet than he did. In the light of the warlike actions of Athens' cleruchs over the past eighteen months and more, especially now that the reactions from their home-city had confirmed the support they enjoyed there, it was a risk that could not be taken. Military support had to be provided and the fleet brought into play. Philip despatched a part of his army to the Chersonesos. Since his troops could not simply march around the coast, the terrain in many places posing formidable barriers to such passage, it is probable that the force was divided into two or more, which then marched in turn to each successive landfall required by the ships.[91] Such an action was technically in breach of the peace, it being unlikely that Philip had obtained prior permission – or even delayed to ask for it – to order troops on to the soil of a state that remained technically his ally. His troops desisted from any hostile action, but the march could well provide Athens with an excuse – if she wanted one – for declaring war. Philip accordingly despatched immediately a message to that city ('Philip's Letter' = [Dem.] XII).[92]

The letter represents an interesting piece of diplomatic bluff, not so much in what it says as in what it is intended to achieve. On the one hand, it is strongly condemnatory of the acts of war committed by Athens since the autumn or winter of 342; it deals firmly with Athenian complaints over Macedonian actions in Thrace, in support of Kardia, against Peparethos and in escorting the fleet past the Chersonesos. On the other hand, there is no sign that this letter is in any way either a declaration of war or even a final ultimatum.[93] As Demosthenes had had occasion to notice only recently, it would have been most uncharacteristic (and not a little naïve) of Philip to broadcast his intention in such a way; he had been more inclined in the past to go to war while protesting friendship. To declare himself at war with Athens at a time when his Hellespontine difficulties were demanding vast resources would have been madness. The letter was intended rather to *delay* any direct Athenian intervention.[94] Philip knew that, since the opening of hostilities by Diopeithes and the approval given to him by the Athenian people, the state had been inevitably committed to war once the opportunity offered. But in nearly two years the level of action had not been significantly increased. The king therefore judged, correctly, that he would best delay Athens' wholehearted entry – which might easily have resulted from his violation of Chersonesan sovereignty – by directing his appeal, in effect, to those Athenians (a minority) who did not want war and those (altogether evidently a majority) who would hesitate until it seemed unquestionably the most profitable course. To this end he designed his argument to show Athens clearly in the wrong and himself as acting only out of necessity. When the letter was read to the assembly, we may imagine, it sparked off sufficient controversy to prevent any move towards committing the state to battle. Athens took no official steps to aid Perinthos. With a little more time at his disposal Philip concentrated on the task at hand.

BYZANTION

By this time there were 30,000 troops under his command. But he still had Byzantion to contend with and, even more seriously, Persian assistance was now complicating the Perinthian siege. Artaxerxes Ochos had written to his satraps in northwestern Asia Minor ordering them to give all possible aid. A force of mercenaries under the Athenian-born mercenary leader Apollodoros, who at the time was in the service of Arsites of Phrygia, was sent to Perinthos, along with money, food, arrows and other reserve materials.[95] The result was that Philip could not take the city; his own fleet was evidently too weak to deny naval entry to the supplies. In assisting its ally, however, Byzantion had seriously depleted its own resources, presumably confident that there would be no Macedonian attack against itself.[96] This, the king decided, would be his next move.

Byzantion, as we have noticed, was well fortified and open to the sea. Whether or not we ought to give much credit to the ancient tradition that its citizens were an unruly and unwarlike lot,[97] we may conclude that, in its weakened state, it might fall more easily if a surprise attack were launched against it. Alternatively, with their own forces inadequate to meet Philip in battle, rather than see their surrounding territory laid waste while they were confined to the defence of their battlements, the Byzantians might well decide to surrender. In this case too, speed would be essential because the greatest obstacle in the way of Byzantian submission would be the blandishments of Athens, whose assurances of support had presumably been conveyed by Demosthenes as early as the preceding autumn and no doubt since.

The siege of Perinthos had failed and must now have been written off. That Philip left a force there, perhaps under Parmenion, who had been called to Thrace,[98] means only that the Macedonian line of communications had at all costs to be preserved; the Perinthians must therefore remain circumscribed by land. For the same reason, while en route to Byzantion, he detailed a small force to invest Selymbria – not because it was a city of any importance but because, as the ally of Byzantion and situated on the coastal road to the latter, it offered to his enemies a base from which his supply-route could be blocked.[99]

On his arrival at Byzantion he found the gates closed to him. The inhabitants were not interested in surrender; the assurances they had received from Athens and from their own allies and the indications they had seen of Artaxerxes' interest in Perinthos gave them the necessary confidence to resist. The king was however not yet deterred, particularly since, with Perinthos intact behind him, his general credibility was at stake. He remembered well the results of his defeat in 353 by Onomarchos, how it had taken him as long as three years to repair the damage caused to his earlier arrangements by news of that failure. A siege was possible, but it would probably be lengthy and would not be complete while his fleet remained too weak to clear the Propontis of the ships of Chares and of Chios, Rhodos and the Persians. However, there was more than one way to cook a boar; as before, his best hope of a quick solution was to induce the Byzantians to surrender. This could be achieved most readily by creating among them the impression of isolation. On the one hand, he could concentrate on detaching those allies – such as Chios and Rhodos – who had no real stake in the issue – provided that they could be assured that their Black Sea interests would not be damaged. On the other, he could demonstrate that Athens was powerless to assist the defenders.

ATHENS DECLARES WAR

At this time of the year (August or September) the great Athenian corn-fleet would be arriving in groups to muster (often with ships from other cities) for the voyage through the Hellespont and down the Aegean.[100] For at least the first part of the route, Chares' warships would provide an escort and he was accordingly waiting near Hieron for the stragglers to arrive, when he was called away to a conference with the satraps who were supporting Perinthos. In his absence the Macedonian fleet descended upon the merchant-ships and captured every one, a total of 230. Of these, 50 appear to have been neutrals (and perhaps Chian and Rhodian), which he let go. The 180 Athenian ships raised for Philip 700 talents' worth of booty plus large quantities of timber of use for the siege of Byzantion, food, hides and other goods.[101]

As soon as word reached him at Byzantion that this coup had been successful, Philip quickly drafted and despatched to Athens another letter. In this he affected to believe that the Athenian merchantmen had been bound for Selymbria, and accused them of giving aid to the enemies of Macedon without even the pretext of a treaty. This he charged, was an act of war. When these words had been read to the Athenian assembly, its response was blunt. Philip, affirmed Demosthenes, had now openly repudiated the Peace of Philokrates. The Athenians were justified in meeting war with war. The *demos* agreed.[102]

It is hardly conceivable that after the capture of the corn-fleet the Athenian decision could have been anything but what it was, and one may therefore wonder why Philip bothered to fabricate an excuse that both he and the Athenians knew to be spurious. No one, friend or foe, could doubt that he had welcomed an injection of funds and supplies for his army. All could see that he had needed to demonstrate the inability of Athens to protect her own interests, let alone those of the Byzantians, whom she had encouraged to take on this war. And, perhaps most of all, he had intended to show his own allies (and perhaps even his Macedonian soldiers) that two unsuccessful sieges reflected no weakening of his power. But if he had good reason for pushing Athens over the brink, it was equally important to him that, in doing so, he provoke the formation of no anti-Macedonian coalition. This was in any case unlikely, for the action was too far from the bulk of the Greek states to produce any panic reaction on their part. But, no doubt, the Athenians would do their very best to win support; and it was to provide the uncommitted majority with a pretext for remaining aloof that the king strove to cloud the issue by charging that the fleet he had captured had been despatched to the aid of his enemies.[103] It would be a war, he hoped, that Athens would have to fight with no more allies than the paltry remnants of her naval league and, at most, the like-minded states already involved in the Propontis.

CHAPTER VII

340–337
THE SECOND GREEK SETTLEMENT

WAR IN THE NORTH

THE SIEGE OF BYZANTION, which in the event turned out for Philip no better than the assault on Perinthos, was nevertheless an event of some significance. So far as we can tell, the Persian assistance of the earlier campaign was not repeated.[1] Artaxerxes Ochos, whose sympathies had been at the very best lukewarm, now decided that after the loss of her corn-fleet Athens would be obliged to involve herself openly in hindering Philip's activities; Persia could accordingly withdraw and allow the Greek powers to do to each other what injuries they might. The Macedonian mountain, constructed by Greek intelligence over the past years, appeared no more than a Balkan molehill.

On the Athenian side, the outbreak of war brought mixed results. We have already noticed an unjustifiable tendency to magnify the diplomatic achievements of Demosthenes between 343 and 340; no less than an anti-Macedonian 'Hellenic League' has been manufactured *ex nihilo* and attributed to the orator's personal efforts.[2] Certainly, after the war transferred to central Greece itself, late in 339, issues that were, a year and more earlier, a good deal less clear, crystallized in Greek thinking; and one might at most say that Demosthenes' diplomacy had created the groundwork for some of the alignments that formed then. But if, as Aischines later alleged, his opponent really boasted early in 340 that he had lined up behind Athens the Akarnanians, all of the Peloponnesians, as well (implicitly) as the Euboians,[3] then the Athenian people, who were so appreciative of his services at the time, must have been sorely disappointed in the autumn of the same year. Although the immediate cause of the war (which Philip admittedly attempted to obscure with his final letter)[4] had been a successful Macedonian strike at her very lifeline, when Athens went to war she attracted no allies beyond the pathetic remnants of her naval alliance. Other than the three principals – Byzantion, Athens and Philip – the only known independent participants were the Chians, Rhodians and Koans, who were all – since their joint revolt during the Social War – the allies not of the Athenians but of Byzantion. It may be that some of the members of Athens' league felt inspired to contribute wholeheartedly (and, not surprisingly, the little island of Tenedos, a mere 20 km. from the mouth of the Hellespont, was foremost among them);[5] and it may be that the aid furnished by the fleets of Chares and then Phokion played a significant role in Philip's failure to take the great city. But the facts are that Athens intervened directly at the Propontis only when her own grain-supply was cut, and, when she did decide to fight the war she herself had provoked, she added to the defence of her new ally little more than that fraction of her own resources that she herself was prepared to commit.

Since Chares was already in the area with a fleet of forty ships and his mercenaries, he was ordered to the relief of Byzantion, whence he drove the Macedonian fleet back into the Bosporos; there, with aid from Byzantian galleys, he struck again, forcing Philip's admiral Demetrios into the Black Sea. At the Propontine entrance to the Bosporos he established a base from which he was able to control the naval passage in both directions.[6] With his fleet paralysed, Philip (with his engineer, Polyeidos) applied all his ingenuity to the assault on the city walls, but to no avail. A nocturnal attempt by stealth came nearest to success, but was thwarted by the barking of dogs.[7]

From Athens a second force was despatched. Chares' fleet was not particularly large and Chares himself was regarded with less than warmth by the Byzantians, in part, perhaps, because he had failed to protect the corn-fleet, but probably, in the main, because of his leading part in the naval campaigns against them and their allies during the Social War.[8] By the time the new force arrived, under Phokion's command, the winter must have been close. The king by now realized that he could not win this war. Maintaining the siege during the winter, he considered what action he should now take.

There is no doubt that these two significant failures, watched with interest and anticipation by the Aegean and Balkan world, had damaged Philip's prestige. The effects on his own soldiers, who suffered their first serious rebuffs for more than a dozen years, must also have given him concern. As if to cast his own ineffectiveness in sharper relief, Alexander, regent in Macedonia since the Byzantian siege had begun, had met only with success in his role. With the invasion-army occupied in the Propontine area, some of the less accessible Thracian tribes not directly subject to Philip had seized the opportunity to revolt, and both Parmenion and Antipatros were involved in their suppression.[9] Near the same time, the Maidoi, a troublesome tribe inhabiting the upper

Strymon valley below (east of) Mt Kerkine, had rebelled, and they may have found support among the Danthaletai, their equally irrepressible neighbours.[10] Alexander himself, sixteen years old, led an army up the Axios valley, then cut eastwards along the course of the present-day Bregalnitsa and descended into Maidic territory.[11] When he had put down the revolt he followed his father's example by founding a military colony, naming it Alexandropolis.[12]

Towards the end of winter 340/39, Philip determined to cut his losses at Byzantion. Shortly beforehand, he had answered a plea from Ateas, the Skythian king, for military assistance. The latter, who had regarded him as a natural ally in the effort to destroy Byzantian influence on the western Pontic coast, found himself hard pressed by some of his neighbours and made his approach through the medium of Apollonia, which had probably been Philip's ally since summer/autumn 341. Troops were detached from the main force and sent to support him, but found, on their arrival, that the problem had been resolved without their aid. They were abruptly and rudely dismissed and reported back to the king that not only had his generosity been rebuffed, but even the expenses of their march had been refused them.[13] This boded ill for the future of the northern and northeastern settlement of Thrace, arranged by means of the treaties with the Getai and the Pontic Greek coastal towns. After the years of cumulative effort expended in Thrace, culminating in its establishment as a Macedonian dependency, the new security could not be permitted to collapse through Skythian pressure.

Not until spring would the weather be suitable for pressing northwards through the Thracian mountains, and, meanwhile, the Macedonian forces – and prestige – had to be extricated from the Black Sea and its approaches with as little further damage as possible. To begin with, Philip sounded out some of the opposing participants with a view to peace. The Chians and Rhodians in particular, since they had little at stake in this war, he cultivated by pointedly returning any of their ships that fell into his hands. Their good offices might assist him in reaching a settlement with the Byzantians,[14] but, in any case, the removal of their ships from the Hellespont – or, at the very least, the reduction of their will to continue the war – would make the escape of his own fleet the easier to effect. However, it still had to elude the Athenian squadron blocking the Bosporos and then to pass along the Chersonesan coast, where, if it had escaped, it would meet with much more overt hostility than had threatened it in the previous summer when it passed in the opposite direction. He laid his plans.[15]

To Antipatros, perhaps still in command of a force in Thrace, he addressed a despatch containing the information that Thrace had risen in revolt and had cut off the Macedonian detachments and garrisons there from supplies and relief. Abandon all other matters, the letter ordered, and leave the Propontine coast for the trouble-spot. The message was false and was designed not for his commander but for the enemy, into whose hands Philip contrived to have it fall. Word quickly reached the Athenian squadron at the Bosporos, which immediately set sail for the Aegean coast of Thrace – and allowed the Macedonian fleet to penetrate into the Propontis without hindrance.[16] Philip had indeed left Byzantion,[17] as his false despatch had said, but it was to lead troops into the Chersonesos, where he now repeated in reverse the action of a year earlier, escorting his fleet along the hostile coast. On this occasion the troops were under no such constraint as had deterred them in the previous summer from adding any hostile act to their actual presence, and, while it is unlikely that they wasted time on capturing cities, as Justin says, they appear to have ravaged some of the countryside on their route.[18] Phokion, when he discovered the trick, remained in northern waters for a time, but in the course of rather futile manœuvres against Macedonian coastal possessions and shipping he was wounded and sailed disconsolately for home.[19] He personally had not wanted this war in the first place; he had been dragooned into replacing Chares, tricked into losing the Macedonian fleet and disheartened by a fruitless campaign against a coastline practically invulnerable to it. His preparedness to talk peace with Philip after (and perhaps even before) Chaironeia, although his support for the ensuing Peace of Demades was qualified, would assist in bringing about a settlement that spared Attika direct invasion by the victorious Macedonians in late 338.[20]

How far Philip went in pressing for peace with his opponents at the Propontis, we do not know. Diodoros refers to a treaty with 'the Athenians and the other Greeks who opposed him', but, as Demosthenes makes clear, Athens made no such agreement.[21] The Chians and Rhodians do not again appear among his enemies, and it should perhaps be assumed that his offers to these islanders were accepted.[22] Whether the alliances of Macedon with Byzantion and Perinthos were now revived is more difficult to answer. The Suda quotes a letter allegedly written by Philip to the people of the former 'when [he] was beaten off from Byzantion', in which he alluded to the receipt of his money by Leon, the pro-Athenian leader of the city. As a result, so the account continues, the people surrounded Leon's house, driving him to suicide.[23] In 336/5, Byzantion was the ally of Macedon; and this story suggests that its return to the former allegiance followed the raising of the siege. It may well be that as the campaign finished the

Byzantians realized how exposed they would now be to Persian interests as their allies came to terms with Philip or, in the case of Athens, concentrated their efforts on their own defence.[24]

THE SKYTHIAN CAMPAIGN

The Skythian campaign, which occupied Philip's forces during the spring and early summer of 339,[25] was presumably undertaken for good reason. During the years of the first war with Athens (357–346), the king had been able for long periods virtually to ignore the existence of his enemy; but now, with the second war declared, with Athens considerably stronger than during and after her Social War and with some doubts raised as to the steadfastness of some of his Greek allies, he will presumably have allowed only serious matters to divert him from his most pressing need, that for a new Greek settlement. It is therefore unfortunate that our sources for this brief expedition are so scant and, except in one case, uncircumstantial.

How far back the king's dealings with Ateas went we do not know. For some time, Skythian influence had been felt south of the Danube, apparently as the result of the expansionist drive of this particular leader, rather than through pressure of more northern population-movements.[26] Philip's expedition to the western coastal areas of the Pontos in 341 can scarcely have been made without some sort of contact with these people, who inhabited the more northerly of the inland areas behind the Greek colonies with which Philip had formed alliances at the time.[27] Indeed, it is hardly more likely that the even earlier contacts with Kothelas and his Getai (late 342) were effected without at least taking their northern neighbours into account.

At any rate, as we have seen, the relationship (whatever its nature) between Ateas and Philip broke down. The victory the king could anticipate winning would compensate his troops for their morale-lowering failures in front of Perinthos and Byzantion and prepare them more effectively for the expected campaign in Greece. As the Macedonian army marched to the north, a despatch was sent ahead, asserting that the king had sworn during the siege of Byzantion to erect a statue of his ancestor Herakles at the mouth of the River Istros (Danube), an obligation he now wished to fulfil. He requested safe passage, as a friend, to that point. Ateas refused, offering at best to erect the statue himself and to leave it unmolested, if Philip would have it consigned to him; but, if he should set it up in spite of the Skythians, they would remove it afterwards and melt it down for arrowheads. The badinage over, the Macedonians arrived in the

Skythian area (the Romanian Dobrudja) and, in a single battle, defeated their opponents. Ateas, aged nearly ninety, fell during the fighting.[28]

It turned out that, so far as precious metals were concerned, the Skythian territory was as barren as Ateas had claimed when refusing to pay the Macedonian military expenses in the previous year; but, the district being very fertile, there was other booty to be had, and the victors struck out westwards for home laden down with 20,000 young prisoners and large numbers of brood mares and cattle. Their route probably took them across the north of Haimos (the Balkan Mountains), through the Isker valley to the area of Sofia and thence down the Strymon to the Doberos (Strumitsa). This, in turn, led farther west to the Axios, whose more spacious passes eventually gave on to the Emathian Plain. But, while still in the Danubian Plain, they had to pass through Triballian territory, and it was here that, weighed down and slowed by their Skythian booty, they suffered a setback. The tribesmen refused to let the army pass until they were given a share of the spoils. Unsatisfied, they attacked. During the fighting, Philip was wounded in the thigh by a blow so heavy that it killed his horse under him. At first thinking him dead, his men made no attempt to save the booty; by the time they realized he was still alive, it was lost. They pressed onwards, arriving back in Pella in middle to late summer.[29]

The battles of the past three years had brought, to the very end, the most mixed fortunes to the Macedonian army. But, in spite of the setbacks, the vast rugged area of Thrace could now be regarded as a dependency and a source of revenue and manpower. If the Hellespontine area was as yet far from secure, that did not matter greatly so long as the Thracian hinterland remained firmly under control. And, if the problem of the Triballoi remained unsolved, that could await a future time; control of the Axios and Hebros passes would in the meantime prevent any large-scale intrusion on their part into the central areas of Macedonia or Thrace.

Although the troops may have arrived home as early as July/August 339, Philip remained inactive for perhaps three months. He had, of course, to recover from his thigh-wound; but, more importantly, the arrangements he had made, before the Skythian campaign, with his Amphiktyonic representatives (Theodoros and Nikanor)[30] had yet to bear the fruit he intended.

AMPHISSA AND THE AMPHIKTYONS

In the early spring, soon after the raising of the siege of Byzantion, the Amphiktyonic Council had convened at Delphoi under its Thessalian president, Kottyphos.[31] It was a meeting probably anticipated with foreboding at Athens, for, whether or not any hints of the king's plan were known before the Athenian elected delegates (the *pylagorai*: Aischines, Meidias and Thrasykles) and the annually appointed *hieromnemon* (Diognetos)* arrived for the Pylaia, the Athenians realized that some move against them was in the air. Although Philip was at the moment far away, the timing of the war between him and Athens was entirely in his hands; and it was so highly probable that he would choose to continue his isolation of the Athenians by means of this Council that they took the precaution of electing as their delegates men who were well regarded by its more influential members.[32] At Delphoi they received word that the Lokrians of Amphissa would propose a motion condemning them for impiety over a matter which had probably arisen during the years in which the temple had been under Phokian control. They had dedicated (or, more probably, re-dedicated) to Apollo shields captured from Persians and Thebans during the Persian Wars, but they had done so before the temple had been re-consecrated. The dedication – 'the Athenians, [captured] from the Medes and Thebans when they fought against the Hellenes' – well reflected Athenian feelings towards Thebes during the Sacred War, but was a source of embarrassment by 339, when Thebes had moved much closer to being a potential ally against Philip. Since Diognetos and Meidias had been struck down by fever (whether pathological or political is never clear), Aischines hastily entered the august synod after the *pylagorai* of the other states had left and the *hieromnemones* were about to begin their deliberations. Attacked by one of the Lokrian councillors (probably one Kallikron from Amphissa), Aischines launched into a bitter counter-attack against Amphissa, which had evidently been in violation for some years of Amphiktyonic regulations governing the use of the sacred Plain of Kirrha below Delphoi and of the adjoining harbour.

Philip's tactics were now clear. Aischines could hardly have doubted that the king stood behind the Lokrian charge. Were it accepted by the Council, Athens would be due for punishment for impiety. In that case, there was every possibility that the *demos* would refuse to pay the fine – which was said to be fifty talents, according to the plan. Another Sacred War would ensue, this time with Athens isolated from all the Amphiktyons and alone facing Philip at the head of all his allies.

Aischines' oratory – and no doubt his standing among the Councillors – carried the debate. Afterwards a herald proclaimed the decision. On

* For the *hieromnemones* present at this meeting see Table 4 on p. 135.

the following morning, all the young men of Delphoi and all the assembled Amphiktyonic officers and delegates would meet to vindicate Apollo's claim on the sacred land and harbour. The question of Athenian impiety was never again raised. The next day, the sacred band tramped down the steep, winding road on to the plain, where it demolished the offending harbour-installations and burned down houses before an Amphissian attack sent it scurrying back to Delphoi. Again the *hieromnemones* conferred and, on the third morning, Kottyphos convened an Amphiktyonic Assembly, to which all delegates and all others in Delphoi on religious business were bidden. At the end of this conclave it was solemnly announced that, before the autumn Pylaia, an extraordinary synod would meet at Thermopylai to declare war on Amphissa – presumably so long as satisfaction were not offered in the meantime.[33]

So far Aischines had done what he had to do; and Demosthenes, although nine years later he was to put a different interpretation to it, must have approved. But it was back in Athens, when both Boulē and Assembly had given their blessing, that the fundamental antithesis in the policies of these two orators clearly emerged. Aischines may have hoped that the promises of Philip in 346 might still be realized, that the king and the Athenians might yet be reconciled and Thebes humbled. Demosthenes, on the other hand, while he had always been circumspect, in his (known) references to Thebes between 346 and 340, had nevertheless worked carefully for the day when he might bring their powerful neighbour into alliance against Philip.[34] It was known that Thebes was sympathetic to Amphissa – probably for the latter's anti-Phokian sentiments during the third Sacred War and, more recently, because of a natural Lokrian antipathy towards the near-by Delphians, whose position in the Amphiktyony Philip had so measurably increased and who no doubt added their two votes constantly to the pro-Macedonian majority. Both Aischines and Demosthenes suspected rightly that Thebes would support the Amphissian cause. If war were declared, then, at Thermopylai, Thebes would abstain. The question was: would Athens? If the Athenians were to join the crusade, they might thereby avert war with Philip, who, if – as was inevitable – he were called upon by his Amphiktyonic allies, would be obliged to treat first with Athens; such was presumably the hope of Aischines. But this would be achieved only at the cost of an irretrievable rift with Thebes; and to this Demosthenes was unwaveringly opposed.

What had been achieved, in fact, was the reconstruction of the situation of Skirophorion 346. Again, and even more clearly than before, the Thebans had been manœuvred on to the wrong side. If they should refuse to assist in the punishment of the Amphissian sacrilege, they would be open to the same charge. Athens, again, had the opportunity to join the majority side. Again, Demosthenes was instrumental in destroying the plan. Operating through a colleague on the Boulē, he had a *probouleuma* framed and, then in the Assembly, passed, declaring that Athens would not participate in the Thermopylai meeting. The city, like Thebes, would abstain. When or if Philip intervened, he would have to do so without the support either of his enemy or of his most dangerous ally. By their initial approval of Aischines' report and recommendations, the people had – perhaps unintentionally – given notice that they would, in effect, support Philip against Thebes. Thanks to Demosthenes, they reversed this decision and made their stand in Thebes' favour against Philip. How much of the implications the majority realized we do not know.[35]

Not long afterwards, perhaps in May or June, the synod convened at Thermopylai declared war as expected and elected Kottyphos general of the Amphiktyons. When the campaign actually began, it became clear that it was a charade. Few members bothered to participate and those that did, largely Thessalians, attempted little more than to impose on Amphissa a fine (to be paid by the autumn Pylaia)[36] and to order into exile certain leaders said to be responsible for the impieties. The only effect – the only possible effect – was to provoke the defendant into refusing to comply. Philip may have been far away in the north, but the scene was already set for his entry into central Greece, again as the defender of Apollo – but this time as the enemy of Athens and, potentially, of Thebes. This was a potential already close to actuality, as Demosthenes knew. Thebes would not re-admit the king to central Greece under such terms, and now, secure in the knowledge that, if the worst happened, Athens must ally herself with them, the Thebans seized the Thessalian garrison at Nikaia, expelled the troops and replaced them with their own.[37] Thermopylai was closed to Philip.

This was the situation of which the king was informed on his return to Pella. He had first to recover from his wound, but, in any case, there was no action he could take before official conferment of the Amphiktyonic hegemony upon him at the autumn Pylaia (October). After that, he had before him substantially the same two alternatives as in 346. Again, the choice between them was in the hands of Athens. But there was a serious difference, which made this second confrontation very much more dangerous than the first: in this, Thebes would probably be against him whatever Athens should decide; and all indications to date were that he would have to face both. It was, in short, the very combination he had striven to avoid through his planned settlement of 346, and it stands, for good or ill, as the greatest achievement of Demosthenes' career.

ELATEIA

At the autumn Pylaia all went according to plan. The Amphissians refused to pay their fine. They had restored the men exiled by Kottyphos' troops and re-exiled those restored at that time. Sacrilege had been committed and now compounded. To the Amphiktyons there remained a simple choice: either they must commit their own tribes to financial levies and the provision of troops or mercenaries, or they must call upon Philip to carry the burden. By late October, the king received word that he was Hegemon of the Amphiktyons.[38]

With all speed he marched south. The main alternative route into central Greece, once he had reached the Gulf of Malia, lay through the mountainous passes of Oitaia to the town of Herakleia Tracheia and thence to Dorian Kytinion. The Oitaians and Dorians were his allies, as also were their immediate neighbours, the Phthiotians, Dolopians, Ainianes and Aitolians. The Amphissians, farther south on the same route, were thus tightly hemmed in, with Delphoi at their rear. At Kytinion the road forks. To the south, between Parnassos and Korax (Mt Giona), ran the road to Amphissa; to the east the upper Kephisos valley led to Elateia and the Boiotian frontier. The former, in view of his commission, was the expected course, but the latter he took. Leaving some troops to fortify Kytinion, the rest of the army hurried down the Kephisos into Phokis and seized and fortified Elateia.[39]

In this march, speed had been vital – not so much to forestall any pre-emptive action by Athens or Thebes, but – even more important – in order to present the latter with an unexpected fait accompli; their defensive position at Nikaia suddenly turned (for Elateia lay between Thermopylai and Thebes), they could now be offered the chance to return to the obligations of their alliance with Macedonia.

In the practice of diplomacy, no matter how stern the ultimatum one decides to issue, it is almost axiomatic that, unless one wishes to drive the recipient to war, one must allow him an avenue for withdrawal without unacceptable loss of face. Five months or less earlier, when Kottyphos, at the head of Amphiktyonic forces, had laid down the terms of the Amphissian punishment, the alternatives for the latter had been to accept a humiliating fine and political intervention, climaxing the already unpalatable events at the spring Pylaia, or to refuse, and so, in effect, to declare war on the League. The Amphissians had really had no choice – and this, no doubt, was the intention of the Amphiktyonic majority. In the November confrontation between Philip and the Thebans, the reverse was the case. In his advance, the king had established himself at Kytinion, opening the way to Amphissa, and at Elateia, opening the way to Thebes; but he had encroached on the territory of neither. He now despatched an embassy to the Thebans. Led by the Macedonians Amyntas and Klearchos and comprising two of the Thessalian tetrarchs, Daochos and Thrasydaios,[40] and representatives from Ainis, Aitolia, Dolopia and Phthiotis, the envoys requested only two concessions of the Thebans: that they should hand over Nikaia and that, as Philip's allies, they either join him in an attack on Attika or at least allow him passage through their territory. The former request was reasonable. Nikaia was now quite irrelevant to the strategic situation, and it was to be surrendered not to Macedonia or to Thessaly but to the Epiknemidian Lokrians, within whose state it lay and whose valid claim to it had been by-passed when it was stripped from Phokis in 346.[41] The latter request was equally palatable. Thebes was not asked to participate in the sacred issue regarding Amphissa, to which she had already, in effect, declared her opposition. She did not even have to endure the distaste of serving the interests of Macedonia, for which she had lost all sympathy. She had not yet repudiated her alliance with Philip, and now all that was required was acquiescence in his passage across her territory. With Athens now committed, thanks to Demosthenes, to maintaining herself at war, Philip, by the terms he offered, made it clear that he did not wish to drive Thebes too into opposition.[42]

THE THEBAN/ATHENIAN ALLIANCE

The occupation of Elateia caused consternation at Thebes, but, although it was practically on the Boiotian border, its impact, since the Thebans' fate lay entirely in their own hands, was felt even more strongly at Athens. It was evening when the news arrived. Preparations for an early morning assembly were made against a background of panic and rumour.[43] As the Boulē met at daybreak, the citizens gathered on the Pnyx. When the *bouleutai* arrived and the news was officially reported, there was silence. Not surprisingly. There was one man who must speak: the man whose provocative policies, whose steadfast opposition to the Peace of Philokrates, which he himself had aborted before it was fully born, and whose motion of war in autumn 340 had now brought Philip almost to the doorstep of Athens.

Demosthenes responded with consummate skill. For years he had worked to moderate the traditional anti-Theban feelings of his fellows.

The time had now come to put into effect the policy on which he had planned since 346. The Athenians, he proposed, must mobilize all men of military age, infantry and cavalry, and march out to Eleusis, the first point on the road to Thebes. So much to demonstrate that the Athenians meant business. Next, ten envoys must be appointed with authority to negotiate, in consultation with the generals, towards alliance with the Thebans, and to regulate the ensuing military campaign. Thirdly, the envoys must offer alliance to the Thebans not as to superiors or to saviours but as to those in need of assistance, as a favour to a Thebes 'in extremities' by an Athens wise enough to assess the common need and strong enough to deliver the goods.[44]

The proposal was accepted with relief. Demosthenes drafted a decree to establish the embassy and was himself appointed its chief negotiator.[45] Travelling with all speed, the envoys reached Thebes to find the enemy embassy already there, ready to put its case. When Philip's ultimatum had been heard, the Athenians took the floor; but on this – on the actual proposals made and on the terms finally agreed upon – Demosthenes, in his account of the whole affair, is absolutely silent, passing quickly from the Macedonian statement to the joining of Athenian and Theban forces when the alliance had been formed.[46]

When we turn to Aischines' account,[47] we appreciate the reason for his opponent's reserve. First, the envoys repudiated all previous Athenian support for the autonomy of the Boiotian cities: 'if any city stand apart from the Thebans, the Athenians will assist the Boiotians, those in Thebes.' Secondly, on the question of leadership and expense: Thebes was given the supreme command by land, but was asked to pay only one third of the costs, Athens bearing the remainder;[48] by sea, the Athenians were to bear the full cost but to share the command. The joint war-office, with responsibility for strategy and troop-dispositions, was to be located (with more justification, since it was closer to the immediate sphere of operations) at Thebes, manned by the Boiotarchs and the Athenian envoys and generals.[49] It is no wonder that Demosthenes preferred to pass over all this, for the contrast between what he had promised the Athenians and what he eventually conceded at Thebes could hardly be sharper. He had left Athens as the confident plenipotentiary of the state with much to offer and little to gain; he had arrived in Thebes cap in hand, prepared to concede anything to achieve his end.[50]

Whatever Philip had really expected to achieve when he despatched his 'panhellenic' embassy to Thebes – and, as we have seen, his terms were such as to allow his ally to back down without serious loss of face – his embassy was ultimately unable to prevail against Theban mistrust and Athenian bellicosity. The Thebans found the Athenian alliance preferable to a return to the uncertainties of their relationship with Philip. Nevertheless, they drove a very hard bargain; and one may speculate that, had the details of it not been easily overlooked in the hectic months ahead, had the Thebans not been defeated and ultimately destroyed (in 335), or had the alliance been victorious and had the victors then turned to the division of spoils, Demosthenes in later years would have disclaimed responsibility as eagerly for the Theban alliance as for the Peace of Philokrates.

THE MANNING OF THE DEFENCES

But, for the moment, the triumph was all his. The army of the Athenians joined forces with the Boiotians in Thebes and the joint strategy was planned. This laid heavy emphasis on the land and, apparently, none at all on the sea. The immediate threat was, of course, by land; but pressure might have been brought to bear on Philip's allies in the north,[51] and, at the very least, a fleet might usefully have been sent to the Korinthian Gulf to strengthen Naupaktos and to back up the efforts by land to prevent Philip's making contact with his Peloponnesian allies. The king controlled Thermopylai itself, which he fortified, but this was of no offensive use to him while Nikaia remained in enemy hands.[52] He held the mountain route to Kytinion and the upper Kephisos valley as far as Elateia, which, as we have seen, put him within striking distance of both Amphissa (and thus the Korinthian Gulf itself) and the Boiotian Plain. The strategy adopted by the allies, therefore, was to block both of these routes. Acting quickly – while Philip continued to negotiate[53] – they despatched 10,000 mercenaries to Amphissa, where, under the command of the Theban Proxenos and the Athenian Chares, they took up a position a few kilometres to the north in the Gravia Pass.[54] The main army established itself at Parapotamioi, where the Kephisos passes, by way of a narrow gap between Mts Parnassos and Hedylion, from the Phokian Plain (the upper Kephisos valley) to the Boiotian Plain. By fortifying such Phokian towns (presumably destroyed in 346) as Lilaia and Ambrysos, they blocked the high routes through Mt Parnassos, thus building a defensive line along its northern slopes, facing the Macedonian line on the northern side of the Kephisos.[55] Provided the passes were not lost, the acropolis of Parapotamioi was a strong position; and, if it were to fall, a retreat of less than ten kilometres would bring the defenders to the gap between Mts Petrachos and Akontion, on the southern side of which the town and acropolis of Chaironeia were situated. Only if that too failed to hold would

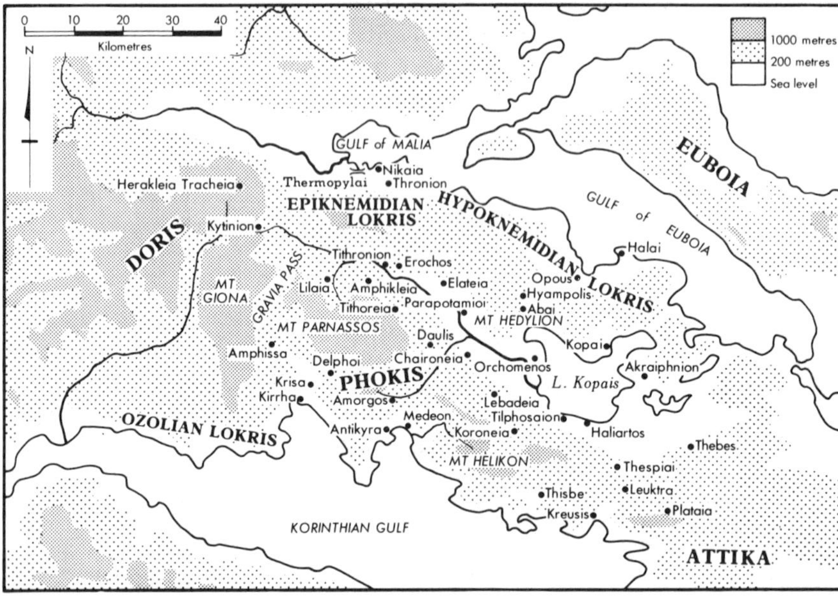

Map 4 Central Greece

Philip win access to the Boiotian Plain, whence he might advance on Thebes and Athens.[56] Both sides thus occupied strong positions, but, in that Philip now needed to force the issue, the allies might be said to hold the advantage.

PHOKIS

The state thus divided between opposing armies was Phokis, and, unfortunately, we have no good information on the attitude of the Phokians to either side. We have no reason to doubt the word of Pausanias, five centuries later, that Ambrysos and probably Lilaia were to some extent reconstructed by the Thebans and Athenians in the course of their fortification of the Parnassian and near-by passes;[57] he visited these towns and, even after so long, should have been able to rely on native traditions as to matters of such significance in the locality. Some other towns in southern Phokis may have been rebuilt, although he does not specify any. On the other hand, there is very good reason to query his general statement that it was Athens and Thebes that restored Phokis before the Battle of Chaironeia.[58] In the first place, the allies controlled at most only southern Phokis and, at that, held it for little more than three months before Philip's capture of Amphissa turned their defensive line and forced their retreat. Secondly, as Pausanias makes clear in a reference to Parapotamioi, not all of the destroyed towns under allied control were even fortified, let alone rebuilt.[59] Given the time available, it is much more likely that the tradition picked up by this traveller was a distorted memory of the fortification of some sites selected for their strategic significance.

It is also difficult to gauge the effects of the 346 settlement on the Phokian attitudes to the two armies poised on their soil. The punishment meted out to them at the conclusion of the Sacred War was not of Philip's making, was indeed contrary to his intentions, and had in fact been greatly moderated by his influence. He had seen then – and in 339/8 still continued to see – that the Phokians were at the least a useful counterbalance to Theban ambitions in central Greece. Whether the Phokians themselves were able to take such a detached view of what they had suffered is another matter. But they must have recognized most of this. They must have seen where responsibility lay for the three-year moratorium on their Delphian repayments and their subsequent halving. And, whatever sympathy they may have retained for the Athens that had supported them (albeit half-heartedly) during the Sacred War, and whether or not they appreciated her role in vitiating the settlement Philip had proposed at its end, any goodwill must have evaporated when she allied herself with the hated Thebans. If we are correct in thinking that Philip had insisted that his troops supervise the dismemberment of the Phokian cities in order to prevent the Theban soldiers from exacting their private vengeance, then the results of his precaution were surely evident in the Phokian villages. Finally, since his arrival in the Phokian Plain, Philip will certainly have made it his business to spread the word that nothing now stood in the way of his intention that Phokis should be reconstructed – nothing, at least, once Theban opposition was removed; it was a task that was, in fact, substantially achieved before 336.[60] All in all, we seem obliged to conclude, in spite of Pausanias, that Phokis was restored by Philip, not by Athens and Thebes, and after Chaironeia, not before – though undoubtedly on the basis of promises delivered by the king in 339/8. It seems likely that, except for those areas directly held by the allies, Philip was able to count on the support of the Phokian people.

However, neither this nor the fact of his final victory should obscure the danger in which he stood. He faced the coalition he had strenuously sought to avoid between early 346 and 339. He had been forced, in more general terms, into an open declaration of his intent to organize Hellenic affairs to his own advantage. Compelled to appear in battle against major Greek powers, he now risked draining the reservoir of good will among the smaller states that he had carefully built up over seven years. He had been prepared to see his partisans in the Greek states rest their claims to power on mere tokens of his support and had worked through the Amphiktyonic Council to broadcast a panhellenic image designed to reassure the Greeks of his benign intentions. Athens, with Thebes shackled and Sparta surrounded by her enemies, might have been the executor of a new Common Peace of all Greek states and the exploiter of a new Aegean and Anatolian naval network guaranteed by Macedonian power. Now, he was reduced to pitting Macedonian against Greek, and the consternation and suspicion this aroused served to bring about what he had attempted to avoid. Several uncommitted states and several whose relations with Athens had been no better than half-hearted were either driven into the enemy camp or into worried neutrality.

BREAKTHROUGH TO AMPHISSA

Both sides sent out embassies seeking support. In Philip's case, the call was not for allies for Macedon but rather for service in the Amphiktyonic cause, which he had so far left deliberately unresolved. If his request should find a response in the Peloponnesos, he might divide his enemies' forces by putting pressure on the isthmus at Korinth and Megara.[61] But, although only three Peloponnesians – Achaia, Megara and Korinth – served on the allied side, not one enlisted in his support. For his allies and sympathizers the dilemma was serious. They saw that the combination already arrayed against the king was extremely formidable, and their forebodings can only have been accentuated by his failures at Perinthos and Byzantion. They took the only reasonable course and remained neutral.[62]

In central Greece his backing was much stronger. Phokis must have been for him. After his attempt to recover Nikaia for the Epiknemidian Lokrians, he could probably count on them. The majority of the Amphiktyons northwest and west of his present position had already declared themselves. Only in Euboia and the far west did the allies secure much support. The Leukadian and Kerkyraian islanders, as well as the Akarnanians, followed Korinth on to the Athenian side.

During the course of these diplomatic manœuvres over the winter, Philip made an attempt to strengthen his position by thrusting across the River Kephisos. If successful, he would in one blow have turned both of his enemies' defensive positions. But he was beaten back.[63] A more difficult alternative could not be evaded.

A pitched battle in the narrow gap below Parapotamioi was out of the question; apart from anything else, he would be unable to use his cavalry to advantage.[64] The only other point at which he might exert pressure was the Gravia Pass. So, using the same stratagem that had successfully extricated his fleet from the Black Sea, he arranged for a false despatch to fall into enemy hands, giving the impression that he was withdrawing from Kytinion. When the mercenaries of Proxenos and Chares relaxed, the Macedonians burst through at night,[65] opening the way to Amphissa. Within two or three hours, with Parmenion at their head, they took the town, with a sympathetic Delphoi now only another few hours ahead.[66] A mass exodus of Theban and Athenian forces from the Parnassian passes must now have followed; and a speedy Macedonian march through Delphoi and along the Sacred Way towards Chaironeia might have hampered their efforts to rejoin the main force. But Parmenion had other orders. With the Amphiktyonic purpose of the campaign now realized, it was essential that the allies of Philip be discouraged from giving up their efforts. In 343/2, at the time of his Epeirote intervention, the king had promised to the Aitolian League that he would restore to it the port of Naupaktos, at the time in the hands of his declared enemies, the Achaians. In early summer 339, Parmenion turned westwards and fulfilled this undertaking.[67]

CHAIRONEIA

During the spring, the allies abandoned their now useless position at Parapotamioi. Dropping back to Chaironeia and Lebadeia, they prepared to make their last stand.[68] This was an excellent position. First, by extending their line across the river plain from Chaironeia itself, on the left flank, to the Kephisos on the right, they blocked the Macedonian passage down the valley. But, since in the event of a retreat the superior Macedonian and Thessalian cavalry could cut down fugitives on the open plain, the position had the added advantage that the battle line could be placed obliquely so as to cover the entrance to the steep Kerata Pass, in which cavalry could not be used, and through which a safer retreat was therefore possible.[69] Philip had no option but to stake his whole programme on this one battle.[70]

At dawn on 7 Metageitnion 338, the two armies deployed in the plain,[71] the Greek allies superior in numbers but not in skill and training, the Macedonians compelled to attack a superior position, but one against which their cavalry could be used to the full. In the battle itself, it was probably the toughness of the king's phalanx and horse that carried the day. The young Alexander, eighteen years old but supported by experienced commanders, led the left wing at the head of the Companion Cavalry,[72] opposed to the Theban Sacred Band, which was stationed against the Kephisos banks or some marshes at its edge. On the opposite flank, Philip, with 'selected' troops, probably the Hypaspists, faced the Athenians. The Macedonian centre must have comprised the bulk of the phalanx, opposed largely to the smaller allied contingents of the defending force.[73] When, at the decisive point of the struggle, both defensive wings crumbled, the Theban troops took extremely heavy casualties and, of the Athenians, 1000 were killed and another 2000 captured; in the centre, Achaian and Boiotian losses were also heavy. No order was given to pursue the defeated (who included Demosthenes) and the fugitives gathered at Lebadeia.[74]

It will be understandable if in the aftermath of the victory the Macedonians were at times unable to cloak their elation.[75] Against the best army their Greek enemies had been able to throw against them, they had won a decisive victory. But this was a time not for celebration but for careful diplomacy. Two premises governed Philip's analysis of the situation. He was master of the Greek mainland – needing, at the most, more time to subjugate it beyond foreseeable hope of reclamation. Virtually any form of settlement, in other words, was within reach. But – and this was very soon to emerge from his actions – his intention remained, as it had been in 346, to make Greece safe not for his overlordship but for his absence; his diplomacy, now as then, was aimed unmistakably at getting himself out of Hellas. He had learnt, at the cost of eight almost wasted years, that Athenian pride and skepticism would not permit of a loose arrangement of Greek states under nominally Athenian, but substantially Macedonian hegemony. More familiar with the rough cohesiveness of the tribal state, he had made the mistake of underestimating the egocentric forces that sustained the separatism of the Greek *poleis* and the deeply ingrained pride of an Athens that would accept no subordination, however discreet or profitable. It might have been expected that Philip would now impose the sort of conditions – garrisons, mass exiles, puppet juntas and an occupying army – that would physically prevent the overthrow of the supremacy he had achieved. But, if he had paid the price of naïveté, he was not about to abandon his analysis of the Macedonian socio-military needs, nor his primary aim to serve these needs in an Asian expedition. In fact, he determined to alter only the method of achieving the Greek settlement he had sought eight years before, not its essential nature. Selecting the orator Demades from among his 2000 Athenian prisoners, he sent him back to Athens with the news that he again wanted peace.

SETTLEMENTS WITH THEBES AND ATHENS

When the army had encamped at Chaironeia and performed the requisite offices for the Macedonian dead,[76] the new plans began to go into effect. Treating the Athenian fallen with respect, Philip refused to let the Thebans recover their dead except on payment of a ransom, and set a similar condition on the release of their prisoners. On the heels of Demades he despatched his own envoys, had the Athenian bodies conveyed unasked to their city and offered the return of the prisoners free of cost.[77] Probably at the same time, he delivered his terms to Thebes. The city was to receive a Macedonian garrison, to recall its exiles (perhaps largely banished at the time of the decisions to seize Nikaia in summer 339 and to ally with Athens in the following November) and to accept a new government favourable to him – one of three hundred men appointed from among the restored exiles. He would then rely upon this body to do what he would prefer not to do himself: if there were further banishments, these would be the new council's responsibility.[78]

This was the settlement applied to an ally which had defected and joined the enemy. But vindictiveness counted probably for much less than the sheer need to destroy Theban military power. Perhaps too by drawing so clear a distinction between his two major foes at Chaironeia he would bring home the contrast in the roles he wished them to play in his new settlement. Losing no opportunity to pay court to the Athenians, he humiliated Thebes at every turn.[79]

The terms offered to Athens could hardly, in the circumstances, have been more generous.[80] Her dead were returned in honour, escorted by the two highest-ranking Macedonians available, other than the king: Alexander and Antipatros, accompanied by Alkimachos.[81] Probably as early as Demades' arrival home, hardly more than two days or so behind news of the battle, the *demos* heard of the offer regarding the prisoners. (They were in fact set free with their battle-damaged clothing replaced.)[82] A reciprocal embassy, apparently comprising (or headed by) Demades, Phokion and Aischines, was appointed to travel to Chaironeia to negotiate.[83] It was to these men that Philip revealed his detailed plan. Oropos would be removed from Boiotia and restored to Athens.[84] The Athenian naval alliance was to be dissolved, but her possession of Lemnos, Imbros and Skyros, to which Samos and, in effect, Delos were added, was confirmed.[85] She would remain free and autonomous, would suffer no garrison or any other Macedonian force by land or sea or any interference in her internal affairs.[86] Her Amphiktyonic role would remain unimpaired (as the documents confirm).[87] Like Thebes, she would be free to join Philip's planned Common Peace of all the Greek states (though, one may suspect, no freer than Thebes *not* to join).

It is not possible to keep precise track of the Athenian changes of mood in the days and weeks following Chaironeia. The initial reaction had been one of grim resignation and preparedness to defend the city walls. Demosthenes, who had fled from the battlefield, contrived to procure for himself, during the discussion of emergency-measures, a commission for collecting supplies (of grain and/or financial contributions), and sailed out of the Peiraieus to levy the allies. His policy had brought the city, so it seemed, to the brink of absolute ruin, and he judged it expedient to be somewhere else.[88] A short time afterwards, the mood had altered completely, and we must suppose Demades' tidings to have been the catalyst. During the period of the negotiations, and perhaps later, the intervention of the Areiopagos to replace the hard-line general Charidemos with Phokion was followed by an apparently unbridled enthusiasm for Philip that produced such unexpected gems as the erection of an equestrian statue of him in the Agora and a grant of citizenship to him and Alexander; presumably some care was taken to keep the latter distinct from similar grants to Theban refugees![89] Yet, on Demosthenes' return, while he was hounded, with some of his colleagues, in the law-courts, he was never convicted on any charge, he was invited to deliver the epitaph over the Athenian dead and he was appointed by his tribe to serve on the board of ten entrusted with continuing work on the city fortifications.[90] After their initial sensations of fear and then relief, that is to say, the Athenians had changed little. But, for Philip, the important result was that he had in some respects cancelled out the previous eight years; he was free to begin again his attempts to draw Athens into a constructive and productive relationship. The difference between 346 and the present was that he was no longer prepared to base his plans only on Athens' goodwill.

The Greek settlement of 338/7, as compared with that of 346, might be characterized in this way. Wishing to make Greece and Macedonia safe for the withdrawal of large forces from the latter for the Asian campaign, Philip, in the former instance, had attempted to organize a superstructure (in the form of a powerful, dual hegemony of himself and the Athenians) which would then impose a security from above upon the rest of Greece. When this had failed, he aimed, through the post-Chaironeia settlement, to reverse his previous order of attack: first, he intended to reorganize the fundamental power-balances of the peninsula so as to impose a system of order and security; and then he might with more confidence re-create very much the same superstructure as before, in order to maintain the new arrangement.

It is within this framework that the peace-treaties negotiated with Athens and Thebes are to be seen. They are not single settlements with defeated enemies, but single elements in a new and larger design. The differences in their respective terms are to be explained as indicating not the relative severity of treatment each merited, but rather the means by which these two states were prepared for their distinct and quite different roles in the new total structure.[91]

ARRANGEMENTS IN CENTRAL GREECE

The treaty with Thebes is itself only one constituent in the restructuring of the power-balance in central Greece. The Boiotian League remained in existence and Thebes retained membership of it.[92] But the disposition of power within it was dramatically altered, not only by the limitations imposed on Theban power, but also by the restoration of those Boiotian cities whose resentment of Theban imperialism had led to their destruction. The Plataian people, who in 373 had fled their ruined city into honourable exile in Athens, were brought home again.[93] Orchomenos, similarly depopulated after Leuktra and, presumably, again after the Peace of Philokrates, was restored;[94] the same was true of Thespiai and perhaps of other towns.[95] The League was again to act as a federal body and no longer as the mere instrument of Theban domination. While Thebes continued to play a role, it was now a much reduced one.[96]

Elsewhere in central Greece, the Epiknemidian Lokrians retained Nikaia and plans were made for the restoration of Phokis.[97] So far as the latter was concerned, of course, the Amphiktyonic decisions of 346 could hardly be wiped out; the penalty for sacrilege, in the absence of Phalaikos and his mercenaries, could fall on no one else. It follows that we should not expect to find a blatant reversal by Philip of the Council's judgement; but we may well look for signs that he attempted to lighten the burden of the punishment. Thus, while Phokis was never readmitted to the Amphiktyony and continued, for the time being (at least until the end of Philip's reign), to pay the reparations at the same rate, half the original 60 talents per annum, at the same time its people must have been permitted to begin the rebuilding of their cities; by the autumn of 337, the Phokian *koinon* appears to have been operating in something like its old manner.[98]

On the western side of central Greece, control of the north-south route was now open to Philip, from Aitolian Naupaktos on the Korinthian Gulf to Epeiros.[99] In Akarnania the news of Chaironeia had brought a change in government, as Macedonian partisans (like their colleagues in many other cities), or those claiming the allegiance, used the discredit of their opponents to win office. Banishments followed, some of the exiles finding refuge and honour in Athens in the summer of 337.[100] The same may have been true on the islands of Leukas, Kephallenia and Kerkyra.[101] This was all to the king's advantage, in that it absolved him from any need for direct intervention; instead, he simply attempted to crystallize in legal form, through the organization he was shortly to establish at Korinth, the new arrangements that had already come about naturally. But, probably in large measure for the security of his client-king in Epeiros, he decided to stabilize the western Greek arrangement and to protect the western route by the additional installation of a garrison in Ambrakia, which provided, like Thebes in the east, a well placed base for the control of north-south traffic.[102]

It may appear strange that the Athenian naval alliance – or what remained of it after the end of the Social War in 355 – was dissolved, while Thebes was neither severed from the Boiotian League nor ordered to disband it. But this was an inevitable result of the quite different power-balances in the two bodies. Philip had left Thebes weak and now intended to use to contro lher the very instrument she had forged for her own power. On the other hand, given that he did not want to interfere any more than necessary with Athens, and given that in any case there were no means of building any Aegean islands into a power-bloc to counterbalance the Athenian navy, there was no option but to destroy that alliance. To do so was only to hamper the Athenian military potential, to make it in fact more heavily dependent on the co-operation of states that were his allies. It involved no deleterious effects upon the Aegean trading-network, which would rest as always on Athenian economic superiority and drive. Even more so than in the aftermath of the Peloponnesian War, while Athens would find her military/naval undertakings limited, her merchant fleet would be able to exploit the Aegean trade unhampered, provided that she maintained a friendly relationship with the ally that controlled the Hellenic coastline and hoped shortly to bring the shores of Asia Minor under his influence.[103]

The Euboian situation must have come under close scrutiny. Philip well knew its importance to Athenian power, and he no doubt dissolved the alliance contracted in 340. But we have no evidence that the new Euboian League was destroyed – only that certain pro-Athenian leaders, notably the Chalkians Kallias and Taurosthenes, sought and found refuge in Athens.[104] It may be that a garrison was set in Chalkis; but no evidence survives for this time, and, with the Theban garrison near by and with easy Macedonian access from the Magnesian coast of

Thessaly, it was hardly necessary before the destruction of Thebes by Alexander and the Hellenic League in 335.[105]

ARRANGEMENTS IN THE PELOPONNESOS

During October or November, Philip crossed the Isthmus of Korinth into the Peloponnesos. After Chaironeia, the Korinthians had followed the Athenian lead in preparing to defend their city. But, either when Athens agreed to peace (which may have precipitated the rise of Philip's partisans to power in Korinth, as probably also in Megara) or when Philip actually approached the cities of the isthmus, both surrendered.[106] Nothing is known of the settlement with Megara, other than that the state continued to send its *naopoios* to Delphoi.[107] Although the Korinthians also retained their status at Delphoi and suffered no known punishment, it seems that the position of what was probably a Macedonian partisan government was not only confirmed (as were all others) by the charter of the Hellenic League, but guaranteed by the installation of a garrison.[108]

Apart from Megara and Korinth, Philip had to deal in the Peloponnesos with a mixture of states, some recently his foes (the Achaian League and the towns on Akte peninsula) and some, albeit neutral in the war, previously his allies (Elis, Argos, Arkadia and Messenia). Sparta alone had remained absolutely aloof, presumably out of frustration in the years after 346 at the growing influence of Philip among her neighbours, but unable to counteract this for fear of Theban intervention. (The decision to send off Archidamos and troops to her ancient colony of Tarentum in 342[109] may have arisen out of this frustration, but there may also have been an element of hope that a successful mission might produce enough funds to hire mercenaries for her own needs.) At any rate, the Spartans had been guilty of no known display of overt anti-Macedonian sentiment.

As with Megara, so with the towns of Akte little is known after their surrender, except that at least Troizen, where internal eruption combined with outside assistance produced a pro-Macedonian government, continued to send a *naopoios* to Delphoi.[110] Like its Boiotian and (probably) Euboian counterparts, the Achaian League was not dismantled.[111] Its claim on Naupaktos, had been at best tenuous.

The settlements with Philip's existing allies were not as straightforward as might be expected. Their neutrality in the recent war was understandable enough: in the first place, Philip's army had been outnumbered, and to commit themselves, isolated in the Peloponnesos as they were, to the losing side would have been suicidal; moreover, with

Korinth and Megara firmly on the allied side, they had no prospect of reaching Philip with any aid they could provide. But this was not the difficulty. It was rather that, with the exception of Elis, all had originally given Philip their allegiance primarily because of territorial conflict with Sparta. The border-areas of Lakonia lay at the heart of the Peloponnesian problem.

From Korinth, Philip went to Argos. His partisans were firmly in control there, but that, in any case, had nothing to do with the reasons for his visit, which were largely connected with matters of propaganda. For not only did his own Argead family lay claim to descent from Herakles, whose traditional home it was, but he was obliged, in the absence of any better pretext for meeting his allies' wishes, to rest his territorial demands to Sparta on their claims to the land, which they had contrived to support by appeal to the mythical division of the Peloponnesos by the Sons of Herakles.[112] Then, at some time very late in the year, he delivered an ultimatum to the Spartans, demanding the surrender of the disputed territories.[113] When they refused, he invaded Lakonia, though not Sparta;[114] as a result, the Argives recovered the long, southerly neck of the Argolid southwards of Thyrea and north and northeast of Sparta itself,[115] the Megalopolitans the Belemina district to Sparta's northwest;[116] the Tegeates the Skiritis district due north of it;[117] and the Messenians the Denthalian area to its west and southwest.[118] Not only did such adjustments satisfy the claims of his allies; their most important result was that Sparta was ringed around completely by states whose possession of their 'restored' territories depended ultimately on Philip's sympathy and support.[119]

Macedonian policy in the Peloponnesos thus parallels closely that enacted elsewhere: in brief, it represented the weakening of the powerful to the advantage of those with a strong stake in maintaining a pro-Macedonian alignment. To the Spartans, in effect, Greece was made 'inaccessible'.[120] It is not at all clear whether all of these arrangements – or even those contracted with previous enemies – were fixed by actual treaties, or whether they were merely informal agreements or *de facto* reapportionments of power. Probably, in general, formal arrangements had been unnecessary. For the present, after all, they were guaranteed by Philip's superior power; and, for the future, they were to be legally enshrined in the panhellic agreement.

CONGRESS AT KORINTH

By now, the winter of 338/7, delegates of all Greek states had been summoned to attend a conference at Korinth.[121] It is likely that it was already generally known that Philip wished to lead a panhellenic army against the Persians. When the three Macedonian envoys had visited Athens not long before to agree the terms of the Athenian settlement, Antipatros had discussed the plans in some detail with the ancient Isokrates, then ninety-eight years old and soon to die. In his last letter shortly afterwards, the old man recalled to Philip the advice he had offered eight years earlier.[122] He had urged then that the king reconcile the four major Greek cities, Athens, Thebes, Sparta and Argos, and build a concord of all the Hellenes in the launching of a joint crusade against Persia. At about the time that he wrote, word reached the author that Philip was indeed planning an Asian campaign, causing him and his friends to wonder whether his advice had provoked the decision or had simply fallen in with an existing intention.[123] Now, after Chaironeia, with Philip within reach of establishing precisely the form of control in Greece that he wished, Isokrates made a last effort to strengthen the king in his intentions. Tact and flattery combined to urge that the victor refuse to sacrifice the glory he might obtain for the sake of grasping more firmly what he already had. He must now strive for the supreme prize – after which, what was left for him but to become a god? – and not allow himself to be seduced by the easier, more immediate (and, for the Hellenes, more uncomfortable) goal of a Macedonian empire of the Greek mainland.[124] There is more than a tinge of anxiety to his words.

At Korinth, delegates of all states except Sparta were present.[125] The general tenor of the king's Asian plans must have been widely known by now, but the purpose of this convention was to hear and then transmit his detailed proposals for the maintenance of peace. What he wished to establish, he announced, was a Common Peace, a general agreement of all Greeks.[126] As precedents he could point to the series of treaties, beginning with the 'King's Peace' of 387/6, which had been full of promise but had grown successively less effective as the signatories perceived the weakness of their sanctions, agreed upon by the Greeks under pressure from the Persian Artaxerxes II. The first difference, in the present case, was that Philip himself, the Macedonian state, would guarantee the agreement to which the signatories would subscribe. But further, he had already achieved – in marked contrast to his predecessor in this regard – a state of peace on the mainland; the role of this arrangement would be to preserve, and not to instil stability.[127]

The plan involved, first, the co-operation of the Greek states, all of whom were invited to participate.[128] All would then be assigned, on the basis of their military capacity, a bloc of votes of appropriate number: ten voices for the Thessalians, three for the Lokrians, etc.,[129] to be exercised in a General Synod of the Common Peace. When the several states had discussed and approved the proposals and selected their synod-representatives (*synedroi*), the new body would be charged with the maintenance of peace. It would have the authority to adjudicate on disturbances and violations, and, in cases of breach, would then authorize the chief executive officer, an elected Hegemon, to levy a force appropriate to the situation.[130] To participate, a state must bind itself to take no hostile action against any other member or against Philip or his descendants, by way either of direct military interference or of aid and encouragement to revolutionary movements in another's state. So much was explicit in the actual oath of allegiance, to which each member would swear (and of which a large part of one copy survives).[131]

But the basis of the settlement was spelt out very much more clearly in sections of the charter that survive in a pseudo-Demosthenic speech (No. XVII = *On the Treaty with Alexander*).[132] In its oath, it emerges, a contracting state would undertake not only to observe the terms of the Common Peace, but also to uphold the individual settlements already negotiated or confirmed after Chaironeia between Philip and his former friends and enemies. That is, first of all, the rearrangements of territory and power made in the previous months were now to be confirmed and guaranteed under the new order. Secondly, a participant must swear not only to refrain from interfering in the internal constitution of another, as it existed at the time of the oath-taking,[133] but, in addition, to eschew such revolutionary actions within its *own* territory as unlawful executions or banishments, or any confiscations of property or dispersals of land, cancellation of debts or emancipation of slaves, where these might lead to the overthrow of the existing constitution.[134] That is to say, while a signatory was not required to leave undisturbed the existing political *balance* within his state, he was forbidden to allow any subversion of his political *system* – which in practice, according to the discretion of the General Synod, might well come to mean the same thing.[135] With these qualifications, each member would otherwise be 'free and autonomous' and would enjoy freedom of passage and trade, at least by sea and probably too by land.[136] Brigandage and piracy could now be dealt with by the whole body of states.

To most of those present at Korinth, the cost of the proposed settlement must have seemed relatively light (especially since they were by and large representatives of governments whose continuance was to be guaranteed by its terms). Although in all matters involving inter-state breaches of the peace or internal upheaval the General Synod bore full deliberative responsibility, and although its decisions were binding on all without further ratification, its sphere of reference apparently went no farther than that. When, soon afterwards, a territorial disagreement arose between the neighbouring islanders of Kimolos and Melos, both parties appear to have requested the Synod's intervention. That this body did not itself arbitrate (presumably because the peace had not been breached) but referred the dispute to an independent body acceptable to both sides, the Argive *demos*, suggests that its competence was carefully circumscribed.[137] How its members were to be selected we do not know; but, in view of the variety of state-organizations represented, it seems unlikely that any uniform method was laid down. (For the safety of the *synedroi* it was probably agreed that no state was entitled to hold its representatives legally responsible for any decision of the whole body.) The Athenians, who may have had title to five,[138] could quite easily select them by the normal process of sortition, or perhaps election. With the Thessalians, who had ten,[139] they may have been provided, as in the case of the Amphiktyonic *naopoioi*, one or two each by the leading cities and their areas, or perhaps in some way by the four tetrarchies and periœcic territories.[140] But much greater difficulties must have arisen over, for example, the apportioning of one vote among 'the islanders' (if this is correctly restored in the Athenian copy of the charter inscription), or five among what appear to be six small areas in the region of Thermopylai. It is interesting to note that, like the Lokrians, the Phokians received three votes – implying that the restoration of the state was by now well under way.[141]

As it happens, the participants whose names survive at the foot of the Athenian decree are invariably central and northern Greek, where there had long been an emphasis on ethnic or federal organizations of one sort or another. It may have been the case that Philip preferred to deal with such units, which tended less towards the extreme chauvinism exhibited by many *poleis*. But the fragmentary evidence is hardly sufficient to put this beyond doubt.[142] What is clear is that with smaller states there was a certain amount of grouping for the purpose of determining representation – presumably the only reasonable expedient, given a need to reflect a proper balance between big and small and the undesirability of constructing a body comprising many hundreds of *synedroi*.

Such, so far as we can reconstruct them, were the terms the envoys at Korinth were to carry back for the ratification of their respective states. Discussion could take place, but it is unlikely that Philip's timetable allowed for much delay. Almost certainly, the choice was simple (whether or not explicit): one might join the Common Peace voluntarily; or one took the risk of allowing those who did participate to decide whether one's abstention was subversive of the common good. In Athens, we are told, Demades proposed acceptance of the charter, the *demos* assented and the *synedroi* were appointed.[143] The fragmentary inscription we possess is probably part of the record of this meeting.[144]

COMMON PEACE

At the second meeting at Korinth, hardly before late winter or early spring, the first item of business before the assembled *synedroi* will have been the constitution of the General Synod itself. Chief among related matters was the appointment of a Hegemon, to which office Philip was elected.[145] A standing committee of *proedroi* was set up to organize the machinery of synod-meetings, to deliberate out of session with the Hegemon or (in his absence) his deputy, and probably to act as the Synod's probouleutic council.[146]

This done, the members turned to the remaining item of business scheduled for this meeting: the question whether a war should be undertaken against the Persians in retaliation for their destruction of Greek temples 150 years before. Such a panhellenic motivation had long been toyed with in Greece, most notably (according to one source) by Perikles at the time of his so-called Congress Decree; all Greeks were at that time to be invited to send representatives to Athens to discuss the defilement of the sanctuaries by the Persian invaders and the fulfilment of the sacred oaths taken as a result.[147] Such a pretext had been conspicuously absent from the recommendations of Isokrates; but then his concern had been with the real justification (especially as Philip would see it) for such a campaign, not with the sort of sugar coating that might appeal to the romantic and the patriotic.[148] But there was a stronger reason for the proposal of such a motive, for it is difficult to see how such a venture could fall technically within the sphere of competence of the General Synod of the Common Peace unless it were argued that the long-past Persian actions detracted from the present general security. Punishment was to be exacted not for the destruction of Greek cities, nor for the deaths of Greek citizens, but for the despoliation of the sacred places of the gods; such sacrilege, it was presumably argued, could remain a *present* cause of the gods' disfavour.

It is probable that Philip's own motives were many: that he had need of such a campaign to ease the military pressures within his own society; that it might provide a unifying influence (as Isokrates thought) among the Greek states, on whose stability he must depend for the security of Macedonia in his absence (and the panhellenic nature of the army would provide him with hostages for the co-operation of their states); that he needed the sort of money that was to be won in Asia Minor or beyond; that he saw the virtue of Isokrates' proposal to settle colonies of the restless, dispossessed, war-produced elements in Greece that provided ready mercenaries to serve any wealthy tyrant. Some of the same motives will also have appealed to the Greek states, for they too might have risen to the old catch-cry of liberation for the Greeks of Asia Minor.[149] But, if the Hellenic League was to serve as an instrument in this venture, Philip had to find the key to activate it; and it was for this reason that he based his appeal to the Synod on what may appear otherwise the most specious reason of all. The *synedroi* accepted the proposal, approved the crusade and authorized their Hegemon to levy the requisite forces from the member-states and to take command of the army so raised. They may have finished by pronouncing an anathema on those Greeks who continued henceforward to fight in the Persian service.[150]

RETROSPECT AND PROSPECT

The business finished, the Synod adjourned, perhaps to re-convene at the Nemean Festival at Argos in the following autumn (unless some emergency should bring it into session in the meantime);[151] Philip, leaving deputies to make arrangements regarding military contributions with the individual states, returned to Pella.[152]

In many ways he could feel satisfied with his achievement. From a position of danger and embarrassment in the winter of 339 he had risen to triumph on the battlefield. In the further, diplomatic triumph that had followed, he had neither annexed nor made tributary to himself any part of central or southern Greece. He had acted at all times so as to align himself with the panhellenic religious notions espoused by many Greeks. The reduction of power and influence he had perpetrated on especially Thebes and Sparta would go unlamented by most; and, while the same was true with Athens, he had attempted to ease the humiliation and win her confidence by other means. He had settled Greek affairs by way finally of a form of peace well known to the fourth century, which he had however modified in fundamental and effective ways. Most obviously, the new Common Peace was guaranteed by the military power of Macedonia – power that, until the unforeseeable dismemberment of Alexander's empire after 323, needed to be exercised only twice, in 335 (as a direct consequence of the disruption following his own death) and in 331 – as well as by the compulsory sanction binding all participants to assist in mending breaches of the general peace. While none of this – other than the military effectiveness of the guarantor of the Common Peace – was entirely new, the role of the General Synod in matters affecting the common security was an effective innovation, reminiscent more of the conciliar bodies of *sympoliteiai* and *koina*.[153] The fact that what otherwise was the most constructive attempt in past history at instilling general peace into the Greek peninsula had been imposed from outside did not – and does not – go unnoticed; but, if the terms of the settlement had the effect of limiting the more powerful states in ways they were not accustomed to finding acceptable, it was equally evident that they limited the conqueror himself. As elected Hegemon of the Common Peace, Philip was technically bound as tightly by the terms of reference of the General Synod as were its other members. It was now up to him to demonstrate by his actions whether he actually regarded himself so bound, or whether this settlement was, in the end, as much of a sham as its predecessors. The most important ingredient still lacking was merely time: time for the new situation to become a part of the Greek furniture and time for the Hegemon to demonstrate his bona fides. Unfortunately, he himself was not to be given that time, and his successor was less concerned to make constructive use of it.

CHAPTER VIII

337–336

PHILIP, ALEXANDER AND PERSIA

PHILIP'S LAST MARRIAGE

ARRIVING HOME after an absence of nearly a year and a half,[1] Philip gave orders for the preparations necessary to begin the Asian offensive in the following spring.[2] He had most of a year in which to settle any difficulties attendant upon the impending absence of himself and a large Macedonian army for a campaign that might well prove difficult, dangerous and protracted. But beyond problems of logistics, which subordinates could handle, and those of Macedonia's Illyrian neighbours, to whom he would shortly need to devote his efforts,[3] we are compelled to assume that unforeseen pressures bearing on the question of Alexander's succession now began to be felt. At such a time as this, it is safe to say, such uncertainties were the last thing the king wanted. It was now, probably in the spring or summer, that he contracted a seventh marriage, to a high-born Macedonian lady, Kleopatra, the niece and apparently the ward of Attalos, a senior and influential noble.[4] A new marriage in itself was of no great consequence, and, to see why this one has occasioned so much comment and speculation, we shall need to look briefly at the whole, somewhat vexed question of Philip's marriages, for which the main source is the third-century Peripatetic biographer Satyros.[5]

> Philip always fought his wars by marriage. In the twenty-two years of his reign . . . he married Audata the Illyrian and had from her a daughter Kynna,[6] and he married Phila, the sister of Derdas and Machatas. Wishing to commandeer the Thessalian nation he had children by two Thessalian women,[7] one the Pheraian Nikesipolis, who bore him Thessalonike, the other the Larisaian Philinna, from whom he had Aridaios. He acquired also the Molossian kingdom by marrying Olympias, from whom he had Alexander and Kleopatra. And when he took Thrace, the Thracian king Kothelas joined him, bringing his daughter Meda and a substantial dowry. By marrying

> her he brought her in besides Olympias. Then, after all these, he married Kleopatra, sister of Hippostratos and niece of Attalos; and the addition of her to Olympias affected his whole life ... And Kleopatra bore him a daughter named Europe.

But this account is clearly unsatisfactory in some ways, especially in that its relative chronology is often suspect and in some respects quite wrong[8] – perhaps because its author was striving at the same time for completeness and to illustrate his opening aphorism to the best possible effect. At least it is clear that, according to Satyros, Olympias preceded Meda, who preceded Kleopatra, who came last of all – and so much is acceptable in the light of independent evidence.[9] But it is difficult to see how the Pheraian marriage could have preceded that with Olympias. The most likely date for it is 352;[10] and it may get its early position in this list on account of the relatively early establishment of Philip's influence in Thessaly, or because the marriage with Philinna, with which it is grouped (but in the wrong order), preceded that with Olympias. The Philinna-marriage probably belongs in 358 at the time of the earliest intervention in Thessaly, which was undertaken at the behest of the Aleuad family of Larisa, to which she most likely belonged. As to the first two mentioned, we have no sure way of dating them with precision; but it has been suggested above that that of the Illyrian will belong in 359 and that of Phila, from the royal house of Elimeia, will fit either before Philip's accession or possibly *c.*358.[11]

A further difficulty may be raised as to the actual status of these women. Out of a wish to preserve for Olympias a position befitting the mother of Alexander the Great, commentators have commonly attempted to introduce artificial distinctions between 'wives' and 'mistresses'. Philip's morals have been more questionable than Alexander's birth! Thus we often find the notion[12] that when Philip married Kleopatra (which cannot be doubted) he must previously have 'divorced' Olympias, who (in turn) must hitherto have been his only surviving wife, her predecessors having conveniently died, been divorced into obscurity or been really concubines all along. The difficulty is that we have no shred of evidence for such a distinction between these liaisons,[13] or, in the one instance for which we have much evidence at all, any sign that Olympias was divorced in order to make room for Kleopatra. No source, to be sure, ever suggests that Alexander was anything but the heir apparent from the moment of his birth – indeed from his conception[14] – but that is no more than we should expect. All surviving sources for Alexander's childhood and early youth were written much later as the result of the achievements of his maturity; and the derivative sources, practically all we have, may be forgiven for the presumption that a man capable of so much had grown from a baby no less capable in potential, and was born of none but the queenliest (since the fatherhood is a constant – if we discount thunderbolts, grapevines and large snakes) of mothers.

But this is to omit Alexander's elder brother from the picture. For Aridaios, son of the Larisaian Philinna, was in all probability born before Alexander, the one in 357 and the other in 356.[15] Aridaios, we are told, was feeble-minded. It is alleged that this was the result of injury done him by Olympias.[16] The former datum must be true; but if the latter is, then at the least it implies that Aridaios posed a threat to Alexander's succession. If only the former is, then we should at least acknowledge that it was most likely several years before a congenital mental defect became apparent or before an accidental injury was sustained. It seems difficult, in other words, to escape the likelihood that at Alexander's birth he was second in line for the throne.[17] In the polygamous situation we are so clearly confronted with, moreover, we should expect that it was – other things, at any rate, being more or less equal – the status of the son that governed that of the mother, and not the reverse, since we have no reason to suppose a mere wife (among many) to have enjoyed any intrinsic status at all.[18] Olympias, that is, became the chief of Philip's (surviving?) wives when it became clear that it was her son and not Philinna's who was destined for the sort of princely training and experience that, barring accidents, would clinch his succession.

All this is of course highly speculative and is intended to prove nothing. But it may assist in clarifying our perspective. We are dealing with polygamous marriages contracted for reasons of state and involving, we may suppose, at least the appearances of proper treatment for a wife at least while the political motivation remained that had produced her marriage. But the first virtue of any wife in such a situation was her fecundity – her daughters serving the same diplomatic purpose as she had herself and her sons receiving the training proper to princes. In general, it was probably anticipated that the eldest of the male children would become king, whatever formal process of selection (or acclamation) he might have to survive when the time arrived. And this primacy will have formed the basis of his mother's position, from which she will have worked to safeguard her progeny's (and therefore her own) interests the more effectively, always conscious that her glory was only reflected – for in the end her son was really her husband's. For this reason her origins did not matter much. It was not because his mother was of royal Hellenic stock or because her marriage represented a union of upland and plain[19] that Alexander was seen as the successor, but rather because he was (after Aridaios' claim was seen to be hopeless) the eldest, indeed the only contender; and it was this that more or less guaranteed his mother's position, at least until 337.

Maternal watchfulness, however, might yet be put to the test; for her son needed two more practical qualifications for acquisition of the throne: he had to be alive when the time came, and he had to be the son of the king. In both, especially so in the latter, he was in the hands of his father, who could, if he wished, kill him, or – with less effort – repudiate him. So that once Alexander's priority over Aridaios was assured Olympias had nothing to fear from other wives; for they, if they now bore sons, were too late – or, if they did not, did not count at all. By 340, when Alexander's regency proclaimed to the world (if it did not already know) that Alexander would be the next king, Olympias must have felt supremely secure in her anticipation of the fruits of her labour. And when Philip announced that he intended to marry Kleopatra there is absolutely no reason why that should disturb her. Yet it seems that it did.

There is no good evidence that Olympias was in any sense divorced. She did not leave the Macedonian court until after the new marriage, and only then, so far as we know, because of a crisis precipitated by her son.[20] At the wedding the bride's guardian-uncle is said to have prayed, while drunk, that Macedonia might at last be given a legitimate successor.[21] It was Alexander's furious challenge – whether Attalos was calling him illegitimate – that led to his flight from Macedonia, taking his mother with him.[22]

So circumstantial an anecdote, which purports to give the actual words of participants, ought to be treated with the utmost caution, and it is surprising that this has not always been the case. The story is preserved by Athenaeus, who takes it, again, from the third-century Satyros; so that, if there was ultimately a contemporary source for it, we do not hear of it. Then, ignoring the inherent difficulties in crediting such memorable repartee from the mouths of people purportedly sodden drunk, the most serious hurdle before us is to explain the meaning of Attalos' inflammatory remark. In what sense could it be taken that Alexander's legitimacy were questionable? It *may* be that among certain of the Macedonian nobility (though, naturally, only the old nobility, who may well have been in a numerical minority by now), it was regarded as preferable that the king should be of pure and noble *Lower* Macedonian descent. But even if we could be sure of this, and even if we were confident that such people could form in the new Macedonia a pressure-group powerful enough to force the king into action he obviously had never contemplated until 337, we should still have to be at least guarded in proposing it as an overt factor in any campaign to oust Alexander; for the king himself was the son of a half *Illyrian* princess.[23] (In what terms, one wonders, do the proponents of this view imagine Alexander's opponents voiced their disapproval to the king?) If we are to attach any significant meaning to Attalos' words, it is likely to be found in their more literal meaning. If Kleopatra could produce a son, the way would at least be open for a challenge to Alexander's paternity. Such an implication from the drunken noble would quite plausibly explain Alexander's ire.

But what of Philip, who, according to Plutarch's version of the story, seized his sword and sprang not at Attalos, but at his own son, only (so it is implied) failing to kill him because alcohol rendered him temporarily incapable?[24] In the much less anecdotal version of Satyros, we may note, the incident terminates with Alexander's hurling his wine-cup at his tormentor and flouncing out of the hall and, with his mother, out of Macedonia.[25] But if we manage to believe that Philip did pursue his son with a sword, are we also obliged to conclude that he agreed with Attalos that at last he might beget for himself a new and somehow more legitimate heir? Or was this merely the (drunken) temper of a king whose own wedding-feast has been soured by a sudden flash of filial paranoia? Alexander and Olympias are said to have left the country immediately; the former, after establishing his mother at the court of her brother at Dodona, pushed northwards into Illyria.[26]

The question remains: why did Philip decide to take a new wife? Did he conceive a *grande passion* for a young girl, and, since she was too well born to take second place, find himself obliged to divorce Olympias, the mother of the next king?[27] This will not do. We have seen reason to doubt the hypothesis that the king wanted a true-blue Lower Macedonian heir to his throne.[28] The suggestion may suffice that, with a real possibility that both Philip and his heir might be killed in Asia, a second-string successor was required;[29] but this will not explain why Alexander himself felt his own position to be under challenge. To accept the view that Philip moved to replace his son because he suspected the youth and his mother of plotting to overthrow him[30] follows largely from the prior assumption that they were plausibly incriminated later in his assassination; and, while a circumstantial case may be made out for the latter, the former does not accord well with Philip's own actions during the previous or following months. A simple answer, of course, is that Philip merely *wished* to take a new wife – six had presented him with only two sons, or less between them – and that our sources represent it as a romantic attachment because they knew of no political motive. The truth is that those interpretations which involve the supposition that Alexander was to be supplanted as heir founder on the matter of time.[31] It is simply incredible that Philip, after years of diplomacy and war designed to protect his kingdom during his absence in Asia, should decide to repudiate his heir almost on the eve of his departure. If Kleopatra should produce a son it would be twenty years before he could rule the throne without being heavily or wholly dependent on a regent – and any Macedonian king who willingly rested his son's hopes on a regent had taken leave of his senses. That Philip was not so foolish, whatever Alexander and his mother might have feared, is demonstrated by the reconciliation he effected soon afterwards and by the subsequent indications he gave that Alexander's position remained unchanged.

It is evident that the sources on which we must rely for the context of this marriage are too suspiciously circumstantial and too vividly anecdotal for us to give much credence to their details. At least, though, we have to reckon with what does appear factual: the exile from the kingdom of Alexander and Olympias.[32] But here we should note that no source alleges that Philip banished them; all concur in stating or implying that their flight was of the fugitives' own choosing.[33]

Shortly afterwards, further action was taken against the Illyrians. Although we know almost no detail, it seems likely that this was a pre-emptive strike designed, in much the same way as Alexander's Danubian campaign of 335, to discourage the build-up of any northern pressures that might ultimately threaten Macedonia itself. It may be that Pleurias, the chieftain against whom Philip is said to have fought, was leader of the Autariatai, the last of the three greatest Illyrian tribes to be subjugated.[34] We know nothing of the military characteristics of the campaign, but, according to Diodoros, who reports (as does Aristotle) the 'official' version of Philip's assassination, it was during a battle with Pleurias that a young man, supposedly Philip's lover, deliberately met his death after confiding to Attalos that he had been driven to it by the jealousy of another member of the king's entourage. Apart from the innate improbability of this story on its own – for, if anyone was driven to suicide, it ought to have been he who *lost* the king's affections, not their new recipient – this has all the appearance of a rationalization after the fact, designed to implicate Attalos in the murder of Philip; for it was the thwarted lover, raped by Attalos for his part in the affair, who commited the regicide some months later.[35]

Before he had been long absent, Alexander was recalled to Macedonia. The Korinthian Demaratos, guest-friend of Philip and well known for his Macedonian sympathies, acted as the king's agent.

Reassured by his entreaties, the prince accepted his father's invitation to return. Whether the same was true of Olympias is not clear – one version of the incident appears to say so – but there seems no good reason for doubting that she did return to Pella and was present in the country during the following sensational months.[36] Apart from anything else, it is not easy, in view of what is implied by their flight together, as well as of their relationship after Alexander's accession to the throne, to believe that the young man was prepared to return unless his mother was offered the same amnesty.

Two further marriages somewhere near this time attract our notice. Attalos himself acquired a daughter of the powerful Parmenion, and Philip gave his daughter Kynnane (or Kynna) by the Illyrian Audata to his nephew Amyntas, son of Perdikkas III. It is possible to read sinister implications into both, and certainly in the turbulent weeks and months after Alexander's succession those involved were to play dubious roles. But so much of what happened then may have arisen directly out of the assassination itself that it is unwise to assume automatically that alignments tempered in the conflagration of mid-336 were already forged nine months or more earlier. On the face of it, certainly, there was nothing ominous in Attalos' choosing to marry. He was about to embark on a dangerous military campaign and, so far as we know, he had no sons of his own. No more portentous was Parmenion's acquiescence. Attalos' status now could scarcely have been higher, and, unless he could win Alexander himself for this daughter (and there is no hint of a suggestion that Alexander, at nineteen, was yet ready to marry), he could hardly find a better son-in-law.[37]

Amyntas was now somewhere between twenty-three and thirty years of age[38] and unmarried. If the worst should happen – if both Philip and Alexander should be killed in Asia Minor, this man's position, whether as king, as protector of the simple-minded Aridaios or as regent for an infant son of Kleopatra, would be crucial. It was time, the king decided, to bind his nephew more closely to his own family. Again, this does not seem calculated to pose any threat to the heir apparent.[39] It is difficult to believe that Philip would elevate his nephew above a son of his own loins; and for that, in the foreseeable future, Alexander was his only option.

PIXODAROS

By now there can have been little left of 337. Only the winter remained before the Macedonian army and that of the Hellenic League would cross the Hellespont to the coastal areas of Asia Minor and its offshore islands and then press into the hinterland. At about this time, it must have been, the dynast/satrap of Karia, Pixodaros, attempted to bolster his growing independence of the Persian King by seeking alliance with Macedonia. Some three years earlier he had driven his sister Ada (widow and successor of the previous ruler, Idreus) out of power. In 338 the strong Artaxerxes Ochos had fallen to the poison of the eunuch Bagoas, who placed on the Persian throne the youngest of the princes, Arses, and killed his brothers. In the difficulties and uncertainties of this situation Pixodaros saw his opportunity to follow the lead of Hermias before him, but, with the Macedonian campaign now imminent, with considerably greater chances of real support than his exemplar.[40] He offered, as token of his friendship, the hand of his daughter in marriage to a son of Philip. This was, of course a diplomatic contrivance well known to the king, who also saw the virtue of gaining a grip on the southwest corner of Asia Minor. He had no intention of marrying his heir to a mere Karian, and it may be, as Plutarch seems to imply, that Pixodaros himself has asked for Aridaios, realistic enough to see that while diplomatic ties were all very well, he could hardly expect his daughter to become the wife of the Macedonian king-to-be. But, innocent as the arrangement probably was, Alexander's apparent insecurity led him into overreaction. Sending as his personal envoy the tragic actor Thessalos, he offered himself in place of his brother. Philip naturally discovered what was happening and reacted sternly. This action, aided and abetted by equally untrustworthy friends who must have helped the prince in obtaining secret information and in making his own clandestine arrangements, was that of an unstable and paranoid young man who would need to be carefully watched.

The young man in question, however, was still the heir apparent, and the king took care to leaven his reproofs with reassurance; it was unworthy of his son's status to wish to become the son-in-law of a Karian, a mere slave of the Persian King. But it was too late to save the alliance. Whatever Thessalos had told Pixodaros, the latter decided that Macedonian royalty was too uncertain a prop for his ambitions, and he withdrew his offer. He evidently judged that Philip's prospects in Asia were not very hopeful, for he now returned to the Persian fold and shared his satrapy with a new son-in-law, Othontopates.[41] At this time a group of friends of Alexander was banished from the kingdom; they did not return until Philip was dead.

These – Harpalos, the brothers Erigyios and Laomedon, Nearchos and Ptolemaios – represented an interesting cross-section of noble Macedonian society, three of them of foreign stock, whose fathers were probably new *hetairoi* of Philip, and two Upper Macedonians, one with royal blood (and himself destined to found the Ptolemaic dynasty of Egypt).[42] The precise cause of their exile is not mentioned, but, since Thessalos, who by now had fled to Korinth, was pursued by an extradition-order, it is clear that Philip took the behaviour of Alexander's confederates seriously. One would imagine that such diplomatic matters needed to be conducted in secret until agreement was reached (most obviously, in this case, Pixodaros' position needed to be protected), and these young men (and Olympias?) and the actor-envoy had been at least guilty of obtaining and then jeopardizing state secrets to the actual disadvantage of their country. In those circumstances, their punishment was not unduly harsh; all, even Thessalos, survived the experience apparently unscathed. But, quite apart from the consequent loss of the Karian alliance, Philip must have been seriously concerned for the stability of his own court. It was disturbing enough that his son and heir persisted in his monomaniac fantasies; but that he had now found a clique of important young men prepared to indulge his paranoia to the detriment of the kingdom raised an internal misunderstanding to a much graver level. This was the atmosphere in which high treason was bred. So it was probably around this time that the king decided to give a more spectacular demonstration of his intentions towards Alexander. Where promises and guarantees had failed, the prince's doubts might be dispelled by a new marriage which would rest on the close patronal links between the Macedonian and Epeirote courts and would implicitly confirm his own status.

PRELIMINARIES IN ASIA

But the first problem to be solved was the launching of the Asian campaign. It was decided to despatch in the following spring a smaller advance-party, apparently comprising entirely Macedonians and mercenaries, to establish bases for the main army and to take the first steps towards involving the Greek states in the great cause. Whether the original plans had included this two-stage advance we do not know; it may have been that the whole Macedonian and Greek army was to cross the Hellespont in a blaze of patriotic glory, but that the importance of Philip's arrangements for the Epeirote marriage now made the alternative preferable. Whichever was the case, there were certain advantages to the plan adopted, apart from the obvious one that the crossing of the main force could proceed more smoothly.

It is clear enough that some (and perhaps many) Greek states were less than wholeheartedly enthusiastic about the coming expedition. We know little about their reasons, but may conjecture that one of the objections lay in the suspicion that they were being forced to contribute to what was really no more than an imperialistic venture for the benefit of the Macedonians.[43] In this case, the advance-party might demonstrate the bona fides of the crusade before the Hellenes themselves were called upon to despatch their levies. While a few months' campaigning by a relatively small force would hardly serve to punish the Persians for their ancient sacrilege, it might begin a task equally important for Macedonian propaganda in Greece, that of 'liberating' the Greek cities of the Anatolian seaboard and the offshore islands. While the religious theme had to serve as the official motive for the participation of Hellenic League troops, the liberation-theme was very much more real. It was a cause that had often received lip-service on the mainland, and to Philip it provided a useful avenue for demonstrating his devotion to the ideals he had proclaimed in founding and undertaking to uphold the Common Peace. So it was with this avowed intent that the 10,000-strong force of Macedonians and mercenaries was ferried across the Hellespont to Abydos.[44]

Whether or not it was known now – as Alexander let it be known later – that the Macedonian treasury would find it difficult to bear the cost of a campaign that did not largely finance itself with booty, this must at least have been a factor in Philip's thinking. He may not have been short of ready cash but he was in debt, and a further advantage to the dual attack was that the first and much cheaper force could devote itself to bringing over as allies the Anatolian Greeks, whereupon the second and expensive army could press on quickly into the interior towards the treasury at Sardis, unhampered by the need to pass time in serving propagandistic ends already catered for by the advance-party.[45]

Unfortunately, next to nothing is known of the progress of these troops, who were led by Parmenion, his son-in-law Attalos and Amyntas, the son of the Lynkestian Arrabaios.[46] What little information does survive relates to the campaigns of 335 and only occasionally and by implication to those of 336. A further difficulty hinders our attempts to assess Philip's policy as carried out by his old and trusted subordinate. Assuming that the advance-party left in about March 336 and that Philip died in July, or thereabouts, of the same year, it appears that very little progress can have been made in that time. Now it may be true that Alexander, once acknowledged as king, is unlikely to have countermanded or perhaps even modified the instructions issued by his father to Parmenion[47] until he had time to turn from the Illyrian and Greek problems that followed his accession; and by that time (late 335) he judged it preferable to recall Parmenion to assist in the planning of the main expeditionary force. On the other hand, it is equally certain that Philip's main force was to set out long before Alexander's actually did; indeed, this was probably planned for later 336. The wedding-celebrations in Aigai at which Philip lost his life were heavily dominated by the imminence of that expedition, which should have got under way in the late summer or the autumn to take all possible advantage of the instability of Persian affairs at the time. It is therefore most unlikely that Parmenion had any orders that would govern his campaigning for longer than the current season. Then, not many weeks later came news of the murder. Amid the uncertainties of the next months, while Alexander was striking out at his rivals, real and imaginary (and Attalos and perhaps Parmenion had cause to feel uneasy until the purge was done), while Illyrians and Greeks, even the Thessalians, were in revolt or planning it, while it must have seemed that the whole crusade must be abandoned, the proclaimed purpose must very easily have been overlooked.[48] It is very easy, in other words – and it must have been at the time – to lose sight of the original aims as they were carried out to Philip's orders.

None the less, it is clear that initially events in Asia Minor went according to plan. As the army of Parmenion crossed the Hellespont and moved southwards down the coast, partisans in several (perhaps many) Greek cities rose in revolt against their Persian-backed governments. The little island of Tenedos was probably quick to come over, along with Lesbos and Chios.[49] On the mainland it is likely that coastal cities at least as far south as Ephesos declared their allegiance and were enrolled, like the islanders, as members of the Hellenic League. Perhaps such realignments were not so much reflections of the anti-Persian aspirations of the crusade as instances of the advantage taken by internal political groups to overthrow the existing governments. This process seems clear in two cases for which some documentation survives: Ephesos and Eresos (a city of Lesbos). In both, it appears, the local democrats (or so called) seized upon the approach or the appearance of the Macedonian army as an opportunity to oust their tyrant-regimes (also so called), whose dominance allegedly derived from Persian patronage. In Eresos, the brothers Hermon, Heraios and Apollodoros were pulled down and the triumphant democracy celebrated its emergence in the erection of altars to Zeus Philippios, in Philip's honour. The intervention here, indeed, may have been brought about by the mediation of Theophrastos, a native of the place, through his friend Aristotle.[50] In Ephesos, similarly, the *demos* must have risen in 336, overturning the tyranny and welcoming Parmenion. Here a statue of Philip was set up in the famous temple of Artemis said to have been burnt out at the moment of Alexander's birth.[51] Although it can not be dated at all precisely – either 336 or 334 is possible – there is evidence to suggest that at Erythrai too the same succession of events obtained.[52] (In the first two cases and possibly the third, the recovery of Persian strength in 335 swung the balance against the democracies, which were subsequently restored by Alexander in 334.)

CELEBRATIONS AT AIGAI

There is thus reason to believe that the role of the advance-party was the dual one of preparing the way for the main army and of establishing the 'credentials' of the crusade in the eyes of the Greeks, and that during the campaign-season of 336 these aims were pursued with considerable success. By the time that, in about July,[53] friends of Macedon and delegations from all over Greece assembled for the lavish celebrations prepared for the royal wedding at Aigai, news of some of these achievements must have been reaching the mainland. It will have compensated in some measure for another event that must have been roughly contemporary: the birth to Kleopatra of a daughter. Yet again the king had demonstrated his limited capacity for producing sons. However, it did at least show that his newest wife was fertile, unlike two of her predecessors. The child was named Europe.[54] (Presumably the next, according to sex, would have been something like Asianike or Asianikos, after the manner of Thessalonike, who was now about fifteen years old.)

During the preparations for the wedding the king despatched a herald to Delphoi to obtain from Apollo a suitable response to serve as rallying-cry for his coming ventures. The priestess' answer, we are told, included the line: *The bull has been garlanded, the end is come, the sacrificer is at hand.*[55] What else it contained is unknown, but its typical ambiguity seems to have attached it unsurprisingly to the coming rituals in Aigai as well as, neatly but non-committally, to the propaganda surrounding the great crusade. The survival of this line (if it is genuine) was due to the even greater impact it gained from the murder that was to climax the nuptial festivities.

As an exercise in public relations, which from every point of view was its purpose, the wedding would have been a resounding success, From all over Greece guests and visitors crowded into Aigai, bringing in many cases official honours conferred by their cities upon the king. In fact the central figure at all times was Philip himself; so far as the Greeks, at least, were concerned the ceremonies only provided an opportunity to fête the new Hegemon of the Common Peace.[56] As a herald from Athens announced the conferment of a golden crown by the Athenian *demos* and added that his city would harbour no man who dared plot against the king, Philip must have felt confident that, in spite of the setbacks of a decade, his diplomacy had finally come near to producing the effect he had desired from the beginning. The sort of elation among the Greek states that could lead even Athens to proffer so generous a token of her respect can have been caused by nothing less than the news of Hellenic democracies in Asia Minor scrambling to power over the oligarchic bodies of their pro-Persian opponents. To the Greek world the panhellenic crusade was becoming a reality.

ASSASSINATION

When the wedding itself was over (or so we must assume, for the attention of our sources is devoted exclusively to celebration of the Persian theme and to the ironic tragedy concurrently unfolding), the stadium at Aigai filled with spectators for a dawn ceremony prefacing the athletic contests of the second day.[57] The official procession began to enter the arena, first statues of the gods[58] and then the royal retinue, the honoured friends and guests of the king. Last of all Philip, resplendent in white cloak and walking between his heir and his new son-in-law, prepared to enter after ordering his body-guards to stand away; one who stood so high among subject and ally alike had no need of guards. But, as he stepped forward, a young man, one of his own body-guards, sprang forward and stabbed him through the heart with a Celtic sword. The king fell. In the mêlée that followed, some body-guards rushed, too late, to his side, while others pursued his attacker. Nearby at the city gates horses awaited the fugitive, but before he could reach them Pausanias tripped, was caught and killed on the spot.[59] In a few minutes the drama was over. Philip and his murderer lay dead.

But the question remained – and remains. Was the assassin alone in his deed or had his hand been guided by others to its target? Rumours abounded, at least in later years, but in circumstances that throw considerable doubt on their implications. However, there is little doubt about the 'official' view, which was that the attacker had acted out of motives of private vengeance.[60]

RATIONALIZATION

Roughly a year earlier,[61] so the story went, a young body-guard of Philip, one Pausanias, who was the king's lover, found himself supplanted in the king's affections by another young man of the same name. Disturbed at his rejection, Pausanias began to insult his rival, who confided to Attalos that he was unable to bear the taunts. In battle shortly afterwards against the Illyrians of Pleurias, he deliberately stepped forward to shield the king from blows aimed at him and so met his death. Attalos chose to hold the surviving Pausanias responsible for the tragedy, invited him to dinner, plied him with alcohol until he lost consciousness and then handed him over to his muleteers for punishment. The young man resentfully complained of his treatment to the king, who however was unable, on account of his own relationship with Attalos, to satisfy his desire for revenge. Instead he sought to mollify the young man, gave him expensive gifts and promoted him to a higher rank among the body-guards.

But Pausanias was not to be appeased. He planned to avenge himself not only upon Attalos, who had done him wrong, but on Philip too, who had failed to assuage his wounded pride.[62] So, posting horses at the gates of Aigai before the ceremony, he carried through his plan. This, the version repeated by Diodoros, is also given, in much abbreviated form, by Aristotle. The latter's publication of it, in view of his connections with the Argead house, justifies our belief that it was either true or at least officially encouraged or sanctioned.

Justin's account contains two versions. He begins with the mistreatment of Pausanias by Attalos and proceeds in much the same way as the official version, adding that Philip had not only failed to act on the complaints but ridiculed the complainant. As usual where the degree of sensationalism is concerned Justin is able to go one better than anyone else. But on this occasion he goes very much further. For he now appears to come under the influence of a second version. Having alleged that the breaking-point for Pausanias came when he saw Attalos not punished but rewarded with a command in the advance-force for Asia Minor,[63] he introduces the additional theme that the assassin was driven to his act by the blandishments of Olympias, with the knowledge of Alexander himself. At this point he inserts the story of Philip's last wedding (to Kleopatra) and his 'repudiation' of Olympias, Alexander's quarrel with Attalos and the flight of mother and son to Epeiros and Illyria respectively. Olympias, he declares, prepared the horses for Pausanias' escape, publicly exulted afterwards in the death of Philip and cruelly murdered Europe and drove Kleopatra to suicide in Alexander's absence.

With such an agglomeration of distortions and implausibilities – such as assassinations have always attracted and always will – the task of assigning responsibility for the murder has become quite impossible. The official version has its weaknesses – not least in the improbabilities of the developing saga of the two Pausaniases; but the primacy given to the unsavoury role of Attalos suggests that it was an explanation that could circulate plausibly shortly after the event; for at the time he was absent (and the absent are always wrong) and before long his own treason made him an eminently suitable villain.[64] The place given in Justin's variant on the official version to the advance-party command of Attalos not only ties in with an independently attested historical datum but provides a credible explanation as to why a twelve-month-old grudge should have been reactivated. Pelion upon Ossa! If it was indeed, as it appears, the story circulated more or less immediately afterwards, then we should hesitate before perceiving smoke in the detail which has three of (apparently) Alexander's own bodyguards killing the assassin before he can be questioned.[65] Apart from the intrinsically short odds against his survival in such circumstances, whoever reached him first, we may surely take it that, if there was really strong suspicion of Alexander at the time, that is one item that would have been suppressed from the record.

With this official version, built around at least a core that is plausible, Justin's second version clashes badly. Whatever we might conclude regarding the character and ambitions of Olympias – whether or not we are prepared to associate her provisionally in the murder – some parts of this account are totally incredible. She could not have openly laid a gold crown on the head of the dead murderer, have cremated his body upon Philip's remains, have had him properly buried or have instituted an annual sacrifice on his behalf.[66] Such fantasies could not have circulated while people remembered the events of that day. In fact this version fits best in the context of *c.* 316, during Kassandros' bitter propaganda-war against Olympias, his capture of her at Pydna and his success in procuring her condemnation and death before the military assembly.[67]

It may be that the overlay of fiction and time is too dense for us to penetrate to the truth. A later fabrication vies for our attention with a version that was acceptable to Alexander and may have been designed to cloak, rather than reveal the facts. But it is worth noting that the presumption of misrepresentation on his part follows from a prior assumption that he was in some way responsible for the murder. That, in turn, rests upon two lines of reasoning: first, that Alexander (and Olympias) stood to gain most by Philip's premature death; and second, that his subsequent ruthless purge of rivals, whether real or imagined, was the action of a guilty man – or, at least, that it reveals the character of a young man who would not be deterred from his ambitions by any distaste for patricide. The more important premise is the former, for its invalidity would render the latter irrelevant. As nearly every commentator has religiously asked: *cui bono?*

Indubitably Alexander did profit most. But, in spite of attempts to suggest otherwise, all he did gain was the hastening of a legacy that was in any case secure for the foreseeable future. His succession was assured when the proper time came, and the difficulties of his early years as king[68] only served to reinforce what he must have known – that he was (or ought to have been) too young and inexperienced to hold his own against the giants of the Macedonian power-élite. Indeed, it might be argued that what Alexander did gain was fortuitous, whereas what he stood to *lose* by the sudden catastrophe and its inevitable aftermath of struggling pretenders was no less than the kingdom and his life. That he lost neither was a tribute not to the timing of his accession, but to his own skill and determination and to the loyalty of those who cast in their lot with him. The same argument governs the case of Olympias almost as effectively. We might pursue it a little further by suggesting that the whole story of the estrangement of Olympias and Philip – by no means the necessary result of the marriage to Kleopatra – is a product of the late anti-Olympias propaganda, for it is in precisely that context that Justin preserves it, whereas Diodoros does not know of it at all. Otherwise it appears only in Athenaios and Plutarch, both of whom probably take it, as the former certainly does, from the third-century biographer Satyros. Its dramatics – the confrontation of Attalos and Alexander, the drawn sword of Philip, the aphorism of Alexander on his father's drunken inelegance – will qualify it for that milieu, where it furnishes a suitably melodramatic motivation for the unbelievable atrocities ascribed to Olympias without seriously denigrating Alexander himself.

The official version, on the other hand, is at least fundamentally plausible, especially when reduced to the bare details on which Aristotle and Justin (in his first version) agree and on which Diodoros embroiders – the story, that is to say, that Attalos abused Pausanias, who, receiving less than the satisfaction he required from his king, was driven to violence when his enemy was given a new position of honour in the advance-party. Some have found it difficult to believe that Pausanias could have wished to kill Philip if his grudge was primarily against Attalos. But who expects rigorous rationality from any assassin, especially one who chose the occasion and the moment Pausanias did, when, as a body-guard, he could presumably have killed Philip in private with less risk to himself and with greater chances of success? Philip was not the first nor, certainly, the last political figure to be cut down by the insensate act of a maniac. Along with the allegations as to Olympias' complicity in the murder we should probably abandon the anecdote which seeks to provide her motivation; this, as we have already seen, makes very poor sense. Whether the account of Pixodaros' bid for Macedonian alliance may be accepted is rather less clear. Only Plutarch knows of it. That in itself does not tell against its truth, except that Arrian, the best source we have for the period after Alexander's accession, conspicuously fails to notice it in a summary of the fortunes of Karia in the years around Pixodaros' reign.[69] All that can be said though, with complete confidence, is that our evidence, taken as a whole, does not suggest that Olympias and Alexander were implicated in the regicide; neither does it attribute to them any credible motive. There is some reason for believing that, while Alexander's succession was under no challenge, he may have thought it was; but this rests entirely on the two very dubious stories of Attalos and Pixodaros (and on the very vaguest of allusions by Arrian); it is worth little. There was trouble of some sort between the king and his son, but we cannot tell what it was.[70]

INTENTIONS, REALIZED AND UNREALIZED

A final problem remains to be considered. The question as to how far Alexander initially intended to go has been put often; more rarely has it been asked of Philip.[71] But there are in reality two separate questions here, the one involving Philip and his (likely) plans, the other tied up more with Macedonia than with the king himself. For this enquiry has been pursued too often as though the Persian crusade of Philip and Alexander was a construct of the one's ambition transmitted with his crown to the other. And yet we should hardly expect so vast a flood of social and military energies to be released by nothing more than the arbitrary decision of one man, however personally outstanding or influential. We may continue to disagree over the extent to which in human affairs the circumstances produce the man, or vice versa, but we have progressed beyond the era in which historians permitted themselves to explain all action in terms of the personal motivation of individuals. We need to consider, then, not only the likely territorial extent of Philip's aims, but also the dynamic forces that led him to cast these plans in the first place and that would have sustained him (as they did his son) in the difficult campaigns ahead.

Without reviving the problem of Isokrates' influence on Philip – or, more to the point, his perception of the forces driving the king and of the directions in which the king himself was giving promise of channelling them – we may nevertheless take as a starting-point the three choices he saw were open to any invader of Persian territory from Greece. They were, in practical terms, the only three.[72] Isokrates' presentation of the possibilities leaves us in no doubt as to his preference, whether it is governed by what he thinks practical or what he considers desirable. 'Most of all', Philip might, he says, 'attempt to lay hold of the whole Persian kingdom.' But he does not elaborate. He passes on so quickly as to give the impression that he does not regard his own suggestion seriously. It is included because it is a logical alternative. Passing on to the second: 'or, if not that, to conquer and sever from it the vast territory of Asia (Minor) . . . "from Kilikia to Sinope".' Here colonies might be planted to draw out from the body of Greece the poisonous effects of the large numbers of displaced men, refugees from impoverished soil, stasis and war, whose presence and availability as mercenaries could transmute a backwoods Jason, given only ambition and cash, into a glittering political leader. Such men might be employed in the task of winning Asia Minor. Then, settled in agrarian prosperity in the hinterland near the Tauros range, they would serve Greece both by their absence and by the buffer their colonies would raise against Persian encroachment. 'But even if you fail in these aims, this much at least will be easily accomplished: you will liberate the Greek cities of Asia Minor.' The first alternative, he seems to say, is but an ideal; the second is realizable, laudable and beneficial; the third will suffice *faute de mieux*.[73]

Such advice as to the courses open to the king is, of course, irrelevant to our search for his aims. But it does gain some significance when we remember that he was attempting to persuade Philip of the virtues of a particular policy and must therefore recommend what was not only attractive, but also practical.

It is possible to speculate at length on the respective virtues of each alternative. Philip was too strongly cognizant of his own successes against the Athenian coastal bases of the northern Aegean to place any faith in the long-term prospects of 'liberated' coastal cities against a hostile hinterland. Such an achievement would be a sham from the outset and would soon collapse. To take on the whole of the Persian Empire, on the other hand, was an aim practical really only after it had been achieved. One may point to the inherent weaknesses of this heterogeneous and unstable edifice. But the vast distances that made the mobilization and deployment of imperial armies difficult rendered logistical and communications problems doubly serious for the intruder. And for all the military inferiority of the Persian fighting-forces, the Great King, while his vast wealth lasted, would always be able to call upon the talents of such Greek commanders and troops as had brought the tottering empire back to its feet in the later 340s. Men of the calibre of Mentor and his brother Memnon were known in the west for their ability and, no less, for their loyalty to their master. It may be true that Persia was ripe for collapse, but from the outside its weaknesses appeared counteracted by its strengths.

Nevertheless, although it is unlikely that Philip had his sights set as high as the empire, it is evident that by July 336 they did reach further than just the coastal cities of Asia Minor. The successes towards this end that could already be laid to the credit of the advance-force of Parmenion could be expected to continue and increase. If that was all that the king required, the first-stage army would win the bulk of the credit, leaving for the stage-two force, the panhellenic army, mainly the chore of holding what had come over voluntarily. It is in fact too easy for us to overlook the achievements of the first stage. The reversals inflicted as Dareios and Memnon took full advantage of the loss of Macedonian impetus on Philip's death were sufficient to negate many of the gains, and the failure of the second stage to materialize when planned has almost wiped the initial successes from our sources. But the exhilarating atmosphere in Aigai, which reflected the optimism of the whole mainland, is our best guide to their magnitude. It should discourage us from dismissing the notion of a panhellenic crusade as utter fraud. It was not yet a strong enough sustaining force to lift the new and still shaky unity over the disruption of Philip's assassination, and it was certainly transmuted into sullen and grudging acquiescence as a result of the methods Alexander used – perhaps was forced to use – to bring Greece back under control. But it is unhistorical to paint the accomplishments of early 336 in the much more sombre hues of post-335. It is difficult to believe that Philip's aims could have been encompassed by Isokrates' third alternative.

When Alexander in 332 was engaged in the siege of Tyre, envoys from Dareios III came to him bearing the Great King's offer to pay ransom of 10,000 talents for his captured harem, to give his daughter in marriage to Alexander, who would then be his friend and ally, and to cede 'all the territory from the Euphrates to the Greek sea'.[74] When Alexander had these proposals read in his Council of the Companions, his senior commander is said to have urged him to accept. The king declined. It has often been remarked that this may represent a sign that Parmenion, who had apparently been Philip's co-planner of the whole crusade and had been commander of its first phase, took it that Dareios' offer fulfilled the original aims of Philip's expedition.[75]

Six months earlier, when Alexander had not penetrated so far into Phoenicia, Dareios had proposed similar terms, but on that occasion he had offered 'the territory and cities of Asia as far as the River Halys'.[76] That this is extremely close to the area envisaged in Isokrates' second alternative is not due to any particular prescience on that author's part, but rather to the fact that this was an obvious and natural unit of control, whether its eastern boundary were defined as 'a line from Kilikia to Sinope' or as the Halys River. Both are approximate ways of saying 'as far as the Tauros range of mountains', which cut off Asia Minor from Armenia, Mesopotamia and the rest of the Persian Empire. The offer at Tyre, although it included a little more territory (in effect Asia Minor plus the Kappadokian satrapy), was similar. On the earlier occasion Alexander's reaction, according to Diodoros, was to suppress Dareios' real letter and to read to his staff a forged version 'more in accord with his interests'. The forgery, perhaps the version preserved without comment by Arrian, couches the offer in terms that will be quite unacceptable to the Macedonian officers; by omitting the territorial offer altogether, Alexander contrived to have his senior staff repudiate the overtures.

No firm argument is possible on the basis of such evidence, but the implication of both incidents is that the leading officers of Alexander's army (who at this time were largely Philip's officers) were prepared, or were likely to accept Dareios' proposals. This in turn raises the presumption that what was being tendered was approximately what had been envisaged in the original plans of the expedition; that, however fluid the whole scheme might have been and however dependent at each point upon success at earlier stages, it was the conquest of Asia Minor that was regarded as the desirable or likely end. It may have been that in the end Philip would have proved as much of an opportunist as his son, but it is nevertheless likely that some statement of the provisional aim of the crusade was in circulation before it began. That no more definite trace of Philip's aims survives in our source is not really surprising. Those in question are Alexander-sources and, whether or not relatively firm territorial aims were announced or rumoured at the outset, they are likely to have been forgotten in the light of what was won, especially by authors who lived long after the event and who were in any case little disposed to credit the great Alexander with ambitions any inferior to his achievements.

It has been observed that Philip's evident proclivity for transferring population-groups within the kingdom as well as in the neighbouring areas arose in part out of an attempt to overcome the serious problems of social and political disunity which had always plagued Macedonia in the past. He transplanted villages and ethnic groups where it was expedient to divide hostile concentrations or to strengthen the well-disposed – no less than where it was desirable for the consolidation of frontiers and communication-routes. Similarly the large-scale augmentation of the *hetairos*-class – with the consequent dilution and weakening of the established nobility – by numbers of new men, together with the obligation he laid upon the *hetairoi*, old and new, to assign their teenage sons to the royal court for training in leadership and for personal service to the king, will have been directed to this end. Through the sons Philip would be able to strengthen his patronal links with the new generation; at the same time they were in effect hostages for the co-operation of their families.

But while such measures indicate a recognition of the old Macedonian duality and a concern to prevent its effects while attempting to superimpose a new unity, it seems that he came to see the army, more than any other single instrument, not only as the guarantor of Macedonian sovereignty and security, but as the catalyst of the new unity. It seems fair to say that, quite literally, the army was expanded so as to become the state. The overriding emphasis on the unity of the former thus fundamentally affected the latter.

But the creation of a powerful army and a powerful military class has its difficulties and constraints. For the army to act effectively and cohesively both as the instrument of security and the catalyst of unity, it required – like any army – military objectives and military achievements. The king, if he wished to maintain an acceptable socio-military harmony, had to reckon with the interests and pressures of a society to which war was a positive benefit. This military factor must have been a crucial determinant of foreign policy, for Philip (and, later, Alexander) was obliged in his policies to give expression to these interests or face the alternative of internal struggle. However, it has been one of the purposes of this book to suggest that Macedonian foreign policy under Philip was not one of undirected and indiscriminate militarism. Militarism, certainly; but guided in directions both identifiable and consistent, and modified or replaced very often by diplomacy.

We have seen that the early years of Philip's reign were devoted to meeting the existing problems of Macedonia's own security, the removal of immediate threats from beyond the borders, the expansion of those borders to well defined and defensible natural frontiers and the creation of a circle of influence by diplomacy or war in the surrounding states. Three of these neighbouring areas, Thessaly, Thrace and, to a lesser extent, Epeiros, were the objects over many years of careful and successive interventions, political manipulation, the cultivation of pro-Macedonian interest-groups and eventually, in the later 340s, when earlier arrangements had proved deficient, of a complete re-ordering of the government. The treatment of these territories contrasts sharply with that accorded to the other neighbouring areas, Illyria, Paionia and northern Thrace, in which Macedonian policy seems to have aimed merely at the building of buffers; these areas were subordinated by the occasional war, when necessary, and held down by the establishment of fortresses on or near the frontiers. A third category, which presents a lesser problem, is represented by the Chalkidike, western Thrace and some of the nearer Epeirote, Illyrian and Paionian areas, which were actually swallowed up in the expansion of the kingdom to the effective natural barriers offered roughly by the Aegean, the Nestos on the east, the Pindos on the west and a succession of ranges and passes across the north.

In all of this the most outstanding feature is the care with which Macedonian interests in Thessaly, Thrace and Epeiros were nurtured. These areas, the first two in particular but the third in emergencies, were, obviously enough, the areas through which Philip most needed access to what lay beyond (or control over who came from beyond), and this would be sufficient to explain their special treatment. But, at the same time, by differentiating so definitely between the two types of territory that comprised the Macedonian circle of influence, Philip was to a considerable extent drawing a blueprint of his own longer-term plans. Whether he felt that the circumstances of the time *obliged* him to ensure security of passage to (and, of course, from) the south and east, or gave shape to Macedonia's policies with positive, quasi-imperial ends in mind, the fact remains that by doing so he was both placing certain limitations upon his own options and, in a way, giving notice of his intentions. Given that there was a high degree of inevitability in the explosion of Macedonian energies and that Philip realized that his policies had to embrace this outward movement, and given that trans-Danubian ambitions, Black Sea, northern Illyrian, even Italian conquests were all, in theory, possible objects for the satisfaction and absorption of these internal but expansive forces, Philip's failure to take the obvious and prerequisite steps in the intervening territories, the areas across which the vital communication-lines must lie, precluded their use in this way for the foreseeable future. The two significant directions, those in which he did open and leave open his options, were south and east – and beyond Thessaly (with Epeiros) and Thrace respectively lay the major Greek states and Asia. It has therefore been a major preoccupation of this work to explore his intentions towards these areas.

Philip's dealings with Greece and his projected dealings with the Persian Empire have normally, almost invariably, been explained in terms of a 'domino' theory. The treaty with Athens in 346, the Peace of Philokrates, has been interpreted – as it was by Demosthenes – as one significant staging-point on the road to the eventual more total subjugation of the Greek states represented by the settlement at Korinth in 338/7, made possible by the Macedonian defeat of the most powerful Greek states at Chaironeia. That accomplished, this standard interpretation continues, Philip turned to the east to find further objects of victory and conquest – an aim that in the event, however, had to be pursued by his like-minded son.

In the present treatment, however, two points have been emphasized. First: in August 338, with victory at Chaironeia behind him, Philip had the Greek states actually – or certainly potentially – at his feet. He could have gone ahead to subjugate them and to control them so as to make even internal autonomy virtually impossible. In the process of achieving this, the Macedonian army would have been provided with useful military objectives for years to come. By contrast, what Philip did was to impose on these states a surprisingly mild settlement, a variant on a form invented by Greeks and well known to them, with as little open coercion as possible. Even Chaironeia occurred only after the failure, through Persian intervention, of a bloodless attempt to achieve the same end by squeezing the Athenian corn-pipeline at the Hellespont. After the decisive battle, further military confrontations were carefully avoided, and, by the individual settlements of 338, many of the old causes of tension on the mainland were eased. But immediately these arrangements had been crystallized in the treaty at Korinth, Philip put his proposal that the united states campaign against Persia. Having achieved his political ends in Greece, that is, his immediate concern was to withdraw and turn eastwards.

Second: in two outstanding ways the peace of Philokrates, more than eight years earlier, appeared to be designed to achieve substantially what the settlement of 338/7 did achieve. It provided for the weakening of Thebes, to the advantage of Athens and several central Greek states; and it too appears to have been associated with the imminence of an Asian campaign. In both of these aims, of course, the Peace was not only unsuccessful; it hardly reached the point, indeed, at which they could be realistically proclaimed. Then, within weeks of its ratification, Demosthenes was urging his fellows to bide their time against the day when they might rise and smash it. Within four years it was irreparably undermined. But the apparent coincidence, in substance, at least, between Philip's aims in 346 and his dispensation of 338/7 suggests that the Demosthenic view, that the Peace of Philokrates was a mere step towards a more thorough-going domination, is untenable. It seems more reasonable to conclude that the arrangement of 346 represented, in Philip's intentions, the final formative step in his relationship with Greece. The Common Peace formed at Korinth was but its replacement, on a firmer, more realistic basis, when it had been sabotaged.

A consequence of this interpretation is that Demosthenes' co-envoys in 346 were right to strive for the settlement that Philip wanted, and they were right to argue, when its intent had been thwarted in late Skirophorion, that the Peace they did have must not be destroyed but preserved for the day on which its deficiencies could be made good. Had it stood, the Greek states might well have seen, after 346, as little of Philip as they did after 337, or of Alexander after 335.

From the Macedonian viewpoint, Greece was poor in all respects but one, that its soldiers were the best, outside their own, in the eastern Mediterranean world. Whether or not Philip wished to make very extensive use of the Greek soldier or sailor in a co-operative eastern venture, he was at the least compelled to protect his kingdom against their use in opposition to him. In military terms, that is, Greece was only incidental to Philip's longer-term aims. His ambitions lay in two directions, south and east. Towards the former he turned for security and coalition, but for a continuing source of military objectives and wealth he turned towards Asia.

APPENDIX

COINAGE UNDER PHILIP AND ALEXANDER: SOME OBSERVATIONS

It is the purpose of this appendix to survey briefly and from the historian's viewpoint some of the recent trends in numismatic studies of Philip's reign as they relate both to Macedonian regal issues and to those of two closely related areas, Philippoi and Thessaly. The conventional picture will no longer do, and, although much work remains to be done (a major step is forthcoming in the publication of the corpus of Philippic gold and silver by Georges le Rider, who has been extremely generous in supplying advance-information of his observations and conclusions), some of the outlines of a new picture are beginning to emerge. In what follows these abbreviations are used:

le Rider: Georges le Rider, by private communication (see above), cited here with permission;

Bellinger (I): A. R. Bellinger, 'Philippi in Macedonia', *ANSMN* 11 (1964) 29ff & Pl. vi–xi;

Bellinger (II): A. R. Bellinger, 'The Thessaly Hoard of 1938', *Congr. Internat. di Numismatica, Roma* ii (1961) 57ff.

Le Rider's general conclusions on the chronology of Philip's regal issues of gold and silver are as follows:

Gold: Philip began striking gold in the second half of his reign (as West, *Num. Chron.*, 1923, 177ff., thought), after 346; this appeared to coincide neatly with Bellinger (I)'s terminal date for the gold of Philippoi – but see below. A fairly limited number of issues appears to have been struck during Philip's lifetime, but a much larger volume posthumously. (This reflects, presumably, the greater national wealth and imperial income of Philip's later reign and of Alexander's period, as well as the disappearance in 348 of the prolific Chalkidian mint at Olynthos.) The coins were struck at two mints, clearly Pella and Amphipolis. The issues appear to run from post-346 down to *c.* 328 and are then interrupted, resuming *c.* 323 or later and running to *c.* 315 or later, with sporadic emissions thereafter.

Silver: Philip began coining silver on the 'Thraco-Macedonian' standard from one mint (certainly Pella) in 349 and, soon afterwards, from another (therefore Amphipolis, from *c.* 357/6). The two distinct styles of silver (distinguished by the respective reverse types of a bearded horseman and a naked young rider bearing a palm: see Head *HN*[2] 223, Babelon, *Monn. Grec. et Rom.* II, 4, pp. 518ff., second and first series, respectively) cover roughly the periods 359 to *c.* 348/346 and *c.* 348/346 to the end of the reign; the second style then continues post-humously until *c.* 328, is interrupted and then resumes *c.* 323 until *c.* 315 or later, with further emissions thereafter, at least from the Amphipolis mint.

In 1964 Bellinger (I) subdivided the gold and silver coins of Philippoi into two clear classes, which he labelled Styles I and II. Style I was identical to the earlier issues from Krenides by the 'Mainland Thasians', except that the legend *ΘΑΣΙΟΝ ΗΠΕΙΡΟ* gave way to *ΦΙΛΙΠΠΩΝ*. In Style II a stylistic change was evident and, with the silver, an increase in weight from the 'Paionian' standard of Damastion to the 'Phoenician' or 'Thraco-Macedonian' standard. For the Style I silver a total of 6 (+?) issues was certain and it therefore lasted at least six years, i.e. *c.* 356–351+. But since the fall of the Olynthian mint, which had coined on the latter standard, appeared to be the determining factor the period was probably *c.* 356–348. Only two issues of Style I gold were known and, since these were of the same style as the silver, they probably covered the same period. With Stlye II Bellinger found only two issues of silver, which he tentatively dated *c.* 348 and 347. Of the Style II gold he found four issues, which might cover *c.* 348–345+, but he acknowledged that these might run as late as the end of Philip's reign, presumably by analogy with the longer-lived gold issues of Style I. (It is to be noted that Bellinger (I)'s study was based on admittedly incomplete evidence, largely the coins available in the trays of the American Numismatic Society.)

Bellinger (I) also treated the bronze coinage of Philip, Alexander the Great and Philippoi and, on Philip's bronze, reached fundamentally the same conclusions as le Rider has for the gold and silver: that there were two mints and large posthumous issues. But he did not attempt to determine the chronology of the posthumous coins.

Bellinger (II) dealt with a hoard of fourth- and third-century silver coins found in Thessaly in 1938. Their burial-date must have been soon after 250 BC. The hoard contained large numbers of Macedonian regal issues representing the reigns of Alexander the Great, Philip III, Lysimachos, Demetrios Poliorketes and Antigonos Gonatas. Other than 72 Old Style (i.e. pre-322, approx.) Athenian tetradrachms, the other large group was 155 drachms of Thessalian Larisa. The general abundance of Larisaian coins in the fourth century, as compared with cities like Pherai and Pharsalos, combined with the fact that the earliest Macedonian regal coins represented in this hoard dated from *c.* 325, led Bellinger to the conclusion that Larisaian silver continued to be minted until that time, when it must have been replaced in Thessalian currency by the Macedonian regal issues of Alexander and then his successors. (This appears to be supported in general terms by the fact that Noe's *Bibliog. of Greek Coin Hoards*[2] lists only two Thessalian hoards containing any coins of Philip and these both belong late in the fourth century, not in Philip's lifetime: Nos. 533 & 595; see Kraay, *Greek Coins & History* 15f.) The absence of Pheraian coins in the hoard suggested to Bellinger that the beginnings of the Larisaian group represented dated after 352 (or 344), when Philip's defeat of Pherai removed it from the position of dominance it had enjoyed in previous decades.

The picture emerging from these studies has certain impressive characteristics when their results are viewed together. Philip's regal gold and silver both (though beginning at different times) ran to *c.* 328, stopped and then resumed *c.* 232 (le Rider); Bellinger (I) did not attempt to date the posthumous bronze and le Rider did not include it in his study, but the same possibility is open there. (However,

Bellinger did note 36 or – by combining similar symbols and monograms – 14+ different issues for the posthumous bronze of Philip, which, at one per year, is of the right order to cover fairly neatly the periods that le Rider postulates for the gold and silver: *c.* 336–328 and *c.* 323–315.) Larisaian silver, it appears, did not terminate in 344, when Philip gained sufficient power in Thessaly to reorganize the government, but continued through his reign and until a point late in that of Alexander. The gold of Philippoi, which Bellinger (I) terminated *c.* 345 *or later*, should in fact go much further than that. There was evidently only one issue of gold by the Mainland Thasians prior to Philip's acquisition of Krenides; this single issue presumably ran *c.* 360–356, a period as long as 4 or 5 years. Gold in the Style I of Philippoi was minted in two issues and these should cover the approximate period 356–348: 8 or 9 years. Bellinger knew of four issues for Style II gold, which, as he admitted, might therefore reach considerably further than *c.* 345; in fact, at the same 4+ years per issue, they will have run to *c.* 330 or later. This hypothesis seems strengthened by the observation of influence by coins of Alexander upon some of the Philippoi Style II (see Kraay *op. cit.*, 17); and le Rider now notes significant similarities between Bellinger (I)'s No. 21 (a *silver* Style II tetradrachm from Philippoi) and some posthumous ½-staters of Philip which he dates between 336 and 328. Thus both gold and silver from Philippoi seem to continue into Alexander's reign.

Some tentative conclusions now seem in order regarding Philip's own coinage and these two other coinage-areas more or less under his control.

Striking in his own name began in the year of his accession at Pella (strengthening the view that he was never regent). His silver from Pella was soon joined (*c.* 357/6) by issues in the same style from Amphipolis. After acquiring Krenides and refounding it as Philippoi, he encouraged the inhabitants of the new colony to continue the issues its first founders had originated, but under the new name. Although he may have begun at this time to exploit the gold resources in this area he did not yet coin it in his own name; gold coinage was perhaps more the currency of international trade and the little that Macedonia needed was presumably provided by the autonomous issues of Philippoi.

The next major *terminus* was the fall of Olynthos. This wealthy state, coining the impressive issues of the Chalkidian League, fell in autumn 348, and the disappearance of its mint no doubt provided the stimulus to Philip to issue his own gold – though perhaps not immediately – and, around the same time, to introduce a new style of silver. The regal gold, bearing the head of Apollo on the obverse, continued the symbol used by the Chalkidians; but at the same time it plausibly alludes to Philip's presidency over the Pythian festival of Apollo in 346. (In fact, the allusion to Delphoi would not compel us to date the first issue of the gold *post*-346; by analogy with the account in Justin 8.2.1ff. of his religious preparations for the Crocus Field battle of 352 we might assume that he adopted this type *before* his intervention in the Sacred War in order to point up in advance the religious basis of the action he had already been invited to take and would embark upon when the circumstances were suitable.) The standard of the gold is Attic, again that of the defunct Chalkidian mint at Olynthos. The new style of silver continued the obverse type with the head of Zeus (or Herakles on the fractions), but replaced the reverse, the bearded horseman, with a naked boy-rider bearing a palm, an agonistic type presumably referring to an Olympic or other victory by one of the king's horses (cf. Plut. *Alex.* 3.5); on the reverse of the gold the two-horse chariot (biga) referred similarly to an Olympic victory (Plut.

Alex. 4.5). The regal bronze throughout the reign (and posthumously) bore Apollo's head on the obverse and a horseman wearing the *kausia* on the reverse.

Shortly afterwards, when it was within his power to enforce his own coinage upon Thessaly (say, in 344), he did not do so, at least as far as silver was concerned. Larisa, his closest ally among the Thessalian cities, continued to strike its own silver throughout Philip's reign and more than halfway through Alexander's. No Thessalian mint had ever coined gold; but the fate of the existing autonomous Thessalian bronzes has yet to be examined (every study to date has been based on the assumption that all autonomous coinage terminated in *c.* 344 but the new evidence for Larisaian silver now raises some doubt). Sordi (*AIIN* 1954, 18ff.) has suggested that some of the bronze coins of the Thessalian *koinon* bearing the legend *ΠΕΤΘΑΛΩΝ* (= *ΘΕΤΤΑΛΩΝ*) belong to its revival by Philip in 344. (Franke, *Arch. Anz.* 1970, 85ff., assigns these and similar coins to the fifth century, but he was evidently not aware of Sordi's argument and the matter needs to be reconsidered.) If this is so, then it may indicate that Philip wished to use the bronze (which had the widest currency inside the country) as an instrument of the new Thessalian unity, while allowing the well established mint at friendly Larisa to continue minting the more selectively used silver.

As regards all of these coinages Philip's death was no *terminus*. Alexander's coinage began shortly after his own accession and it was emitted parallel with his father's posthumous issues. In 336 his position was shaky in that his youth made him heavily dependent on powerful Philippic appointees of the stature of Antipatros, Parmenion, Kleitos, etc. But by 330 he had built a sufficiently stable power-base of his own to allow him, for example, to risk murdering Parmenion and to get away with it (see especially Badian, 'The Death of Parmenion', *TAPA* 1960, 324ff., 'Alexander the Great and the Loneliness of Power', *AUMLA* 1962 = *Studies in G. & R. Hist.* 192ff.). Shortly before, the Persian monarch Dareios III had died at the hands of Bessos, his Baktrian satrap. In 329 the latter was captured and in July 328 executed. Alexander's claim to be Persian King was indisputable. In the autumn of the same year he murdered Kleitos, amid general resentment over the king's autocratic demeanour and his attempts to orientalize his court. In spring 327 he married the Iranian noblewoman Roxane; and shortly afterwards followed the so-called Pages Conspiracy and the liquidation of Kallisthenes. By 328/7, that is, Alexander had quite openly cut most of the ties inherited from Philip and had established himself in his own right as King of Persia.

What may be suggested is that at roughly this time he sent an order to his Macedonian regent. There were still three non-Alexander coinages operating under Antipatros' oversight, the posthumous Philippic gold and silver (and bronze?) from Pella and Amphipolis alongside Alexander's own types (which by now were also emitted from eastern mints and, from about this time, Sikyon), the autonomous silver of Larisa (and perhaps a federal bronze of the Thessalian *koinon*) and the autonomous issues of Philippoi. It may be conjectured that he instructed Antipatros to terminate all coinages under Macedonian control that were not the king's own. Thus the posthumous Philippic issues stopped *c.* 328 or later (le Rider), the Larisaian silver stopped (to be replaced shortly in Thessaly by regal silver) and the gold and silver of Philippoi stopped.

Finally, we have evidence of declining relations between Alexander and Antipatros, in which Olympias was involved, towards 323. If what many of the older Macedonians resented most about the later Alexander was his orientalizing tendencies and the implications these bore for Macedonians and Macedonia, and their place in what the king saw as his new empire, then an order to terminate all coinage but his own would likely be interpreted (as, perhaps, he intended it) as a further step in the progressive devaluation of things Macedonian and towards the transfer eastwards of the imperial centre of gravity. The terminated coinages of Larisa (and the Thessalian *koinon?*) and Philippoi never resumed. But the posthumous issues of Philip did, *c.* 323 or later (le Rider), which raises the presumption that, as soon as Alexander was dead, Antipatros repudiated his late master's orders – and perhaps he was by then thinking more of the queen mother than of her dead son – and resumed the Philippic issues alongside those of Philip III Aridaios.

SELECT BIBLIOGRAPHY

BOOKS

Accame, S. *La lega ateniese del sec. IV a.C.*, Rome 1941.

Beloch, K. J. *Griechische Geschichte* Vols III and IV, Berlin and Leipzig 1922/3 and 1925/7.

Bengtson, H. *Die Verträge der griechisch-römischen Welt*, Munich and Berlin 1962.

Berve, H. *Das Alexanderreich aus prosopographischer Grundlage*, 2 vols, Munich 1926.

Bickermann, E. and Sykutris, J. *Speusipps Brief an König Philipp*, Leipzig 1928.

Bourguet, E. *L'Administration financière du Sanctuaire Pythique au IVᵉ S. av. J.-C.*, Paris 1905.

Busolt, G. *Griechische Staatskunde*, 2 vols (rev. Swoboda) Munich 1926.

Casson, S. *Macedonia, Thrace and Illyria*, Oxford 1926.

Chroust, A.-H. *Aristotle, New light on his life and on some of his lost Works*, Vol. I, London 1973.

Cloché, P. *Démosthènes et la fin de la démocratie athénienne*, Paris 1937.

—— *Un Fondateur d'Empire, Philippe II, Roi de Macédoine*, Saint-Étienne 1955.

—— *Histoire de la Macédoine*, Paris 1960.

Collart, P. *Philippes, Ville de Macédoine*, Paris 1937.

Cross, G. N. *Epirus*, Cambridge 1932.

Crum, R. H. *Philip II of Macedon and the City-State*, diss. Columbia 1966.

Ellis, J. R. and Milns, R. D. *The Spectre of Philip*, Sydney 1970.

Geyer, F. *Makedonien bis zur Thronbesteigung Philipps II*, Munich and Berlin 1930.

Glotz, G. (and Cohen, R.) *Histoire Grecque* Vol. III, Paris 1936.

Granier, F. *Die makedonische Heeresversammlung*, Munich 1931.

Green, P. *Alexander of Macedon; a Historical Biography*, Harmondsworth 1974.

Gude, M. *A History of Olynthus*, Baltimore 1933.

Habicht, C. *Gottmenschentum und griechische Städte* (= Zetemata No. 14), Munich 1956.

Hamilton, J. R. *Plutarch Alexander. A Commentary*, Oxford 1969.

Hammond, N. G. L. *Epirus*, Oxford 1967.

—— *A History of Macedonia*, Vol. I: *Historical Geography and Prehistory*, Oxford 1971.

Hampl, F. *Der König der Makedonen*, Weida 1934.

Head, B. V. *Historia Numorum*, 2nd edn, Oxford 1911.

Helly, B. *Gonnoi (Thessalie)*, Vol. I: *La cité et son histoire*, Amsterdam 1973.

Hoffmann, O. *Die Makedonen, ihre Sprache und ihr Volkstum*, Göttingen 1906.

Jacoby, F. *Die Fragmente der griechischen Historiker*, Leiden 1923–.

Kaerst, J. *Geschichte des Hellenismus*, Vol. 2, 2nd edn, Leipzig 1926.

Kienast, D. *Philipp II von Makedonien und das Reich der Achaimeniden* (Abhandl. der Marburger Gelehrten Gesellschaft, No. 6), Munich 1973.

Klotsch, C. *Epeirotische Geschichte bis zum J. 280*, Berlin 1911.
Kraay, C. M. *Greek Coins and History*, Oxford 1969.
Kraft, K. *Der 'rationale' Alexander* (Frankfurter Althistorische Studien, No. 5), Frankfurt 1971.
Kromayer, J. and Veith, G. *Heerwesen und Kriegführung der Griechen und Römer*, Munich 1928.
Larsen, J. A. O. *Greek Federal States; Their Institutions and History*, Oxford 1968.
Markle, M. M., III *The Peace of Philocrates*, diss. Princeton 1970.
Marsden, E. W. *Greek and Roman A)tillery*, 2 vols, Oxford 1969.
Marshall, F. H. *The Second Athenian Confederacy*, Cambridge 1905.
May, J. M. F. *The Coinage of Abdera (540–345 BC)*, (ed. Kraay and Jenkins), London 1966.
—— *The Coinage of Damastion*, Oxford 1939.
Momigliano, A. D. *Filippo il Macedone*, Florence 1934.
Parke, H. W. *Greek Mercenary Soldiers*, Oxford 1933.
Parke, H. W. and Wormell, D. E. W. *The Delphic Oracle*, 2 vols, Oxford 1956.
Pickard-Cambridge, A. W. *Demosthenes and the Last Days of Greek Freedom*, New York and London 1914.
Robinson, D. M. and Clement, P. A. *Excavations at Olynthus*, Part ix: *The Chalcidic Mint and the Excavation Coins found in 1928–1934*, Baltimore 1938.
Roebuck, C. *A History of Messenia*, publ. diss. Chicago 1941.
Ryder, T. T. B. *Koine Eirene*, Oxford 1965.
Schachermeyer, F. *Alexander der Grosse*, Vienna 1973 (= Sitzb. Vienna Vol. 285).
Schaefer, A. *Demosthenes und seine Zeit*, 3 vols, Leipzig 1885–87.
Schwahn, W. *Heeresmatrikel und Landfriede Philipps von Makedonien* (Klio Beiheft 21), Leipzig 1930.
Sordi, M. *La lega tessala fino ad Alessandro Magno*, Rome 1958.
Tarn, W. W. *Alexander the Great*, 2 vols, Cambridge 1948.
Tod, M. N. *Greek Historical Inscriptions*, Vol. ii: *From 403 to 323 BC*, Oxford 1948.
West, A. B. *The History of the Chalcidic League*, Madison 1919.
Westlake, H. D. *Thessaly in the Fourth Century BC*, London 1935.
Wilcken, U. *Alexander the Great* (English transl.) New York 1967.
Wüst, F. R. *Philipp II von Makedonien und Griechenland (346–338)*, Munich 1938.

JOURNALS AND PERIODICALS

Adams, C. D. 'Recent views of the political influence of Isocrates', *CPh* 7 (1912) 343–350.
Aymard, A. 'Basileus Makedonon', *RIDA* 4 (1950) 61–97.
—— 'Philippe de Macédoine, otage à Thèbes', *REA* 56 (1954) 15–36.
—— 'Sur l'assemblée macédonienne', *REA* 52 (1950) 115–137.
Badian, E. 'Alexander the Great and the Greeks of Asia', *Ancient Society and Institutions* (Ehrenberg Studies), Oxford 1966, 37–69.
—— 'The Death of Philip II', *Phoenix* 17 (1963) 244–250.
Bellinger, A. R. 'Philippi in Macedonia', *ANSMN* 11 (1964) 29–52 and pls vi–xi.
—— 'The Thessaly hoard of 1938', *Congr. Internaz. di Numismatica, Roma* ii, Rome 1961, 57–60.
Bosworth, A. B. 'Asthetairoi', *CQ* 23 (1973) 245–252.
—— 'Philip II and Upper Macedonia', *CQ* 21 (1971) 93–105.

Brunt, P. A. 'The aims of Alexander', *G&R* 12 (1965) 205–215.
—— 'Alexander's Macedonian cavalry', *JHS* 83 (1963) 27–46.
—— 'Euboea in the time of Philip II', *CQ* 19 (1969) 245–265.
Carter, J. M. 'Athens, Euboea and Olynthus', *Historia* 20 (1971) 418–429.
Cawkwell, G. L. 'Aeschines and the Peace of Philocrates', *REG* 73 (1960) 416–438.
—— 'Aeschines and the ruin of Phocis', *REG* 75 (1962) 453–459.
—— 'The Defence of Olynthus', *CQ* 12 (1962) 122–140.
—— 'Demosthenes' policy after the Peace of Philocrates', *CQ* 13 (1963) 120–138 (Part I) and 200–213 (Part II).
—— 'Eubulus', *JHS* 83 (1963) 47–67.
—— 'Notes on the Social War', *C&M* 23 (1962) 34–49.
Chroust, A.-H. 'Aristotle and the foreign policy of Macedonia', *Review of Politics* (Indiana) 34 (1972) 367–394.
Coste-Messelière, P. de la, 'Listes amphictyoniques du IVe s.', *BCH* 73 (1949) 201–247.
Dell, H. 'The western frontier of the Macedonian monarchy', *Archaia Makedonia* x i (Thessaloniki 1970), 115–126.
Edson, C. F. 'Early Macedonia', *ibid.*, 17–44.
Ehrhardt, C. 'Two notes on Philip of Macedon's first intervention in Thessaly', *CQ* 17 (1967) 296–301.
Ellis, J. R. 'Amyntas Perdikka, Philip II and Alexander the Great; a study in conspiracy', *JHS* 91 (1971) 15–24.
—— 'Philip's Thracian campaign of 352/351', forthcoming in *CPh.*
—— 'Population-transplants under Philip II' *Makedonika* 9 (1969) 9–16.
—— 'The stepbrothers of Philip II', *Historia* 22 (1973) 350–344.
Foucart, M. P. 'Les Athéniens dans la Chersonèse de Thrace au IVe s.', *Mém. de l'acad. de l'insc.* 38 (1909) 83–120.
Glotz, G. 'Philippe et la surprise d'Élatée', *BCH* 33 (1909) 526–546.
Griffith, G. T. 'The letter of Darius at Arrian 2.14', *PCPhS* 14 (1968) 33–48.
—— 'The Macedonian background', *G&R* 12 (1965) 125–139.
—— 'Makedonika: notes on the Macedonians of Philip and Alexander', *PCPhS* 4 (1956/7) 3–10.
—— 'Philip of Macedon's early interventions in Thessaly', *CQ* 20 (1970) 67–80.
Hamilton, J. R. 'Alexander's early life', *G&R* 12 (1965) 117–124.
Hammond, N. G. L. 'Diodorus' narrative of the Sacred War', *JHS* 57 (1937) 44–78.
—— 'The Illyrian kingdoms c. 400–167 BC', *ABSA* 61 (1966) 239–253.
—— 'The Sources of Diodorus Siculus XVI. Part I: the Macedonian, Greek and Persian narrative', *CQ* 21 (1937) 79–91.
—— 'The two battles of Chaeronea', *Klio* 13 (1938) 186–218.
Höck, A. 'Das Odrysenreich in Thrakien', *Hermes* 26 (1891) 76–117.
Kahrstedt, U. 'Städte in Makedonien', *Hermes* 81 (1953) 85–111.
Kanatsulis, D. 'Antipatros als Feldherr und Staatsmann', *Ellenika* 16 (1958/9) 14–64.
Larsen, J. A. O. 'Federation for peace in ancient Greece', *CPh* 39 (1944) 145–162.
—— 'Representative government in the panhellenic leagues', *CPh* 20 (1925) 313–329.
Macurdy, G. H. 'Queen Eurydice and woman power in early Macedonia', *AJP* 48 (1927) 201–214.
Markle, M. M. III, 'The strategy of Philip in 346', *CQ* 24 (1974) 253–268.

Merker, I. L. 'The ancient kingdom of Paionia', *Balkan Studies* 6 (1965) 35–54.
Mihailov, G. 'La Thrace aux IVe et IIIe siècles avant notre ère', *Athenaeum* 39 (1961) 33–44.
—— 'La Thrace et la Macédoine jusqu'à l'invasion des Celtes', *Archaia Makedonia* i (Thessaloniki (1970) 76–85.
Milns, R. D. 'Alexander's Macedonian cavalry and DS XVII.17.4', *JHS* 86 (1966) 167–168.
—— 'Philip II and the hypaspists, *Historia* 16 (1967) 509–512.
Perlman, S. 'The coins of Philip II and Alexander the Great and their panhellenic propaganda', *Num Chron* 1965, 57–67.
—— 'Isocrates' Philippus – a reinterpretation', *Historia* 6 (1957) 306–317.
Petsas, Ph.M. 'Pella: literary tradition and archaeological research', *Balkan Studies* 1 (1960) 113–128.
Pohlenz, M. 'Der Ausbruch des zweiten Krieges zwischen Philipp und Athen', *Gött. Nachr.* 1924, 38–42.
—— 'Philipps Schreiben an Athen', *Hermes* 46 (1929) 41–62.
Pritchett, W. K. 'Observations on Chaeronea', *AJA* 62 (1958) 307–311 and pls 80–81.
Raven, E. J. P. 'The Amphictyonic coinage of Delphi, 336–334', *NumChron* 10 (1950) 1–22.
Roebuck, C. 'The settlements of Philip II with the Greek states in 338 BC', *CPh* 43 (1948) 73–91.
Rohrmoser, J. 'Kritische Betrachtungen über den philokrateischen Frieden', *Zeitschr. für die Österreichischen Gymnasien* 25 (1874) 789–815.
Ste Croix, G. E. M. de, 'The alleged secret pact between Athens and Philip II', *CQ* 13 (1963) 110–119.
Sinclair, R. K. 'Diodorus Siculus and fighting in relays', *CQ* 16 (1966) 249–255.
Sordi, M. 'La dracma di Aleuas e l'origine di uno tipo monetario di Alessandro Magno', *Ann. dell'Ist. Ital. di Numism.* 1954, 9–22.
Treves, P. 'The meaning of *consenesco* and King Arybbas of Epirus, *AJP* 63 (1942) 129–143.
West, A. B. 'The early diplomacy of Philip II of Macedon, illustrated by his coins', *NumChron* 1923, 169–210.
Wilcken, U. 'Beiträge zur Geschichte des korinthischen Bundes', *Sitzb. München* 1917, 3–40.
—— 'Philipp II von Makedonien und die panhellenische Idee', *Sitzb. Berlin* 1929, 291–318.
Willrich, H. 'Wer liess K. Philipp von Makedonien ermordern?', Hermes 34 (1899) 174–182.
Wormell, D. E. W. 'The literary tradition concerning Hermias of Atarneus', *YCS* 5 (1935) 57–92.

ABBREVIATIONS

In references to ancient authors I have followed with little change the conventions used by the editors of *The Oxford Classical Dictionary*; the minor differences should not hamper identification. All fragments of the ancient historians are (unless noted otherwise) from F. Jacoby's *Die Fragmente der griechischen Historiker* and are given in the simple form: author plus fragment-number (Theopompos F27). References to periodicals are in standard form. For modern works often cited a shortened form of the title is commonly used (Bengtson *Verträge* No. 307; Hampl *KM* 36; or simply Beloch III, 1.529 or Tod ii 177); these will be readily identified from the Bibliography. Standard epigraphical, numismatic and general works are abbreviated as under.

BMC Mac. = *British Museum Catalogue of Greek Coins,* No. V: *Macedonia* (ed. Head), 1879.
BMV Thess. to Aetolia = *id.*, No. VI: *Thessaly to Aetolia* (ed. Gardner), 1883.
CAH VI = *Cambridge Ancient History* Vol. VI: *Macedon, 401–301 BC*, Cambridge 1954.
FD iii 5 = *Fouilles de Delphes* Tome iii: *Epigraphie,* fasc. 5: *Les Comptes du IV*[e] *siècle* (ed. Bourguet), Paris 1932.
IG = *Inscriptiones Graecae,* Berlin 1873–.
RE = *Real-Encyclopädie der classischen Altertumswissenschaft* (ed. Pauly, Wissowa, Kroll, etc.), Stuttgart 1893–.
SIG = *Sylloge Inscriptionum Graecarum* (ed. Dittenberger), Vol. I, 3rd ed., Leipzig 1915.

NOTES

NOTES ON TABLES 2–4

The data shown in these tables are derived from the inscriptions and tables in *Sylloge Inscriptionum Graecarum*, Vol. I (ed. Dittenberger) and *Fouilles de Delphes*, Vol. iii fa c. 5 (ed. Bourguet), but modified in the light of de la Coste Messelière's revision of the Delphic archon dates (*BCH* 1949, 200ff.). Tables 2 and 3, in particular, are based closely on those of de la Coste Messelière on pp. 235f., 248ff.

CHAPTER I

1 See, for example, (aside from the Macedonian regal coins of the fifth century and the first two-thirds of the fourth) Tod ii 111; [Dem.] 7.30ff.; 12.5, 11; Dem. 18.40; 19.48; Arrian 1.16.7; Plut. *Alex.* 16. There is no need to resort to Beloch's expedient (IV, 1.4 n. 3) of assuming that in documents involving Hellenic League troops the Macedonians were subsumed under the heading of 'the Hellenes'; they were embodied in the king himself. It is a confusion of this order that led Hampl (*KM* 10ff.; also 47f., 63, 64ff.) to his fantastic theory of the twofold entity of the king.

2 As in *IG* VII 3055.8f., which, even though this probably represents not an actual king but a pretender (as I have argued in *JHS* 1971, 15ff.), should give the correct title. See also Aymard *RIDA* 1950, 64ff., who lists other documentary uses of the full title (to which *Hesperia* 1961, 207 1.7 may be added, though it depends on restoration), which he finds dubious before Alexander's conquests. This, I suspect, is due to the nature of our pre-hellenistic sources. As an individual a king might have his title added for identification, but there is no doubt that, in common with contemporary diplomatic usage, his name served alone on documents of state.

3 From the time of Antigonos Doson the Macedonian people were officially styled 'The Macedonian Koinon' and the state could be referred to as 'King Antigonos and the Macedonians': *IG* XI 4, 1097, Tarn *JHS* 1909, 269ff., Tarn/Griffith *Hell. Civ.* 48.

4 Caesar *BG* 6.23.4, Tac. *Germ.* 7.11.11; cf. Granier *Mak. Heer.* 14 n. 70f.

5 Edson *Arch.Mak.* i, 22.

6 The latter view has been urged for Macedonia by de Francisci *Arcana Imperii* ii, esp. 364f., 369f., 380ff.

7 The *patrios nomos* in the religious context: Arrian 3.16.9, 5.3.6, 8.3, 29.2, 6.3.1f., 7.11.8, etc. (see also Hampl *KM* 17 n. 1).

8 Arrian 4.11.6, Tarn *Alex.* ii 287.

9 Polyb. 15.25.11, Curtius 10.7.9, Justin 24.5.14.

10 Plut. *Pyrr.* 5.2. On the similarity of the Macedonian and Molossian states see Klotsch *Epirot. Gesch.* 26ff., Granier *Mak. Heer.* 103ff. In general on the oaths: Hampl *KM* 16f., Aymard *REA* 1950, 128, de Francisci *Arc. Imp.* ii 381 (though modified on p. 379).

11 On the powers of the military assembly see Granier *Mak. Heer.* 14 and *passim*, Tarn/Griffith *Hell. Civ.*

47f., Hampl *KM* 12ff., Aymard *REA* 1950, 117ff., Edson *Arch. Mak.* i 22f.; compare the cautionary remarks of Badian, *HSCP* 1968, 197f., but see Ellis 'The Dynamics of 4th-C. Mac. Imperialism', forthcoming in *Arch. Mak.* ii, esp. n. 12. For the evidence on treason-cases (or capital cases generally): Curtius 6.8.25 (which depends on an emendation, convincing in the context); on acclamation: Curtius 10.6.ff., esp. 10.6.8.

12 Curtius 10.6ff.

13 Curtius 10.6.8, 7.7f.

14 Curtius 10.7.12.

15 Justin 7.5.9f. claims that Philip was first regent to his young nephew Amyntas, the son of Perdikkas III; but, as I have argued elsewhere (*JHS* 1971, 15ff.), there is reason to doubt this. I owe to Georges le Rider, whose corpus of Philip's gold and silver coinage is almost complete at the time of writing, the observation that Philip appears to coin in his own name from 359 and that there is no coinage of Amyntas 'IV' (see Appendix). See also Chap. 2 n. 10.

16 In the trial of Philotas, for example; see Arrian 3.26.2, Curtius 6.8f., with the remarks of Milns *GRBS* 1966, 159ff., Badian *TAPA* 1960, 324ff.

17 Polyb. 6.13.4, 14.7, referring to the end of the third century (6.11.1f.).

18 Curtius 6.8.25: *in pace erat vulgi.*

19 Arrian 4.4.1; cf. Curtius 6.8.23, who refers to *lixae* and *calones.*

20 Anaximenes F4 (J), Diod. 17.17.4 with Arrian 1.14.1, 7.11.6, Tarn *Alex.* ii 139.

21 Diod. 17.17.4, Tarn *Alex.* ii 139 n. 3, 154ff., Brunt *JHS* 1963, 35, Milns *JHS* 1966, 167. In Alexander's expeditionary force there were eight squadrons of Companions including the Royal Squadron – thus perhaps seven at 200+ horsemen each and one at 300+. But 1500 cavalry were left with Antipatros in Macedonia and there is no reason to assume that these too were not Companions. The seven territorial squadrons used in Asia represent nothing like the whole of Macedonia, especially old Macedonia. For the regions see Arrian 2.9.3, 1.2.5, 12.7, 14.1ff., 15.13; cf. Hampl *KM* 31ff., Beloch III, 1.497 n. 1, Tarn *Alex.* ii 154f., Ferguson *Gnomon* 1935, 520, Griffith *G&R* 1965, 135 n. 4.

22 Theopompos F224, 225b (J), Ferguson *Gnomon* 1935, 521.

23 Curtius 6.9.21, 10.7.20.

24 See for example Arrian 1.17.7, 25.1, 3.25.2, etc.

25 Kalleris *Les anc. Macédoniens* i 242ff., Edson *Arch. Mak.* i 22, 30.

26 For the best brief introduction to Macedonian society see Edson *Arch. Mak.* i 17ff.

27 Hampl *KM* 66ff., esp. 73 has studied the land-grants in most detail, although some of his conclusions are now rightly rejected. It was thus possible for squadrons of Companion Cavalry (and presumably *pezetairoi*) to be levied from areas like Anthemous and Amphipolis (see n. 23).

28 On the *pezetairoi* see Berve i 112ff., Tarn *Alex.* ii 153ff., Milns *Historia* 1967, 509f. Bosworth *CQ* 1973, 245ff. suggests that the term *asthetairoi* should not be emended into oblivion (cf. Arrian 4.23.1, 5.22.6, 6.6.1, 21.3) but applied to the three (+?) divisions of the phalanx from Upper Macedonia, which were incorporated into the national army by Philip.

29 On the *hypaspistai* see Berve i 122ff., Tarn *Alex.* ii 153ff., 140, 148ff., Milns *Historia* 1967, 509ff., and below, Chap. 2.

30 On the light cavalry see Berve i 129. Brunt *JHS* 1963, 27f. and Milns *JHS* 1966, 167ff. have shown that Berve was right to believe that a substantial part of the light horse taken by Alexander to Asia was Macedonian (*contra* Tarn *Alex.* ii

157f., who however is probably correct in rejecting Berve's suggestion that the 1800 cavalry given by Diod. 17.17.4 included such horsemen). Milns argues for a total of 900 in the expeditionary force, including a probable 600 that crossed with the advance-party in 336.

31 Diod. 17.17.3ff. (whose figures are said to represent the forces that crossed the Hellespont in spring 334; to these must be added a proportion of the advance-party of perhaps 11,000, some of whom were mercenaries and 1000 cavalry: Diod. 17.17.10, Polyainos *Strat.* 5.44.4, Brunt *JHS* 1963, 32ff., Milns *JHS* 1966, 167f.). The *pezetairoi* accompanying Alexander appear to have served in divisions (*taxeis*) of up to 2500-strong, of which there were six; since the king presumably took the whole Hypaspist body (whose function as the Bodyguard was to accompany him), Antipatros' force of 12,000 foot will have represented (allowing for a lighter levy for the home guard) another six or so divisions. It is therefore possible that Philip left a total of 12 to 14 recruitment-areas in Macedonia for the levying of both cavalry and infantry – but the evidence is far from conclusive. Only three phalanx-*taxeis* are known: Elimeia, Orestis/Lynkos and Tymphaia (Diod. 17.57.2), which are all Upper Macedonian; among the squadrons of Companion Cavalry Arrian mentions 'the cavalry of Upper Macedonia' (1.2.5) but does not say whether this represented only one squadron (which would automatically destroy the rough coincidence of infantry/cavalry regions) or more.

32 See n. 30.

33 Beloch III, 1.296 reckons them as outnumbering Macedonian citizens. See n. 19.

34 Arrian 1.16.4f. A tax *κατὰ τὴν χώραν* (district-tax?) was presumably one that related to the individual administrative districts and one *κατὰ τὰς κτήσεις* a land-tax presumably owing to the state itself. But such distinctions are highly conjectural in the absence of other evidence.

35 These are the districts named in Arrian's trierarch-list (*Ind.* 18), on which see Geyer *Mak.* 101ff., Kahrstedt *Hermes* 1953, 85ff., Hampl *KM* 78ff., Tarn *Antig.Gon.* 184 with n.57, Ehrenberg *Gnomon* 1931, 583.

36 Edson *Arch. Mak.* i 19 (and, on the Macedonians as a 'frontier people', 17f.).

37 Cic. *Pis.* 16.38.

38 A caveat: it is of course anachronistic to speak glibly – even with reference to the end of Philip's reign – of frontiers in the modern sense, and the practice is adopted here largely for convenience. But it is nevertheless true that certain of Philip's activities in those areas of his kingdom bordering on the land of neighbouring tribes and states are difficult to regard otherwise than as attempts to define a frontier, and suggest that the concept was beginning to emerge. See pp. 58ff. and 134ff.

39 Hammond *Mac.* i 3 defines Macedonia in avowedly geographical terms as comprising the drainage areas of the Haliakmon and Vardar (Axios), but this is limiting, based apparently on a desire for geographical unity rather than on the actual area given the name Macedonia by its inhabitants (cf. the remarks of Ph. M. Petsas, *Μακεδονία καί Μακεδονες μία ἄποψη*', forthcoming in *Arch. Mak.* ii). Admittedly, an all-embracing definition, in view of the shifting borders, becomes impossible on the latter basis. Here, however, our interest is specifically in Philip's Macedonia.

40 The figures are taken from the *Handbook of Macedonia & Surrounding Territories* (British War Office, 1916) 54ff. and Hammond *Ep.* 17 n. 1.

41 Hammond *Mac.* i 208.

42 Theophr. *Caus. Pl.* 4.5.5, Hdt. 5.23, Xen. *Hell.* 5.2.11f., Tod ii 111.9, Casson *Mac. Thrace & Illyria* 53.

43 Hdt. 7.125f.

44 Ath. I 18a.

45 Hammond *Mac.* i 312ff.

46 Strabo 7 C326. On the location of Damastion see May *Coinage of Dam.* esp. 28ff., with modifications by Hammond *Mac.* i 93f.

47 Hdt. 5.17. On the location see Casson *op. cit.* (in n. 42) 62f., Hammond *Mac.* i 194.

48 Strabo 7 F36, Appian *BC* 4.106.

49 Perdrizet *Klio* 1911, 26, Casson *op. cit.* (in n. 42) 75, Diod. 16.8.6.

50 Plut. *de exil.* 605, Marcellin. *vit. Thuc.* 19, Plut. *Kim.* 4.

51 For the population see the calculations of Beloch III, 1.294ff.; cf. Glotz *Hist. Grec.* III 233, Griffith *G&R* 1965, 142ff.

52 This Beloch attempts in his calculations. See also the modern census-figures cited by Hammond *Mac.* i 16f.

53 Hammond *Mac.* i 420ff., who treats in detail the prehistory of Macedonia and its early history to *c.* 550 BC.

54 M. Andronikos *Vergina* (in Greek; Athens 1969), Hammond *loc. cit.*

55 Hdt. 7.127.1, 131.1.

56 Hdt. 4.12, 7.20.

57 Hammond *Mac.* i 428, 438f.

58 Hdt. 8.137.1, Thuc. 2.99.3, 5.80.2. The point has been hotly contested in modern times on patriotic as much as scholarly grounds, the central point at issue being whether the Macedonians were (as the ancient Greeks conceded their ruling family to be) of Greek blood or (as some of their enemies charged) barbarian.

59 Hdt. 8.137f.; see Hammond *Mac.* i 433f.

60 Aigai has until recently been identified with modern Edessa (and equated with ancient Edessa; cf. Justin 7.1) on the eastern slopes of Mt Bermion. Hammond *Arch. Mak.* i 65 n. 17, *Mac.* i 156ff., 435 has now shown convincing grounds for regarding the identification as false (and see Fox *Alex.* 19, 553). See Chap. 2 n. 25.

61 Hdt. 8.138.3, Thuc. 2.99, Hammond *Mac.* i 435ff.

62 Hdt. 5.94.

63 Hdt. 8.116; 5.15ff.; cf. Thuc. 2.99.2, 6.

64 Strabo 7 C324, 9 C434; Hekataios F107 (J).

65 Thuc. 2.99.2, 4.81.3.

66 See Hdt. 7.131 with Geyer *Mak.* 45f.

67 Schol. Thuc. 1.57.3; cf. Beloch III, 2.62f.

68 Beloch *loc. cit.* for the former view, Geyer *Mak.* 78f. for the latter.

69 Thuc. 2.99.

70 For the generally accepted dates see Beloch III, 2.53f., but also Raymond *Mac. Regal Coinage* 129ff., who finds 451 more suitable for the end of Alexander's reign than for the beginning of Perdikkas'.

71 Thuc. 4.76, 83f., 124ff.

72 Thuc. 1.57.3, 59.

73 Xen. *Hell.* 5.2.38ff., 3.9.

74 Satyros *ap.* Ath. 13.557d; below p. 46.

75 Xen. *Hell.* 5.2.38ff., 3.9.

76 Ath. 10.436c, 13.557b (cf. *RE* V, 1.239 No. 3).

77 The one Orestian king known is an Antiochos, who aided (as did Perdikkas secretly but ineffectively) the Spartan forces under Knemos against Ambrakia: Thuc. 2.80.6. So far as we know there were no marriages in the fifth century between the Orestian and Argead houses (Beloch III, 2.74f., 78 thinks the Irrhas of Arist. *Pol.* 5.1311b was Orestian, but he misreads an admittedly confusing passage; see n. 98 below). In the fourth century the only likely contender for Orestian royalty seems to be Perdikkas, son of Orontes (Arrian 1.14.2, 3.11.9, *succ. Al.*2, *Ind.* 18.5), who is said to be of royal stock (Curtius 10.7.8) and from Orestis (Arrian 6.28.4, *Ind.* 18.5). But we do not know what royal stock is meant, Orestian or Argead. Another possibility is Lagos, father of Ptolemaios; although Arrian calls him Eordaian (6.28.4, *Ind.* 18.5), Steph. Byz. (*s.* 'Orestia') believed him Orestian.

78 Strabo 7 C326.

79 *IG* II^2 71.75ff.; his inclusion was perhaps on Athens' insistence.

80 Arist. *Pol.* 5.1311b.

81 Tod ii 143 (= *IG* II^2 110), 148 (= *SIG* 188), Dem. 4.27.

82 Ael. *VH* 14.17, Diod. 16.92, Geyer *Mak.* 98.

83 Thuc. 2.99.4, Livy 44.10, Pliny *NH* 4.34, Plut. *Demet.* 43. Cf. Struck's map *ap.* Casson *Mac., Thrace & Illyria* 14, but compare Geyer *RE* XIX, 1.647ff., who modifies this on the basis of Hdt. 7.127. See now also Hammond *Mac.* i 152f. and his map of the Thermaic Gulf *c.* 356 (p. 150).

84 Diod. 13.49, Xen. *Hell.* 1.1.12.

85 Pl. *Grg.* 471 (surely exaggerated); Ael. *VH* 12.43 calls him *tyrannos.*

86 Xen. *Hell.* 5.2.13.

87 That this occurred is undoubted (see Arrian *Ind.* 18), but for its authorship by Archelaos see Geyer *Mak.* 101ff.; see n. 35 above.

88 Thuc. 2.100.1f.

89 See Griffith *PCPS* 1956/7, 7ff.

90 Thuc. 2.100.3ff. See Granier *Mak. Heer.* 9f. (with refs), who understandably confesses uncertainty but finally rejects the suggestion that Thucydides had anything but cavalry in mind.

91 Edson *Arch. Mak.* 39ff. (with refs).

92 It has been commonly said (e.g. by Abel *Mak.* 204, Droysen *Hell.*^{2} I, 1. 77, Kaerst *RE* I 679) that Aeropos and Pausanias were Lynkestians. But, as Beloch III, 2.65 and Geyer *Mak.* 107 have argued, this is impossible. It is highly unlikely that a Lynkestian regent would have been appointed for Archelaos' son, especially since all indications are that during Archelaos' reign the Lynkestian king Arrabaios was strongly independent of and opposed to the Argeads (Arist. *Pol.* 5. 1311b). More probably Aeropos was an Argead. His son Pausanias, as Beloch III, 2.65 suggests, may have been the father of the Pausanias who attempted to seize the throne during the reigns of Ptolemaios Alorites (Ais. 2.28ff.) and Philip (Diod. 16.2.6) and who is said on both occasions to be a member of the royal house.

93 For the tangled chronology of this six-year period see Geyer *Mak.* 107, who makes better sense than Beloch III, 2.55f.

94 Diod. 14.89.2, Arist. *Pol.* 5.1311b.

95 For a more detailed study of what follows see Ellis *Makedonika* 1969, 1ff.

96 Tod ii 111. On the power of Olynthos (obviously, from the terms, the dominant signatory of this alliance) at this time: Geyer *Mak.* 113f., Busolt *Gr. Staatsk.* 2.1501ff., West *Hist. Chalc. Lg.* 97ff.

97 Isok. 5.46, Diod. 14.92.3, 16.2.2, Costanzi *Klio* 1907, 300ff., Geyer *Mak.* 117, Dell *Arch. Mak.* i 116ff.

98 So Hoffmann *Die Makedonen* 160ff., Momigliano *Fil.* 30 n. 2. The issue of Eurydike's provenance has been clouded unnecessarily by Beloch III, 2.78ff. (who makes her father Orestian), Geyer *Mak.* 79ff. (Elimiote, following Abel, Kaerst and Droysen) and now Hammond *ABSA* 1966, 244 (Lynkestian). The fact is that (*contra* Hammond) no source calls Eurydike Lynkestian, while the conjectures of Beloch, Geyer, *et al.* are quite desperate. Strabo 7 C326 says that she was the granddaughter of the Lynkestian Arrabaios but observes, without giving his ethnic, that her father was a certain Irrhas (emended wrongly by Meinecke to Sirrhas; see Beloch *loc. cit.*), which is confirmed by Plut. *de lib. educ.* 20

(*Mor.* 14). Those sources who give her an ethnic (*Plut. loc. cit.*, Suda *s.* 'Karanos', Lib. *vit. Demosth.* p. 296, Westermann) are in no doubt that she was Illyrian. The confusion arises from attempts to take in isolation the enigmatic reference to Irrhas in Arist. *Pol.* 5.1311b, which neither gives nor even implies his provenance. See n. 77.

99 Diod. 14.92.2ff., Xen. *Hell.* 5.2.11ff., 2.38ff.

100 Tod ii 129, Ais. 2.28ff., Beloch III, 2.57, Geyer *Mak.* 122ff.

101 Diod. 15.61, 67, Plut. *Pel.* 26, Justin 7.5.2.

102 Ais. 2.28ff., Diod. 15.71.1, 77.5, Synkellos p. 500, Beloch III, 2.61f., Geyer *Mak.* 134.

103 Plut. *Pel.* 27, Ais. 2.29. On Philip's hostageship: *ibidd.* and Plut. *Pel.* 26, Diod. 15.67, Justin 6.9.6f., 7.5.1, Suda *s.* 'Karanos', Aymard *REA* 1954, 15ff.

104 Ais. 2.30f., schol. Ais. 2.31, Dem. 23.149ff., 2.14, Diod. 15.81.6, 16.3.3, Nepos *Tim.* 1,2, Plut. *Pel.* 35, Polyainos *Strat.* 3.10.8, 14, Isok. 15.108, 113, Beloch III, 1.220, 2.244, 247.

105 Diod. 16.2.2, Justin 7.5.1.

106 Polyainos *Strat.* 15.10.1, Diod. 16.2, Lib. *vit. Demosth.* p. 110, Westermann, Justin 7.4.5, 5.9, 8.3.10; and see Chap. 2 *init.*

CHAPTER II

1 Diod. 16.2.5ff. describes the general situation on Philip's accession.

2 Lykkeios or Lykpeios: *BMC Macedonia* 13; also Tod ii 157 (= *IG* II[2] 127), where the name is spelt Lyppeios.

3 Dardanoi; see Hammond *ABSA* 1966, 244, 247ff.

4 Diod. 14.92.4; for refs and discussion see Ellis *Makedonika* 1969, 1ff.

5 Kotys died after Philip's accession: Theopompos F 31 (J), Hegesandros *ap.* Ath. 6.248e, Höck *Hermes* 1891, 99f., Schaefer II 17 and n., *RE* XI, 2.1551f., III, 1.294. Some, for no good reason, have reversed the order and consequently assume the king in question to have been one of Kotys' successors, probably Berisades: Glotz *Hist. Grec.* III 228, *CAH* VI 203, Beloch III, 1.224.

6 Ais. 2.28ff., Diod. 14.89.2. Pausanias may also have had support in eastern Macedonia; the same name appears in a list at Epidauros of 360/59 beside the town of Kalindoia in Mygdonia: *IG* IV[2] 94/95.13.

7 Ath. 11.506ef, 508de, Pl. *Ep.*5, Speusippos *Ep.* 12. On Philip's hostageship see pp. 43f. above.

8 Ath. 13.557d (= Satyros in Müller *FHG* III 161).

9 Ath. 10.436c, 13.557b, above p. 38.

10 I have argued elsewhere (*JHS* 1971, 15ff.) that the slender evidence for Philip's alleged regency for his nephew Amyntas is suspect. It depends on the unsupported word of Justin 5.7.9f. and is contradicted by the words used by Diodoros (Ephoros) 16.1.3 to describe the accession (and cf. schol. Ais. 3.51) and by the silence on the matter not only of Demosthenes and the other Philip-sources but also of those Alexander-sources who record the later activities of Philip's 'ward' with never a suggestion that this conspirator against Alexander's crown was none other than the 'ex-king of the Macedonians' (Arrian *Succ. Al.*22, Polyainos *Strat.* 8.60, Plut. *de fort. Al.*1.3, Curtius 6.9.17, 10.24, Justin 12.6.14). The inscription (*IG* VII 3055.7f.) naming Amyntas King of the Macedonians, I have argued, belongs not at the beginning of Philip's reign but early in Alexander's, in association with *IG* VII 4250 and 4251 and a newly published stone (Petrakos *Arch. Delt.* 1966, 45ff.); all seem to hint at the activities of a group of Macedonians seeking external support to replace Alexander with Amyntas in 335. See also Appendix.

11 Ellis *Historia* 1973, 350ff.
12 See note 10 and pp. 24f. above.
13 As Köhler *Hermes* 1889, 642 noted. His father Perdikkas had needed a regent in 368 and is therefore unlikely to have married before his accession in 365. Amyntas was not married until 337 (p. 217 below), which suggests that he was born late rather than early in his father's reign.
14 Arrian *Succ. Al.* 22, Polyainos *Strat.* 8.60.
15 Ath. 13.557b, 560f., 4.155a, Polyainos *Strat.* 8.20.
16 Arrian *Succ. Al.* 22.
17 Refs in n. 15; also Diod. 19.52.5, Arrian 1.5.4, *Succ. Al.* 23, Polyainos *Strat.* 8.60.
18 Diod. 16.3.3: Amphipolis; 16.3.4: Paiones.
19 *IG* IV² 94/95.18, Geyer *Mak.* 138.
20 Diod. 16.3.4.
21 Ais. 2.29, Dem. 2.6f., 23.116, [Dem.] 7.27f.
22 Note 5 for refs.
23 Höck *Hermes* 1891, 99ff., Lenk *RE* VIA, 1.423ff.; further refs in Tod ii pp. 152ff.
24 For the attempt of Argaios: Diod. 16.2.6, 3.3ff., Justin 7.6, Dem. 23.121.
25 For the location of Aigai, Chapter 1 n. 60. Hammond *Mac.* i 157f. (cf. *Arch. Mak.* i 64ff.) has already drawn attention to the difficulty of making sense of Argaios' attempt to approach the place normally identified as Aigai (i.e. mod. Edessa). Such a journey (at least 60 km. as the crow flies) would have taken the pretender very close to Pella, allowing him no chance of reaching his destination in the first place, let alone of returning safely to Methone if unsuccessful.
26 Diod. 16.3.6, Dem. 23.121.
27 Diod. 16.3.6.
28 For Olynthian/Athenian relations in the previous decade see West *Hist. Chalc. Lg.* 108ff., Robinson/Clement *Excavs at Olynthus* IX 158ff., Gude *Hist. of Olynthus* 24ff. On the Chalkidian link with the mines of Damastion see May *Coinage of Damastion* 38ff. and, on their location, Hammond *Mac.* i 93f. (cf. May 28ff.).
29 Published by Meritt *Hesperia* 1961, 207f. and Pl. 35.2.
30 Diod. 16.4.1, Dem. 2.6f. and schol. (Dindorf 83.19), Theopompos F30a (J), Polyainos *Strat.* 4.2.17.
31 Dem. 2.6; see de Ste Croix *CQ* 1963, 110ff., who points out that a secret bargain between Philip and Athens, involving a promised exchange of Amphipolis and Pydna, is neither possible nor what Demosthenes says (his meaning is irretrievable) – whatever the scholiast (n. 30) says or modern scholars have believed. See note 33.
32 Ais. 2.25ff. The worst Aischines was able to say (or to claim later to have said) was that Philip 'in his turn took up the war against our city' (s. 30).
33 See note 31. According to Theopompos F30 (Book I, referring to the earliest year of Philip's reign) two Athenian envoys, Antiphon and Charidemos, were sent to arrange friendship with Philip and they tried privately to arrange the exchange of Amphipolis for Pydna. On their return they reported their bid only to the boulē for fear that a public report would reach Pydnaian ears. From this account it would seem that any initiative was taken not by Philip (as Demosthenes was to imply a decade later; n. 31) but by Athenians perhaps acting at their own discretion (see Mosley *Envoys & Diplom.* 13). Whatever they might have hoped to achieve, Athens could not be committed secretly to such a deal, as de Ste Croix has shown (n. 31).
34 See n. 107.
35 Diod. 16.3.1ff.; on the sources of Diod. Book XVI see Hammond *CQ* 1937, 79ff.
36 Anaximenes F4 (J), Momigliano *Fil.* 9ff., Edson *Arch. Mak.* i 31 and n. 80; cf., for example, Jacoby *FGH*

IIC p. 107, Griffith *PCPS* 1956/7, 7, who prefer Alexander II (370/69–369/8), on the grounds that in Thucydides' time the Macedonian infantry was still (again?) worthless. The objection is well founded, so far as it goes, but the extremely short reign of Alexander II is quite unsuitable. As another alternative 'Archelaos' sounds plausible, but is not what Anaximenes says. However ineffective in the longer term any military reform by Alexander I, it might nevertheless explain his remarkable success in expanding the kingdom (p. 35 above).

37 See n. 35.

38 Theopompos F348 (J), Milns *Historia* 1967, 510f.

39 *Contra* Tarn *Alex.* ii 138–140 and Milns *loc. cit* (in n. 38). As Milns notes, Demosthenes (2.17) is aware of the *pezetairoi* in 349 and might be expected to include the *hypaspistai* at this point had he known of them. But he was probably no less ignorant of Macedonia (especially before he visited it in 346) than were most Greeks. In the case of other contemporaries the argument from silence is even weaker, since in the key case (that of Anaximenes F4) the fragment in question (which mentions *hetairoi* and *pezetairoi* but not *hypaspistai*) is one of only eleven preserved from the author's *Philippic History* and survives through being excerpted by Harpokration and the Suda only to define the term *pezetairoi*. The argument might in fact be reversed with more profit, for it is surely *less* likely that contemporaries could have overlooked the Hypaspists had Philip himself brought them into being.

40 On the Hypaspists in general see Tarn *Alex.* ii 138ff., Hamilton *CQ* 1955, 218ff., Milns *Historia* 1967, 509ff., Ellis 'Alexander's Hypaspists Again', forthcoming in *Historia*. For Hypaspists as bodyguards: Arrian 3.17.2, 4.30.3, 5.13.4; and, for an instance of their performance of this function (at Opis): Arrian 7.11.1f.

41 Tarn *ibid.*

42 Ellis *loc. cit.* (in n. 40). Best *Thracian Peltasts* 139ff. suggests that the hypaspist was a peltast, though not of the javelin-slinging type. This may be so, but it does not invalidate the arguments (refs in n. 40) for the coincidence of hypaspist and phalangite armament, since the Macedonian phalanx was in any case more lightly armed than the Greek hoplite (Griffith *PCPS* 1956/7, 3ff.).

43 Diod. 16.4.3; and see below.

44 Diod. 17.17 with Griffith *G&R* 1965, 129ff., Brunt *JHS* 1963, 32ff., Milns *JHS* 1966, 167f., Green *Alex.* 157ff., 530f.

45 Arrian 1.14.2; see Tarn *Alex.* ii 148.

46 So we may judge from their higher rate of pay (see below). On recruitment, as distinct from territorial levy, I am aware of no evidence for this, Tarn's assertion, but there is no good reason to doubt it. Kromayer *Heerwesen* 100 n. 1 claimed that they were raised by levy but he wrongly cited Arrian 3.16.11, which refers to *pezetairoi*. Their élite function as well as the small number of divisions (three) justify the assumption.

47 Theopompos F224 (J).

48 Theopompos F225b (J).

49 Arrian 7.23.3, cf. 6.9.3.

50 Tod ii 183 = *IG* II² 329.

51 For different interpretations see Griffith *Hell. Merc.* 299 n. 1, Berve i 193ff., Kromayer *Heerwesen* 111 and n. 3, the last of whom badly misreads Diod. 17.64.6. Bellinger *Coinage of Alex.* 36f. and n. assumes a rate of dr. 20 per month for ordinary soldiers, but this would put the *dimoirites* on the same level as the *dekastateros*, contrary to Arrian 7.23.3. See also Green *Alex.* 530 n. 7.

52 Parke *Gk Merc. Soldiers* 158.

53 On which see *ibid.* 161ff., Griffith *Hell. Merc.* 8ff.

54 Griffith *G&R* 1965, 134.

55 *Ibid.* 138. Dem. 2.15ff. is so vague as to strengthen the presumption that he had absolutely no evidence for his claims. The amusing story of Polyainos *Strat.* 4.2.6 centring upon Philip's lack of funds to meet the needs of military pay (which Green *Alex.* 96 dates to 337/6 – plausibly, but without evidence), is – if evidence for anything – proof that Philip did pay his soldiers.

56 Diod. 16.35.2, Polyainos *Strat.* 2.38.2 (352 BC); see pp. 78ff. below.

57 Revenues: Diod. 16.8.6f., 71.2, Dem. 1.22, 6.22, 19.89, Arrian 1.16.5.

58 Plut. *Alex.* 15; above pp. 25f.

59 Diod. 16.34.5. Such evidence is however poor and Griffith's cautious remarks (*G&R* 1965, 136f.) go as far as is permitted.

60 Chapter 1 n. 21.

61 See for example Diod. 16.3, Front. *Strat.* 4.1.6, 2.4, Polyainos *Strat.* 4.2.1, 3,10.

62 Best *Thracian Peltasts* 139ff. On armament see Polyainos *Strat.* 4.2.10, Snodgrass *Arms & Armour* Chap. 5, Wilcken *Alex.* 30ff., Kromayer *Heerwesen* 95ff., Griffith *PCPS* 1956/7, 3ff., Milns *Alex.* 45ff.

63 Arrian 1.15.5, Diod. 17.60.2; note also the Alexander-mosaic (Nat. Mus. Naples), copied from an original by Philoxenos of Eretria painted perhaps a generation after Philip's death.

64 Arrian 1.15.7f., Plut. *Alex.* 16, 32, Curtius 4.6.7, 13.25, 7.5.16, 8.3, the Alexander-mosaic (n. 63), Berve i 104.

65 On Philip's Paionian campaign see Diod. 16.4.1f. For a recent survey of sources on the Paiones: Merker *BS* 1965, 35ff. No information survives for the period between the Peloponnesian War and *c.* 360, but during this period Agis appears to have built up an unprecedented conglomeration of tribes. For Agis' successor see n. 2 above.

66 Diodoros dates the accession of Philip (and therefore the defeat of Perdikkas, presumably not long before) to 360/59 and the first Illyrian campaign to 359/8. The latter fits more comfortably in the first half of 358, following a Paionian campaign in the second half of 359.

67 Strabo 7 C315.

68 Diod. 14.92.3, 15.2.2, 15.13, 15.19.2, Kallisthenes F27 (J), Justin 7.5.1, Front. *Strat.* 2.5.19, Theopompos F18, 40, 286 (J). See Hammond *ABSA* 1966, 239ff., Dell *Arch. Mak.* i 115, 126.

69 For Philip's Illyrian campaign: Diod. 16.4.3ff., 8.1, Justin 7.6.7, Front. *Strat.* 2.3.2 (and possibly Polyainos *Strat.* 4.2.5).

70 See Beloch III, 1.226 and n. 2. C. F. Edson, in an exploratory, unpublished paper entitled 'Who was Parmenion?', suggests that P. stemmed from the ruling family of Pelagonia. The identification, depending primarily on the uncertain restoration of his name in *IG* II/III^2 190 is possible but far from certain. However his son Philotas may have an association with the Upper Macedonian cavalry of Alexander (Chapter 8 n. 23).

71 Dell *Arch. Mak.* i 121ff., Ellis *Makedonika* 1969, 15f.

72 Arrian 7.9; see Griffith *G&R* 1965, 137.

73 See notes 8 and 9 above; I have suggested (p. 46) that the marriage of Philip to Phila took place before 359 (and see Beloch III, 2.66, Kaerst *RE* V, 1.239, *s.* Derdas No. 3).

74 Tod ii 143 = *IG* II^2 110.

75 Tod ii 148 = *SIG* 188 (and cf. Dem. 4.27; the identification of this man by Harpokration, *sv*, with the stepbrother of Philip is generally rejected: Loeb note on Dem. 4.27).

76 Bosworth *CQ* 1971, 99 n. 9.

77 *Ibid.*, Hoffmann *Die Makedonen*

165f., Geyer *Mak.* 81f., Beloch III, 2.76f.

78 Dem. 23.154ff. The name of the Pelagonian king began with the letter 'P' (in 365/4: *IG* II/III^2 190; see note 70); Ferguson *Klio* 1915, 393 n. 5.

79 Menelaos appears to have continued his Athenian citizenship and is found fighting with Athens against Philip in Thrace in 351: Dem. 4.27, Geyer *Mak.* 82 n. 3.

80 See n. 70.

81 For refs see Berve ii No. 37; also Chapter 6 n. 53.

82 Justin 10.7.8, Arrian 6.28.4, *Ind.* 18.5.

83 Diod. 16.92.3, Justin 9.6.4ff.

84 Droysen *Gesch. Hell.* I^2 1.86 n. 7 – although as Beloch III, 2.75 cautions this identification is far from certain.

85 See n. 28 above; also May *Coinage of Damastion* 82ff., 105f., 110ff.

86 Griffith *CQ* 1970, 73f., Sordi *LT* 148ff.

87 Larisa and Krannon: Diod. 15.61.3ff.

88 Diod. 16.14.1f.

89 Diod. 14.92.3, Ellis *Makedonika* 1969, 1ff.

90 Diod. 16.14.1f., Justin 7.6.6ff., Ath. 13.557bd, Theopompos F34, 35, 48 (J). This evidence came under attack by Ehrhardt *CQ* 1967, 298ff., but, as Griffith *CQ* 1970, 67ff. has shown, there is no good reason to doubt its substance. For the dating: Sordi *LT* 230ff., esp. 230 n. 3.

91 Plut. *Pyrr.* 1.4, Justin 17.3.10f.; cf. Thuc. 2.80.6, Reuss *RhM* 1881, 161, Klotsch *Ep. Gesch.* 24ff., Schwahn *RE* VA 1308f., Marshall *SAC* 63, Hammond *Ep.* 508, 511.

92 For refs: Tod ii p. 216 (No. 173). This Athenian inscription, apparently erected largely at Arybbas' own expense, bears no mention of a royal title and refers to his – by then lost – kingdom as a dominion (*archē*), features regarded by Tod as significant, but wrongly so, since it was a standard feature of protocol, reflected in decrees from many northern Greek and non-Greek kingdoms at least in their dealings with Greek states, that kings were officially referred to by name alone, without title: Aymard *Études d'Hist. Anc.* 85ff. On Arybbas' status before 350 and between 350–342 see Chapter 4 n. 16.

93 Plut. *Alex.* 2.1f., Curtius 8.1.26 (and for other refs Strasburger *RE* XVIII, 1.177ff.); see also Reuss *RhM* 1881, 161ff., Berve ii pp. 283ff., Macurdy *Hell. Queens* 22–46.

94 Front. *Strat.* 2.5.19, Hammond *Ep.* 533, Klotsch *Ep. Gesch.* 58f. On Epeirote organization: Cross *Epirus* 30ff., Hammond *Ep.* 527ff., Beloch III, 2.177ff., Kaerst *RE* V, 2.2723ff.

95 Ath. 13.557bd; here all of Philip's wives and offspring are listed. See pp. 211f. below.

96 Aridaios: *ibid.*, Arrian *Succ. Al.* 1, Plut. *Alex.* 77, Justin 9.8.2, 13.2.11, Ath. 13.578a; his mental deficiency: Plut. *de fort. Al.* 1.3, Justin 13.2.11, 14.5.2, Appian *Syr.* 52. Attempts have been made to divide Philip's women into wives and concubines (Chapter 8 n. 4), but there seems no good reason for doing so. Presumably at the time of her marriage the status of a new wife will have been affected by the diplomatic situation in which it was contracted and, as time passed and that situation changed, so perhaps did her status. But most importantly by far, her role at court (in so far as she had one at all) must have been determined by her success in producing children for the king. Thus, if Olympias enjoyed a position of stature in Philip's later reign it was because her son was being groomed for responsibility and, ultimately, kingship. But it seems more likely than not that at Alexander's birth he was second in line to Aridaios, whose mental deficiency, unless it was accompanied by serious physical deformity, was surely not recognized for several years. His mother's marriage probably fell as much as one year before that of Olympias. Our (mainly derivative) sources, largely ignorant of internal matters, are concerned almost exclusively with the childhood of Alexander, who did become king, and ignore Aridaios, who may have been destined for the role in his early years. The assertion that Olympias herself was responsible for Aridaios' retardation may be no more than part of the substantial body of later anti-Olympias propaganda; it may, however, reflect some need to explain why the younger man should have succeeded to the throne in place of the elder.

97 Arrian *Succ. Al.* 22, Polyainos *Strat.* 8.60.

98 Macurdy, *AJP* 1927, 201ff.

99 Marshall *SAC* 100ff., Accame *LA* 186f.

100 Tod ii 151 = *IG* II/III^2 124, Dem. 23.173, Höck *Hermes* 1891, 103f., Cloché *RevPhil.* 1922, 5ff., *Mélanges Glotz* i 215ff., Accame *LA* 181f.

101 The main source for the Social War is Diod. 16.7, 21–22.2. On the date of the outbreak see Cawkwell *C&M* 1962, 34ff.

102 Diod. 16.7.2; Tod ii 153, 154 for the effect of the campaign, the rejoining of Athens' alliance by the major cities of Euboia. See Brunt *CQ* 1969, 247f.

103 Dem. 1.8; the main source for Amphipolis is Diod. 16.8.2.

104 Theopompos F42 (J).

105 Tod ii 150 = *SIG* 194.

106 Especially since, as the inscription (n. 72) shows, in l. 1, he wished the city to *look* autonomous, whatever its actual status.

107 Above pp. 47f. According to Aristeides (*Symmachikos* A = *Or.* 38, Vol. i p. 715d), there was a cult of Philip in Amphipolis at this time, before the Macedonian capture of the city. This was possibly – if the evidence is to be trusted – raised in gratitude for Philip's action of 359. See Habicht *Gottmenschentum und griechische Städte* 12f.

108 Outbreak of the Social War: Diod. 16.7.2f.; capture of Amphipolis: 16.8.2 (both under the year 358/7). Beloch III, 1.229 reversed the order, placing the latter in summer/autumn 357 and the former, on independent criteria, in autumn/winter 357/6 (III, 2.258ff., 458). Cawkwell *C&M* 1962, 34ff. supports Beloch, rightly I believe, on the Social War but does not deal with the relativity of Amphipolis.

109 The population of the Chalkidike is discussed by Beloch III, 1.295. While I find his estimate of the total population somewhat low, I have no quarrel with his military figures.

CHAPTER III

1 Diod. 16.8, using Ephoros as source (Hammond *CQ* 1937, 78ff.).

2 Tod ii 150 = *SIG* 194.

3 Diod. 16.8.2; see n, 1.

4 Hampl *KM* 22–28, Perdrizet *BCH* 1897, 102ff., esp. 111, Köhler *SB Berlin* 1891, 475f.

5 Dem. 1.5.

6 Plut. *Mor.* 293ab for its 8th C. foundation by Eretria. Like Pydna it was not (as Kahrstedt *Hermes* 1953, 85ff. argues) a native Macedonian town; Edson *Arch. Mak.* i 24 n. 38 and n. 57 below. For their autonomous coinage in the years before this see Head *HN* 218.

7 Hammond *ABSA* 1966, 239ff., esp. 244, 252.

8 Robinson *TAPA* 1938, 44ff., No. 2 with Pl. II, Bengtson *Verträge* No. 307. The stone recording the alliance between Grabos and the Chalkidians was found in an unfinished state in the river-bed near Olynthos. On the Chalkidians and Damastion see Chapter 2 n. 28.

9 West *Num. Chron.* 1923, 199ff., Robinson/Clement *Excavs. at Olynthus* IX. 158ff., Head *HN* 223f., Seltman *Gk Coins* 199ff. See also Appendix.

10 Dem. 23.107f., 2.14, 6.20, Diod. 16.8.3.

11 Tod ii 146 = *IG* II² 144, Habicht *Gnomon* 1959, 707.

12 Tod ii 158, Robinson *TAPA* 1934, 103ff.. Diod. 16.8.3ff., Dem. 2.6ff., 6.20, 23.107f., Libanius *Hyp.* to Dem. I, Gude *Olynthus* 32ff.

13 On the foundation and coinage: Diod. 16.3.7, Beloch III, 1.230 n. 4, Collart *Philippes* 134ff., Bellinger *ANSMN* 1964, 29ff., Appendix below. For the role of the exiled Athenian Kallistratos: Collart 133ff., Kirschner *PA* I 541 (No. 8157), Cloché *REA* 1923, 5ff.

14 *IG* II² 126 = Tod ii 151 (and pp. 152f. for refs), Höck *Hermes* 1891, 99ff.

15 On the death of Berisades in late 357 or early 356 his three sons inherited the westernmost Thracian kingdom. Ketriporis was evidently the most influential; another was [Mono] unios (Tod ii 157 = *IG* II² 127.9; cf. ll.14, 29) and the third was possibly Shostokes, known from contemporary coins: Head *HN* 241.

16 Collart *Philippes* 152ff. has demolished the common view that the aggressor was Ketriporis. Dem. 23.10, 179 alludes to what was certainly this campaign as a war by Kersebleptes against his Thracian colleagues.

17 Isok. 5.20.

18 For the remains: Collart *Philippes* 168ff. and Pl. ii, xxv, etc. For the colonists: Diod. 16.3.7, 8.6.

19 The suggestion was made by P. A. Mackay in discussion at the second International Symposium on Ancient Macedonia, Thessaloniki, August 1973.

20 Momigliano *Fil.* 49ff. for the most useful examination of the likely income from this source.

21 The attribution of this clearing and drainage to Philip is by Hammond *Mac.* i 149, 160, 207; see Theophrastos *Caus. Pl.* 5.14.6.

22 On the coinage: Collart *Philippes* 162ff., with plates, n. 23 below.

23 Bellinger *ANSMN* 1964, 29ff., Kraay *Gk Coins & Hist.* 17, Appendix below.

24 Momigliano *Fil.* 48 refers to Philippoi as a military colony.

25 Perhaps the Grabaioi: Hammond *ABSA* 1966, 244, 252.

26 Tod ii 157 = *IG* II² 127.

27 Diod. 16.21, Beloch III, 1.239, Marshall *SAC* 111f., *CAH* VI 210f.

28 Diod. 16.22.3.

29 Plut. *Alex.* 3.5; cf. Justin 12.16.6.

30 Dem. 4.35.

31 Diod. 16.8.3ff.

32 It is listed independently in a list at Epidauros in 360/59: *IG* IV² 94/95.12.

33 See Habicht *Gnomon* 1959, 707.

34 [Dem.] 7.10; cf. Dem. 6.20, Arist. *Oec.* 2.1347a; also Diod. 16.8.5, Dem. 2.7, 8.62, 65, 20.61, 23.107.

35 [Dem.] 7.9ff.

36 Cf. Habicht, *loc. cit.* (in n. 33).

37 Diod. 16.8.5, Paus. 5.23.3. For the unhappy relationship between Poteidaia and Olynthos: Alexander *Potidaea* 82ff. and refs in Tod ii pp. 142f.

38 Casson *Mac., Thrace & Illyria* 27f. notes the limitations of the harbour but his qualification applies more to larger vessels that cannot be beached in bad weather. When Chares lay in wait at Neapolis for Philip in spring 353 it was evidently with his ships out of the water: Polyainos *Strat.* 4.2.22.

39 Strabo 7 C331 F35, Collart *Philippes* 140, Scymn. 656ff. = *GGM* I 221.

40 Tod ii 159 = *SIG* 197.

41 Chares was able to use Neapolis as a base probably in spring 353 (p. 77 and see n. 38 above). That he could beach his ships there has been taken to mean that Neapolis was at that time still free of Philip. But a fragment of Herakleides (Kock II 435, quoted by Parke *Gk Merc. Soldiers* 145) commemorates a defeat by Chares over Philip's mercenaries under the command of Adaios 'the Cock', a success which Chares is said to have celebrated in Athens with funds given him by Onomarchos (Theopompos F241, Oxford text). Since it seems most unlikely that Philip would have allowed Neapolis to remain untouched for so long (with near-by Galepsos, Apollonia and Oisyme already taken; n. 39 for refs), it seems possible that the city was taken at some time between summer 355 and late 354 and that Chares liberated it in or before spring 353, defeating Adaios in the process. Since Onomarchos was Phokian commander from autumn 354 till early summer 352 and most likely made payments to Chares as part of his preparations during the spring of 353 or early 352, the latter's celebration of the victory would plausibly have taken place either in very late 353, when (and *if*) he returned to Athens after his successful Chersonesan campaign, or possibly late in 352, when, with Onomarchos and Pagasai fallen in spite of Athenian hopes, he may have wished to draw attention to his own successes to offset his Thessalian failure. See also n. 93 below.

42 Marshall *SAC* 78ff., 105ff.

43 Diod. 16.22, Plut. *Arat.* 16.

44 On the situation in Athens see Isok. 8, *passim*, but esp. 19, 21, 69, 7.9, Dem. 18.234, Marshall *SAC* 115f. On the finances: Cawkwell *JHS* 1963, 46ff., Thomsen *Eisphora* 230f.

45 For the chronology of the Sacred War I follow largely the reconstruction of Hammond *JHS* 1937, 44ff. See also Sordi *Riv. Fil.* 1958, 134ff.

46 On the origins of the Sacred War between spring 356 and mid-355 see Diod. 16.23–28, Hammond *loc. cit.* (in n. 45). For the membership of the Amphictyonic League we are dependent on Ais. 2.116 and Paus. 10.8.2, the latter of whom omits the Boiotians, Ionians and Perrhaibians. Aischines rightly includes the Oitaians but does not mention that they counted as Ainianes. For membership-lists see, most conveniently, *SIG* I pp. 314f. and Table 3 on pp. 132/3. A majority at this time were subject to either the Thessalian or the Boiotian League (the latter itself dominated by Thebes). Athens and Sparta represented only one voice each in the Ionian and Dorian tribes respectively. Each tribe wielded two votes.

47 Demosthenes' confidence (14.33) a year later in Theban philhellenism is heavily qualified and additionally highlights the fear of Persian invasion felt by at least some Athenians; cf. 14.40.

48 Suggested by Griffith *CQ* 1970, 79; while, as Griffith is careful to add, there is no direct evidence for this intervention, he adduces compelling reasons for its plausibility. Such neighbourly actions on Philip's part seem *de rigueur* to explain the remarkable honours and powers heaped on him by the *koinon* in 353 or 352. See also Westlake *Thessaly* 167 and n. 4, Sordi *LT* 233f.

49 Diod. 16.23.1, 28.4, Hammond *op. cit.* (in n. 45) 75; also Diod. 16.29, Ais. 2.116, Pickard-Cambridge *Dem.* 172, Table 4 on p. 135 for voting strengths.

50 Diod. 16.30.1, Parke *Gk Merc. Soldiers* 133ff.; cf. Diod. 16.56.5 for a contradictory account, in the interpretation of which I follow Parke 134 n. 4.

51 Lenk *RE* XV, 2.1385; the exact site has not been found but its approximate location is known: Hammond *Mac.* i 129, 425f.

52 Diod. 16.34.4f.

53 *IG* II[2] 1.130.

54 Justin 7.6.14ff., Theopompos F52 (J), Dem. 18.67, Strabo 7 F22, C374, Pliny *HN* 7.37, Plut. *Mor.* 307d; also, on the assault, Polyainos *Strat.* 4.2.15.

55 Dem. 1.9, 4.35. Demosthenes' implication that there was some delay before the *despatch* of relief is used by Hammond *JHS* 1937, 58 to extend the length of the siege until late summer 354; but there is no warrant for manufacturing an additional delay *en route*, as he urges.

56 Momigliano *Fil.* 53 suggests spring 354 for the date of capture.

57 Diod. 16.34.5. Plut. *vit. X orat.* 851a claims that Philip took prisoners at Methone and released them on ransom – paid, among others, by Demosthenes. But this is contradicted by Diod. *loc. cit.* and Justin 7.6.13ff. The departure of the citizens almost empty-handed suggests (against Kahrstedt *Hermes* 1953, 85ff.; see n. 6 above) that they were non-Macedonians and were now expelled from the country.

58 Hammond *Mac.* i 129 (on the fertility of the area); on the division of Methonaian territory: Diod. 16.31.6, 34.4f. (a doublet) and p. 55 above with Chapter 2 n. 59.

59 Diod. 16.30.3.

60 Diod. 16.30.4; the reference is no more specific than is shown in the translated phrase, but the 'neighbouring allies' of Thessaly were the Perrhaiboi, Ainianes, Dolopes, Athamanes, Achaioi Phthiotai and Magnetes – though the two last, under Phokian influence or control, would have been unable to contribute. The force is not large, hardly a token.

61 Diod. 16.30.4, *SIG* 203. The defeated Thessalians appear to have returned home: Sordi *LT* 239 and n. 4, Hammond *JHS* 1937, 67; cf. Beloch III, 1.250 n. 1, Westlake *Thessaly* 171.

62 Diod. 16.31, Paus. 10.2.4.

63 Diod. 16.31.6; on the reading 'Pagai' see Ehrhardt *CQ* 1967, 298ff. The words 'he compelled it to submit' or '. . . to be subject' may suggest that Pagai was either a Macedonian town or that it lay in territory that was later to become part of the kingdom.

64 May *Coinage of Abdera* 286ff. argues for *c.* 346. His Period IX, the beginning of which he dates to 365/60, contains 13 mint-issues and may therefore extend past 350, but the difficulties of dating his Period VIII (pp. 264ff.) leave open the possibility of starting Period IX earlier than 365 and ending it *c.* 354. Beloch III, 2.283 dates the capture to 347/6.

65 Polyainos *Strat.* 4.2.22, Dem. 23.183; Collart *Philippes* 166 n. 3 for this reason dates the capture of the two cities between 354 and 352.

66 Dem. 23.183; see Höck *Hermes* 1891, 102 and n. 6. On Kersebleptes and on the antagonism of Byzantion and Perinthos towards Athens: Dem. 23 *passim*, Isok. 8.22, Höck 104, 107f., Cloché *Mélanges Glotz* 215ff. Höck believes that Kersebleptes and his adviser Charidemos wished to gain Philip's assistance to counter Athenian ambitions in the Chersonesos and that they sent the Kardian Apollonios for that reason. This is likely and – but for the countermeasures of Chares in the following year – might have been most detrimental to Athenian interests there; but for the moment Philip could not oblige; the Thessalian request for aid may now have reached him, Amadokos was blocking the path between Maroneia and the Chersonesos and Chares was operating on the coast behind him.

67 Dem. 23.183 and see n. 66. There can be little doubt that by this time Macedonia and Thebes were allies, although no direct evidence establishes it. (Cf. Paus. 10.2.5, which however does not help much.) The fact that the Thebans sent their hoplites overland to Phrygia (and therefore via Macedonia) suggests that an alliance was already in force. See Griffith *CQ* 1970, 74 and n.

68 Cloche *Ét. Class.* 1939, 195f.

69 Diod. 16.34.1f., Polyainos *Strat.* 5.16.2, Frontinus *Strat.* 2.3.3.

70 Plut. *Pel.* 26, Suda *s.* Karanos; cf. Justin 7.5.3.

71 Polyainos *Strat.* 4.2.22. See n. 41.

72 See Hammond *JHS* 1937, 62ff. also Diod. 16.32.2. The presence of Lokrian delegates implies both that parts of Lokris were now under Phokian control and that the Phokians wished the meeting to appear as official as possible, with (therefore) as many of the proper participants as could be mustered.

73 Diod. 16.32–33.

74 Diod. 16.33.3. Cf. Schaefer I 504 n. 4 and Westlake *Thessaly* 172 and n. 1, but the latter, following Beloch's chronology, has this one year too early. The outbreak of *stasis* in Krannon – at a date unknown but possibly at this time – may also help to account for Thessalian preoccupation with internal matters (Polysanos *Strat.* 2.34, Westlake *Thessaly* 172f.

75 He was 'summoned *back*' μετακληθείς): Diod. 16.35.1, Griffith *CQ* 1970, 68 and n. 2. See also Polyainos *Strat.* 4.2.19. Westlake *Thessaly* 168 thinks Philip may, while preserving the appearances of alliance, have in reality attempted to preserve a balance of power between the league and the tyrants until he was ready to ensure that any settlement worked in his favour. This (premonitions of Macchiavelli!) is intrinsically plausible, in the light of his half-hearted intervention against Phokis in 347 (pp. 103f. below), but seems unlikely in view of the unprecedented honour given him by the *koinon* before the campaign that culminated at Crocus Field.

76 See n. 67. Justin 8.2.1f. has this request for aid coming from both Thessalians and Thebans, which Westlake *Thessaly* 174 n. 3 puts down to confusion (cf. Justin 8.4.4 in the context of 347/6), but the objection is weak. See also n. 104.

77 Diod. 16.35.1.

78 Diod. 16.35.2.

79 *Ibid.*

80 Polyainos *Strat.* 2.38.2.

81 Dem. 2.15f.; see Griffith (*op. cit.* in n. 75) 138 and above Chapter 2 n. 55.

82 Marsden *G. & R. Artillery* 58.

83 Griffith (*op. cit.* in n. 75) 138.

84 Diod. 16.74, Ath. Mechanicus W 10. 5ff., Wüst 130 n. 3, Marsden (*op. cit.* in n. 82) 60.

85 See Marsden (*op. cit.* in n. 82) 59f.

86 Diod. 16.34.3; on the dating of the chapter see Hammond *JHS* 1937, 65, 69f.

87 Theopompos F101 (in his Bk XI, which deals with northern events between the Thessalian campaign of 353–352 and the Chalkidian campaign beginning in 349) refers to an alliance between Philip and Amadokos in 'the war against Kersebleptes', evidently the Thracian campaign of 352–351. Both Perinthos and Byzantion also combined with the allies in this war: schol. Ais. 2.81 (Dindorf 57.12), Ellis 'Philip's Thracian Campaign of 352/351' forthcoming in *CPh.*

88 Diod. 16.34.4, Dem. 23.14 (Amphipolis), 103 (cleruchs), 110, 177 (revenues), 181 (Kardia). In the navy-list for 353/2 there is reference to equipment for triremes in use by colonists at the Chersonesos: *IG* II^2 795.134.

89 Dem. 23.107ff.

90 Demosthenes himself classes the Olynthians with the Thessalians as invariably faithless and makes no recommendation that his fellow citizens take the offer seriously.

91 Dem. 1.12f., in a catalogue of Philip's misdeeds, lists in order the campaigns against Amphipolis, Pydna, Poteidaia, Methone, in Thessaly, in Thrace and against Olynthos (351) and then concludes: 'not to speak of his campaigns against the Illyrians and Paionians and against Arybbas'. It is not at all certain that this may be taken as a sequential continuaton of the preceding list. But we know of no war against Arybbas of Epeiros before 351 (it probably took place in 350), and perhaps all three were conducted between 351 and 349. If so, it is likely that they were brought about by defections from existing alliances with Philip, rather in 353, when Macedonian fortunes were low, than in the following two or three years, when they were being rebuilt.

92 Diod. 16.35.3, Ephoros F95 (J). This campaign was not (as Westlake *Thessaly* 174) the product of Onomarchos' overconfidence. Koroneia was offered him by the anti-Theban group there (Ephoros) and, when he had successfully taken it, near-by Korsiai and possibly Tilphosaion may have joined him (Diod. 16.58.1, Dem. 19.141, Beloch III, 1.254 n. 3). Such gains reduced the ability of the Boiotians to take Onomarchos in the rear during the impending campaign in Thessaly. When Philip advanced to Thermopylai in mid-352 the Boiotian aid without which his attempt would be at best difficult and drawn out showed no sigh of materializing, and he was obliged to withdraw. Arist. *Eth. Nik.* 3.1116b has an interesting comment on the capture of Koroneia.

93 See n. 41 on the Phokian funds paid to Chares. Diod. 16.57.1, in a moralistic digression, comments that Athens and Sparta, both allies of Phokis in the Sacred War, received payments from Apollo's funds out of proportion to their services, and thus shared the guilt with successive Phokian commanders for the despoliation of sacred property.

94 Justin 8.2.1ff.; see n. 76.

95 Ehrhardt *CQ* 1967 298ff. shows that Pagasai fell at the time of the Pheraian defeat. Its capture must have preceded the Crocus Field battle. The Athenian aid for Pagasai arrived too late (Dem. 4.35); since Chares and his fleet were in the immediate vicinity during the battle on the shore, it follows that Pagasai had already fallen.

96 The site of the battle is not given by any source, but to judge from its proximity to the shore and from the decisive role played there by cavalry (Diod. 16.35.5) it was probably the Krokion (or Krokoton) Plain: Strabo 9 C443, Steph. Byz. *s.* 'Demetrion', Beloch III, 1.477 n. 1.

97 Diod. 16.35.5f. Justin 8.2 adds little but rhetoric and romance.

98 For variant accounts of Onomarchos' death: Diod. 16.35.5, 35.6, 61.2, Paus. 10.2.3, Euseb. *Praep. Evang.* 8.14.33.

99 Diod. 16.35.6.

100 Diod. 16.37.

101 Sordi *LT* 244 n. 1 applies it to the capture of Pagasai, which she dates in 354 after the fall of Methone, but this is based on a false emendation of 'Pagai' in Diod. 16.31.6 (see Ehrhardt, cited in n. 95).

102 Hammond *JHS* 1937, 58 dates it to late summer 354; but see n. 55.

103 The election is nowhere affirmed explicitly but see Justin 11.3.2 and Diod. 17.4.1 with Isok. 5.20, Beloch III, 1.529 n. 1, Sordi *LT* 249ff., Larsen *Gk Fed. States* 24 and n. 4, 26, Westlake *Thessaly* 200f., Griffith *CQ* 1970, 73ff. The date has been disputed but is not later than 352 (Sordi and Griffith). If we accept the conferment as factual we ought not to reject (as, e.g., Westlake does) the one moderately explicit piece of evidence: Justin 8.2.1; and this would assign it to 353. On the office under its older, now discredited title (*tagos*) see Sordi 334ff., with refs, Beloch III, 1.529 n. 1, I, 2.200. Larsen 24 suggests that the new title was adopted to indicate that the bearer was a magistrate, not a monarch. An Athenian decree of 361/0 (Tod ii 147

= *IG* II² 116.18, 23, 34) uses the title *archon*. Dem. 2.7 probably refers to inducements Philip offered in exchange for the offer: the restoration of Magnesia to the *koinon* and the settlement of the Sacred War in its favour.

104 See n. 103.

105 Dem. 1.22 (349 BC), referring to a Pheraian revival in that year. The involvement of the *koinon* implied by the orator is not so certain; the actions referred to in Dem. 2.11, 1.22 may have been taken by the restored Pheraian tyrant (see Diod. 16.52.9 and p. 96 below). For the various types of duty on foreign trade: Hasebroek *Trade & Politics* 161f. The commonest rate was the *pentecostos* ('one fiftieth'), a 2% *ad valorem* levy on imports and exports, collected (in Athens, at any rate: Dem. 34.7) in cash, not goods.

106 Dem. 1.22; see the comments of Griffith (cited in n. 103).

107 Dem. 4.34, Ellis/Milns *Spectre of Philip* 28 n. 57.

108 Ath. 13.557, Plut. *Mor.* 141bc. The assertion of Steph. Byz. *s.* 'Thessalonike' that Nikesipolis was of the tyrant family is hardly credible and perhaps represents confusion with a plausible alternative, that her family, certainly one of distinction, had collaborated with the tyrants. On this marriage see also Chapter 8 n. 7.

108a Dem. 2.7, note 103 above.

109 Dem. 2.11, 1.22. In the latter, Dem. appears to mean that by the time he spoke (autumn 349) no fortification had yet begun.

110 Strabo 9 C440, Isok. 5.20; for Amphictyonic League membership at this time see Ais. 2.116, Diod. 16.29.

111 Westlake *Thessaly* 179; not the whole of Perrhaibia was ceded.

112 The Perrhaibian district was governed for Philip by a Thessalian friend Agathokles: Theopompos F81 (J).

113 Hdt. 7.128.

114 On Gonnoi see now the detailed study by B. Helly (*Gonnoi*, esp. i 81ff.).

115 Polyainos *Strat.* 4.2.18f., Westlake *Thessaly* 177f., Sordi *LT* 253ff. Theopompos F82 (in Bk IX) dealt with Pharkadon; if this war was the subject of the reference then it would be dated 353 or 352.

116 Steph. Byz. *s.* Philippoi; see Westlake *Thessaly* 178 n. 5 and, for full references, Sordi *LT* 256 n. 2.

117 Diod. 16.36, 37, Justin 8.2.8, Dem. 19.84, Libanius *Hyp.* to Dem. V, 2. Dem. 19.319 implies that only Athenians defended the pass, but his intention was limited.

118 Figures for the allies, totalling perhaps 10,000, are given by Diod. 16.37.

119 See above pp. 80f.

120 Dem. 23.183. Whatever the precise terms forced on Kersebleptes, his undertaking to support Athenian claims over Amphipolis was a repudiation of his relationship with Philip.

121 Schol. Ais. 2.81 (Dindorf 57.12). Although Aischines is not referring to the war of 351 his scholiast is; it was then that Philip acquired these allies: n. 87 above, to which add Theopompos F62 (J), Dem. 15.26.

122 Dem. 3.4f., Ellis 'Philip's Thracian Campaign of 352/351' forthcoming in *CPh*.

123 Dem. 1.13, Ellis *Makedonika* 1969, 16f.

124 Dem. 3.5, 4.10f., 1.13.

125 Dem. 4.17 refers emotively to the whole campaign as being 'against' (or 'towards') the Chersonesos.

126 Schol. Ais. 2.81 (see n. 121) mentions the successful conclusion of this campaign and the restoration of the 'disputed' territory, but does not mention Heraion by name nor the rightful owner, which was by implication, however, one of Philip's three allies, possibly Perinthos, which was the closest to Heraion.

127 See n. 91.

128 Dem. 23.107f., p. 81 above.

129 Dem. 1.13, Theopompos F127 (cf. Babrius *Fable* 70). Theopompos' Bk XX dates to 351/0.

CHAPTER IV

1 Isok. 5.21, Dem. 1.13; see Merker *BS* 1965, 35ff. and, on the current Paionian chieftain, esp. 44.

2 See above p. 70, Hammond *ABSA* 1966, 244f. Which tribes were involved we do not certainly know. The attested campaigns into Illyria during Philip's reign are those of 358 (against Bardylis of the Dardanoi), 356 (against Grabos, perhaps of the Grabaioi), 345 (against Pleuratos of the Ardiaioi., 339 (against the Triballoi) and 337 (against Pleurias, perhaps of the Autariatai); on these and for refs see Hammond *loc. cit.* At least one more campaign is likely, that currently under discussion, in 351/0. Dem. 4.48, 1.13 are not very helpful except for the implication in the former that it may have been in progress at the time of the speech. In mid-346 Isokrates was able to say (5.21) that Philip then ruled 'most of the Illyrians apart from those on the Adriatic'; this implies that the significant advance between the campaign of 356, which appears to have been brief, and those of 345 and later was to the shores of the Ionian Sea, an area inhabited by smaller tribes recently subject to the Dardanoi.

3 Justin 8.6.5. The date of this war is unknown, but it was fought before 349, when Demosthenes' *Philippic* 1 (cf. § 13) was spoken. See Reuss *RhM* 1881, 162, Hammond *Ep.* 533, whose date I accept; cf. Beloch III, 2.282, Treves *AJP* 1942, 144.

4 Diod. 16.72.1 gives 342/1 as the date at which Arybbas, 'King of the Molossians, died after a rule of ten years'. Treves *AJP* 1942, 129ff., dating the Philip/Arybbas war to 352 (see n. 3), assumed that the latter until that time had been regent for his nephew Alexandros, and became, for the next ten years, king *de iure.* But no such campaign will fit in 352 and, since Philip is unlikely to have allowed Arybbas to become king at the very time that his plans to replace him with Alexandros began to go into effect, this alternative seems preferable. We might save some credit for Diodoros' figure by assuming that he knew Arybbas was king for 10 years, but, by wrongly connecting his expulsion with his deposition and death (see Treves), simply got his decades mixed. This would mean that Arybbas became king *c.* 360 (the very date established independently for the death of his predecessor: Klotsch *Ep. Gesch.* 58, Hammond *Ep.* 278 n. 2, 517f.), was forced to step down to the regency in 350 and was expelled in 342.

5 Klotsch *Ep. Gesch.* 80, Cross *Ep.* 38f., Beloch III, 1.491, 2.180f., Hammond *Ep.* 534.

6 Diod. 16.34, 52, Olmstead *Hist. Persian Emp.* 429, 486.

7 See Table 2 on p. 123.

8 Hammond *JHS* 1937, 63, Diod. 16.40.1f. Beloch III, 1.483 points out that the Persian gift must have been inspired by the resumption of the old Theban friendship, as is seen in their aid in the unsuccessful bid by Ochos in 351 to recover Egypt.

9 Diod. 16.56–58.

10 See p. 95f. Dem. 2.11 and 1.22, although avowedly referring to decisions of 'the Thessalians', may well be in fact allusions to Pheraian attempts to subvert Philip's earlier arrangements; cf. Diod. 16.52.9.

11 Dem. 59.90f., 9.56–66, 8.40. The date of the banishment is unknown (cf. the indecisive attempt of Robinson/Clement *Excavs at Olynthus* ix 133f., 158ff.). If, as I think, Philip's warning march into the Chalkidike is to be dated to late 351, then 350 is possible for the political change; but 351 or even 349 would be possible.

12 Justin 8.3.10.
13 Justin 7.4.5, 8.3.10, Ellis *Historia* 1973, 350ff.
14 Dem. 9.11.
15 Diod. 16.52f. (under 349/8). On the date: Cawkwell *CQ* 1962, 130ff., Carter *Historia* 1971, 418ff. Stageira: this is the likely reading, but the mss at Diod. 16.52.9 show Geira or Zeira; see Beloch III, 1.494.
16 At least Apollonia and Akanthos may still have resented Olynthian ambitions, as they had three decades before: Xen. *Hell.* 5.2.11ff.
17 Sept./Oct. 349; see Philochoros F49–51.
18 On the order of the Olynthiacs: Dion. Hal. *ep. ad Amm.* i 4, Ellis *Historia* 1967, 108ff.
19 Dem. 3.7f., 21.161, Philochoros F49–51.
20 Dem. 2.11. What he means by 'to hold discussions about Magnesia' the orator does not explain.
21 Dem. 1.22. On Philip's Thessalian settlement see p. 83ff.
22 The suggestion that the *koinon* itself, and not merely Pherai, was involved in this affair comes alone from Dem. 1.22.
23 Diod. 16.52.9, Westlake *Thessaly* 183 n. 3. Although Sordi *LT* 244ff. agrees that a Philippic intervention took place at this time (and see Polyb. 9.28.3, cf. 33.2, Justin 8.3.12), she denies that Pherai was involved (see *LT* 358ff.). But her main argument (that Dem. 19.320 expressly excludes it) is false, based on a dubious translation of *prōton*, which more naturally here means 'primarily' – not 'for the first time'.
24 Cawkwell *CQ* 1963, 127ff., Brunt *CQ* 1969, 247ff.
25 Plut. *Phok.* 12–14, Ais. 3.86ff. On the date (Feb./Mar. 348): Dem. 39.16. See also Carter *Historia* 1971, 418ff. Phokion's release of his prisoners before the Athenians could vent their fury on them (Plut. *Phok.* 13.4) suggests that he had realized the Athenians had taken the wrong side and was attempting to prevent even worse damage to their image in Euboia.
26 He, Chares and Charidemos are in Lesbos by May 348. Charidemos may in the meantime have served briefly at Olynthos. Refs in n. 35.
27 [Dem.] 7.38, Dem. 19.326, Brunt *CQ* 1969, 249ff.
28 Cawkwell *JHS* 1963, 47ff. See also Dem. 21.162, 59.3ff., Buchanan *Theorika* 60ff. Demosthenes' opposition to the Euboian involvement proves that Philip was not yet involved there, and was known (then and later) not to be: Cawkwell *CQ* 1963, 129f.
29 Dion. Hal. *ep. ad Amm.* i. 5, Theopompos F250, Did. *in Dem.* 5.27ff., Pl. *ep.* 6, Strabo 13 C610, *SIG* 229, Jaeger *Aristotle* 111ff., Wormell *YCS* 1935, 57ff.
30 Chroust *Rev. Pol.* 1972, 370ff. brings together a number of little-known sources containing a tradition quite different from the standard. These are difficult to control and need further study, but Chroust makes out a plausible case for a closer relationship between Philip and Aristotle than is generally recognized.
31 Jaeger *Aristotle* 120 dates the formation of the treaty between Philip and Hermias to *c.* 342, but see Chroust *Rev. Pol.* 1972, 373f.
32 Philochoros F50 shows that Bottiaia and Pallene had fallen away from the Chalkidian League.
33 Dem. 3.4f., and p. 88 above.
34 Dem. 21.197, cf. 132, 164. Carter *Historia* 1971, 424ff. shows that the cavalry used by Charidemos are unlikely to have been those sent on from Euboia, who probably served in the third Athenian force; cf. Cawkwell *CQ* 1962, 130f.
35 Philochoros F50. Theopompos F143 has him in Olynthos and may also provide the reason for his early departure (by May: *IG* II[2] 207).

36 Diod. 16.53.2, Philochoros F51; cf. Cawkwell *CQ* 1962, 131. Philochoros clearly believes that some of the Athenians and mercenaries already there – presumably those who had gone under Charidemos' command – remained; but at least their leader had been ordered elsewhere: n. 35.

37 Philochoros F51, showing overall totals of (at most) 35 triremes, 4000 mercenaries (or perhaps 6000), 2000 citizens and either 300 or 450 cavalry: compare with Dem. 19.265, whose context is tendentious.

38 Suda *s.* 'Karanos'; on the timing see Cawkwell *CQ* 1962, 130f.

39 Ais. 2.12. On the terms: Dem. 5.5 with schol. (Dindorf 161.12). The arrival of this embassy will have been in June; it shortly preceded the Olympian truce (Ais. *loc. cit.*), which (by analogy with that for the Lesser Mysteries in Athens: *IG* I^2 6.76ff.) probably ran from early July to mid- or late August.

40 In the catalogue of pre-346 peace-moves in Ais. 2.12ff., Aischines makes no attempt to show that his opponent reacted favourably towards any before his defence of Philokrates; it was clearly the first (or first plausible) instance. Something must have occurred to change Demosthenes from anti- to pro-peace; and this – certainly the fall of Olynthos – Aischines carefully avoids placing in its proper context within his account, so as to make Demosthenes not only inconsistent but irrationally so.

41 Dem. 8.40, 9.56ff., 19.265,342, Diod. 16.53.2f., Hypereides F76 (Oxford = Loeb B19.1). The source-tradition on the traitors, largely Demosthenic in origin, is too distorting for us to reconstruct their actual roles. Polyb. 18.14 (a useful corrective in general terms) does not mention these; perhaps he knew as little as we do.

42 Refs in n. 41. Hypereides casts doubt on Demosthenes' claim (8.40) that the traitors 'suffered the worst fate of all'. His assertion (9.26) that the Chalkidian cities were utterly destroyed is refuted by Köhler *SB Berlin* 1891, 473ff.; see also Beloch III, 1. 416 n. 1. For cities not destroyed (Akanthos, Aineia, Apollonia, Mekyberna, Skione, Mende, Torone and perhaps Poteidaia) see Dem. 34.36, 35.10, Diod. 19.52, Strabo 7 F21, Livy 31.45, 44.10. Others *if* destroyed were soon rebuilt (e.g. Aphytis, Dion, Olophyxos, etc., were known to later geographers: Strabo 7 F27, 33, 35). See the useful discussion of sites, in connection with their earlier coinage, in Robinson/Clement *Excavs at Olynthus* ix 261ff.

43 Ais. 2.15, Dem. 6.21, Diod. 16.53, Arrian 1.2.5 (referring probably to Chalkidian Bottiaia), 1.12.7, 2.9.3; see Chapter 1 n. 21. On land-allotments see *SIG* 332.

44 In condemning Philip's treatment of Olynthos the Athenians overlooked Chares' more brutal handling of Sestos in 353 (Diod. 16.34.3). See Tod ii 166 = *IG* II^2 211, Dem. 19.263ff.

45 Ais. 2.12ff. Cawkwell *CQ* 1962, 130 and *REG* 1960, 417 argues that these events took place before the fall of Olynthos, but Demosthenes' change of policy (see n. 40) belongs most comfortably in the context of the sense of relief felt in Athens following the return of Ktesiphon; with Olynthos fallen, Athens might have been next! Cawkwell cites Diod. 16.55.1 and Dem. 19.192 to demonstrate that the city was taken 'during the Macedonian Olympia', but, although the chronological references are at best indefinite, their most natural meaning is that the festival (held at Dion in autumn, as Cawkwell shows) took place *after* the victory. See Markle *The Peace of Philocrates* 33ff.

46 Ais. 2.18f.; the association is also suggested by his defence of Philokrates.

47 Ais. 2.13. This is not disputed by

Demosthenes in 343. But, of course, Aischines spoke last; and, in any case, Demosthenes was safer to avoid the subject altogether.

48 Compare, for example, Tod ii 147 = *IG* II[2] 116.31ff. and Tod ii 157 = *IG* II[2] 127.42ff.

49 Ais. 2.14, 3.62. This must have been in late 348 or early 347, probably the former.

50 Dem. 19.10ff., 303f.

51 Refs in n. 50. The date of this decree was not (as Cawkwell *REG* 1960, 416ff. argues) early 346; he conflates two separate decrees aimed at slightly different ends and passed probably more than a year apart (see Markle *The Peace of Philocrates* App. 1). Diod. 16.54 refers to a despatch of envoys soon after the fall of Olynthos, but wrongly credits this to Demosthenes. See below with n. 66.

52 Dem. 4.32, 1.17f. As regards Dem. 19.315, we are justified in assuming that the forces recorded by Philochoros F49–51 represent the only Athenian ships currently in the north. Even if daring enough to venture this sort of campaign, they were too few to cause damage; as a fully land-based power in no way dependent on the Aegean, Macedonia presented no vulnerable points to a sea-borne raiding force.

53 Rohrmoser *ZÖG* 1874, 789ff., Pickard-Cambridge *Dem.* 273ff.; this theme is developed most convincingly by Markle in the dissertation cited in n. 51; see now also his 'Strategy of Philip in 346', *CQ* 1974.

54 Diod. 16.56. Theopompos F158 (Bk XXV) and 159 (Bk XXVI) probably refer, as Jacoby suggests, to the trial of Philon – following F157, which refers to the preceding military engagements (cf. Dem. 19.148 for Hedyleion). On the affairs of 351 see Diod. 16.38–40; this author then leaves the subject entirely until 16.56 (347).

55 Diod. 16.58.1; for Koroneia and Korsiai see Chapter 3 n. 92; for Orchomenos: Diod. 16.33.4.

56 Diod. 16.58.3.

57 Diod. 16.58.4ff., Paus. 10.2.5–3.2.

58 Ais. 2.79.

59 According to Ais. 3.62 (cf. 2.3, 3.3), by bribery. Whether or not we credit that, blind chance seems out of the question. Probably sortition was practised only when candidates outnumbered the bouleutic quota of their deme; *i.e.*, to guarantee appointment one did not need to bribe city or deme *officials*, but merely (somehow) to dissuade other candidates from standing if there was an excess. Stavely *G & R Voting & Elections* 110f., with this sort of explanation in mind, suggests that Demosthenes came from a small deme in which it was easy to buy off rivals. But Paiania was one of the very largest in the state: see Bicknell *Stud. in Ath. Pol. & Geneal.* 8, 25, who also makes some interesting observations on the powers of demarchs, pp. 5f. Significant for our understanding of Athenian democracy is the link implied between pursuit of a vital policy and the procurement of a bouleutic seat. Compare Ais. 3.125, in which Demosthenes, not then (340/39) a *bouleutes*, operates through a colleague. It is very likely that Philokrates too, the man chosen to move all the operative decrees of the peace, was a *bouleutes* for 347/6.

60 Dion. Hal. *ep. ad Amm.* i. 11, Dem. 18.70.

61 Dem. 9.15f., 8.63, 19.156, 10.8, 18.27, 70, [Dem.] 7.36f., Ais. 2.90, 3.82, Strabo 7 F47. Ais. 3.82 also mentions Ganias (cf. Harpokration *sv*), which may be the Ganiai between Ganos and Perinthos (Ps-Skylax 67). Markle *Peace of Philoc.* 49ff., 129f., in a useful discussion of these places, attempts with little success to distinguish between those garrisoned by Athens and those held by Kersebleptes. It seems more probable that none was actually manned by Athenians, who merely assisted Kersebleptes to establish them. Certainly by the time of their capture by Philip (in the two months after 23 Elaphebolion 346) there will have been no Athenians there, when even cleruchs in the Chersonesos, which Philip had guaranteed not to touch, were abandoning their posts: Ais. 2.72.

62 We have only a chance ref. to this preliminary campaign in Theopompos F160 (and perhaps 161), which has Antipatros devastating near-by Apros (for a description of the area: Strabo 7 F55). The Theopompos-fragment is from Bk XXVI, which deals with events before the negotiation of the Peace of Philokrates, which is itself covered in Bk XXVII and perhaps the end of Bk XXVI; this suggests a date in the second half of 347 and implies that the action was a response to the efforts of Kersebleptes and Chares.

63 Ais. 2.132ff., Diod. 16.59.1.

64 Dem. 19.36 with schol. (Dindorf 359.22), 39, 159, 163, 174, 334.

65 For the chronology of what follows see Cloché *Étude chronol. sur la 3ᵉ guerre sacrée* 119ff., with important modifications by Sealey *WS* 1955, 145ff. and especially Cawkwell *REG* 1960, 427ff. I follow Cawkwell approximately in the dating of this decree but not in his identification of it with that of Euboulos; see n. 51 above.

66 Ais. 2.57ff., esp. 60 (with Markle *Peace of Philoc.* App. 1). Dem. 19.16 accuses Aischines of having advised the *demos* to make this move; Aischines evades the charge: 2.57.

67 We must assume that when Phalaikos returned to power he had already been in communication with Philip; one of his first actions was to reverse the Athenian and Spartan alignment adopted by the triumvirate – hardly the response of one who had to fear Macedonian intervention against himself. Perhaps Philip promised him substantially what he promised Athens: to preserve Phokis but to destroy Theban power.

68 On the actor Neoptolemos: Dem. 5.6; also 19.12, 315.

69 Ais. 2.15ff. Key Athenian *bouleutai* must have conspired to delay this report, probably for fear that Athenian enthusiasm for peace would hamper the dealings with Phokis and with the Greek states who were being canvassed for support. If these were successful, then a better peace could be negotiated.

70 For the synchronism: Ais. 2.132ff. Sealey *WS* 1955, 145ff. misdates this assembly by misreading Ais. 2.36f. What seems likely is that when intelligence arrived of the change in Phokian leadership, soon after the offer of the Thermopylai towns, Proxenos was sent to discover whether the arrangements still held. Spurned, like the Spartans, by Phalaikos, he remained near by to watch developments and conveyed his report by letter to the *demos*. At this point the first embassy departed. As Demosthenes (allegedly) said, the large force had been voted but it would never be manned (Ais. 2.37). See Cawkwell *REG* 1960, 416ff.

The Julian equivalences given for the second half of 347/6 are based on the suggestions of Dinsmoor *Archons of Ath.* 428 (and are close to those assumed by Pickard-Cambridge *Dem.* 247f., 277f., etc., and Glotz *Hist. Grec.* III 291), which I follow out of consistency more than confidence.

71 By 343 he had switched to charging Aristodemos with submitting misleading reports (Dem. 19.12, 18, 97) and by 330 he could pass over his own role in this Assembly as if it had never happened (18.21).

72 As Cawkwell *REG* 1960, 424f. suggests, early Gamelion (= approx.

the end of January) or thereabouts is the likely date of their departure.

73 According to Cawkwell *art. cit.* 438 (and see Ryder *Koine Eirene* 97), Dem. 19.16 implies that some did eventually come. That may be the implication, but, since the substance of Demosthenes' assertion here is a lie that Aischines (2.57ff.) easily refutes, its implications deserve little credence. In 330 Aischines (3.64ff.), speaking first on this occasion, accuses Demosthenes of taking the decisive steps towards peace before the return of the Athenian envoys sent to the Hellenes (which, as he had shown 13 years earlier, was true). The point is effective – but not nearly so much as if he were able to say (the obvious thing if true or even plausible) that Demosthenes' action had in fact undercut embassies that were going to arrive to discuss common war or common peace. This he does not say; he cannot say that his opponent destroyed the common cause against Philip, but merely that he disobeyed the public will by acting before any response was received. When that was known, it must have been unfavourable – or he would have made no secret of the contrary. Demosthenes' only defence (18.23f.) is to ridicule the notion that he had prevented a panhellenic alliance against Philip (which Aischines, as we have noticed, was careful not to allege) and to assert that no envoys were out of Athens then for that purpose, because the Hellenes had all been sounded long ago (which is either a blatant lie, as Cawkwell argues, or a skilful attempt to confuse the jury into thinking that the envoys in question were those despatched by Euboulos' decree more than a year before).

74 Dem. 19.163f.

75 Ais. 2.18.

76 Ais. 2.22ff. (and see Mosley *Envoys & Diplom.* 27). Dem. 19.253 denies that Aischines mentioned Amphipolis; cf. Ais. 2.43ff., Dem. 19.254.

77 So Ais. 2.34f., 38 asserts in the presence of most or all of the envoys.

78 Although the ambassadors were well aware that Philip's Thracian campaign was about to begin, they evidently did not consider the question of peace materially affected by it, at least after the king had undertaken to keep his hands off the Chersonesos (Ais. 2.81f.). In 341, when Demosthenes wished to argue that Philip had acted faithlessly over Thrace, he could do so only by a lie: Dem. 9.15 (Pickard-Cambridge *Dem.* 266f.). As Rohrmoser *art. cit.* (in n. 53) 799 pointed out long ago, the forts the Athenians were holding (if indeed they, as distinct from their ally Kersebleptes, held any; see n. 61) belonged not to them but to their ally (and, it may be added, to the successor of Philip's ally, Amadokos, in whose territory at least two lay).

79 This is implicit in [Dem.] 7.24ff.

80 Dem. 19.321f.

81 Dem. 19.40.

82 [Dem.] 7.38; cf. Dem. 19.166ff., Ais. 2.99ff.

83 Dem. 5.10, 15, 6.30, 19.21, Ais. 2.119f.

84 [Dem.] 7.33, Dem. 19.40; also 19.316, Ais. 2.45, 50.

85 Ais. 2.81; he was still there in 343. Aischines may mean that Kersebleptes' son was in Pella only by the time the second embassy left it, and was therefore taken hostage not in 351 but during the campaign just finished; but the sense is not clear. A scholiast commenting on the passage refers to the 352/351 campaign (see Chapter 3 n. 121), but it does not follow necessarily that Kersebleptes' son was taken at the same time.

86 Ais. 2.90, Dem. 19.156, 158 with Ais. 2.91f.

87 See n. 61.

88 See Justin 8.3.14ff., who implies that on the pretext of arbitrating a dispute between two brothers (*these* brothers?) Philip took their (Thracian) territory for himself; also Dem. 1.13, Schaefer I 446, Höck *Hermes* 1891, 108.

89 Höck *Hermes* 1891, 85ff., 109f.

90 Dem. 12.8, Höck *Hermes* 1891, 110ff. If this is the 92-year-old Odrysian mentioned by Theopompos (F310, and see Schaefer I 446), then he can hardly be the son of Amadokos, who had only recently died.

91 Theopompos F164 with the *Hypoth.* to Dem. XIX (2.5). It is not clear from Dem. 19.163 whether Parmenion had accompanied the first embassy north from Halos, but that is unlikely. It is likely that Antipatros and Eurylochos collected their colleague *en route* to Athens.

92 Ais. 2.61.

93 The *demos* not only wanted, but positively expected to make peace: Cawkwell *Mnemosyne* 1962, 381 on Tod ii 167 = *IG* II² 212.39ff. Further action arising from this business was then scheduled to be taken at the assembly set down for 18 Elaphebolion.

94 See n. 93. In my reconstruction of the events of the following Assemblies I am in substantial agreement with Markle *Peace of Philoc.* 91ff.

95 Dem. 19.159, 174, [Dem.] 7.24ff.

96 Ais. 3.68ff. and cf. 2.60. See Cawkwell *REG* 1960, 420 n. 1, 435, Ryder *Koine Eirene* 97 n. 3 and (for Common Peaces in general) *passim* but esp. xi ff. and 118ff.

97 Ais. 3.71, Dem. 19.15.

98 Ais. 3.71f. Cawkwell *REG* 1960, 436 suggests that Aischines still hoped that Philip wanted peace badly enough to agree to it on the allied synod's terms and that he therefore wished to give Antipatros the night to cogitate over the unanimous Athenian support for it. But this would seem unduly naïve on Aischines' part. Perhaps, rather, all the envoys had been taken aback by the strength of opposition to the exclusion-clause and Aischines wished to canvass means of circumventing that *impasse* before Antipatros was obliged to lay all the cards on the table. On 24 Elaphebolion the clause which was indeed excised on the 19th, was reinstated *de facto*; and it was perhaps this tactical manoeuvre that was hammered out (and, necessarily, approved by the Macedonians) during the night of the 18/19th and that Aischines had in mind when he moved for the adjournment of proceedings on the evening of the former.

99 Aischines' charge (3.71f.: in 330 BC) that Demosthenes himself spoke in favour of alliance must be false or he would have quoted him thirteen years earlier in answer to Dem. 19.15.

100 (As it must have been!) Ais. 2.63ff. denies that discussion took place on the 19th, but his proof is transparently unconvincing (and compare 2.74ff., which can refer only to the 19th if his speech on the previous day was, as he also claimed, in favour only of the allies' dogma).

101 Ais. 2.67 claims that Demosthenes had a draft-motion of his own which was very similar to that of Philokrates. The charge must be false, for such an expedient was quite unnecessary. But only by such means could Aischines point to the line Demosthenes was actually taking while pretending to do otherwise. But the fact that such a story had to be fabricated implies that Aischines (and the jurors) knew Demosthenes had never spoken in favour of Philokrates' motion.

102 Dem. 18.21, Theopompos F166, Ais. 2.74ff.

103 Dem. 19.159, 291 and see Ais. 2.74ff.

104 Ais. 3.73f.

105 Gilbert *Const. Antiquities* 285ff., Stavely *Gr. & R. Voting & Elections* 79. In fact Kersebleptes was to surrender on 23 Elaphebolion, so that by the

24th, although the Athenians did not know it at the time, it was too late to claim him for a co-signatory.

106 Ais. 2.83f. [Dem.] 12.8 gives a slightly different version, which is perhaps complementary rather than contradictory; see n. 110.

107 Ais. 2.111, 3.76.

108 Demosthenes asserts that this *probouleuma*, which he moved, ordered them to meet Philip wherever he might be, and he has the resolution read in confirmation (19.54, cf. 18.25). He knew as well as his colleagues that there was absolutely nothing they could do in Thrace, even if they found and reached Philip there. His aim in drafting the resolution, therefore, must have been to give himself a pretext for dissociating himself from his colleagues in the formation of the peace. This is the first sign that he wished to bring about a result different from that anticipated by the others.

109 Dem. 19.155ff. The embassy left Athens on 3 Mounychion (= *c.* 29 April) and arrived in Pella *c.* 26 Mounychion; Philip arrived *c.* 23 Thargelion (= *c.* 17 June); the oaths were taken at Pherai shortly before 10 Skirophorion (= *c.* 4 July) and the envoys returned to Athens on the 13th: see Dem. *loc. cit.*, Ais. 2.91f. and Dem. 19.58.

110 Dem. 19.174. Thus in Philip's letter ([Dem.] 12.8) there is no reference to their positive exclusion but merely to their non-inclusion. See above with nn. 98, 106.

111 It was represented as bribery by Dem. 19.167f. (but cf. 19.235), but see Mosley *Envoys & Diplom.* 39f. If Demosthenes, as he claims, did spurn Philip's hospitality at the time, it must have been another sign that he was preparing to dissociate himself from his colleagues; see n. 108.

112 Dem. 19.166ff., Ais. 2.99f. That Demosthenes went armed with no more than a silver talent (if true) suggests that he was merely making a gesture which would enable him to attack Philip, when the time was ripe, from firmer ground. Since, in any case, all knew that Philip had promised to release the prisoners without cost, Demosthenes' colleagues must now have become seriously concerned as to his intentions (see nn. 108, 111).

113 Ais. 2.113ff. (cf. 122), Dem. 19.19ff. Such discussion was *inter alia* the legitimate concern of the embassy, which was under instructions 'to negotiate about any other advantages within their power to achieve' (Ais. 2.104). That such matters were later considered of less importance than the reception of oaths, etc., was the result of the collapse of the peace they were trying to construct.

114 See Ais. 2.104, which makes this clear.

115 Dem. 9.11 and cf. Ais. 2.137, referring to the time after 13 Skirophorion.

116 Ais. 2.136. The Thessalians were convinced that Thebes was not to be the object of Philip's favour; they no doubt anticipated that the planned settlement would strengthen their already powerful position in the Amphiktyonic League.

117 Dem. 19.76, schol. 19.72 (Dindorf 377.3).

118 Argos, Messenia and Megalopolis were so deeply concerned as to the outcome (Isok. 5.74) that we should expect them to have had envoys present.

119 For the contemporary situation in the Peloponnesos and central Greece see Isok. 5.47–56. In particular, this author makes it clear that the Spartans at the time were faced with complete isolation were they unable to join Philip and Athens against Thebes.

120 Isok. *loc. cit.* Arkadia should presumably be added, to judge by

Aischines' failure there against the pro-Macedonians in late 348: Dem. 19.10f., 303f., Ais. 2.79.

121 Dem. 9.11, who could afterwards pass off Philip's friendliness towards the Phokians as a pretence because by then his plan had failed.

122 Ais. 2.137. A scholiast on Dem. 19.22 (Dindorf 353.5ff.) states that hostility between Thebes and Athens was sufficiently high (and we should remember that both were now allies of Philip) to deter the envoys from travelling home from Pherai via Boiotia.

123 Dem. 19.278.

124 Perhaps the Euboians (Ais. 2.20) or the Oitaians, Ainianes and Malians, whose hatred for Phokis was well known. Markle *Peace of Philoc.* 182ff. points to several scholia which suggest that the Thessalians alone signed as Philip's allies (and cf. Dem. 12.5).

125 Ais. 3.74. *Hypoth.* 2 to Dem. XIX (Dindorf 337.3ff.) claims that Philip's oath was 'to the Athenians and the allies of the Athenians *except for the Halians and the Phokians*', but the author is a casualty of Demosthenes' attempts (by suppressing the events of 24 Elaphebolion and playing up those of the 19th) to claim that these allies should have been sworn in as participants (see Dem. 19.44, 159, 174, 278).

126 Philip undertook in writing to send representatives of his other allies to Athens (Ais. 2.129). Clearly he did not object to their participation, but simply wished to avoid a public declaration of his allies before the reshuffle that would be involved in his plan for the settlement of the Sacred War.

127 Dem. 19.36ff.; when the siege ended, Halos was handed over to Pharsalos and its citizens were exiled: [Dem.] 11.1, Dem. 19.39.

128 Dem. 19.173f., 323.

129 Dem. 19.58.

130 Cawkwell *REG* 1962, 454f. suggests that he camped at Nikaia, but this was the base of the Phokian commander: Diod. 16.59.2.

131 Dem. 19.51; at 19.52 he misrepresents Aischines' advice at the time, as is proved by 19.113: Markle *Peace of Philoc.* 237. This letter was probably despatched between 16 and 18 Skirophorion.

132 Dem. 19.17f., 31f. for the Council's resultant resolution (Aischines' lame rejoinder fails to refute this: 2.121ff.); cf. Wüst *Phil.* 7; also Cawkwell *REG* 1962, 455ff., who disbelieves Demosthenes' account of his own part in this meeting.

133 Dem. 19.48ff. The orator here misrepresents the intention of this clause and claims as its result the failure of the *demos* to send the hoplites – which in fact was the work of Demosthenes a few days later. See Markle *Peace of Philoc.* 219.

134 P. 115 above, schol. Dem. 19.72, Diod. 16.59.1. Dem. 19.76 implies that the Spartans had actually gone to Thermopylai in all innocence, only to withdraw when they perceived Philip's real intention. This is the reverse of the truth.

135 See Schaefer II 275 and n. 1. This was during the same Assembly.

136 Dem. 19.121f., Ais. 2.94f., and see Mosley *Envoys & Diplom.* 39.

137 Schol. Ais. 2.94.

138 Dem. 19.122. I believe that it was at this time that Demosthenes and Timarchos initiated their prosecution of Aischines for *parapressbeia*. In this I follow Markle *Peace of Philoc.* 239ff., who cites schol. Ais. 1.169. (Alternatively, see Schaefer II 280 and n. 3, who dates it after the surrender of Phokis.) The central and decisive point, it seems to me, is that the charge was levelled at *Aischines* and not at Philokrates, who was (by virtue of his far closer association with the peace) much easier game. This proves that the prosecution was aimed at discrediting Aischines personally, rather than at attacking the peace itself. In that case, the only suitable time for it was when Aischines was excused from embassy-service and remained behind to oppose Demosthenes' machinations. By 343, when the trial was finally held, the situation was quite different. By then, the peace itself was unpopular – and in those circumstances, significantly, it was Philokrates who was prosecuted (and Aischines only when the former's flight made his former colleagues more vulnerable to attack). The original charge against Aischines was made, in all probability, without any intention on the complainants' part of actual prosecution; they simply wished to smear his name at this most crucial point.

139 Ais. 2.137. On the existing hostages see above pp. 109 and 114 with n. 112.

140 This I take to be the implication of Ais. 2.138 (*fin.*), 139, where the author suggests that if the Athenians had acted when they should they would have done so in concord not only with Philip but with the Thessalians 'and the other Amphiktyons'. See also Dem. 5.23.

141 Dem. 6.13, Diod. 16.59.2.

142 Dem. 5.23. As Ais. 2.140 points out, Philip had in any case to reckon with traditional Thessalian hostility towards Phokis; and he makes it clear that the Thessalians (previously supporters of the planned settlement: Ais. 2.138 and nn. 116, 140 above) at this critical point began to press for action. A further spur to speedy action lay in the difficulties of the food supply, for in this area no corn had been sown during the last spring (Dem. 19.123). While food could be brought into the Pass from the Oitaian and Malian districts, this made Philip more susceptible to pressure from these bitterly anti-Phokian allies.

143 Orchomenos and Koroneia (Dem. 5.21f., 6.13, Ais. 2.141) and presumably Korsiai and Tilphosaion (Dem. 19.141). Diod. 16.60.1 mentions three cities but it is not clear whether he refers here to cities in Phokian or Boiotian territory; Sherman's reading (Loeb) plausibly makes them three Boiotian towns 'in the possession of the Phokians'. See n. 162.

144 Diod. 16.59.2 shows that the expectation of all was that the issue would be settled not by negotiation, as Isokrates (5.30ff. and cf. Ais. 2.114) wished, but by war.

145 Dem. 19.123. Phokis might not, if desperate, be easy to subdue and a campaign might last several weeks. Knowing that capitulation under those circumstances would mean the harshest possible treatment, the Phokians must fight to the end. The casualties would be extremely high.

146 Dem. 19.62f., Diod. 16.59.3. On the subsequent fate of Phalaikos: Diod. 16.61.3–64 with Beloch III, 1.510 and n.3. No Phokian towns resisted the surrender: Dem. 19.61.

147 Diod. 16.59.4, Dem. 19.53ff., 61.

148 Dem. 19.50, cf. 19.62 and schol. Ais. 2.94.

149 Once the regular meetings began the Boiotian votes on the Council were exercised (at least until autumn 339 and perhaps until autumn 337) by a succession of pairs of delegates with their communities not designated, contrary to the Ionian and Dorian practice. This almost certainly means, as in the past, that Thebes supplied both *hieromnemones* for the Boiotians. See Table 3 on pp. 132/3 (and also Table 4 on p. 135 for a similar situation among the *naopoioi*); also Ais. 2.116.

150 Dem. 19.62, 18.63, Ais. 2.142.

151 Dem. 5.14, Ais. 2.116.

152 Diod. 16.60.1, *Hypoth.* to Dem. V (Dindorf 158.1ff.), Dem. 19.237, Paus. 10.3.2, 8.2.

153 *SIG* 221B. The special position

accorded to Macedonia in the Amphiktyony is evident in the decrees that list the *hieromnemones* present at various sessions of the Council. The names of 'those from Philip' (see p. 21 above) followed immediately after those of the Thessalian delegates, whose traditional claim to precedence placed them first. Among the *naopoioi*, however, they took third place to Delphoi and Thessaly. See Parke/Wormell *Delphic Oracle* i 233; also Table 3 on pp. 132/3 and Table 4 on p. 135.

154 Busolt/Swoboda *Gr. Staatskunde* 1296, Perlman *Num. Chron.* 1965, 57f.

155 Reaction to the Phokian surrender: Dem. 19.125f.; the embassy: Ais. 2.95; Demosthenes' refusal to serve: Dem. 19.172, Ais. 2.140; Aischines' role: Ais. 2.140ff. (cf. Dem. 19.80, which is too weak to need comment). In 343, Demosthenes 19. 126, 129, 131 attempted to devalue Aischines' efforts by accusing him of participating in the embassy although he had declined service for health reasons. But he is here clouding the issue by pretending that the fourth embassy was the same as the third – a lie he himself refutes at 19.172. One wonders whether he was attempting to confuse the jurors. Would they assume (those, that is, who did not know) that he had not refused the fourth mission (which was morally inexcusable) but rather had not been *able* to serve, having declined service on the third (which he consequently equated with it)?

156 Ais. 2.142 and schol., Paus. 10.2.2. See also Parke/Wormell *Delphic Oracle* I 234, who however misinterpret the role of Philip in the determination of the punishment. The overblown rhetoric of Justin 8.5 needs no attention. If Demosthenes (19.64f., 9.19, 26, 18.36) speaks in later years of atrocities, we may note that in the most immediate of his speeches (when exaggeration was more easily perceived) he makes no such charges.

157 See n. 165. On the humiliations of Athens and Korinth see Dem. 19. 327 (loss of Athenian *promanteia*), Diod. 16.60.2 (loss of Korinthian right to participate in running of Pythia). According to Paus. 10.8.2, Sparta lost its Amphiktyonic rights altogether. However, as the *naopoioi*-lists show, none of these three lost its membership, and perhaps Pausanias is confusing expulsion with censure. See Table 4 on p. 135.

158 Paus. 10.2.4, schol. Ais. 2.142, Dem. 19.327 for the seriousness with which sacrilege could be regarded.

159 Diod. 16.60.1, Dem. 5.19. Dem. 19.127, 141, 149 claims in 343 that Thebes acquired Phokian territory, but he is uninterested in specifying which areas; Diod. 16.60.2 affirms that the Phokians retained all their land. The rhetorical nonsense in Justin 8.5 is worthless. See Wüst *Phil.* 17 and n. 3.

160 16.56.6.

161 See Table 2 on p. 123, Diod. 16.60.2. The payments appear to have terminated around 320, by which time rather less than 500 talents had been repaid.

162 Diod. 16.60, Dem. 19.81. Dem. 19.123 mentions 22 Phokian towns and Pausanias names 21 (10.3.2: including Abai, which was not harmed). Beloch III, 1.512 wishes to emend the second sentence of Diod. 16.60.1 but Sherman's reading (Loeb) is preferable; see n. 143 above. The effect of this *metoikesis* (Diod. 16.60.2), or *dioikesis* (cf. Xen. *Hell.* 5.2.5), on the government of Phokis is not altogether clear. Glotz *BCH* 1909, 533 states bluntly: 'plus de gouvernement commun'; but the only relevant evidence to survive, the records of the Phokian reparations, lend him uncertain support. The Phokians continued to be styled by their common name; and the fact that duplicate records of those in Delphoi were inscribed and preserved in Elateia suggests that this city continued to play its central role in Phokian affairs – as well as that at least some vestige of common government survived for the execution of such tasks. See for example Tod ii 172B.

163 Diod. 16.60.3f. has been misread (see esp. Wüst *Phil.* 20ff.) as indicating that a Common Peace (in the technical sense) was arranged by the Amphiktyony. Griffith *JHS* 1939, 71ff. has shown that this is not the meaning of the passage, which indeed positively indicates that there was no Common Peace. See also Ryder *Koine Eirene* 145ff., Hampl Gr. *Staatsverträge* 64ff.

164 Dem. 5.15, 20ff. Indeed, since the orator's aim was to avoid provoking the Amphiktyons, we should expect him to *understate* any tensions believed to exist among them, since the unhappier their relationships the greater the likelihood that his fellow Athenians might feel disposed to defy them.

165 The roles of both Sparta and Korinth in the Sacred War had seriously compromised their standing among the Dorians in the Amphiktyony: see n. 157. Many commentators have been unhappy about Diodoros' reference (16.60.2) to the Korinthians alone, and Schaefer II 286 n. 2 suggests emending the text to include Sparta.

166 We are not to be misled by Philip's nomination *by name* to the presidency (Dem. 5.22, 9.32) or by the styling of the Macedonian *hieromnemones* as 'those from Philip'. See p. 21 above. At the Pylaia of autumn 346, alongside the otherwise unknown Timanoridas, sat (apparently; see Bourguet *BCH* 1896, 233) Philip himself: *SIG* 241B = *FD* iii 5, No. 19.74 (see Table 4 on p. 135, which however does not give names).

CHAPTER V

1 Cawkwell *JHS* 1963, 50 n. 27, cf. *REG* 1960, 416ff.

2 Pp. 112f. above and Ais. 2.83ff.

3 As we have noticed (p. 114), some of the fault in this attaches to Philip himself, whose insistence on holding Athenians prisoner until his ends were attained was used to great advantage against him.

4 Diod. 16.60.4f. Isok. 5.12ff. and *passim*, writing during the peace-negotiations, urged Philip to engage in an Asian campaign at the head of a unified Hellenic force. In autumn 338, in a subsequent letter, he implied that Philip's intentions had become known at about the same time as he had raised the subject eight years earlier (*Ep.* 3.2f.); had his submission, he wondered, inspired or merely coincided with Philip's plans?

5 The Panathenaia began on 28 Hekatombaion (= *c.* 21 August, in the year 364/5: Deubner *Attische Feste* 23. The prisoners were returned ([Dem.] 7.38) – clearly before the promised deadline (Dem. 19.168), or Demosthenes would have said so.

6 For Philip's letter see Dem. 18.39f., in which, however, the alleged text is a forgery and the words apparently cited by the orator (s. 40) are, by his own admission, a tendentious paraphrase; see Grote xi 229 and n. 1, Schaefer II 294, Pickard-Cambridge *Dem.* 286 n. 2, Beloch III, 1.513, Wüst *Phil.* 39 and n. 4.

7 Dem. 19.128, and see Beloch III, 1.513, *CAH* VI 241, Wüst *Phil.* 39 n. 5. However, as a Delphic *naopoioi*-list (*SIG* 241B = *FD* iii 5 No. 19.74; and see Table 4 in p. 135) shows, Athens did participate in the autumn Pylaia two months later.

8 Ais. 1.166ff. (delivered in autumn/winter 346) for the line he took; also Dem. 19.111ff., who ignores his own part in these proceedings, which however is preserved for us in his fifth speech (*On the Peace*).

9 Dem. 5.14ff., 22, 19.128, 132, 327. They were responsible, probably about this time, for the despatch to Philip of Eukleides, who was charged to demand that Kersebleptes be included in the peace: Dem. 19.162, 181, schol. 19.149 (Dindorf 408.20).

10 Dem. 19.111ff. oversimplifies the purpose and composition of this embassy by referring only to Macedonian and Thessalian members and by stating that it requested support only over the matter of Philip's admission to the Council. This, however, is certainly the occasion on which he delivered his extant speech *On the Peace*, which is more revealing.

11 Dem. 5.13ff. and *passim*.

12 The Pythian festival was probably held in the early autumnal weather of the Delphic month Boukatios (corresponding to Attic Hekatombaion), followed in Heraios (Boedromion) by the Pylaia. See Bourguet *L'Admin. financ.* 142f., Dittenberger *SIG* i p. 630 n. 1, cf. No. 145.45, Schaefer II 295 n. 2 and especially Markle *The Peace of Philocrates* 305ff.

13 Dem. 19.111ff.

14 Diod. 16.60, Dem. 5.18f., 19.80, 310, 327, 18.36.

15 For the date: Ais. 1.80, 159 (with Schaefer II 336, Beloch III, 1.532 n. 1); for the charge: 1.28ff.; for the penalty: 1.19ff.

16 Ais. 1.94, 119, Beloch III, 1.532, Pickard-Cambridge *Dem.* 302.

17 The citizen-review: Dem. 18.132, Suda *s.* '*apopsephisthenta*', Harpokration *s.* '*diapsephisis*'; Antiphon: Dem. 18.132ff., Plut. *Dem.* 14, Deinarchos 1.63. For the date: Wüst *Phil.* 47ff.

18 For the date see Isok. 5.7.

19 See, for example, *CAH* VI 510.

20 As, for example, does Cawkwell *CQ* 1963, 121.

21 Isok. 5.3, 19ff., 120ff.; cf. *Ep.* 9.9 (356 BC), 4 (*Paneg.*). 24 (355).

22 Isok. 5.39, 49ff., 73ff.

23 Perlman *Historia* 1957, 306ff., esp. 311.

24 Pp. 96f. above.

25 Dem. 18.134, Hypereides F76 (Oxf. = Loeb F19.1). For the date of this appeal, probably at the spring Pylaia of 345, see Wüst *Phil.* 52. For the pretext over which Athens appears to have justified her control of the Delian temple see Thuc. 3.107, 5.1, 32 with Hypereides F67–75 (= Loeb F19.1–5).

26 Such an interpretation is implied by Dem. 18.134. He does not say that the Areiopagos Council branded Aischines a traitor, but merely that it rejected him and appointed Hypereides. By that action, *he* interpolates, 'the Council branded him traitor and enemy of the people'. What the action implied, that is, was simply that Hypereides was the more appropriate appointee, as the accompanying (and possibly forged) document (s. 135) says. On the Areiopagos' powers in such matters see Sealey *CPh* 1964, 12ff. = *Essays in Gk Politics* 43ff., but note that Dem. 18.34 says explicitly that this body was authorized by the Assembly to act as it did. That fact, plus the acceptance of the reversal without demur, suggest that it was a matter not of internal politics but of international strategy.

27 Dittenberger *SIG* i p. 340; see Table 4 on p. 135.

28 Didymos *in Dem.* 4.1ff. In line 11 another petitioner is enrolled as a member, but the name is unreadable; Dittenberger *SIG* No. 224 suggests the Elians.

29 Table 3 on pp. 132/3.

30 Justin 8.5.7–6.2.

31 Cf. Arrian 7.9 and, on the general

subject of such population-'transplants': Ellis *Makedonika* 1969, 9ff.

32 Justin 8.6. For Pleuratos: Didymos *in Dem.* 12.64ff.; for his tribe (not the Dardanoi of Justin): Hammond *ABSA* 1966, 241ff. Strabo 7 C315 names the Autariatai, Ardiaioi and Dardanoi as the three most powerful Illyrian tribes.

33 Diod. 16.69.7.

34 Isok. *ep.* 2.3; for the synchronism see s. 11. For the date of the campaign, 345 rather than 344, see Cawkwell *CQ* 1963, 126f.; there is certainly no room for it in 344 before the Thessalian intervention.

35 Didymos *in Dem.* 12.37ff., Sen. *Controv.* 10.5.6. Dem. 18.67 (and schol.) believed that the injury was to the king's collar-bone, but, as Meyer *SB Berlin* 1909, 759 has pointed out, the sources employed by Didymos (Theopompos, Marsyas of Pella and the Samian Douris) are preferable: Did. *in Dem.* 12.48ff.

36 Pp. 95f. above.

37 *Ibid.* and Dem. 2.7, cf. 2.11. 1.22.

38 Dem. 6.22. Nikaia, originally (so Thebes alleged) a Theban foundation (schol. [Dem.] 11.4), was claimed by them in vain (Ais. 3.140). On the basis of [Dem.] 11.4 (and see Didymos *in Dem.* 11.40ff.), it has been concluded by some that Philip later ousted the Thessalians from Nikaia (e.g., Glotz *BCH* 1909, 529, *Hist. Grec.* III 317 n. 61, who dates this to 344 or 342), but this is probably not so; he is unlikely to have risked unnecessary offence to his closest allies. Thc confusion perhaps arises out of Philip's dual role as Macedonian king and Thessalian archon.

39 Dem. 5.23.

40 Table 3 on pp. 132/3. Ais. 3.124, 128 refers to Kottyphos as president at least in 339; see also schol. Ais. 3.128, Westlake *Thessaly* 189, Sordi *LT* 286 n. 2.

41 Table 4 on p. 135. There was also a *naopoios* from Perrhaibia, the only one from the Thessalian *perioikis*. In 337 there were seven Thessalians and in 334 six.

42 Arist. *Pol.* 5.1306a, Dem. 18.48, Dem. 59.24, 108, Harpokration *s.* 'Simos'. For a complementary tradition that the Aleuadai, Philip's traditional allies, turned against him at some stage, see Dem. 2.14, schol. 1.22, Polyainos *Strat.* 4.2.11. This belongs most appropriately in the context of 344; Westlake *Thessaly* 190ff., Sordi *LT* 285f., 364ff. On Simos' coinage: Head *HN* 297,299; his minting forms part of a series of issues (no doubt Aleuad-controlled) that had run at Larisa for perhaps half a century, from which only the addition of his name distinguishes these. Gardiner *Cat. of Gk Coins, Thess. to Aetolia* xxivff., *BMC Thessaly* xxv, Head *HN* 297 thought Simos a tetrarch appointed by Philip, but Aristotle's evidence refutes this.

43 Diod. 16.69.8 implies that there were tyrannies in a number of cities (and see Isok. *ep.* 2.20: a people 'full of stasis', written soon after, or even during the present campaign).

44 For the date: Beloch III, 2.289, Wüst *Phil.* 54ff.

45 Diod. 16.69.8, Dem. 8.59, 9.12, 19.260, [Dem.] 7.32.

46 Dem. 6.22, on whose interpretation there are two schools of thought (cf. Westlake *Thessaly* 196f., Wüst *Phil.* 56, 99ff. and Beloch III, 1.529, Sordi *LT* 275ff.); the view adopted here is, with modifications, that of Sordi. There is no need to emend away Demosthenes' reference to a dekadarchy, which, as Wüst noticed, was an appropriate safeguard against further trouble from Pherai and is not at all incompatible with the overall reintroduction of the tetrarchies. The consequence of this more straightforward interpretation is that there is now no evidence for a separate intervention by Philip in 342 (for which, in any case, there is no room); Dem. 9.26, in summer 341, is only an *ante quem* for the tetrarchies; Theopompos F208 belongs to Bk XLIV, the date of which is indeterminate (Jacoby *FGH Komm.* IIB p. 385f.).

47 Westlake *Thessaly* Chap. 2, Sordi *LT* Chaps 2 and 3. On the new organization see Momigliano *Athenaeum* 1932, 47ff., Schnitzer *Hermes* 1954, 451ff., Sordi *LT* 313ff., Larsen *Gk Fed. States* 12ff.

48 *SIG* 55, Xen. *Hell.* 6.1.8, 12; for the title *basileus* see Pind. *Pyth.* 10, Hdt. 5.63, 7.6, Thuc. 1.111.1, Polyainos *Strat.* 8.44, Suda *s.* 'Aleuadai'.

49 *SIG* 274, Nos. 2 and 8. No. 8, a Daochos, was also a Thessalian *hieromnemon* at Delphoi from 336–332 or later.

50 Dem. 23.199, [Dem.] 13.23; see Larsen *Gk Fed. States* 14.

51 Head *HN* 291ff., Seltman *Gk Coins* 160ff. For a useful summary of the evidence see Larsen *op. cit.* 20f.

52 Xen. *Hell.* 6.1.2ff., esp. 19. On the earlier system of levying troops (on the basis of *kleroi*, or allotments) see Arist. F497, 498 (Rose), quoted and discussed by Wade-Gery *JHS* 1294, 55ff., Cary *CAH* III 600, Sordi *LT* 66ff., Larsen *op. cit.* 16ff.

53 The most useful treatment of the dynasty is by Beloch III, 2.80ff. On Jason: Stählin *RE* IX, 1.771ff., Westlake *Thessaly* 67ff., Sordi *LT* Chap. 7. On Jason's successors: Beloch *loc. cit.*, Westlake 126ff.

54 Westlake *Thessaly* 133ff., Sordi *LT* 193ff.

55 By 361: Tod ii 147 = IG II[2] 116.18, 23, 34.

56 Westlake *Thessaly* 133ff., Sordi *LT* 193ff., 313ff., Larsen *Gk Fed. States* 24.

57 Diod. 15.61, 67, Plut. *Pel.* 26.

58 Pp. 61, 74, 78ff. above.

59 Diod. 15.80, Plut. *Pel.* 35, Isok. 5.53, Westlake *Thessaly* 151f.

60 As well as his traditional rights to mobilize the army and to control finance: Justin 11.3.2.

61 As Westlake *Thessaly* 201f.; he is clearly right about the increased powers of the tetrarchies and the emphasis now laid upon them, but it is impossible that Thessaly could have been organized entirely on the basis of such large units. Larsen *Gk Fed. States* 24, 26 sees the system as a *sympoliteia*, a federal state made up of cities.

62 *Naopoioi*: Table 4 on p. 135; *hieromnemones*: Table 3 on pp. 132/3.

63 Theopompos F209

64 Theopompos F209 and *SIG* 274 No. 8; on the former see also *SIG* 240H.11 and n. 7. A third possibility, Kineas (Dem. 18.295; perhaps a Larisaian: Theopompos F35 with 34), cannot be confirmed. Sordi *LT* 287f. thinks that Pharsalos now replaced Larisa as the dominant city of the *koinon*; but her arguments are indefinite and now appear contradicted by numismatic evidence (see Appendix below).

65 *SIG* 274 No. 8; his great great grandfather, one Aknonios (*ibid.* No. 2), bore the same title in the fifth century.

66 Dem. 18.295f.; but cf. Polyb. 18.13ff., on which see Aymard *Rev. Hist.* 1938, 79, *REA* 1940, 9ff., Cloché *AC* 1939' 361ff.

67 *SIG* 249II.22; cf. 274 No. 8.

68 Head *HN* 291; cf. Westlake *Thessaly* 204, Hammond *HG*[1] 559.

69 Noe *Bibliog. of Gk Coin Hoards*[2] lists only two: Nos. 533 (Karditsa) and 595 (Lamia), both late fourth-century burials.

70 Kraay *Gk Coins & Hist.* 14ff.

71 For refs see Appendix.

72 Table 4 on p. 135.

73 Diod. 16.69.8, Didymos *in Dem.* 11.40ff., Westlake *Thessaly* 192.

74 Dem. 6.19ff., 18.79.

75 Dem. 18.136, [Dem.] 7.18ff.,

Hypoth. to Dem. VI, s. 2. Demosthenes' *Philippic* II belongs to this context; see Dem. 6.5, 34, Cawkwell *CQ* 1963, 121ff. (cf. Brunt *CQ* 1969, 262 n. 3). Hegesippos' speech ([Dem.] VII), delivered in early 342 (Wüst *Phil.* 95, modified by Cawkwell 202 and Brunt 252f.), alludes not only to these events but also to later offers by Philip. There seem to have been two sets, the first conveyed by Python's embassy and the second (possibly in a series of despatches, but culminating in the 'recent' letter mentioned by [Dem.] 7.39), a reiteration of the first, general offer of negotiation with the addition of specific bids on points of difference arising out of the first offer or out of interim developments.

76 Paus. 4.28.2, Cawkwell *CQ* 1963, 132.

77 [Dem.] 7.20f., Dem. VI *passim*, *Hypoth.* to Dem. VI s. 2, Dem. 18.136, and see refs cited in n. 75.

78 [Dem.] 7.20f.

79 [Dem.] 7.18, 31f., Grote *HG* xi 250, Wüst *Phil.* 69ff., Ryder *Koine Eirene* 100f., Cawkwell *CQ* 1963, 132 (cf. Brunt *CQ* 1969, 262 n. 2).

80 [Dem.] 7.18, 36f., p. 110 above. It is not clear whether this issue arose out of Python's embassy or at a later time. When it did, Philip offered to submit it to arbitration. He was on safe ground, for no impartial adjudicator could hold that the Peace of Philokrates had been in force before *both* parties had signed. In any case, the Athenian claim was absurd, for the fortresses had been on the territory of Amadokos' successor and Philip's ally, Teres, and on that of Kersebleptes, who, before Athens signed the peace on 24 Elaphebolion, had surrendered to Philip, also becoming, in the process, his 'ally'.

81 [Dem.] 7.2ff., 12.12ff. (Philip's letter).

82 [Dem.] 7.18ff.

83 [Dem.] 7.26ff. (Amphipolis and the Chalkidike), 41ff. (Kardia), 32 (Pherai), Dem. 6.7 (Thermopylai and Phokis), 13 (Orchomenos and Koroneia). Instances of unresolvable disputes arising from any strict application of the amended peace might be extended indefinitely; see n. 84.

84 The Athenian claim to Amphipolis rested on her ownership of the site (having plundered it from the Thracians) for a mere dozen years in the fifth century. Her claims upon the Chersonesos, in particular, and upon Lemnos, Imbros and Skyros, which were late-sixth and fifth-century acquisitions (see most conveniently Meiggs *Athenian Empire* 69, 160), would likewise have to be asserted against others with prior claims. The principle was quite unworkable unless applied extremely selectively.

85 That the proposed amendments to the peace (other than Common Peace, at any rate) were not in the recommendation of the Boulē seems to follow from [Dem.] 7.19; they were tacked on in the Assembly. See Cawkwell *CQ* 1963, 133.

86 Dem. 19.331.

87 [Dem.] 7.30.

88 Philochoros F157, cited in context by Didymos *in Dem.* 8.5ff.; cf. Diod. 16.44.1 (misdated), [Dem.] 12.6. The synchronism of the two embassies need not be taken absolutely literally; certainly we should not infer that the same Assembly had to deal with both. (Hence, I find unconvincing Brunt's view, *CQ* 1969, 262 n. 3, that the lack of reference in Dem. VI to the Persians dissociates the speech *ipso facto* from Python's embassy.) As Cawkwell *CQ* 1963, 133 shows, the rebuff to the Persians naturally follows after a decision to accept Philip's offer of an amended and enlarged peace.

89 On current Persian affairs see Diod. 16.40ff., who however conflates the unsuccessful Egyptian campaign of 351/0 with the final and successful series against Phoenicia, Cyprus and Egypt several years later. The final fall of Egypt now seems securely dated to late autumn/winter 343 (Cawkwell *CQ* 1963, 121ff., 136ff., *q.v.* also on the recapture of Phoenicia; *contra* Olmstead *Hist. of the Persian Emp.* 437, Sordi *Kokalos* 1959, 107).

90 Isok. 12.159, [Dem.] 12.6, *IG* IV 556. On the Greeks in mercenary service on both sides: Parke *Gk Merc. Soldiers* 165ff. Theban compliance with the Persian request indicates her deteriorating relationship with Philip; Argive compliance appears to reflect a recent change in leadership: Cawkwell *CQ* 1963, 129f.

91 Philochoros F157; cf. the milder version of the reply in Diod. 16.44.1. [Dem.] 12.6 should *perhaps* be taken to imply that the Athenians called in this event upon all their allies, and not upon '[Philip] and the rest of the Greeks'.

92 Dem. 6.44; there was even a rumour, possibly well founded, that Philip intended to fortify Elateia, thus barring the Theban path to Phokis. Such, however, would depend on the success of his overtures to Athens.

93 Cloché BCH 1920, 133, *CAH* VI 246, Bickermann/Sykutris *Speusipps Brief* 42, Wüst *Phil.* 64. The repayments actually began at the next, the autumn Pylaia of 343. It is open to speculation whether, had Philip's recent attempt to win over Athenian opinion to Common Peace been successful, the reparation-payments would ever have begun. As it did happen, the rate of payment was reduced by half after two years. See Table 2 on p. 123.

94 At this point, Wüst *Phil.* 89ff. has conjectured, a treaty was negotiated between Philip and Artaxerxes Ochos as another consequence of Hegesippos' embassy. (See also Cloché *Un fondateur* 202, *CAH* VI 250, Bengtson *Verträge* No. 333.) Plausible enough superficially, there is however hardly enough urgency in the current situation to demand so compromising an action on Philip's part (Cawkwell *CQ* 1963, 128). The sole evidence for any such treaty is in Arrian 2.14, containing a letter purportedly from Dareios III to Alexander in 333; but Griffith *PCPS* 1968, 33ff., esp. 46ff. not only follows others in doubting its authenticity, but argues convincingly that its real author (probably Alexander himself) concocted this particular item as a deliberate falsehood. Dem. 4.48 in early 350 reported a rumour (in which he himself professed no faith) that Philip had sent envoys to the Great King (and Schaefer II 33, on this basis, dates a treaty to 352; also Pickard-Cambridge *Dem.* 191); but Demosthenes' own doubt and his failure ever to mention it again, even as a possibility, combine to refute the suggestion (*contra* Cawkwell *loc. cit.*).

95 Dem. 6.28ff. and *Hypoth.* s. 3ff. The date of Philokrates' trial is fixed approximately (by Dem. 19.116) relative to the trial of Aischines (on the date of which see Beloch III, 2.287, 291).

96 Chapter 4 n. 138.

97 Perhaps by this time internal struggles in Megara and Elis, responsibility for which Demosthenes later laboured hard to pin on Philip (19.260, 294f., 326, 10.10), were also influencing Athenian opinion. But their date is uncertain and they may have occurred after Philokrates' trial but before Aischines'. However, the Athenian *demos* may not have been so naïve as to assume that behind every stasis lay Philip's intervention, even when one of the contending parties claimed to be pro-Macedonian. They had heard Demosthenes assert in mid-344 that Philip and his mercenaries were poised to strike on behalf of Argos and Messene (6.15); but, a year later, nothing had happened.

98 Hypereides 4.29f.; Dem. 19.114,

145, 146 (but on the Olynthian evidence cf. Ais. 2.154f.), 309, Ais. 2.14ff., 3.79ff.

99 Dem. 19.116ff.

100 Two other trials were heard at about this time, those of Proxenos and Thrasyboulos, but they appear unrelated to these issues. See Dem. 19.280f. with schol. (Dindorf 441.1), 290, Deinarchos 1.63, Schaefer II 368f.

101 See Cawkwell *CQ* 1963, 200ff., the only serious attempt to probe beyond Demosthenes' tendentious assessments of what were probably (at least in their earlier stages) instances of internal stasis in the second half of the 340s. Some challenges to details have been made by Brunt *CQ* 1969, 245ff., but the substance of the study is unaffected.

102 Dem. 19.294f., cf. 87, 204, 326, 334, 9.17f., 27, 18.71, cf. 295. Plutarch's story (*Phok.* 15) of Athenian intervention in Megara is difficult to reconcile with whatever Demosthenes had in mind, at least without serious modification of one or both sources. See Cawkwell *art. cit.* (in n. 101) esp. 203, Brunt *art. cit.* (in n. 101) 264f. We may note that the conflict between Megara and Athens in 350/49 (Did. *in Dem.* 13.42ff.= Androtion F30 + Philochoros F155, *IG* II[2] 204, Dem. 13.32, 3.20 with schol.) left a residue of anti-Athenian feeling in both Megara and Korinth (Aristeides *Panath.* 1.311), which, in the case of at least the former, was still evident in 347/6 (Did. *in Dem.* 14.55ff. = Theopompos F164); this is a further indication that Demosthenes' picture of a pro-Athenian *demos* resisting the pro-Macedonian few is false.

103 On the background: Beloch III, 1.541; for the coup: Dem. 19.260, 294 (also Paus. 4.28.4, which clearly derives from Demosthenes). Soon after the event, Demosthenes attributed it to Philippizers, with no hint of outside intervention (*loc. cit.*); by 341 he could refer to Elis as a 'possession' of Philip (9.27) and to the stasis as an instance of his direct interference (10.10). This author, as Cawkwell (*loc. cit.* in n. 102) points out, 'was not constrained by a strict regard for truth'.

104 Dem. 19.8. For the trial in general: Dem. XIX answered by Ais. II. I hope shortly to examine this trial elsewhere in more detail than is appropriate or possible here.

105 Aischines' policy-switch: Dem. 19.10ff., 15f., 302ff.; delay on the second embassy: 19.5f., 150ff.; effects on Phokis: 19.19ff., 34ff., 45ff., 53ff., 61ff.

106 The difficulty inherent in so necessarily distorted a reconstruction of 346 is illustrated clearly in what the Loeb editors (p. 240f.) refer to as the 'scattered and disorderly' nature of Dem. XIX. As the orator reminds his auditors on one occasion, the sequence and dating of events are important; in fact his presentation effectively obscures the sequence in most respects. Both orators are of course selective in their allusions and emphases, but it is noticeable that Aischines too knew the importance of a proper sequential treatment for his defence, and his speech is very largely set out in careful correspondence with the relative chronology of events.

107 Cawkwell *CQ* 1963, 127–134.

108 For Euboian events 343–340 see Cawkwell *CQ* 1963, 201ff., 210ff., Brunt *CQ* 1969, 251ff.

109 The refs to Euboia in Dem. XIX (87, 204, 326, 334) show by their vagueness that the unpalatable nature of the Euboian situation might be expressed in anti-Macedonian terms, but not convincingly. If Philip's influence was strong, the Athenians had their own ill-chosen policy of 349/8 to thank for it. By the beginning of 342 there was still no sign that

Philip was taking more than a diplomatic interest in his Euboian sympathizers; hence Hegesippos' failure to list any action here among Philip's 'misdemeanours' ([Dem.] 7.32). Since that débâcle only Karystos remained loyal to Athens: [Dem.] 7.38, Dem. 19.326.

110 Pp. 90f. above.

111 Pp. 61f. above.

112 Beloch III, 1.546f., Wüst *Phil.* 95 and Hammond *HG*[1] 561 place the offers discussed in [Dem.] VII after Philip's withdrawal from the vicinity of Ambrakia, but Hegesippos in that speech makes no mention of the Athenian action supposedly responsible for that withdrawal (Dem. 9.72) and indeed appears to say that the two were synchronous ([Dem.] 7.32).

113 [Dem.] 7.18ff. and esp. 31f.

114 N. 75 above.

115 [Dem.] 12.12ff.

116 N. 84 above.

117 [Dem.] 7.39ff.; the most useful map showing Kardia relative to the rest of the Chersonesan peninsula is that of Casson *Mac. Thrace & Illyria* facing p. 210. Kardia became Philip's ally before the Peace of Philokrates (Dem. 5.25, [Dem.] 12.11), probably immediately before; it had remained apart from the other Chersonesan towns bludgeoned by Chares from Kersebleptes in 353 (p. 80 and Chapter 3 n. 88 above). See Cawkwell *CQ* 1963, 200.

118 [Dem.] 7.9ff. Harrison *CQ* 1960, 248ff. has attempted to elucidate Hegesippos' antithesis in s. 13, but without success, mainly because he has treated the passage outside its political context. Two comments appear called for. With a speech designed to persuade the Athenians to reject offers that were arguably as attractive as Philip could reasonably make them, it is surely unacceptable to start from the premise that what Hegesippos says (if only we can make out what it means) must be so. Secondly, the whole passage in question is so riddled with falsehood and distortion (e.g. s. 12, that Macedonia had been 'tributary' to Athens, on which see Gomme *Comm. Thuc.* i 238; s. 10, that the Athenian cleruchs in Poteidaia were Philip's allies when he took the city in 356, on which see pp. 71f. above) that it leads one, on the contrary, almost to *expect* that s. 13 will contain a misrepresentation of Philip's offer. See also Hopper *JHS* 1943, 44.

119 [Dem.] 7.13ff.

120 [Dem.] 7.15f.

121 Dem. 48.24. At 9.72 Demosthenes prides himself (with others) on having *prevented* any invasion of Ambrakia, so that [Dem.] 7.32, Dem. 9.27 and 10.10 must be taken as at best ambiguous and possibly deliberately misleading. No action had taken place before Hegesippos spoke ([Dem.] 7.32), and, with the debate on the peace still open, Philip is unlikely to have negated his efforts by any attack on Ambrakia. See below and n. 125.

122 On the possible routes see Hammond *ABSA* 1932, 141f., *Ep.* 34.

123 Justin 8.6.4ff., Diod. 16.72.1 (confused; see Treves *AJP* 1942, 129ff.), Tod ii 173 = *IG* II[2] 226.

124 Tod ii 173 with commentary. On the organization of the Molossian *koinon* and its dominant role in Epeiros see Hammond *Ep.* 525ff., esp. 538f.

125 Speusippos *Letter* 7 (Bickermann/Sykutris p. 15 and n. 3); cf. Dem. 9.34, which seems designed to assert Korinthian priority over this claim (Wüst *Phil.* 94). This promise (if the inference from Speusippos is justified) is the best support that may be adduced for Demosthenes' claim that Philip intended to attack (or did attack) Ambrakia at the time; see n. 121.

126 [Dem.] 7.32, Theopompos F206–207, Beloch III, 1.545.

127 Dem. 48.24, 9.72, 18.244, Schaefer II 424, Wüst *Phil.* 92f.

128 The recapture of Egypt was probably in the autumn/winter of 343/2, just as Philip's Epeirote campaign was beginning.

129 Dem. 9.34, Philochoros F56, Strabo 9 C427, Theopompos F235, Glotz *Hist. Grec.* III 359.

130 Dem. 19.260f.

131 Schol. Ais. 3.83. *IG* II/III^2 225 (Bengtson *Verträge* No. 337), a fragment of an Athenian/Messenian alliance, is probably to be dated at this time.

132 Dem. 9.28ff., 71.

133 Beloch III, 1.546 and, on the date, 595f.

134 Dem. 18.244, schol. Ais. 3.83.

135 Attempts to attribute the foundation of the so-called Hellenic League (340) to Demosthenes' efforts in 342 (Beloch *Att. Pol.* 367 – but cf. *Gr. Gesch.* III, 1.546 n. 3, 554 – von Scala *Staatsverträge* I 204) are groundless; see Schaefer II 427, Pickard-Cambridge *Dem.* 356 n. 5, Wüst *Phil.* 93.

CHAPTER VI

1 Pp. 96f., 130.

2 On the dating of these see Chapter 5 note 89.

3 Dion. Hal. *ep. ad Amm.* i 5, Strabo 13 C608 (whose romantic version is corrected by Did. *in Dem.* 6.15ff.), Jaeger *Aristotle* 115ff., Wormell *YCS* 1935, 75, Chroust *Rev. Pol.* 1972, 376f., Fox *Alex.* 53. Diog. Laert. 5.10 gives the date of the appointment as 343/2, but wrongly puts Alexander's age at 15 years.

4 Speusippos *Letter* (dated to winter 343/2 by the ref. to Ambrakia, s. 7), Theopompos F255–6. Fox *Alex.* 509 suggests that Isokrates' *ep.* 5 (*To Alexander*) is a product of this mentor's pique at the failure of his ex-pupil. See also Theopompos F250 and 291, the latter of which (= Did. *in Dem.* 4.63ff.) belongs to Bk XLVI of his *Philippika* (compare Diels/Schubart on Did. 4.66f. with Jacoby's commentary *ad loc.*, *FGH* IIB p. 393); the historian's envy is perhaps sufficient to explain the viciousness of his attack on the father-in-law of Aristotle (Berve ii No. 365, Wormell *YCS* 1935, 71), and perhaps the ambivalence often remarked in his attitude towards Philip (e.g. Wormell 71f.) was at least partly on the same account. In general, Murray *Greek Studies* 149ff. is useful on Theopompos.

5 Ath. 9.398e, Diog. Laert. 5.2, Sen. *Dial.* 5.12–16, Aul. Gell. *NA* 3.17, Thompson *PCPS* 1948, 7. Cf. Chroust *Historia* 1972, 175, who suggests that the appointment represents the recall of an agent in danger of falling into Persian hands.

6 Mieza is probably to be identified with modern Gastra, close to Naoussa (Hammond *Mac.* i 163f.); and the Nymphaion, it seems likely, was the near-by group of caves examined by Ph. Petsas recently, with vertical walls cut into the adjoining rock-face (*Ergon* 1965, 21ff., *Makedonika* 1967, 33 and Pl. 50). A few kilometres farther northeast is the magnificent tomb of Levkadhia, also excavated by Petsas and tentatively identified by him as that of the noble Peukestas (Berve ii No. 634; Hammond *Mac.* i 201), a native of the Mieza district. See also Fredricksmeyer *CPh* 1961, 160ff. on the Gardens of Midas and their relationship to a significant event later in Alexander's life, at Gordion.

7 Plut. *Alex.* 7, Ael. *VH* 14.1, Paus. 6.4.8, Suda *s.* 'Antipatros', Diog. Laert. 5.1.12, 5.9, Berve ii No. 94 (Antipatros) and 135 (Aristotle).

8 For refs see most conveniently Berve ii Nos 462 (Lanike, Alexander's nurse), 581 (Olympias), 481 (Lysimachos) and for Leonidas: Plut. *Alex.* 5.4f., 22.5, 25.4f. These influences on

Alexander's young life have been well discussed recently by Fox *Alex.* 43ff. and Green *Alex.* 35ff.; also Hamilton *G&R* 1965, 117ff.

9 Title: Arrian 4.16.6, Diod. 17.79.4, Berve i 37 n. 4; high birth: Ael. *VH* 14.48, Curtius 5.1.42, 8.6.2; duties and training: Diod. 17.65.1, Curtius 5.1.42, 8.6.2ff., Arrian 4.13.1.

10 Arrian 4.13.1, Ael. *VH* 14.48.

11 Pp. 52ff. above.

12 Harpalos: Hoffman *Die Makedonen* 164f., Berve ii No. 143; his brothers (?), Tauron and Philippos (Berve ii Nos 741, 780), especially the former, who certainly held a command as early as 331/0, may also have been Philip's pages. Ptolemaios: Hoffmann 154, Berve ii p. 330. Philotas: on Parmenion see Chapter 2 n. 70.

13 Berve ii Nos 544, 302, 464.

14 It may be conjectured that the Tymphaian sons of Andromenes (Berve ii Nos 57, 181, 644, 704; Hoffmann *Die Makedonen* 156f.), since they were close friends of Philotas, were also pages of Philip.

15 Berve ii Nos 250, 466 (cf. Curtius 10.7.8, Suda *s.* 'Leonnatos', Diod. 16.94.4), 489; and see n. 12 above.

16 Ais. 3.88ff., Wüst *Phil.* 108f.; the weakness of Aischines' explanation of Kallias' failure to win Philip's support suggests that he knew of no reason. Philip had of course promised Euboian authority to the Athenians (Dem. 6.30), but had been unable to carry this out without turning Thebes (as well as Euboia) against himself. That he now passed up this chance to increase his already impressive influence in Euboia suggests that Kallias' request belongs in the period before Athens' final rejection of Philip's offers to renegotiate the peace, and that the king at that time still genuinely hoped to enact his original intentions; at least, he wished to keep the possibility open. On the anti-Athenian movement in Euboia in 349/8, in which Kallias had played a leading part, see pp. 95f. and nn. above.

17 Dem. 9.58, Karystios *ap.* Ath. 11.508e, Brunt *CQ* 1969, 251ff., esp. 253f., Cawkwell *CQ* 1963, 210ff.

18 Wüst *Phil.* 102ff., in his treatment of the Thracian campaign, makes no reference to the possiblity of a regent in Pella and even implies (p. 105) that the first bearer of such a *Reichsverweserschaft* was Alexander during the siege of Byzantion in late 340.

19 Antipatros' presence in Macedonia during the time of the Thracian expedition – or at least in its earlier stages – may have provided the opportunity for the growth of friendship between him and Aristotle; see n. 7.

20 Dem. 9.32.

21 Dem. 9.34 and schol., 10.9. For the date for Echinos see Wüst *Phil.* 120. Antron was acquired earlier, probably in 344 (*contra* Schaefer II 429f.).

22 See Chapter 5 nn. 108f. This had taken place before the autumn of 343, when the trial of Aischines was held (Dem. 19.83,87, 204, 326), and probably in the summer (see n. 23); but, in spite of Demosthenes' dark warnings on that occasion, it was not until almost a year later that any Macedonian action occurred.

23 Dem. 9.59ff., giving a date one year earlier than the Macedonian intervention of summer 342 in Eretria; the two successful coups, at Eretria and Oreos, were therefore almost synchronous (see n. 22). The relationship between these events and Kallias' attempt to win Macedonian backing (above and n. 16) is not clear; perhaps Kallias wished to capitalize on strong pro-Macedonian feeling in Euboia in summer 343. But, whereas Philip had been content to see his partisans rise to power in Eretria and Oreos, he was not prepared to give active backing to Kallias (see n. 16). Athenian recognition that events in Eretria and Oreos were internal matters is shown by the failure even of Demosthenes soon afterwards to advance anything worse than gloomy forecasts as to the future there (see n. 22). His vague allusions (19.87, 326) to Macedonian forces on the island (which, if true, would have attracted far more explicit condemnation – and would presumably have produced some result before the lapse of a whole year) may be explained, as Cawkwell *CQ* 1963, 202f, suggests, as refs to what in reality were mercenaries maintained by the now pro-Macedonian cities on Euboia. On Euphraios of Oreos, who claimed to have had a hand in Philip's accession to the throne through influence with his brother and predecessor Perdikkas, see Pl. *ep*. 5.

24 On Karystos: [Dem.] 7.38, Dem. 19.326, Beloch III, 1.495; the near-by Cape Geraistos made Karystos vital to Athens' corn-route (Strabo 10 C444, cf. Dem. 4.34).

25 Dem. 9.33, 57ff., 18.71. The absence of any Athenian charge to the contrary makes it clear that the Eretrians were not harmed.

26 See also Dem. 8.36, 9.17, 10.8, Ais. 3.103, Diod. 16.74.1. Cawkwell *CQ* 1963, 203f. draws attention to Demosthenes' free use of the smear-word 'tyrant' to characterize 'political leaders who pursued distasteful policies'; for some qualification see Brunt *CQ* 1969, 259 n. 3 and 260.

27 Dem. 9.57f.

28 On Parmenion's presence (with mercenaries): Karystios F1–2 (but cf. Dem. 9.62), Dem. 9.33; on Antron: Dem. 10.9 and n. 21 above; for the size of Oreos' territory see Dem. 23.213. Whether this 'one quarter' is to be taken literally is not clear; it may conceivably imply simply that Euboia contained only four cities of importance. For the date: Wüst *Phil.* 109f.; but it cannot be determined with any precision.

29 Dem. 9.59ff., naming as the rulers of Oreos (in summer 341) Philistides, Menippos, Sokrates, Thoas and Agapaios (cf. 8.36, 9.33, 18.71, where the orator refers to a tyranny of an individual, Philistides; also 18.295); also 8.18, 9.17f., 27. For Parmenion's disclaimer: 8.59, 9.12f. Although Demosthenes refers to the 'capture' of the city, he nowhere mentions any fighting; the only violence ever alluded to (apart from the suicide of Euphraios: 9.62) is attributed specifically to the new 'rulers and tyrants' (*ibid.*).

30 It is unfortunate that no speech of Aischines from this period is preserved. In 330, in his few refs to Euboian affairs, he is silent on the events of 342. In the long term, of course, Macedonian activities in Euboia had harmed his own political standing (since they were no doubt taken by most to confirm Demosthenes' dire warnings since 346 and before 348), so that this omission is readily explained. But our impression of the affair might have been rather different had there survived a speech of his contemporary with Demosthenes' three orations of 341 (*On the Chersonesos* and *Philippics* III and IV).

31 So, for example, Brunt takes it: *CQ* 1969, 261f.

32 n. 24 above.

33 Brunt *loc. cit.* (in n. 31).

34 Hdt. 5.3, Mihailov *Athenaeum* 1961, 33ff., *Arch. Mak.* i 76ff.

35 Diod. 16.71.1f. (on the source of which see Hammond *CQ* 1937. 90f.).

36 With the rather pro-Macedonian account of Diodoros (n. 35) compare the highly unfavourable version of Justin 9.1, in which the aim from the beginning is stated to be the securing of Byzantion for Macedonia (s. 2). Two comments are called for. The defection of Byzantion from its alliance with

Philip occurs in 341/0 after the latter's activities on the Black Sea coast in the latter half of 341; it is thus a result of the Thracian campaign, which had its own justification, and not its final goal.

37 Ath. 13.557b–e, Steph. Byz. *s.* 'Getia', Jordanus *Getica* 10. Theopompos (F216) appears to treat this in his Bk XLVI and, since the bulk of the Thracian campaign falls in Bks XLVII–XLIX (F217ff.), it should be placed at the beginning of it: Wüst *Phil.* 103 and n. 1 (cf., for example, Schaefer II 450 n. 1; also Beloch III, 1.549, *CAH* VI 251, Momigliano *Athenaeum* 1933, 341, *Fil.* 146 and n. 1, who date it after the Thracian campaign proper but before Philip's activities on the Black Sea coast and against Perinthos and Byzantion).

38 See Pippidi, 'Les Macédoniens en Scythie Mineure de Phil. II à Lysim.', forthcoming in *Arch. Mak.* ii.

39 Plut. *Eum.* 1, Nepos *Eum.* 1: Philip is said to have met the Kardian Eumenes in Kardia, the latter to have served Philip for seven years until the king's death; reckoning inclusively, we may therefore date the meeting to 342: Schaefer II 446 n. 2, Wüst *Phil.* 102 n. 4. Schaefer (*loc. cit.*) also dates the subjection of Ainos to this time, which is very likely; but cf. Beloch III, 1.557, *CAH* VI 251; Wüst 102 n. 5 is unsure.

40 Dem. 8.35, cf. 8.2.

41 Diod. 16.71.2, Polyainos *Strat.* 4.2.13.

42 Dem. 8.44f., Diod. *loc. cit.* On the colonists see pp. 134ff. above, Ellis *Makedonika* 1969, 9ff., Mihailov *Arch. Mak.* i 82f.

43 Bellinger *ANSMN* 1964, 29ff.; on the duration of the Philippian autonomous issues see Appendix. See also Babelon *Monn. Gr. & Rom.* ii 4, Nos 1177ff.

44 Strabo 7 C320 (Kalybe for Kabyle?; cf. Dem. 8.44, Ptol. *Geog.* 3.11), Theopompos F110; Pliny *NH* 4.18 says that Philippopolis had been Poneropolis; cf. Steph. Byz. *s.* 'Philippou polis', Front. *Strat.* 1.3.13.

45 [Dem.] 7.39ff., and see Casson *Mac. Thrace & Illyr.* 219 with Map xii facing p. 210.

46 Dem. 23.181, 19.174, [Dem.] 12.11.

47 Lib. *Hypoth.* to Dem. VIII, s. 2, [Dem.] 12.11.

48 This incident is known only from Philip's letter, [Dem.] XII. On the date, genuineness and context of this document see Wüst *Phil.* 133ff. Also Mosley *Envoys & Diplom.* 84ff. and Appendix ii.

49 Lib. *loc. cit.* (in n. 47), Dem. 8.9, 16, [Dem.] 12.3, Mosley *op. cit.*, Appendix ii.

50 [Dem.] 12.2: apparently referring to *c.* winter 342/1, Philip complains that Thasian action in opening their harbour to Byzantian wargalleys was an unfriendly action. But, a few months later, Demosthenes (8.14f.) thinks Byzantion is still pro-Macedonian.

51 Dem. 8.14, 58, 64, 9.16, 35, 10.60, 65, [Dem.] 12.11. (Note that the Loeb editor mistranslates 8.58 and 10.60 so as to have Philip going 'against' Kardia.) Reinforcements: Dem. 8.14.

52 See n. 50. In his Speech VIII, although Demosthenes urges that support for Diopeithes' actions be continued (there being strong opposition to it: s. 2ff.), his overall feeling appears to be that Philip's general position is strong (see esp. s. 66f., Wüst *Phil.* 116).

53 At some time during the previous months Demosthenes had travelled as envoy to Illyria and Thrace, so he claims in 330 (18.244). The fact that this does not appear in his contemporary speeches implies that he failed in these missions. The Thracian embassy may be connected with Diopeithes' raid in Thrace in late winter 341 (Wüst *Phil.* 116f.).

54 On the date see Wüst *Phil.* 111 n. 4, Cloché *Un fondateur* 238. Brunt (*CQ* 1969, 255ff.) refutes the case made by Cawkwell (*CQ* 1963, 210ff.) for an earlier date. It would be surprising that Demosthenes made no mention of an existing alliance in his speeches soon afterwards (e.g. in the context of 9.57ff.), and we should probably therefore date its conclusion not long before midsummer rather than in spring. See also n. 57.

55 Ais. 3.91ff., Did. *in Dem.* 1.15ff.

56 This is the line of attack Aischines adopts eleven years later (*loc. cit.*): that Demosthenes (as the result of 'bribery') had sold Athens' prestige and her Euboian revenues to the slick opportunist Kallias.

57 Plut. *Dem.* 17.1, Did. *in Dem.* 1.13ff. (= Philochoros F159, dating the Oreitan coup to Skirophorion 341, apparently immediately after the alliance was formed), schol. Ais. 3.85, 3.105, Diod. 16.74.1. Eretria was taken in the autumn. *IG* II² 230 (on which see Wüst *Phil.* 113, Bengtson *Verträge* No. 340 with text) will belong soon afterwards, but unfortunately only two fragments remain, containing the oath of allegiance between Eretria and Athens alone.

58 [Dem.] 12.5, *IG* II² 809C.42ff. For the date: Wüst *Phil.* 111 n.6, Brunt *CQ* 1966, 255. Neither at the time of Kallias' raid nor when Oreos and Eretria were taken does any contact seem to have been made with Macedonian troops, citizen or mercenary; Philip had perhaps withdrawn them for use in the far northeast.

59 [Dem.] 12.8; the date is uncertain but follows the delivery of Dem. VIII in late spring, at which time Philip was awaiting his reinforcements (8.14).

60 Arrian 1.25.1f. Wüst (*Phil.* 105 with n. 4) doubts whether the office was introduced so early, assuming that while Philip remained in the general area (until 339) he himself would have commanded the Thracian area. But it is more likely that, since the commander was responsible among other things for the collection of the tithe and the command of Thracian auxiliaries, an appointment was made immediately; Philip himself was concerned with matters of more moment.

61 Dem. 1.13.

62 Theopompos F217, Kaerst *Gesch. Hell.* i 255.

63 Arrian 1.1.6 speaks of 'independent Thracians' in 336/5, and cf. 7.9.3; Wüst *Phil.* 104, Mihailov *Athenaeum* 1961, 34, *Arch. Mak.* i 81f.

64 Wüst *Phil.* 105f. considers that the office was created, when the necessity arose, on the model of the Persian satrapy (see n. 60). Hampl (*KM* 42) hypothesizes, in keeping with his general theory of Macedonian kingship, that Thrace now became Philip's personal property and was therefore governed by his own deputy rather than by an officer of state. His key evidence ([Dem.] 12.5, referring to Thrace as 'my territory') however does not imply this at all; as the personification of the state Philip himself stood for the whole state. Thus, for example, in the same letter Pagasaian towns (s. 5), Kardia (s. 11) and Athens (s. 22) are styled 'my allies' (see also 35. 6, 12ff., 16, 17, 23). See pp. 21f. above.

65 Diod. 16.71.1, Hampl *KM* 40.

66 Diod. 17.17.4 (cf. Milns *JHS* 1966, 167f.), Arrian 1.14.3.

67 Berve i 134f., 136f.

68 Justin 9.2.1.

69 Diod. 16.71.2. Strabo 7 C319 lists the coastal towns southwards from the Danube as Istros (a Milesian colony) – Tomis – Kallatis (Herakleiote colony) – Bizone – Krounoi – Odessos (Milesian; mod. Varna) – Naulochos (Mesymbriote) – Mesymbria (Megarian; mod. Mesembrija)

– Anchiale (Apollonian) – Apollonia (mod. Sozopol) – Thynias (mod. Cape Iniada in Turkey) – Phinopolis – Andriaka.

70 Dem. 18.244, 302.

71 Plut. *Vit. X or.* 850a (Hypereides), Hypereides F5–6 (Loeb); cf. Dem. 9.71.

72 Dem. 10.31ff. and scholia.

73 Diod. 16.52 (and cf. 16.22, 34), Polyainos *Strat.* 6.48, Arist. *Econ.* 2.2.28, Diog. Laert. 5.6, Did. *in Dem.* 5.64ff.

74 Did. *in Dem.* 6.15ff., p. 160 above. See Chroust *Rev. Pol.* 1972, 374f., who suggests the following embellishments: that Demosthenes may have passed on to the Persians intelligence of Hermias' suspected dealings with Philip by medium of Aristotle (which would seem to be unnecessary) and (more reasonably) that letters said to have been written to a Mentor by Aristotle (Diog. Laert. 5.27) were addressed to the Rhodian mercenary in a bid to win him over to Hermias' cause (or perhaps to Philip's, since his brother had been a refugee in Pella; see p. 92 above). See also on the whole affair von der Mühll *RE* Suppl. III 1126ff., Jaeger *Aristotle* 117ff., Wormell *YCS* 1935, 57ff.; on the later tradition Wormell pp. 82ff.

75 [Dem.] 12.6 shows that no alliance was established. This is often explained as Artaxerxes' reluctance to repudiate as yet his alliance with Philip (e.g. Kaerst *Gesch. Hell.* i 253, Momigliano *Fil.* 150 n. 2, Wüst *Phil.* 126); but there was no such alliance (see Chapter 5 n. 94). For the Athenian failure to win alliance from the Persian King, the obvious explanation is that his imperial power, with his empire rebuilt and comparatively strong, was simply not put at the disposal of some tiny state beyond the frontiers. If Greek states wanted the King's support they might ask for it; if the King's interests were suited he might give it. But the lion did not bind itself to serve the purposes of the rabbit.

76 Plut. *Vit. X or.* 847f., Arist. *Rhet.* 1386a. Ais. 3.238f. has nothing to do with this occasion (*contra* Wüst *Phil.* 126 n. 5 and Beloch III, 1.551, 552 n. 1; cf. Kahrstedt *Forschungen* 150 n. 123, Cloché *BCH* 1920, 152 n. 4); according to Aischines' own words, the occasion to which he refers (and on which the Athenians *rejected* the King's *unbidden* gift) was during the reign of Dareios III, thus early during Alexander's Asian campaign. The large series of coins emitted from Perinthos at about this time, its first known issues, was evidently struck for this defence and was probably financed in large part by Persian gold; see Babelon *Monn. Gr. & Rom.* ii 4.967ff.; cf. Head *HN* 270.

77 Ais. 3.95ff.; the contributions alluded to in connection with Demosthenes' report (s. 97) as being sufficient to man 100 fast ships and to hire 10,000 foot and 1000 horse are presumably those promised by Kallias. 4000 citizen-hoplites were also said to be committed.

78 *Ibid.*, esp. 100f. and cf. 91ff. Although, contrary to Aischines' implication, Athens had collected no Euboian *syntaxeis* since 348, he is nevertheless correct in saying that the establishment of the Euboian League involved for Athens the surrender of her own collection rights; whether or not she had in fact decided to reimpose *syntaxeis* on Oreos and Eretria, she was at any rate now in a position to do so.

79 Brunt (*CQ* 1969, 254 with 257 and 263 n. 2) sidesteps the question whether the promised congress was, as Aischines implies, a sham. It seems certain that at this assembly Demosthenes and Kallias painted a far rosier picture of their achievements than they were entitled to, probably with the intention of persuading the *demos* to surrender its Euboian claims in a wave of gratitude and goodwill. When it came to the battlefield at Chaironeia, the states most strongly anti-Macedonian did indeed fight on the Athenian (*and* – much more significantly – *Theban*) side, but there is no shadow of evidence that they committed themselves to such a course as early as late winter 340. Wüst *Phil.* 119 goes to the extent of manufacturing a Hellenic League led by Athens, its members represented in a *synedrion*, paying *syntaxeis* and supplying troops! It is amusing that Aischines' sarcasm should have been responsible for fabricating one of the greatest of his opponent's achievements two years before the proper time.

80 Jacoby *FGH* IIIB Suppl. I, Text p. 331 raises a doubt as to the date of this attack, noting that Philochoros F54 appears to date it to midsummer 340.

81 Paus. 4.31.5.

82 The title is used by Marsden, 'Heavy Military Equipment & its Designers under Philip II and Alexander the Great', forthcoming in *Arch. Mak.* ii; see also his *Gk & Rom. Artillery: Hist. Dev.* 59f.

83 Berve ii Nos 267 and 821.

84 This seems likely, as Marsden (see n. 82) has pointed out.

85 Dem. 18.72, 87; cf. Justin 9.1.1f.: '... he decided to make war on all of Greece. Realizing that his scheme would be best promoted if he could lay hold of Byzantion, ... which would provide a base for his land and naval forces, he proceeded, when it closed its gates to him, to lay siege to it.' Also Plut. *Phok.* 14.2.

86 On whose genuineness see Wüst *Phil.* 133ff.; the letter appears to predate by some weeks the investment of Selymbria and Byzantion and the capture of the corn-fleet. But it clearly was written while the siege of Perinthos was in progress – but contains no allusion to it, even in relation to the complaint over the necessity to escort the Macedonian fleet past a hostile Chersonesos (s. 16; see below).

87 Diod. 16.74.2; on Ephoros: Hammond *CQ* 1937, 81f., 85ff. See also Arrian 2.14.5 (in a letter from Alexander to Dareios): 'You assisted Perinthos, which wronged my father.'

88 On Diopeithes' death: Arist. *Rhet.* 2.1386a. Chares at Thasos: Plut. *Vit. X or.* 845f., schol. [Dem.] 7.15 (Dindorf 173.19ff.). Chares at the Chersonesos: *SIG* 255 = Hicks & Hill *GHI* 145 (dated 29th of 7th prytany 341/0 = *c.* March 340).

89 Dem. 18.70 and schol. (Dindorf 287.15ff.), [Dem.] 12.12ff.

90 On the siege see Diod. 16.74.2–76, which is preoccupied with military and technical detail (on the fighting in relays, perhaps a later insertion by Diodoros himself, see Sinclair *CQ* 1966, 249ff.). See Marsden *op. cit.* (in n. 82) 56ff., 100f., Kromayer *Antike Schlachtfelder* I 172ff., Wüst *Phil.* 127ff.

91 [Dem.] 12(Philip's Letter).16; on the terrain see Casson *Mac. Thrace & Illyria* 210ff.

92 See n. 86.

93 The last section (s. 23) is certainly threatening: 'since you were the original aggressors ... and persist ... I shall ... deal firmly with you'.

94 Dem. 9.10ff.; see also Wüst's excellent treatment of the letter, pp. 133ff., esp. 134.

95 Macedonian troops: Diod. 16.74.5. Persian intervention: 16.75.1f., Paus. 1.29.7, Arrian 2.14.5, [Dem.] 12.5, Schaefer II 516. Wüst *Phil.* 130 n. 1 argues that no landing of Persian troops took place in Thrace because this would have been in direct contravention of Artaxerxes' policy, which he takes to have been the maintenance of the alleged alliance with Philip (see n. 75 and Chapter 5 n. 94).

96 Diod. 16.76.3f.
97 Theopompos F62, Ath. 10.442c, Ael. *VH* 3.14.
98 Diod. 16.76.3f., Theopompos F217, Front. *Strat.* 1.4.13, Schaefer II 503.
99 On Selymbria see *Hypoth.* to [Dem.] 11 (Dindorf 209ff.), schol. Dem. 18.76 (Dindorf 289.32ff.) with Wüst *Phil.* 136ff., who argues convincingly for the essential credibility of these two sources, but against that of the false documents included in Dem. 18.73–79 (cf. Pickard-Cambridge *Dem.* 356f.). The most convenient route between Perinthos and Byzantion (other than by sea) is that which follows the modern road between Alexandroupolis in Greek Thraki and Istanbul, passing through Silivri (Selymbria). The inland route followed by the railway is very much more circuitous.
100 Foucart *Mém. de l'Inst. Nat. de France* 1909, 117.
101 Did. *in Dem.* 10.45ff., Front. *Strat.* 1.4.13 (Chios and Rhodes), Dem. 18.139, Justin 9.1.5ff. Justin gives 170 ships, Theopompos 180 and Philochoros 230 – both *ap.* Did. *loc. cit.*, who himself gives the *grand* total as 'no less than 230'. Diels (D./Schubart *ed. princeps*, n. to 11.2, p. 50) suggests that Didymos actually implies that some ships were released, which might reconcile the numerical discrepancy between Theopompos and Philochoros.
102 *Hypoth.* to [Dem.] 11 (Dindorf 209.4–11), schol. Dem. 18.76 (Dindorf 290.1ff.), interpreted by Pohlenz *Gött. Nachr.* 1924, 38ff. and Wüst *Phil.* 136ff. Since Hieron, near which the fleet was captured (Did. *in Dem.* 10.56, 62), was further from the Bosporos than Perinthos and Selymbria, the ships must already have passed by Philip's forces at the narrows, whence news of their passage was probably relayed to the fleet. In view of the point at which the capture was made, it must be presumed that Philip's attempt to mislead Greek opinion assumed general ignorance of the area or aimed to create the misapprehension that these particular ships were coming not from the Bosporos but from the Hellespont. That Philip's letter makes no mention of Perinthos may suggest that the siege of the city had now been raised – although presumably Macedonian forces will have remained in the area to protect the supply-lines.
103 See Wüst *Phil.* 139. It might be added that the falsehood did not even need to be particularly plausible; all that was required was half a pretext to enable those with no real interest in the issue to stand apart from Athens.

CHAPTER VII

1 Ephialtes' procurement of Persian funds (Plut. *vit X or.* 848e) seems to fit the circumstances just before Diopeithes' death, when, as the result of an embassy (presumably that of Ephialtes), money was sent to the Chersonesan commander, who however died before it arrived (Arist. *Rhet.* 2.1386a). Since, as *SIG* 255 shows, Chares was at the Chersonesos by *c.* March 340, the Persian aid appears to relate to Perinthos, not Byzantion. Alexander later charged the Persians with having assisted Perinthos and having landed a force in Thrace, but not with having intervened at Byzantion (Arrian 2.14.5). Wüst *Phil.* 143, cf. 126 explains this as the result of new negotiations between Ochos and Philip over their existing peace of 343, but, as we have seen, there is no evidence that there ever was such a peace (Chapter 5 n. 94).
2 Pp. 189f. and Chapter 6 n. 79.
3 Ais. 3.95ff., esp. 97.
4 Pp. 173f. and Chapter 6 nn. 102f.

5 Diod. 16.77.2, Tod ii 175 (= *SIG* 256).

6 Diod. 16.77.2, Plut. *Phok.* 14, Hesychios F26–28 (Müller *FHG*), Front. *Strat.* 1.4.13.

7 Ath. 10.442c, Ael. *VH* 3.4, Suda *s.* 'Leon' – probably alluding to this siege. For further detail and refs see Schaefer's exhaustive account, II 509ff.

8 Plut. *Phok.* 14, *vit X or.* 848f., 851a, *IG* II[2] 1629.957.

9 Theopompos F217. Schachermeyer *Alex.* 93 n. 74 notes that this fragment puts both Antipatros and Parmenion in Thrace at the time of the Perinthian siege, and suggests Eumenes as Alexander's adviser. But, except at the time of this emergency, Antipatros is more likely to have advised the prince (as Isok. *ep.* 4 suggests): Berve ii 46 n. 4, Wilcken *Alex.* 58, Hamilton *G&R* 1965, 119, *PAComm.* 22, *Alex.* 35, Green *Alex.* 65.

10 Location of Maidoi and Danthaletai: Thuc. 2.98, Strabo 7 C318, Hammond *Mac.* i 197f., 202 (and Map 17 p. 180), Danov *Kl. Pauly s.* 'Maidoi', 'Danthaletai', 'Pantalia', Lenk *RE* XIV 541f., Oberhummer *RE* IV 210f. Theopompos F221 mentions the Danthaletai at this time (also F223, on the Thracian 'millet-eaters'). See Schaefer II 515 n. 1.

11 This was the route followed in 181 BC by Philip V (Livy 40.21.1) and was the easiest means of reaching the area.

12 Plut. *Alex.* 9.1. Tarn *Alex.* ii 248f. doubts this foundation.

13 Clem. Al. *Strom.* 5.31.3, Justin 9.2. The latter gives Ateas' enemies as the 'Istriani'. If the name is entirely wrong it would not surprise us of this author; it would refer most naturally to the people of the small Milesian colony Istros (Strabo 7 C319), but Justin 9.2.2 claims that the pressure on Ateas was removed by the death of the *rex Istrianorum*, which renders that identification suspect. See Pippidi, 'Les Macédoniens en Scythie Mineure . . .' forthcoming in *Arch. Mak.* ii; also n. 27 below. On Apollonia see p. 171.

14 Front. *Strat.* 1.4.13a.

15 Justin 9.1.8, alone among our sources, has Philip giving Alexander his first field experience apparently at Byzantion or in the Chersonesos. Only Schaefer II 445, to my knowledge, takes this seriously. It is perhaps a confused reference to Alexander's promotion to the regency *in Macedonia* during the siege of Byzantion.

16 Front. *Strat.* 1.4.13; the whereabouts of Antipatros in this affair is not mentioned.

17 One may wonder whether the curious stratagem retailed by Polyainos (*Strat.* 4.2.21), referring to the Byzantian siege, belongs at this point; it may even be a garbled version of the ploy designed to release the fleet from the Pontos (Front. *Strat.* 1.4.13; see n. 16), which Polyainos (*Strat.* 4.2.8) has Philip repeating a year later near Amphissa.

18 Justin 9.1.7, Dem. 18.139, Porph. Tyr. (Müller *FHG* iii 692f.); this can not be equated with the similar episode in summer 340 (during which no damage was done to Chersonesan property) as Momigliano Fil. 152 and n. 2 thinks; cf. Schaefer II 515, Beloch III, 1.557, *CAH* VI 256.

19 Plut. *Phok.* 14.5. Dem. 18.145f. later claims that this (?) campaign of harassment was directed at the Macedonian coast and merchant shipping, and that Philip 'suffered badly' from it. The extent of Philip's concern was in fact shown by his immediate departure for the Romanian Dobrudja! Cf. Wüst *Phil.* 144, who, while well aware that Macedonia was not at all seriously vulnerable by way of her coastline, nevertheless wishes to give some credence to this tendentious oratory.

20 Plut. *Phok.* 16.

21 Diod. 16.77.3; at 84.1 he begins his account of the year 338/7 with the words 'In this year King Philip, having won over to friendship most of the Greeks . . .' But cf. Dem. 18.145f.

22 Schaefer II 516, Wüst *Phil.* 144f.

23 Suda *s.* 'Leon'; cf. Plut. *Nik.* 22, which gives to the story an irony that suggests Plutarch too knew of it.

24 So Hammond *Hist. of Gce* 564 suggests. Schaefer II 516 n. 1 denies that Byzantion made peace in 339, but misinterprets his only evidence (Dem. 18.230, which proves only that Philip did not *capture* Byzantion and that its inhabitants and the Athenians prevented his doing so). Wüst *Phil.* 144f. is non-committal. Schaefer III 51 (followed by Pickard-Cambridge *CAH* VI 266, who was earlier undecided: *Dem.* 358) puts the revival of the alliance in 337, giving no particular reason other than (implicitly) that many of Philip's previous enemies came to terms with him after Chaironeia.

25 The campaign was evidently brief, involving (according to the almost solitary source: Justin 9.2) only a single battle followed by the march through Triballian territory across to and down the Axios valley to Pella; no more than six months can have been devoted to it and possibly only four or five. See Schaefer II 522 n. 3, Wüst *Phil.* 144, 146 n. 3.

26 See Pippidi *art. cit.* in n. 13, who suggests that the dealings culminating in the campaign of 339 had extended over several years.

27 Dem. 18.44, Schaefer II 343f. For a war between Ateas and the Triballoi see Front. *Strat.* 2.4.20 and (probably) Polyainos *Strat.* 7.4. In fact it is probable, as Schaefer II 520f. remarks, that the 'Istriani' against whom Ateas had asked for Macedonian help in 340/39 were the Triballoi and not the people of Istros; see n. 13.

28 Some anecdotes preserved by Plutarch (*Mor.* 174e, 334b, 792c, 1095e; also Strabo 7 C307) suggest that Ateas had a reputation for bluntness in his dealings with the neighbouring Greek cities. For his answer to Philip: Justin 9.2.7f.

29 Justin 9.2.9ff., Front. *Strat.* 2.8.14. In Theopompos only a single name (Karos, a Thracian district) survives for this campaign: F226. This is unlikely to be the Karai (?) of Polyainos 4.2.20, which probably refers to 340 or even late 342, Schaefer II 518. For the battle against the Triballoi see Justin 9.3.1ff.; for its date: the refs in n. 25.

30 See Table 3 on pp. 132/3.

31 The chronology of the Fourth Sacred War has been the subject of some controversy, for the most part unnecessarily; for, provided that the Skythian campaign is dated to the spring and summer of 339, then there is no doubt about the key dates, which follow from Ais. 3.113ff., esp. 115, 124f., 128, 129, Dem. 18.143ff., esp. 151. On the chronology see Schaefer II 542ff., Kaerst *Gesch. Hell.* I 257 and esp. n. 1, Wüst *Phil.* 153ff., whose arguments I follow; *contra* Beloch *Att. Pol.* 224, *Gr. Gesch.* III, 2.295, Momigliano *Fil.* 155, Kromayer *Antike Schlachtfelder* i 182ff., Pickard-Cambridge *Dem.* 359ff., *CAH* VI 256.

32 For Amphiktyonic matters between spring and autumn 339 see Ais. 3.113ff. and Dem. 18.143ff. Although Aischines claims to have learnt of the Amphissian plan in Delphoi, I take it that the election of delegates one of whom was well known to be respected by many Amphiktyons and another a close colleague of his was not fortuitous. For the Lokrian delegate in question see Table 3 on pp. 132/3.

33 All Amphiktyonic meetings, it appears, convened in the first instance at Thermopylai, the original centre of the League (hence the name Pylagorai for the tribal delegates), and then proceeded to Delphoi. See Ais. 3.124ff., Burn *OCD*[2] *s.* 'Thermopylae), Larsen *OCD*[2] *s.* 'Amphictyonies'.

34 In 346, after the Peace of Philokrates, Demosthenes' stance had been every bit as anti-Theban as it needed to be in that context, although he had urged a moderation that would not bring down Thebes with the rest of the Amphiktyons upon Athens (5.10, 14; cf. 18f., 24). In 344, in response to Python's embassy, he had little to say on the matter, only denigrating Thebes mildly to emphasize Athens' achievements (6.7ff.). But in the three speeches of spring/summer 341 a quite different tack is observable: Thebes is now treated as a fellow-sufferer at Philip's hands. Thebes, to be sure, was not among the states to which envoys should be sent to canvass alliance (a fruitless task while Philip and the Thebans remained allies), but it was to be regarded with sympathy rather than jealousy and enmity (8.63, 9.27, 34f., cf. 71, 10.47, 64; cf. [Dem.] 11.4). When it became more expedient for Thebes to consider alliance with Athens, and Demosthenes was sure this would happen, there must be sufficient fellow-feeling among the Athenians to ensure a favourable reaction.

35 Aischines (3.125ff.) explains Demosthenes' success in this as a subterfuge enacted in Aischines' absence from the assembly; but perhaps all that was necessary was for his opponent to point out the implications of the *demos*' initial decision. Cf. Dem. 18.143f.

36 Ais. 3.129: a date was specified, but Aischines does not give it.

37 Didymos *in Dem.* 11.44ff.: this happened 'when [Philip] was in Skythia', thus in spring or summer; it is likely to have occurred after the Amphiktyonic decision at Thermopylai but before the sacred command was conferred on the king at the autumn *pylaia,* since by then he was in Pella. The garrison expelled was probably not Macedonian but Thessalian; see Chapter 5 n. 38.

38 Ais. 3.128f., Dem. 18.151.

39 Dem. 18.152, Ais. 3.140, Philochoros F56, Did. *in Dem.* 11.40ff., Diod. 16.84.1, Plut. *Dem.* 18.1. The argument by Glotz (*BCH* 1909, 526ff., esp. 535f.) that, as a result of a rescission in autumn 339 of the 346 *dogma* under which the Phokian towns were destroyed and their *koinon* dissolved, the Phokian League was reconstituted by spring 338, falls with the re-dating of the relevant Delphic archonship, that of Palaios (de la Coste Messelière *BCH* 1949, 201ff., esp. 235ff.).

40 Plut. *Dem.* 18.1, Philochoros F56. The two Thessalian tetrarchs were to become their *koinon*'s representatives on the Amphiktyonic Council, but not until early 336 (Table 3 on pp. 132/3), after having evidently played some role in the establishment of the new College of Tamiai in autumn 337 (see *FD* iii 5 No. 47 I.2). There is no need to doubt that these men were loyal to Philip and were called upon by him on occasions of importance (see Theopompos F209, Dem. 18.211, Polyb. 18.14.4). See also Ais. 3.148ff.

41 Philochoros F56 *ap.* Did. *in Dem.* 11.40ff., Glotz *BCH* 1909, 530ff., and Chapter 5 n. 38 above. Diod. 16.85.3f. includes the Byzantian Python among these, but he is probably confusing the occasion with the embassy to Athens in 344 (cf. Diod. 16.85.4 with Dem. 18.136).

42 Cloché *Un fondateur* 259 wonders whether Philip might not have preferred and aimed at Theban rejection of his proposals, deciding that after the seizure of Nikaia there was no alternative to war. But in that case his terms might so easily have been made far less acceptable. We note that in the negotiations that produced the Athenian/Theban alliance it was the former who did the pushing, not the latter; presumably in Thebes, then, the issue was still open.

43 The main source for the Athenian reaction is Dem. 18.169–179; cf. Diod. 16.84.2ff., which must derive ultimately from it. Glotz *BCH* 1909, 526ff. rightly emphasizes the element of surprise and shock among the Athenians. Philip had moved with lightning speed, had not even gone through the motions of punishing Amphissa and was without warning threatening to isolate an Athens that had no time – should he press on quickly – to call on her allies.

44 Dem. 18.177f.

45 Diod. 16.85.1, Dem. 18.179, 211, 213, Plut. *Dem.* 18.1f.

46 Macedonian proposals (for which see above): Dem. 18.213. In 18.214 Demosthenes explicitly omits the Athenian arguments on the grounds that to include them would be 'useless and vexatious'. He then has the Theban acceptance read and immediately proceeds to the military sequel (18.215). On the alliance see also Ais. 3.84, 106, 142f., 237, 239, 256, Philochoros F56, Justin 9.3.5, Diod. 16.85.1, Plut. *Dem.* 18.3f.

47 Ais. 3.142ff.

48 Athens' share of the burden may admittedly have been eased later by contributions from the allies (Wüst *Phil.* 162 n. 1), but in November 339 it was not yet clear which, if any allies would join the defence-effort, and this large portion of the costs was accepted on Athens' behalf in the knowledge that she would be liable for all or most of what was required.

49 Ais. 3.145: '. . . he got hold of the city's Council-House and the democracy and carted them off root and branch to the Theban Kadmeia by his arrangement with the Boiotarchs for joint control.' This had been authorized in part (Dem. 18.178), but if Demosthenes' words there represent what was actually decided – and this is likely, since he drafted the enabling-decree (Diod. 16.85.1) – then the surrender of part-control to Thebes went beyond what had been approved and authorized. The high level of Athenian financial commitment had probably been made feasible a few months earlier by Demosthenes' successful motion to transfer all state funds (including the theoric monies) to the Military Chest (*stratiotikon*): Cawkwell *JHS* 1963, 61, *Mnemosyne* 1962, 377ff.

50 Wüst *Phil.* 157f. leans over backwards to rationalize this discrepancy. One may sympathize with Demosthenes to the extent that, it having been his policy that had brought things to this pass, he now found it absolutely essential to succeed in Thebes, whatever the price, especially since in some respects his anti-Macedonian policy had been an abject failure thanks to Philip's speed of movement. Demosthenes' so-called Hellenic League is a myth, but, even had it existed, it was for the moment irrelevant, with Philip poised to strike almost before any of Athens' sympathizers knew he was south of Thermopylai. Beloch III, 1.565 considers the agreement cheaply bought – which is true in the sense that no new territorial concessions were incurred on Athens' part. But the discrepancy between what Demosthenes promised in Athens and conceded in Thebes, combined with his coyness over the negotiations even a decade later, proves that his fellow-citizens were likely to think otherwise.

51 For example, at Pagasai and Pherai. Hammond *Hist. of Gce*[1] 567 (citing Plut. *Phok.* 14.8, 16.1) has a fleet under Phokion sailing north in spring 338, but this more probably belongs at the end of the siege of Byzantion; see above and n. 19.

52 *IG* IX, 1.316, Hammond *loc. cit.*

53 Such an assumption seems necessary to explain Philip's failure to prevent the seizure of Parapotamioi and the passes west of there. The two main positions, at Parapotamioi and in the Gravia Pass, were within 20 km. of his own troops. See Kromayer *Antike Schlachtfelder* 134f., Wüst *Phil.* 158.

54 Ais. 3.146, Polyainos *Strat.* 4.2.8; cf. Dem. 18.215ff.

55 Paus. 10.3.3, 3.8, 33.4, 36.2, Polyainos *Strat.* 4.2.14. For useful maps see Pickard-Cambridge *Dem.* facing p. 378, Kromayer *Antike Schlachtfelder* Karten, I, 4, *Schlachtenatlas* IV 36f., Hammond *Klio* 1938, 189.

56 The topography is well explained by Hammond *Klio* 1938, 186ff. See also Strabo 9 C424.

57 Ambrysos: Paus. 10.36.2f., cf. 4.31.5. He does not say that Lilaia was fortified or rebuilt at this time, though he perhaps implies as much at 10.33.2; it is in any case likely since Lilaia controlled one of the three passes across Parnassos from the Kephisos valley. Polyainos *Strat.* 4.2.14.

58 Paus. 10.3.3; he continues with the assertion that the Phokians took part (implicitly) on the allied side at Chaironeia (Beloch III, 2.300 accordingly estimates their troop-contribution as 1000 or less), but this is most unlikely, although it may be that the Athenians and Thebans levied some troops when they fell back to Chaironeia and abandoned the southern Phokian passes.

59 Paus. 10.33.4f.: because Parapotamioi was weak and poor, its population was divided among other towns. The allies, who had fortified the heights of Hedylion for their defensive position, were not interested in the town below.

60 A Phokian record of the eighth repayment to Delphoi at the spring *pylaia* of 336 (see Table 2 on p. 123) appears to lay stress on the Phokian towns – by comparison with a similar record surviving from either autumn 342 or spring 341 (*SIG* 231), and may indicate that, at least in legal terms (since actual rebuilding may have taken some time), the towns and the *koinon* had been reconstituted as early as 339/8, but certainly by 337. (Cf. Glotz *BCH* 1909, 535ff., who however argues on the basis of an earlier dating of the relevant Delphic archon. He also suggests that Philip promised a further reduction in the Phokian repayments and implemented this in 338; but the redating of the archonship – see n. 39 – means that the reduction from 30 to 10 talents per year was not effected until spring 335 or later.

61 Dem. 18.156, 158, Justin 9.3, Wüst *Phil.* 159.

62 There is little to be said with confidence of the gathering of allies at this time. In practice we have only the combattants at Chaironeia to guide us, and even here no source gives us what is incontrovertibly a full and accurate list. See Dem. 18.237 (which is the only actual list, but ignores the Akarnanians, who did serve on the allied side in the final battle: Tod ii 178.11ff., 23ff.), which is perhaps a list of those for whose participation Demosthenes thought he could plausibly claim the credit. See also Plut. *Dem.* 17.3 (with Cawkwell *CQ* 1963, 205f. n. 9), Strabo 9 C414, Paus. 7.6.5 (and 4.28.2, 5.4.9, 8.6.2 for the neutrality of Messenia, Elis and Arkadia; Dem. 18.64 for that of Argos). Ael. *VH* 6.1 (cf. Lykourgos *Leokr.* 42) also names the towns of Akte peninsula, which is likely enough, although Demosthenes again is silent. Paus. 10.3.3 also names the Phokians (but see n. 58) and Plut. *Mor.* 851b (cf. Wüst *Phil.* 160, 163 n. 1) the Amphissian Lokrians.

63 Dem. 18.215ff., *IG* II^2 1155 with Beloch III, 1.566.

64 According to Plut. *Dem.* 17.3,

who gives figures for allied troops raised by Demosthenes, allied states other than Thebes and Athens contributed 15,000 foot and 2000 horse plus citizen forces. But something appears suspect here, for Diod. 16.85.5f. puts Philip's numbers at more than 30,000 foot and no fewer than 2000 horse – larger forces, he says, than the defenders could muster. In this case, however, we should need to assume that the Athenians and Thebans themselves provided fewer than 15,000 soldiers and no cavalry, which seems impossibly low, hardly such as to inspire enough confidence in their other allies to attract the latter's contributions. There seem two alternatives: either Plutarch overstates Demosthenes' achievements (which is very likely; see Chapter 6 n. 79) or the total allied force was superior in numbers to that of Philip, as indeed Justin 9.3.9 says.

65 Polyainos *Strat.* 4.2.8, Ais. 3.146f., Deinarchos *Dem.* 74.

66 Strabo 9 C419, 427 thinks that Amphissa was destroyed by the Amphiktyons, but this was not so; see Diod. 18.56, Paus. 10.23.2, 2. 8. 3, 7.14.4. Plut. *Dem.* 18 wrongly puts the capture of Amphissa before that of Elateia. Kromayer *Antike Schlachtfelder* 187 dates the capture of Amphissa approximately to June, but the presence of the Macedonian *hieromnemones* at the spring *pylaia* at Delphoi shows that the Gravia Pass had been cleared by that time (Wüst *Phil.* 164); see *FD* 21 (dated, with reservations, by de la Coste Messelière to spring 338; see n. 39).

67 Dem. 9.34, Strabo 9 C426f. Theopompos dealt with this in his Bk LII (F235) before Chaironeia in Bk LIII (Oldfather *RE* XIII, 1213 reverses the order).

68 Pp. 193f. above. Lebadeia was essential to the defensive position at Chaironeia, for the Macedonians might otherwise send a small force to cross behind and above Chaironeia to Lebadeia and thence to double back through the Kerata Pass or the main Kephisos valley to take them in the rear.

69 Hammond *Klio* 1938, 203. The site has been examined also by Soteriades (*AM* 1903, 311ff., 1905, 113ff.), Kromayer (*Antike Schlachtenfelder* i 158ff. with maps and *Schlachtenatlas* iv, text and maps pp. 36f.) and, since Hammond, Braun (*JÖAI* 1948, 80ff.) and Pritchett (*AJA* 1958, 307ff.; and 308 n. 19 for a complete list of Soteriades' excavation-reports).

70 Wüst *Phil.* 164 n. 6 follows several other modern scholars in using Ais. 3.148–151 to argue that Philip tried to avoid the issue by reopening negotiations with Thebes, only to be foiled by Demosthenes. But, although Aischines appears at first sight to refer to this time (s. 148), his general context shows that he means the period before Thebes accepted Athens' alliance. His implicit reference to the impending battle was anachronistic.

71 For the date (= probably 2 August) see Plut. *Cam.* 19.5. Diod. 16.86 provides the only even moderately detailed account of the battle but is vague in some respects and heavily pro-Athenian in outlook; also Polyainos *Strat.* 4.2.2, 4.2.7 (cf. Front. *Strat.* 2.1.9), Plut. *Alex.* 9.2, *Dem.* 19. While following Hammond's reconstruction of the battle-lines (see n. 69) I do not fully share his confidence in the credibility of Polyainos *Strat.* 4.2.2 for the allegedly decisive manoeuvre on the Macedonian right wing; see Pritchett, *art. cit.* (in n. 69) 310.

72 This is not directly attested, but see Hammond *art. cit.* (in n. 69) 210.

73 Hammond's reconstruction of the battle-lines takes no account of Philip's allies (Diod. 16.85.5), only of the Macedonian troops; but in general his version of the dispositions is convincing. For the course of the battle (with reservations; n. 71 above) see Hammond 211ff.

74 Diod. 16.86–88, Plut. *Dem.* 20f., *Mor.* 845f., 849a, Lykourgos F10.1 (Loeb), Demades *On the XII Years* 10.

75 Compare Diod. 16.87 and Plut. *Dem.* 20 with Justin 9.4.1ff. Schaefer III 4 n. 1 attempts to reconcile the conflict by suggesting that Justin refers only to the latter stage of Philip's reaction, but this perhaps accords too much weight to the wild and moralistic rumours that are to be expected at such a time.

76 Diod. 16.86.6 (corrected by Paus. 9.40.7); the common tomb (Plut. *Alex.* 9.2) of the Macedonian dead was excavated by Soteriades; it stood near the River Kephisos on the left of the Macedonian battle-line. The Lion of Chaironeia (which Hammond follows Beloch III, 2.303f. in attributing to Philip) stands above another mass grave containing 254 skeletons, which must contain the Theban dead of the 300-strong Sacred Band (Pritchett pp. 310f.).

77 Polyb. 5.10.1ff., Justin 9.4.6, Diod. 16.87.3, Plut. *Phok.* 16.4, Demades *On the XII Years* 10, Dem. *ep.* 3.11f. The details of the terms, however, may have been presented by the king to the formal Athenian embassy comprising (or led by) Demades, Aischines and Phokion (see below).

78 Diod. 16.87.3, Paus. 9.1.8, 6.5, Justin 9.4.7ff.

79 At the meeting of the Delphic *naopoioi* in autumn 337 a Theban representative was present, which represents (although admittedly this list is inexplicably abbreviated) a reduction from three. In the spring 335 list, before the Theban participation was removed altogether, all of the previous three Boiotian *naopoioi* were non-Theban. On the Amphiktyonic Council itself, there was no Theban at the spring 336 meeting and the same was probably true in autumn 337. See Tables 3 and 4 on pp. 132/3 and 135.

80 Pickard-Cambridge *Dem.* 396 and n. 1 suggests that this was because the hostilities with Athens had begun with a proper declaration of war. That is debatable, and in any case the most naïve of reasons.

81 Philip himself wisely forebore from ever setting foot on Attic soil. For the panic-measures initially adopted by the Athenians but now countermanded see Hypereides F18 (Loeb), Lykourgos *Leokr.* 16, 37, 39ff., Plut. *Phok.* 16, Dem. 18.248, Plut. *Dem.* 21, Ais. 3.159. For Alkimachos see Berve ii No. 47 and Tod ii 180.

82 Polyb. 5.10.1ff., Diod. 32.4, Plut. *Mor.* 177ef, 819a, Demades *On the XII Years* 9, Diod. 16.87.3, Justin 9.4.4.

83 Dem. 18.282, Ais. 3.227, Schaefer III 24f.

84 Paus. 1.34.1, schol. Dem. 18.99 (Dindorf 259.10), Demades *On the XII Years* 9. It had been seized by Thebes in 366: schol. Ais. 3.85, Diod. 15.76.1. Athens again lost Oropos after the Lamian War (331): Beloch IV, 2.427. Hypereides IV (*In Defence of Euxenippos*) concerns a dispute arising out of the division of Oropian territory among the Athenian tribes (see esp. s. 16), and this apportionment of the land might be taken to explain what may therefore be a misconception in the Suda (*s.* 'Demades'), that Philip procured Boiotian land for Demades.

85 Paus. 1.25.3, 7.10.5, Arist. *Ath. Pol.* 61.6, 62.2, Plut. *Alex.* 28, Diod. 18.56, 32.4. For Delos see *IG* II² 1652. Athens also, of course, retained Salamis: Schaefer III 28 n. 1.

86 Paus. 7.10.5, Plut. *Phok.* 16.4ff., Schaefer III 27 n. 6, Roebuck *CPh* 1948, 81f.

87 See Tables 3 and 4 on pp. 132/3 and 135. In every extant *hieromnemon-*

list after 338 the Athenians provided, as before, one of the Ionian delegates. Among the *naopoioi* there was no Athenian in autumn 337 (but in this inexplicably abbreviated list there is no Macedonian either); in spring 335, the next for which a list is extant, the Athenian names are missing; in autumn 334 there were three (compared with two in 346).

88 Ais. 3.159, Dem. 18.248, Deinarchos *Dem.* 80f., Lykourgos *Leokr.* 42, Plut. *Dem.* 21. I find it hard to swallow the specious rationalizations of, for example, Pickard-Cambridge *Dem.* 304. It may indeed have been thought vital to organize such supplies, but it was something less than obligatory that Demosthenes himself should have taken on the task. He preferred to absent himself from the reckoning brought about by his own policies.

89 Polyb. 5.10.5, Justin 9.4.5, Plut. *Dem.* 22.3, Hypereides F19.2 (Loeb), Paus. 1.9.4.

90 Dem. 18.113, 248, 286ff., 299, Plut. *Vit. X or.* 845f., 849a, Ais. 3.17, 27, 31. His appointment to the 'wall-building' trierarchy perhaps belongs in 337 (Beloch III, 1.611).

91 This has often been recognized, but its best statement is in the detailed survey by Roebuck (*CPh* 1948, 73ff.) of Philip's settlements with the Greek states after Chaironeia, on which I am heavily dependent in the pages that follow. See also Schaefer III 37ff., Wüst *Phil.* 173f.

92 The survival of the league is proved by Arrian 1.7.11 (335 BC) and Hypereides 1.18 (324 BC); see Roebuck 80 n. 45.

93 Paus. 9.1.8, 4.27.10.

94 Paus. 4.27.10, 9.37.8; some of the cost may have been borne by Philip as it later was by Alexander and members of the Hellenic League: Arrian 1.9.10.

95 Schaefer III 19 n. 1 notes this implication of Dio Chrys. 37.42, who alludes to a statue raised by the Thespians to Philip. In late 335, after the suppression of the Theban revolt, Plataia, Orchomenos and Thespiai are remarked among the Hellenic allies who assisted in the destruction of Thebes: Diod. 17.3.5, Arrian 1.8.8, Justin 11.3.8 (who also includes Phokis).

96 See n. 79, Tables 3 and 4 on pp. 132/3 and 135.

97 See n. 60.

98 On Phokian participation in the Common Peace arranged at Korinth in 338/7 see p. 207 and Tod ii 177.31.

99 See p. 197 above. The settlement with the Aitolians, however, can not have been without its own tensions if Diod. 17.3.3 is correct in making the Aitolians vote after the king's death to restore the Akarnanians expelled 'on Philip's account' (see n. 100); in the same passage (17.3.4f.) he completely reverses the roles of Arkadia and Lakedaimon in Philip's settlements.

100 Tod ii 178 (= *IG* II^2 237), Diod. 17.3.3 (see n. 99).

101 Roebuck *CPh* 1948, 77.

102 Diod. 17.3.3.

103 Kaerst *Gesch. Hell.* i 264f., Wüst *Phil.* 169f., Roebuck *CPh* 1948, 80f.

104 Hypereides 5 (*Against Dem.*) col. 20, Deinarchos 1.44, Ais. 3.85, 87; *contra* Schaefer III 38, Wüst *Phil.* 174. The league was in existence in the 290s (*IG* XII, 9.207), but it may have been refounded (Roebuck *CPh* 1948, 82).

105 Polyb. 38.3.3 (and cf. Strabo 10 C447) says that it was temporarily garrisoned but does not say when or by whom. Our evidence for the series of settlements in 338, however, is surprisingly scant, and the possibility of a garrison at Chalkis, though it seems unlikely, cannot be dismissed. Whether or not Chalkis was garrisoned, its role in the Euboian League after the settlement seems to parallel that of Thebes in Boiotia, with the most powerful and expansionist member strictly controlled and the lesser members allowed a greater role; although the evidence is most fragmentary, this conclusion seems justified by the *naopoioi*-list for spring 334 (compared with that for 346); see Table 4 on p. 135.

106 Ael. *VH* 6.1, Lucian *Hist. conscr.* 3, Schaefer III 39, Roebuck *CPh* 1948, 83. Diod. 16.89.3 dates Philip's entry into the Peloponnesos to 337/6, but see Beloch III, 2.299 and, with more detailed argument, Wilcken *SB München* 1917, 3ff. (esp. 20ff., on the date of the first meeting of the Greek states at Korinth in winter 338/7).

107 See Table 4 on p. 135. A delegate is recorded both for spring 335 and autumn 334, although there is none at the small meeting of autumn 337.

108 *Ibid.*, Plut. *Arat.* 73, Polyb. 38.3.3, Schaefer III 53 n. 1.

109 Diod. 16.62.4, 63.1; further refs in Beloch III, 1.595 n. 1.

110 Table 4 on p. 135. The case of Troizen is straightforward, so far as Delphic representation is concerned, but Epidauros appears to withdraw or lose its *naopoios* from this time onwards. Later lists (for which see *SIG* I p. 341) show Troizen continuing to participate, but Epidauros never again sends a delegate to this body. On the standing of the towns on Akte at Chaironeia see Ael. *VH* 6.1. On the establishment of a partisan government at Troizen see Hypereides 3.29ff., Lykourgos *Leokr.* 42.

111 So Hypereides 5 (*Against Dem.*) col. 18, referring to 324 BC. Polyb. 2.40.5 says the league was dissolved, but gives no date and presumably refers to the period between 323 and *c.* 284, which he does specify in slightly different terms at 2.41.9.

112 On the Herakleidai: Apollodoros 2.167ff., Paus. 1.41.2, 3.1.6, 5.3.5ff., 8.5.1, Hdt. 9.26.4ff. On the claims: Paus. 2.20.1, 7.11.1, Isok. 5.24, 29, 91, Schwarz *Philologus* 1937, 19ff. (with refs), Roebuck *Hist. of Messenia* 43ff.

113 Beloch (III, 1.574, 2.173ff.) misdates *SIG* 183 to argue that Philip went from Argos to Arkadia, where he healed a rift in the Arkadian League; the decree belongs in the early 360s: Paus. 8.27.3f., Cary *JHS* 1922, 188ff., Roebuck *CPh* 1948, 85f. and n. That Philip first issued a series of demands to the Spartans before intervening directly is suggested by a number of *apophthegmata* relating (if sometimes anachronistically) to this time: Plut. *Mor.* 216ab, 218e, 219e, 233e, 235a (and Stob. *Flor.* 7.59, Front. *Strat.* 4.5.12, Val. Max. 6.4.E4, Cic. *Tusc. Disp.* 5.14.42. See Roebuck *CPh* 1948, 87 n. 104.

114 Plut. *Mor.* 216a, 218f., 220e, 235ab, Paus. 3.24.6, 5.4.9, 7.10.3, Polyb. 9.28.6f., 33.8ff. The Eleians, though not directly involved, joined Philip in this campaign as a token of loyalty after their neutrality at Chaironeia: Paus. 5.4.9.

115 Paus. 2.38.5; also Paus. 2.20.1, 7.11.1f. Lakedaimonian control of Thyreatis would have barred the Argives from their territory farther south, between the Parnon range and the Aegean.

116 Livy 38.44, Paus. 8.35.4, Polyb. 9.28. Belemina was located about 30 km. to the northwest of Sparta, near the western end of the common border of the present *nomoi* of Arkadia and Lakonia.

117 So Beloch III, 1.575 n. 1 relying on Theopompos F238 (which alludes to Karyai).

118 Tac. *Ann.* 4.43.3.

119 In general on these territorial adjustments see Polyb. 9.28 and Theopompos F238–245. Their encircling effect is clearly observable from the map (p. 18f.) of Greece in *c.* 330 BC in the *Grosser historischer Weltatlas* (Bayerischer Schulbuch-Verlag, 1953 and subsequent printings), Erster Teil (*Vorgeschichte u. Altertum*). For more detailed discussion see Roebuck *CPh* 1948, 84ff.

120 Plut. *Mor.* 216a.

121 For the date see Wilcken *SB München* 1917, 20ff., who establishes a firm case for Philip's having convened two separate meetings of the Greeks at Korinth: the first a 'constituting assembly', at which details of the Hellenic League/Common Peace were announced and perhaps the body was actually established (as Wilcken thinks); the second the business meeting at which war was declared on the Persian King. At the first meeting *legati* (Justin 9.5.1; cf. Diod. 17.4.9, under relevant circumstances: *presbeis* as well as *synedroi*) attended.

122 Isok. *ep.* 3.1ff.; the fundamental content of Isokrates' proposals was first presented in his *Panegyrikos* 133f., 170ff.

123 Isok. *ep.* 3.1ff. Green *Alex.* 84 puts this down to tact, which is no doubt true. But there is reason to believe that Philip's intention *had* already crystallized by that time; and, if so, then Isokrates would know of it better than we.

124 Isok. *ep.* 3.5.

125 The Spartans refused to bind themselves to any agreement with Philip or to take part in the Common Peace: Plut. *Mor.* 240a, Strabo 8 C365, Justin 9.5.3. The Spartans were now too weak to pose by themselves a serious threat to Philip and were surrounded by those with a stake in containing them. Their absence, in fact, served neatly to underscore the 'voluntary' nature of the whole settlement. Conversely, the continuation of a perceptible amount of Spartan recalcitrance would reinforce her neighbours' dependence upon Philip (Burn *Alex. the Great & the Mid. East* 46f., Green *Alex.* 85).

126 The question whether this was a Common Peace (*koine eirene*), an alliance (*symmachia*), or both combined, has been much discussed. The most useful bibliography of the controversy is provided in Ryder *Koine Eirene* 150 and nn., who deals with the whole subject comprehensively and usefully: pp. 102ff., 150ff. Like all previous Common Peaces (see n. 127) it was to be upheld by joint military action (which must *ipso facto* involve *symmachoi* – cofighters – though not technically a *symmachia*; it is notable that in the oath members were referred to as 'participants', not 'allies': Tod ii p. 228), but, unlike them, it was to have built into its structure the machinery essential for deciding upon and organizing joint action. The central primary sources for this treaty (= the 'Hellenic League' or the 'League of Korinth') are Tod ii 177 = *IG* II[2] 236, [Dem.] XVII, *SEG* i 75 (referring actually to a renewal of it more than three decades later); and see Justin 9.5, Dio. 16.89. Significant modern discussions will be cited in subsequent notes.

127 On the earlier Common Peace treaties see Ryder *Koine Eirene* Chaps 2–5 with appendices.

128 [Dem.] 17.30 cites a clause appended to the agreement by which a state joined the Peace: '*if* we wish to participate in the Common Peace'. In one case, that of Sparta, a state did not wish and was not coerced (above n. 125), but this was probably no more than 'window-dressing' on Philip's part.

129 Tod ii 177.26ff.: a few surviving names of the original members, each followed by a figure representing almost certainly the number of representatives or votes to which it was entitled in the Synod (Wilhelm *SB Wien* 1911, 1ff.). Schwahn (*Klio* 1930,

7ff.) has restored others plausibly but without certainty and has attempted to devise a full list complete with representatives and military resources (*ibid.*, 25).

130 Tod ii 177.17–22 (a section of the oath sworn by participant states): 'if anyone shall act in a way contrary to the agreements I shall give military assistance as the injured require and shall go to war against the offender against the Common Peace as the General Synod requires and the Hegemon orders.' It was probably understood that in case of a particular violation troops would be levied in proportion to the size of the emergency. Schwahn *Klio* 1930, 25 estimates a maximum levy of 36,000 hoplites, nearly 6000 cavalry and 320 ships, which is well above any numbers likely to be required in any foreseeable situation; but if votes in the Synod were allocated in proportion to military capacity then the basis of calculation must in fairness have been the maximum reasonably possible from each member (*contra* Tarn *CR* 1931, 88, who suggests a League force of 500 hoplites, 200 cavalry and 5 triremes – apart from any Macedonian contribution; this may in practice have been enough to deal with minor breaches of the peace, but it cannot have formed the basis of calculation for representation in the Synod).

131 Tod ii 177.6ff.

132 It is generally agreed that, since Alexander at his accession needed only to have himself elected to the Hegemony for the military command against Persia (Arrian 1.1.1ff., Diod. 17.2.2, 4.1), the terms of the Common Peace itself, which already related to Philip *and his descendants* (Tod ii 177.11f.), will have remained unaltered. Therefore those applying at the time of this speech, early in Alexander's reign, were those laid down by Philip.

133 Tod ii 177.11–14, [Dem.] 17.10, 16.

134 [Dem.] 17.15. While such a restriction did not in theory preclude the possibility, in a democracy at least, that opposing political groups might win power by legal means, it did mean, presumably, that the adjudication of the legality or otherwise of such changes lay in the hands of the common body.

135 See previous note.

136 [Dem.] 17.8, 19. Whether this reference to freedom of the seas (s. 19) was designed specifically to reassure Athens or was simply the portion in which the Athenians were interested of a more comprehensive guarantee of passage we cannot know; but there seems no good reason, in view of the selective nature of the surviving evidence, to deny the latter interpretation. The prohibition against forcing ships into harbour (s. 19) might be applied as much to the 'legal' piracy of the sort commonly practised by Chalkedon, Byzantion, Kyzikos and, recently, Rhodes (Lykourgos *Leokr.* 18) as to the illegal variety. See Hasebroek *Trade & Politics* 144, 149. On the central importance of Athenian trade and Philip's recognition of it see Wüst *Phil.* 169f.; on the relationship between sea-trade and naval imperialism: Hasebroek 130ff.

137 Tod ii 179; this interpretation is not obligatory but seems the likely one, on the assumption that, a breach of the peace having not actually arisen, the Synod had no competence to intervene but might nevertheless oblige petitioners by finding a mutually suitable arbitrator (*contra* Badian *Anc. Soc. & Insts* 38f. By contrast see Tod ii 192 (the restoration of democracy in Chios, 332), which shows Alexander, presumably as Hegemon of the League (see lines 10–15 and Lenschau *Klio* 1942, 204ff.) executing a decision that therefore properly belongs within the

Synod's (and therefore *his*) sphere of reference (*contra* Ehrenberg *Alex. & the Greeks* 23ff.). That the Synod's decisions were made binding is made explicit in a record of Demetrios' renewal of the League in 302 (*SEG* i 75 u. 18f.),which probably applies equally to the original structure of 338/7.

138 Schwahn *Klio* 1930, 25; an estimate only.

139 Tod ii 177.25; the following members and levels of representation (see n. 130) are contained in what survives of the subsequent lines of this decree.

140 In view of his reform of 344, it would seem more appropriate had Philip allocated these votes among the four tetrarchies, but that would give us the task of dividing ten votes among four tetrarchies. Perhaps two of the ten were allocated to periœcic territories, but the fragmentary nature of Tod ii 177 prevents our discovering whether these were granted votes in their own right. If Schwahn (*Klio* 1930, 14f.) is correct in restoring the Magnetes and the Achaian Phthiotians in lines 26f., this suggestion is invalidated, but his reconstruction is born out of desperation, not conviction.

141 See n. 60.

142 The view, which has occasioned some controversy, is succinctly stated by Larsen *CPh* 1925, 320ff.; cf. Ryder *Koine Eirene* 160.

143 Plut. *Phok.* 16.4. Schwahn *RhM* 1929, 188ff. may be correct in thinking that a second column of the *stele*, of which only the smallest handful of letters survives, represents the reciprocal oath sworn by Philip. His reconstruction (p. 188), based on the Athenian oath and on [Dem.] XVII, is one of those masterpieces of prose-composition that render the mere remains quite redundant.

144 Tod ii 177.

145 Justin 9.5.4 mentions the appointment of Philip as *dux* (= Hegemon), after alluding to the constitution of the *consilium* (Synod). This may be taken to confirm the implication of the Athenian oath, which refers to the Hegemon but does not name him, that the election was not held until the second meeting at Korinth. The words *hegemon* and *hegemonia* are used commonly by Greek authors in an informal sense, but among Diodoros' references to the position now filled some are certainly technical (16.64.3, 91.1, several times in 17.4; see Ryder *Koine Eirene* 155f.), and there is little doubt that the office was a permanent one closely related to the Common Peace machinery and somewhat distinct from the military command subsequently voted against Persia; see n. 150.

146 [Dem.] 17.15: '. . . it shall be the function of the *synedroi* and those appointed for the general security to see that in the participating states there shall be no unlawful executions . . .' Tod ii 183.12f.: 'This treaty shall be inscribed . . . by those appointed for the general security . . .' (There is no reference to this group in Tod ii 177, but since only the oath survives here, this is not disturbing.) The expression is used also in the 302-renewal (*SEG* i 75 ii.11ff.): '. . . the *synedroi* are to assemble in peacetime at the sacred games and in wartime as often as is deemed necessary by the *proedroi* (*synedroi* is inscribed here, presumably by mistake) and the General left behind by the Kings for the general security. They shall deliberate as many days as the *proedroi* of the Synod shall order. Meetings shall continue until the common war is resolved, which shall be announced by the *proedroi* and the Kings or the General designated by the Kings.' From the interchangeability and vagueness of the term it appears that 'those appointed for the general security' could be the whole Synod, as well as its executive officers and its Hegemon or his alternate; it was a useful expression for designating responsibility for activities or functions relating to the Common Peace in a non-specific way, without, that is, itemizing whichever of its administrative and executive organs might be appropriate to a particular matter.

147 Plut. *Per.* 17.1.

148 Polyb. 3.6.9ff., in a discussion of the crusade, distinguishes this pretext (*prophasis*) from the real causes (*aitiai*), which were, he thought, the perceived weakness of the Persians as demonstrated in their failure to defeat the retreating Greeks under Xenophon in 401/0 or the troops of the Spartan Agesilaos five years later. See also Diod. 16.89.2, Arrian 2.14.4.

149 See Milns *Alex.* 14f., Green *Alex.* 94f.

150 Diod. 16.89.3, Justin 9.5.4ff. There has been much dispute as to whether Philip was designated Supreme Commander (*strategos autokrator*), as Diodoros says, quite separately from his existing position as Hegemon of the Common Peace (see also *Pap. Oxy.* 1.26ff.); for bibliography and discussion see Ryder *Koine Eirene* 154ff. Much has turned on the precision with which Diodoros uses the term. Notably, Polybios (9.33.7) and Arrian (esp. 2.14.4, where Alexander refers to himself as *hegemon* of the Greeks; also 7.9.5, where Alexander calls Philip *hegemon autokrator*) do not know it, and Justin refers to him as *dux*, rather than *imperator*. The correct explanation may well be the simplest. As elected Hegemon Philip was the chief executive and probably *ex officio* chairman of the General Synod in time both of peace and of war. A declaration of war, when necessary, was made by the Synod, which would then, presumably, need to confer the actual command of the League's troops on the appropriate commander, the Hegemon if he were present and willing, or a deputy if that were his instruction. Whether or not he would then assume a separate title in keeping with his *ad hoc* military role does not matter much, and the evidence in any case is uncertain. But since, in the Persian expedition at least, the League's army would need to campaign for a long period far from the supervision of the Synod, clearly its commander would be (*de facto*, whether or not *de iure*) in full control, *autokrator*. On the Greeks in Persian service see Arrian 1.16.6.

151 See the regulations cited in *SEG* i 75 ii.11f. (translated in n. 146 above), which probably applied at the outset. The regular meeting of the Synod in 332 was held at Korinth at the time of the Isthmian Games (Curtius 4.5.11) and that for 330 at Delphoi with the Pythia (Ais. 3.254). The only panhellenic games due in 337 was the Nemea. In 336 there would be a choice of the Olympia or the Isthmia, the latter of which fell, like the Nemea but in alternate years, every second year. See Berve i 229f., Busolt/Swoboda *Staatskunde* II 1394.1.

152 I take it that the implication of Plut. *Phok.* 16.4 is that the Athenians agreed during winter 338/7 to the relativity of troops suppliable and votes exercisable in the Synod, expecting in any case that no military demands would be made on them in the near future. What upset them was that the Persian campaign was adopted by the Synod and their military contribution then demanded.

153 Larsen *CPh* 1944, 160.

CHAPTER VIII

1 Diod. 16.89.3 has Philip returning to Macedonia after arrangements had been completed in Korinth for the Asian crusade. No source gives the slightest hint of his having been anywhere but in central Greece and the Peloponnesos since November 339. Some scholars have been driven, however, by their wish to have Kleopatra bear two children before Philip's death, into postulating an earlier, flying visit to Pella. See notes 4, 54.

2 Justin 9.5.8 dates this in the spring following the conclusion of affairs in Korinth. The chronology in Diodoros (see 16.89, under the year 337/6; and 16.91.1f., under 336/5) is confused; see Beloch III, 2.297ff.

3 Probably in summer 337 Philip is found in battle with Pleurias, 'king of the Illyrians' (Diod. 16.93.6, who dates this after the marriage of Philip to Kleopatra in 337). On the sole basis of a similarity between this chieftain's name and that of the (perhaps) Ardiaian chief Pleuratos (whom Philip defeated in 345; Chapter 5 nn. 32–35), many scholars have conflated the two campaigns (as Hammond *ABSA* 1966, 245 n. 27 explains). But Plut. *Alex.* 10.4 confirms the date in a slightly different way, also showing that the event whose origin Diodoros puts in the Illyrian battle began after the marriage to Kleopatra. There is no reason to reject both of these sources.

4 Satyros *ap.* Ath. 13.557b–e, Plut. *Alex.* 9.4 (and for other refs Berve ii No. 434). Green *Alex.* 87ff. dates this marriage to October 338, but no evidence suggests that Philip returned to Pella before spring 337 (see n. 1); Fox *Alex.* 503 dates the marriage, more acceptably, to early spring 337, but surmises that Kleopatra might already have been pregnant – although he does not suggest how the admittedly resourceful but absent king managed that. Both authors wish to fit in two full pregnancies before Philip's death – for which they need Kleopatra impregnated (putting Philip's death at midsummer 336) for the first time by late autumn or early winter 338. See n. 54.

5 *ap.* Ath. 13.557b–e.

6 Alternatively, Kynnane. On the form of the name see Hoffmann *Die Makedonen* 220; also Berve ii No. 456.

7 Green (*Alex.* 27f. and esp. 515 n. 55. believes that Satyros distinguishes here between Philip's marriages proper and the mere liaisons (with the two Thessalians), but it is doubtful whether this is the author's intention. If Satyros wished to illustrate his observation that Philip made war by *marriage*, did he imagine that he had succeeded by listing third and fourth two women the king did not marry. Perhaps, while wishing to preserve the pungency of his aphorism, he really meant that it was the children of these two liaisons that won Thessaly for Philip, not the marriages themselves, since they were not marriages? It may be arguable that this is what he means, but it is in no sense true. It is easier to take the whole passage at face value and to assume that Satyros was not interested in repeating a precise formula wife after wife merely to ease the task of future historians.

8 As noticed by Beloch III, 2.68ff.; also Griffith *CQ* 1970, 70f.

9 Kleopatra's marriage falls in 337 (see above) and it is likely that Meda's belongs in 342 (p. 166 above). That of Olympias was in 357, preceding the birth of Alexander in the summer of 356 (pp. 62, 71 above).

10 See pp. 84f. Berve ii No. 370 dates this marriage to 346 (followed by Kraft *Der 'rationale' Alexander* 16 n. 10), but the name of the daughter, Thessalonike, probably reflects the circumstances of 352; see Ehrhardt *CQ* 1967, 298ff.

11 Philinna: p. 61f.; Audata: pp. 47f.; Phila: p. 46.

12 In the ancient world only by Justin (9.5.9, 7.2, 11.11.5), but even here in senses not implying divorce in any modern sense. See n. 20.

13 See n. 7.

14 Plut. *Alex.* 2.

15 See notes 9 and 11 for refs to the dates of the marriages.

16 Refs collected by Berve *sv* (ii No. 781).

17 The earliest contemporary reference to Alexander, so far as I can discover, is when he is ten years old (Ais. 1.168f.); it is here implicit (but no more) that by now he enjoys primary status. The next earliest is in the letter Isokrates addressed to the young man four years later, in 342 (*ep.* 5), which is unmistakably addressed to the heir apparent (see esp. s. 3). Certainly by 342, that is, and probably by 346, Alexander is known outside Macedonia as Philip's likely successor; but we have no knowledge of how early this was known, or how much earlier still it was recognized inside the country and the court.

18 Macurdy *AJP* 1927, 201ff.: the *mother* of a king was a different matter altogether.

19 Hammond *Hist. Gce*[1] 571; Bosworth *CQ* 1971, 101f.

20 See n. 12. Justin refers at 9.5.9 to the banishment of Olympias on suspicion of adultery (*expulsa . . . Olympiade propter stupri suspicionem*) and at 9.7.2 to her resentment over her *repudium* and the preferment of Kleopatra. At 11.11.3ff. he alleges that Alexander consulted the oracle of Ammon in 332/1 to inquire *inter alia* into his own birth, and explains this as the result of Philip's denial of paternity and his divorce of Olympias for adultery. But, first, Arrian (3.3.2), Diodoros (17.51.3) and Curtius (4.7.27ff.), who all refer to the same incident, interpret the request quite differently – as an inquiry into his divine descent, not his immediate paternity. Justin's rationalization therefore appears to be an interpolation designed to explain a query which was misunderstood in the first place. Secondly, debatable as the facts of Philip's last year or so may be, it is absolutely impossible to credit that he denied paternity, which, apart from being Justin's explicit affirmation, is in any case implicit in a charge of adultery against Olympias. Thirdly, the only sources we have for the time in question (and these admittedly are poor) have Olympias in Macedon during the wedding festivities, which strongly suggests that she had not been repudiated: Plut. *Alex.* 9.5, Justin 9.7.5.

21 Plut. *Alex.* 9.4f., Ath. 13.557e; cf. Justin 9.7.2ff.

22 According to Arrian 3.6.4f., Alexander's closest friends too went into exile 'when Alexander fell under Philip's suspicion when Philip had taken Eurydike (i.e. Kleopatra) to wife and had treated Olympias, the mother of Alexander, as unworthy'. In spite of Kraft's objection (*Der rat. Alex.* 27 n. 36), we are probably obliged to take Arrian's indication as a general one, merely placing these exiles in the period of disruptions after the new marriage. Plut. *Alex.* 10.3 puts them unequivocally after the Pixodaros affair, which must fall later in 337 or in early 336; see Badian *Phoenix* 1963, 246, Hamilton *G&R* 1965, 121 n. 5.

23 For Eurydike's provenance see Chapter 1 n. 98. Bosworth (*CQ* 1971, 93ff.) makes the whole business a conflict between plain and mountain, but his connection between the Molossian royalty and the hill-tribes of Upper Macedonia is suspect, he overlooks Philip's own (part-Illyrian) parentage (how, one wonders, would Attalos have expressed his objections to the king?), and he ignores much of the evidence, some uncertain but some solid, bearing on the circumstances of Philip's last year. While Attalos and

Kleopatra *may* have been from the plains (we do not know even this), it is more than possible that Attalos' father-in-law-shortly-to-be, Parmenion, was Upper Macedonian. Edson, in an unpublished paper ('Who was Parmenion?') argues inconclusively for this (the nature of the evidence permits of no better) on epigraphical grounds and draws attention to the association of his son Philotas with the cavalry from Upper Macedonia (Arrian 1.2.5 with Berve ii No. 802; and see Curtius 5.2.6). Philip's assassin was from upland Orestis (Diod. 16.93.3), but then so too were at least two of the bodyguards who killed the killer (Diod. 16.94.4, Berve ii Nos 466, 627, 181). In all this it is difficult to see signs of highland *vs* lowland enmity.

24 According to Justin 9.7.4, it was the entreaties of friends that saved the prince.

25 *ap*. Ath. 13.557de.

26 Refs in n. 21. It has been suggested that the 'Illyrian king' to whom he is said to have fled (Justin 9.7.6) was Langaros, the Agrianian chieftain (Badian *Phoenix* 1963, 244 n. 8) followed by Green *Alex*. 90). Although in view of the attested friendship between the two men (Arrian 1.5.2) this seems credible, it is far from certain – the main difficulty being that (whether or not Langaros or Longaros was an Illyrian name: so Tomaschek cited by Berve ii No. 460) the Agrianes were Paionians (Thuc. 2.96.3, Steph. Byz. s. 'Agriai'; for their location at the headwaters of the Strymon see Hammond *Mac*. i 202). Alexander may have met the Paionians during his own campaign against the more southerly Maidoi in 340/39; see pp. 182f.

27 Burn *Alex. the Great & the Mid. East* 47f.; cf. Grote xi 317f., Wilcken *Alex*. 59, Pickard-Cambridge *Dem*. 405.

28 Badian *Phoenix* 1963, 244, 246, Hamilton *G&R* 1965, 120, Bosworth *CQ* 1971, 93ff.; cf. Willrich *Hermes* 1899, 174ff. Milns *Alex*. 27f. additionally suggests a motive in the unpopularity of the overbearing Olympias, which is plausible enough (although we really have no evidence on what Olympias was like at this time; only on what others claimed she was like later), but will not alone explain why Alexander's own position should thereby come under challenge.

29 Hammond *Hist. Gce*. 573.

30 Green *Alex*. 91ff., depending on a presumption of Alexander's and Olympias' complicity in Philip's assassination, an argument revived by Badian *Phoenix* 1963, 244ff. (cf., on less convincing grounds, Köhler *SB Berlin* 1892, 497ff., who was attacked by Willrich *Hermes* 1899, 174ff.).

31 Kraft *Der rat. Alex*. 16ff., esp. 23ff., reviews the analyses of recent authors, especially Badian (see n. 30), concluding that the purpose of the marriage was innocent of political connotations and was unconnected in any significant way with the murder of the king.

32 See nn. 21, 26. Justin 9.7.7 asserts that Olympias passed her time in Epeiros in trying to persuade her brother to make war on Philip but that her entreaties were undercut by Philip's arrangement of a marriage between his daughter Kleopatra and the Molossian Alexandros. No more than a (lone) allegation as to unrealized intentions, this is worthless. Kraft 18 reminds us that Kleopatra was also *Olympias'* daughter and for that reason finds it unacceptable that she could have been used to drive a wedge between her uncle/husband and her mother (as Badian 246 implies).

33 Plut. *Alex*. 9.5, Satyros *ap*. Ath. 13.557e, Justin 9, 7, 4ff., Arrian 3.6.4f.

34 For Pleurias: Diod. 16.93.6 (and, for the date, 16.93.7–9); see n. 3 and Hammond *ABSA* 1966, 245.

35 On the implication of Attalos here see Fox *Alex.* 22 and 505.

36 Plut. *Alex.* 9.6, Justin 9.7.6; Plut. *Mor.* 179c has Philip reconciled to both Alexander and Olympias. If this is so, we should expect Olympias to have attended the wedding of her daughter and her brother at Aigai in the following summer.

37 Curtius 6.9.17, where Alexander's attitude – at least his *later* attitude – is shown; but, in the context of Philotas' trial and after Attalos' treason following the death of Philip, Alexander's slanders should not be given too much weight. We may note that in Plut. *Alex.* 10.3 Philotas, the son of Parmenion and now brother-in-law of Attalos, is said to have been one of Alexander's friends at this time. Compare the interpretation of Badian *Phoenix* 1963, 245.

38 Ellis *JHS* 1971, 18, 22. That he was now married for (apparently) the first time suggests that he was nearer the lower than the higher figure – reinforcing the possibility that he was little more than a babe in arms at Philip's accession; see Chapter 2 n. 10.

39 Cf. Green *Alex.* 102, 112.

40 Plut. *Alex.* 10; cf. Diod. 16.69.2, 74.2, 17.5.3; also Berve ii No. 640, Hamilton *PAComm* 25, Olmstead *Hist. Pers. Emp.* 489f. dates the Pixodaros affair to spring or later 336, after the Macedonian advance-party had arrived in Asia Minor. This is a possible context, though it makes Pixodaros' abandonment of the projected alliance a little harder to explain.

41 Note 40 for refs. Badian *Phoenix* 1963, 245 has suggested that there were grounds for Alexander's fears, but, as he admits, all the incident proves is that Alexander himself felt insecure. As Kraft *Der rat. Alex.* 26 counters, Pixodaros' preference for Alexander shows that, at least outside Macedonia, there was no question as to whose prospects of succession stood higher. See Green *Alex.* 99ff.

42 For refs see Berve ii Nos 143 (Harpalos, probably Elimiote), 302 and 464 (Erygios and Laomedon, Mytilenean), 544 (Nearchos, Kretan) and 668 (Ptolemaios, son of Lagos from Eordaia and of Arsinoë from family cognate with Argeadai). Plut. *Alex.* 10.3 gives only four names and Arrian 3.6.5 adds Laomedon. On the date see n. 22.

43 Little direct evidence survives for the presumed unwillingness of the Greek states to serve (though see Plut. *Phok.* 16.5, referring either to the decisions made at Korinth in 338/7 or possibly to the actual levies of 334).

44 Diod. 16.91.2, 17.24.1, Justin 7.5.8; cf. Diod. 16.89.2 for the aim proclaimed at Korinth. For the size and composition of the advance-party: Polyainos *Strat.* 5.44.4, Diod. 17.7.10, Milns *JHS* 1966, 167f.

45 On the financial difficulties inherited by Alexander see Plut. *Alex.* 15.1, *Mor.* 327d, Arrian 7.9.6. For indications of the cost of maintaining soldiers in the field see Tod ii 183 with discussion by Berve i 193ff., Griffith *Hell. Mercs* 299, Parke *Gk Merc. Soldiers* 232ff., Bellinger *Essays on the Coinage of Alex.* 36ff., Hamilton *PAComm.* 36f., Green *Alex.* 530 n. 7. Bellinger (under-) calculates the cost of maintaining Alexander's army at approx. 200 talents per month. On Philip's alleged lack of financial ability: Theopompos F224.

46 Diod. 16.91.2, Justin 11.5.8.

47 See Badian *Anc. Soc. & Insts* 40ff.

48 For this reason I am in disagreement with Badian (*art. cit.* in previous note). I agree that Alexander is unlikely to have countermanded Philip's orders in late 336 or even 335, but doubt that under the circumstances Parmenion was likely to be following *any* orders at all. When the campaign turned sour after Philip's death and especially on the appointment in 335 (now by Dareios III) of Memnon to recover the ground lost in the previous year to the Macedonians, the latter are even less likely to have been acting upon orders from Macedonia; their natural concern will have been to preserve by whatever means necessary the foothold they had won. The treatment of Gryneion (Diod. 17.7) I should attribute to neither Philip's nor Alexander's policies but to Parmenion's reactions to the exigencies of the moment.

49 Tenedos: Arrian 2.2.2ff. (referring to an agreement with *Alexander* and the Greeks, probably representing a renewal of one concluded initially with Philip). Chios: Tod ii 192 with refs. Lesbos: [Dem.] 17.7. It is admittedly not certain that these islands joined Philip now rather than Alexander later.

50 Tod ii 191 (= *IG* XII, 2.526.1ff. and 43ff.; and see Tod's commentary and *IG* XII Suppl. 65ff.), Habicht *Gottmenschentum* 14f.

51 Arrian 1.17.9ff. (cf. Plut. *Alex.* 3), Habicht *op. cit.* 15f., Badian *Anc. Soc. & Insts* 40f. On the question of Philip's alleged deification, which is not implied by the honours paid by Eresos and Ephesos, see below.

52 *SIG* 284, Badian *loc. cit.* Here too a statue was overthrown by oligarchs when the democracy was suppressed either in 335 or 333; in this case it was a representation of a certain Philitos (on the name see Croenert *Hermes* 1902, 212), who had slain the previous tyrant: *SIG* 284.2f.

53 The date of Philip's assassination: Arrian 1.1.1 places it in the archonship of Pythodemos (wrongly for Pythodelos), 336/5 (cf. Tod ii 181 = *IG* II^2 240, dated June/July 336, at which time Philip is said to be still alive). Alexander's reign was conventionally dated, it seems, from the beginning of the Macedonian year, which began with the month Dios (= *c.* October; see Beloch III, 2.59f. with refs), but the round figure may be a matter of convenience. It is likely that Philip intended the main force to cross to Asia Minor before the end of the campaign season and that he planned the wedding to allow for this. The date, therefore, should be later than early July but as long as possible before October.

54 Satyros *ap.* Ath. 13.557d. Justin (implicitly at 9.7.3 and explicitly at 11.2.3) gives Kleopatra a son Karanos. Although the sources are divided (cf. Paus. 8.7.7, Justin 9.7.12, Diod. 17.2.3), all agree that Kleopatra bore only one child (and there was insufficient time for more; see notes 1 and 4), which must have been the daughter named by Satyros. Tarn, however unhistorical his motive in the matter (see *Alex.* ii 260ff.; 262: 'Alexander did commit two murders in his day; there is no need to invent one which he could not have committed'), was correct to assassinate 'Karanos'. According to Diod. 17.2.3 the 'child' (*paidion*) was born only days before Philip's death.

55 Diod. 16.91.2, Paus. 8.7.6. Translation from Parke/Wormell *Delphic Oracle* ii 238.

56 Diod. 16.91f., Justin 9.6. Diodoros' account (Justin's is extremely abbreviated) derives probably from the Hellenistic Athenian historian Diyllos, which should alert us to the likelihood of an even greater degree of rhetorical adornment than the occasion by its own nature invited. See Schubert *Untersuch. über die Quellen zur Gesch. Phil. II von Mak.* (Königsberg 1904), 32, Hammond *CQ* 1937, 91.

57 Diod. 16.92ff., Justin 9.6.3. Diodoros says the assassination took place at the entrance to the *theatron*, which is either loosely used (since games were held in *stadia*) or presupposes that a separate opening ceremony was held in the theatre.

58 According to Diod. 16.92.5 and 95.1 (and see Welles' note, Loeb Vol. VIII p. 101 n. 3), Philip exhibited his own image with the other twelve in the opening procession. This has provoked some modern discussion, which, by combining this with three other data, has arrived at the general view that Philip felt by now that 'he was in some fashion the equal of the Twelve and entitled like them to worship' (so Welles; and see Momigliano *Fil.* 172ff., Badian *Phoenix* 1963, 246f., *Anc. Soc. & Insts* 41, Fox *Alex.* 504). These need separate treatment. The Philippeion at Olympia was built, according to Pausanias (5.20.9f., cf. 5.17.4, Plut. *Mor.* 170e), by Philip after Chaironeia and contained statues of Alexander, Philip, Olympias and Philip's parents Amyntas and Eurydike (the inclusion of Olympias surely discomfitting at least those who see only antagonism between her and the king at this time; on the excavations see Gardiner *Olympia; Its Hist. & Remains* 133ff.). But, as has long been recognized (Momigliano *Fil.* 175; cf. Curtius 9.6.26, 10.5.30), it was in fact erected by Alexander, probably very late in his reign, and was probably built not as a sanctuary but as a treasury (Crum *Phil. II of Mac. & the City-State*, diss. Columbia 1966, 240ff.). Special ('divine') honours granted to Philip by Eresian and Ephesian democrats in the course of Parmenion's first campaign-season in Asia Minor can hardly have been conceived before Philip's death, let alone enacted in accord with his wishes; in any case, it is doubtful whether they imply any acknowledgement of divinity (Fox *loc. cit.*). As Crum has seen, the whole notion of 'the thirteenth god' has about it an 'apocryphal flavour' reminiscent more of the Hellenistic ruler-cult than of Philip's time, and he argues convincingly that its attribution in embryo to Philip derives ultimately from sources no earlier than the late reign of Alexander. It is in any case, one would think, incredible that Philip could – with his experience – have been so poor a judge of his Macedonians' character, who, even several years later, when their globe-trotting should have made them less intolerant, strongly resented and successfully resisted Alexander's attempts to have himself ceremonially exalted as a king in the Persian manner.

59 Cf. Bosworth *CQ* 1971, 93ff., who attempts to make *Pap. Oxy.* 1798 (= *FGH* 148) say that Pausanias the assassin was captured and later executed by the Macedonian military assembly. All it does say, however, is that someone was executed in the aftermath of the murder, and, as Green *Alex.* 524 n. 65 points out, it could equally well refer to one of the Lynkestian brothers put to death at this time, among how many others we do not know. See Arrian 1.25.1f., Curtius 7.1.6f.; also Diod. 17.2.1, Justin 11.2.1.

60 Diod. 16.93f., Justin 9.6f., Arist. *Pol.* 5.1311b.

61 See n. 3 above.

62 In this he is said to have been encouraged by one Hermokrates or Hermokles; see Welles' note on Diod. 16.94.1 (Loeb VIII), Val. Max. 8.14.

63 Justin 9.6.8 (cf. Diod. 16.93.9, who also appears to see this as a factor, though the relative chronology is confused).

64 For Attalos' treason see Diod. 17.2, 17.5.1, Plut. *Dem.* 23.2.

65 See n. 23.

66 Justin 9.7.10ff.; s. 14: 'All this was done so openly that it seemed that she feared it might *not* be evident that the crime was committed by her'!

67 Diod. 19.50f., Granier *Mak. Heer.* 86ff., Tarn *Alex.* ii 261f., Edson *Hesperia* 1949, 87.

68 See, most usefully, Badian *AUMLA* 1962, 80ff., repr. in *Studies in G&R Hist.* 192ff.

69 Arrian 1.23.7f. and Strabo 14 C656f.

70 Arrian 3.6.5, it seems to me, the only reasonably credible evidence for some disturbance between Philip and Alexander in the last months of the former's life; and even he may have been misled by the anti-Olympias tradition.

71 Most works on Alexander deal with the question at least in passing. For Philip, however (with whom the answer may well be different), two works are of particular interest: Schachermeyer *Alex.* (1973) 58ff. (with whose view I agree substantially), and the skilfully imaginative treatment by Toynbee: 'If Ochus and Philip had Lived on' (*Some Problems of Gk History* Part iv Chap. 2, pp. 421ff.). See also Brunt *G&R* 1965, 205ff.

72 The possibility that Philip, after securing Asia Minor, would have tried to guarantee his possession of the Aegean world by attempting to bring the eastern Mediterranean seaboard under his power has been rightly dismissed by Brunt *G&R* 1965, 207. Macedonian power and interests were continental and they were no more capable of controlling the seas than Sparta in the fifth century.

73 Isok. 5.119ff.; on the mercenary problem see Burn *Alex. the Great & the Mid. East* 36f., Parke *Gk Merc. Soldiers* 113ff.

74 Arrian 2.25.1f.; cf. Justin 11.12.3ff., Curtius 4.5.1ff. (who dates this letter *after* the siege of Tyre and who defines the extent of the territorial cession in the same terms as had been proposed in an earlier offer: cf. Curtius 4.1.7ff.) and Diod. 17.54.1 (who makes similar mistakes). There is good reason here to accept Arrian's version: Griffith *PCPS* 1968, 33ff.

75 Most recently Schachermeyer *Alex.* (1973) 62 and n. 39; *contra* Brunt *G&R* 1965, 207.

76 Arrian 2.14.1ff., Diod. 17.39.1ff., Curtius 4.1.7ff., Justin 11.12.1f. with Griffith *PCPS* 1968, 33ff., who offers a brilliantly plausible explanation of the discrepancies between the versions of Arrian and Diodoros.

SELECT INDEX

of names and subjects

Abdera 32f., 69, 76f.
Achaia 86, 158f., 173, 196, 198, 203f.
Achaia Phthiotis 85, 143, 258, 300
Agis 45, 57, 70
Aigai 28, 35f., 40, 49ff., 161, 222ff., 229
Ainis 121, 190f., 257f., 270
Ainos 167
Aischines 7, 48f., 100f., 108ff., 111ff., 117ff., 125f., 127f., 131f., 148ff., 187ff., 199, 270ff.
Aitolia 90, 143, 158, 190f., 201
Akarnania 158, 173, 181, 196, 201f.
Aleuadai 61, 137ff., 212
Alexander III 12, 24f., 52ff., 71, 141f., 160ff., 168, 170f., 174, 182f., 198f., 202f., 211ff., 216, 220ff., 229ff., 238f., 246f., 278, 286, 296, 305
Alexandropolis 183
Alexandros (k. of Epeiros) 62, 91, 154, 157, 215, 219, 222f.
Alexandros (s. of Aeropos) 60, 170
Amadokos 63, 68, 70, 76, 80, 87f., 104, 166, 277
Ambrakia 86, 90, 156ff., 202
Amphiktyonic League 73ff., 85, 93, 102ff., 114f., 117ff., 126ff., 130ff., 137, 140f., 142, 150, 154, 186ff., 196ff., 201, 203ff., 271f., 291
Amphilochos 169
Amphipolis 28, 43, 45, 48ff., 63ff., 108, 114, 145ff., 167, 235ff.
Amphissa 78, 158, 187ff., 193ff.
Amyntas III 42f., 61, 98, 136
Amyntas (s. of Perdikkas III) 44ff., 48, 91, 217
Amyntas (s. of Arrhabaios) 220ff.
Anthemous 36, 42, 68, 99
Antipatros 60, 103f., 110f., 161, 163, 170f., 182ff., 199, 205, 238f., 245, 266
Antiphon 128, 251
Apollonia (opp. Thasos) 72
Apollonia (Chalk.) 95, 99
Apollonia (= Sozopol) 171, 183
Apollonides 93f.
Archelaos (k. of Mac.) 38, 40ff., 67, 252
Archelaos (s/b. of Philip) 46, 94
Archidamos 74, 159, 203
Ardiaian Illyrians 57, 135f., 262, 274
Areiopagos Council 128, 131f., 200
Argaios 42, 44ff., 75, 94
Argos 35, 74, 115, 121, 134, 144, 146, 150, 158f., 203f., 209, 269, 278
Aridaios (s. of Philip) 211ff., 218, 239, 254
Aridaios (s/b. of Philip) 46, 94
Aristodemos 106f.
Aristotle 97f., 160ff., 221
Arkadia 93, 101, 158f., 203f.
Arrhabaios (s. of Aeropos) 60
Arses 218
Artabazos 73, 77, 91f., 172f.
Artaxerxes III Ochos 74, 77, 91ff., 93, 98, 146f., 160, 172f., 174, 178f., 181, 205, 218, 278
Arybbas 62, 90f., 154, 156ff., 262
Asia Minor 11, 92, 102, 147, 160, 172f., 196, 202, 209, 217ff., 223, 228ff.
Asyla mines 33f., 69
Ateas 166, 174, 183, 185f.
Athenian prisoners at Olynthos 99, 102, 106, 109, 114, 117, 119, 127
Athens:
and Amphipolis 43, 45, 48ff., 63ff., 108, 114, 145ff.; and the Chalkidike 44, 51, 68, 71f., 95ff.; and the Chersonesos 80f., 87f., 109, 155, 168f., 176f.; and the corn-supply 12, 165, 175, 179f., 182, 233; and Euboia 63, 96f., 99, 109, 153, 162ff., 169f., 173, 181; and the Peace of Philokrates 105ff., 111ff., 125ff., 143ff., 158f., 175, 191; and Persia 146f., 173, 181; and the Sacred War (355–346) 74, 78, 86, 93, 105, 111ff.; and the second naval alliance 63ff., 73, 97, 171f., 182, 185, 199ff.; and Thebes 74, 96, 109, 125f., 147f., 187ff., 191ff., 199ff., 290f.; and Thessaly 105, 159; and Thrace 68, 70f., 72f., 77, 104, 107f., 110, 155, 171f.
Attalos 211ff., 217, 220ff.
Audata 46, 47f., 211, 217
Autariatan Illyrians 57, 216, 262, 274
Axios, R. 29, 32, 57, 186, 247

Bardylis 44f., 47f., 53f., 57ff., 62, 67, 262
Berisades 63, 67f., 70, 80
Black Sea 12, 109, 171, 179, 183, 185f., 285
Boiotia/Boiotian League 78, 86, 103, 107, 109, 114f., 118, 121, 139f., 192f., 198ff., 257, 271
Byzantion 77, 87f., 108, 169, 171f., 174ff., 181ff., 196

Chaironeia 78, 93, 150, 184, 193f., 197ff., 233f., 286
Chalkidike/Chalkidian League 29, 33, 36, 40, 65, 67f., 81, 88f., 92ff., 98f., 136, 146, 167, 235ff., 264
Chalkis 118, 164f., 169f., 173, 202f., 296
Chares 73, 77, 80f., 82, 87f., 104, 145, 175ff., 182ff., 193ff., 256f., 263, 264
Charidemos 98, 200, 251, 258, 263
Chersonesos 65, 80f., 87f., 104, 109, 155f., 168f., 176f., 183f., 257
Chios 63, 66, 73, 171f., 179, 181f., 183f., 221f.
common peace (*see also* Hellenic League) 9ff., 111ff., 144ff., 154ff., 196, 199ff., 233f., 273, 298

Damastion 33, 60, 67, 236
Danube (Istros), R. 166, 171, 185, 216
Daochos 141, 191
Dardanian Illyrians 44f., 47f., 57ff., 62, 67, 90, 262, 274
Dareios III 229f., 238, 278, 286
Delphoi (*see also* Amphiktyonic League) 74ff., 78, 86, 121ff., 163, 222
Delos 130f., 199
Demades/Peace of D. 184, 198ff.
Demaratos 216f.
Demosthenes 7, 9, 81, 95f., 97, 99, 100f., 106ff., 111ff., 117ff., 125ff., 143ff., 148, 158f., 188ff., 200, 265, 270f., 272
Derdas (b. of Phila) 38, 46, 59, 211
Diopeithes 104, 169, 175, 177
Dolopia 121, 143, 190f., 258
Dorian tribe 121, 124, 134, 257, 271
Doris 78, 121, 190

Egypt 146, 160, 172
Elateia 190ff.
Elimeia 36ff., 46, 58ff., 85, 162, 212
Elis 151, 153, 203f., 278
Emathian Plain 29, 32, 57, 69, 186
Eordaia 28, 36, 162
Epeiros 29, 61f., 81, 86, 90f., 154, 156ff., 202, 215, 219, 231f.
Ephesos 221f.
Epidauros 78, 93, 134
Eresos 221f.
Eretria 96f., 153, 164ff., 170, 255
Erigon, R. 29, 32, 58
Erigyios 162, 218f.
Erythrai 222
Etesian Winds (Meltemi) 29, 64, 97
Euboia 63, 73, 96f., 99, 107, 109, 121, 150f., 162ff., 169f., 173, 175, 181, 196, 202f., 270
Euboulos 97, 100f., 103ff., 112, 266, 267
Europe (d. of Philip) 212, 222, 224
Eurydike 42ff., 215
Eurylochos 110f., 163ff.

Getai 166f., 183, 185f., 211
Gonnoi 86, 96
Grabaian Illyrians 67f., 70f., 90, 262
Grabos 67f., 70f., 73, 262

Haliakmon, R. 29, 32, 156, 247
Halonnesos 145ff., 154, 175
Halos 103, 105, 107f., 112f., 116, 268
Harpalos 60, 162, 218f.
Hebros, R. 29, 32, 77, 104, 157, 167f., 171
Hedyleion, Mt 193, 265, 293
Hegesippos 145ff., 153ff.
Hellenic League 11f., 200, 203ff., 219ff., 233f.
Hellespont 65, 70f., 173ff., 219ff., 233
Hephaistion 161f.
Heraion Teichos 87
Herakleia Lynkestis 33, 58
Herakleia Tracheia 190
Hermias 97f., 160, 172f., 218
Heromenes (s. of Aeropos) 60
Hieron Oros 104, 110, 179
Hipponikos 163ff.
Hypereides 131f., 148ff., 171ff.

Iatrokles 106
Illyrians 8, 34f., 44f., 47f., 57ff., 62, 67f., 70f., 81, 90f., 134ff., 143, 157, 159, 167, 211, 215f., 224, 232, 262
Ionian tribe 121, 257, 271
Irrhas 247, 249f.
Isokrates 128ff., 143, 160, 205, 227ff.

Kallias 162ff., 169f., 173, 202, 282
'Karanos' 306
Kardia 81, 146, 155, 167, 168f., 179
Karia 218f., **227**
Karystos 97, 164f., 279
Kassopeia 157f.
Kephisos, R. 190ff., 196
Kersebleptes 63, 68ff., 77, 80f., 87f., 104, 107, 110, 112f., 116, 145, 166ff., 277
Ketriporis 68, 70, 73, 80, 110
Kleopatra (d. of Philip) 211, 219, 222ff.
Kleopatra (w. of Philip) 211ff., 222, 224
Kolosimmos 137, 140
Korinth 74, 78, 93, 122, 134, 158, 196, 203ff., 233
Korinth, League of (*see* Hellenic League)
Koroneia 81, 87, 103, 146, 271
Korsiai 81, 87, 103, 271
Kos 63, 181f.
Kothelas 166f., 185f., 211
Kottyphos 137, 140, 186ff.
Kotys 45, 49
Krenides (*see* Philippoi)
Krannon 137, 259
Krokion Plain ('Crocus Field') 82f., 105, 237
Ktesiphon 100, 170
Kynnane (Kynna) 48, 62, 211, 217
Kytinion 190ff.

Larisa 43, 61, 74, 85, 105, 108, 137ff., 211, 236ff.

Lokris 74, 78, 121f., 187ff., 196, 201, 205f.
Lychnitis, L. 29, 33, 58
Lykophron 77ff., 82ff.
Lynkos 36ff., 58f., 136
Lyppeios 70, 73, 90

Macedonia:
army 8ff., 24ff., 34, 41f., 52ff., 99, 161f., 171, 174f., 231ff., 245ff.; artillery and siege-warfare 79f., 174ff.; climate 33; coinage 67, 167f., 235ff., 245; court 8, 42, 161f., 231; earlier history 34ff.; economy 8, 32ff., 58f.; fleet 40, 175ff., 182ff.; frontiers and growth 28f., 52, 58ff., 136, 216, 230ff.; geography 21, 28ff.; kingship 21ff.; Lower Macedonia 8, 38, 41; mercenaries 55, 163ff., 220, 256f.; military assembly 24ff.; organization 27f.; population 34; society 8, 21ff., 32ff., 54f., 58ff., 99, 161f., 231; taxes 28, 247; Upper Macedonia 8, 36ff., 48, 58ff., 136, 162.
Maidoi 182f.
Magnesia 85f., 95f., 121, 137, 202f., 258, 300
Malia, G. of 163, 190
Malis 78, 121, 270, 271
Mantineia 158f.
Maroneia 76f., 80
Meda 166f., 211f.
Megalopolis 93, 115, 134, 158f., 204, 269
Megara 78, 134, 151, 153, 170, 173, 196, 203f., 278
Memnon 92, 172f., 229
Menelaos 46, 94
Mentor 92, 172f., 229
mercenaries, Greek 129, 209, 228, 263f.
Messene/Messenia 115, 134, 144, 150, 158f., 203f., 269
Methone 35, 40, 49ff., 66f., 75f., 83
Mieza 28, 161f.
Molossians (*see also* Epeiros) 35, 61f., 157f., 211

Naupaktos 158f., 193, 201, 203
Neapolis 32f., 69, 72f., 76f., 256
Neon 76f.
Nestos, R. 29, 32, 110, 167ff., 232
Nikaia 78, 119, 137, 146, 190f., 193, 196, 199, 201, 270
Nikesipolis 84f., 211f.

Oitaia 121f., 190, 257, 270f.
Olympias 61f., 90, 154, 161, 211ff., 224ff., 238f.
Olynthos (*see also* Chalkidike) 8, 11, 38, 42f., 45, 51, 60, 80, 102
Onomarchos 76, 78ff., 81ff., 86f., 179, 256f.
Orchomenos 78, 87, 103f., 146, 201, 271
Oreos 107, 164f., 170
Orestis 28, 37ff., 58ff.
Oropos 109, 199

Pagai 258, 260
Pagasai 82ff., 85, 93, 95f., 105, 163, 170, 257, 285
Paionians 44, 56ff., 81, 90f., 167, 232
Pammenes 77. 91f.
Pangaion, Mt 8, 32, 33f.
Parmenion 58, 60, 103, 107, 110f., 163ff., 171, 182, 217, 220ff., 229, 238
Pausanias (assassin) 60, 223ff.
Pausanias (pretender) 44, 45f., 49
Pelagonia 37ff., 162
Pella 28, 40, 42, 92, 107f., 161, 167, 235ff.
Peloponnesos 90, 103, 115, 127, 130, 134, 143f., 150f., 158f., 181, 196, 203f.
Peneios, R. 29, 85
Peparethos 155, 175, 177
Perdikkas III 38, 43f., 45f., 47, 59f., 91
Perinthos 77, 80, 87f., 108, 169, 171f., 174ff., 184, 196
Perrhaibia 85f., 96, 121, 257, 258, 275
Persia (*see also* Arses, Artabazos, Artaxerxes, Asia Minor and Dareios) 174, 179, 181, 227ff., 277f., 286, 288
Persian campaign 11f., 91f., 101f., 127, 160, 172f., 175, 205, 208ff., 211, 219ff., 227ff., 273
Phalaikos 92f., 102, 103f., 106f., 119ff., 201
Pharsalos 105, 137, 141, 231
Phayllos 78, 83, 86f., 92
Pherai 43, 61, 74, 77ff., 82ff., 86, 93, 96, 105, 116ff., 129f., 137ff., 211
Phila 38, 46, 61, 211f.
Philinna 61, 211ff.
Philip:
accession 25f., 44, 45ff., 91; alleged divinity 255, 306f.; alleged regency 246, 250; alleged treaty with Persia 278, 286; colonies 69f., 86, 136, 167f., 230ff.; foreign policies 8ff., 48f., 64f., 67f., 73, 77, 88f., 90, 92ff., 98, 101ff., 105ff., 125ff., 147f., 166, 204ff., 227ff.; marriages 38, 46, 47f., 61f., 84f., 166f., 211ff., 224; pre-accession 43f., 45f.; unification of Macedonia 8ff., 58ff., 230f.
Philippoi 32ff., 68ff., 72f., 167f., 235ff.
Philokrates/Peace of P. 11f., 101, 106ff., 111ff., 117ff., 125f., 148ff., 233f., 270f.
Philomelos 74, 76
Philotas 162, 246, 253, 304
Phoenicia 160, 229f., 277
Phokion 97, 170, 182ff., 199, 200
Phokis (*see also* Sacred War) 73, 78, 93, 102, 104f., 109, 112ff., 129f., 146, 147f., 150f., 154, 187ff., 194ff., 201, 272f.
Pixodaros 217ff., 227, 303
Plataia 109, 201
Pleuratos 136, 143, 262, 302

Pleurias 216, 224, 262, 302
Poteidaia 37, 68, 71f., 156
Propontis 87, 104, 110, 175, 179f., 182ff.
Proxenos (Ath.) 106f., 278
Proxenos (Theb.) 193ff.
Pydna 28, 40, 66f., 75, 225
Pythian festival 124, 127f., 163, 237, 301
Python 143ff., 153f., 291

Rhodos 63, 171f., 179, 181f., 183f.

Sacred War (355–346) 73ff., 81, 92f., 102, 103f., 109, 114ff., 137, 146f., 150, 194ff., 201; (339–338) 186ff.
Selymbria 171f., 174ff., 179
Sestos 80f., 264
Sikyon 74, 134, 238
Skythians 166, 183, 185f.
Sparta 8, 42f., 74, 78, 86, 93, 105, 113ff., 117, 122, 130, 134, 158f., 196, 203f.
Speusippos 98, 160
Stageira 94f., 97f.
Strymon, R. and Gulf 8, 29, 60, 95, 167, 182f.

Teres 110, 166ff., 170, 277
Thasos 68, 72f., 156, 167, 175, 236f.
Thebes 8, 11f., 43, 73ff., 86, 93, 101f., 103, 109, 113ff., 117, 119ff., 125ff., 130, 134, 139f., 146, 147f., 162f., 187ff., 199ff.
Theopompos 160
Thermopylai 78, 83, 86f., 100, 104f., 116ff., 127, 188f., 190, 193
Thessalonike 211, 222
Thessalos 218f.
Thessaly 10f., 42f., 61, 74, 76, 78ff., 82ff., 95f., 102, 113ff., 119, 137ff., 159, 170, 205f., 211f., 231f., 235ff., 258, 259
Thrace 10f., 32, 45, 63f., 67ff., 75f., 80f., 83, 87ff., 103f., 107f., 110, 113, 117, 145f., 155, 157f., 161, 166ff., 170f., 174ff., 182ff., 231f.
Thrasydaios 140f., 191
Tilphosaion 81, 87, 271
Timarchos 128, 148, 270f.
Triballoi 186, 262
Troizen 134, 203
Tymphaia 28, 37ff., 91